AF787075

Applications of Stochastic Optimal Control to Economics and Finance

Applications of Stochastic Optimal Control to Economics and Finance

Special Issue Editors

Salvatore Federico
Giorgio Ferrari
Luca Regis

MDPI • Basel • Beijing • Wuhan • Barcelona • Belgrade • Manchester • Tokyo • Cluj • Tianjin

MDPI

Special Issue Editors
Salvatore Federico
University of Siena
Italy

Giorgio Ferrari
Bielefeld University
Germany

Luca Regis
University of Torino
Italy

Editorial Office
MDPI
St. Alban-Anlage 66
4052 Basel, Switzerland

This is a reprint of articles from the Special Issue published online in the open access journal *Risks* (ISSN 2227-9091) (available at: https://www.mdpi.com/journal/risks/special_issues/Stochastic_Optimal_Control).

For citation purposes, cite each article independently as indicated on the article page online and as indicated below:

LastName, A.A.; LastName, B.B.; LastName, C.C. Article Title. *Journal Name* **Year**, *Article Number*, Page Range.

ISBN 978-3-03936-058-1 (Hbk)
ISBN 978-3-03936-059-8 (PDF)

© 2020 by the authors. Articles in this book are Open Access and distributed under the Creative Commons Attribution (CC BY) license, which allows users to download, copy and build upon published articles, as long as the author and publisher are properly credited, which ensures maximum dissemination and a wider impact of our publications.
The book as a whole is distributed by MDPI under the terms and conditions of the Creative Commons license CC BY-NC-ND.

Contents

About the Special Issue Editors

Salvatore Federico is an Associate Professor of mathematics for economics and finance at the University of Siena. He holds a PhD from Scuola Normale Superiore in the field of financial mathematics.

Giorgio Ferrari is an Associate Professor of mathematical finance at the Center for Mathematical Economics at Bielefeld University. He holds a PhD in mathematics for economic-financial applications from the University of Rome "La Sapienza". His main research interests are the theory and application of singular stochastic control, optimal stopping, and stochastic games.

Luca Regis is an Associate Professor of mathematics for finance and insurance at the University of Torino, ESOMAS Department. His research interests are in the interplay between financial and actuarial mathematics, and include corporate finance.

Preface to "Applications of Stochastic Optimal Control to Economics and Finance"

In a world dominated by uncertainty, the modeling and understanding of the optimal behavior of agents are of the utmost importance. Many problems in economics, finance, and actuarial science naturally require decision-makers to undertake choices in stochastic environments. Examples include optimal individual consumption and retirement choices, optimal management of portfolios and risk, hedging, optimal timing issues in pricing American options, or in investment decisions. Stochastic control theory provides the methods and results to tackle all such problems. This book collects the papers published in the 2019 Special Issue of *Risks* "Applications of Stochastic Optimal Control to Economics and Finance" and contains 7 peer-reviewed papers dealing with stochastic control models motivated by important questions in Economics and Finance. Each model is mathematically rigorously funded and treated, and numerical methods are also possibly employed to derive the optimal solution. The topics of the book's chapters range from optimal public debt management, to optimal reinsurance, real options in energy markets, and optimal portfolio choice in partial and complete information setting, just to mention a few. From a mathematical point of view, techniques and arguments from dynamic programming theory, filtering theory, optimal stopping, one-dimensional diffusions, and multi-dimensional jump processes are used.

The paper by Anquandah and Bogachev deals with unemployment insurance and proposes a simple model of optimal agent entrance in a scheme. The paper analyzes individual decisions regarding optimal entry time, the dependence of the optimal solution on macroeconomic variables, and individual preferences.

In the second paper of the Special Issue, Rotondi documents a bias that may arise when American options are monetarily valued using the traditional least square method. The estimates on which this method is based utilize a regression run of the in-the-money paths of the Monte Carlo simulation. Therefore, large biases may occur if, for instance, the option is far out of the money. The paper proposes two approaches that completely overcome this problem and evaluates their performance, using the standard least square method.

In the third paper, Ceci and Brachetta study optimal excess-of-loss reinsurance problems when both the intensity of the claims' arrival and the claims' size are influenced by an exogenous stochastic factor. The model allows for stochastic risk premia, which takes into account risk fluctuations. Using stochastic control theory, based on the Hamilton–Jacobi–Bellman equation, the authors analyze the optimal reinsurance strategy under the criterion of maximizing the expected exponential utility of terminal wealth.

In the fourth paper, Moriarty and Palczewski study a real option problem arising in the context of energy markets. They assess the real option value of an arrangement under which an autonomous energy-limited storage unit sells incremental balancing reserve. The problem is set as a perpetual American swing put option with random refraction times.

In the fifth paper, Palmowski, Stettner, and Sulima study a portfolio selection problem in a continuous-time Itô–Markov additive market, where the prices of financial assets are described by the Markov additive processes that combines Lévy processes and regime-switching models. The model takes into account two sources of risk: the jump-diffusion risk and the regime-switching risk. The resulting market is incomplete and the authors give conditions under which the market is asymptotic arbitrage-free. The portfolio selection problem is explicitly solved in the case of power and logarithmic utility function.

The work by De Franco, Nicolle, and Pham considers the Markowitz portfolio problem in a setting in which the drift of the underlying asset prices is uncertain. The authors use a Bayesian learning approach to solve the problem and provide a simple and practical procedure to implement the optimal policy. The strategy obtained via the Bayesian learning approach is then compared in three different investment universes to a naive non-learning strategy in which the drift is kept constant at all times.

The last paper in our Special Issue proposes a control-theoretic model for the optimal reduction of debt-to-GDP ratio. In particular, Cadenillas and Huamán-Aguilar consider a government that has limited ability in generating primary surpluses to optimally reduce the level of the stochastic time-dependent debt ratio. The authors explicitly solve the resulting stochastic control problem and identify the endogenous debt ceiling at which a reduction policy should be implemented. A detailed study of the effects of the model's parameters on the optimal policy is also provided.

We hope that the contents of this book might be helpful for senior scholars working in mathematical economics and finance, practitioners of the financial industry, and for younger researchers approaching this exciting field of research. We would once more like to thank all the authors of this book's chapters and we hope that our readers find this work both enjoyable and useful.

Salvatore Federico, Giorgio Ferrari, Luca Regis
Special Issue Editors

risks

MDPI

Article

Optimal Stopping and Utility in a Simple Model of Unemployment Insurance

Jason S. Anquandah * and Leonid V. Bogachev

Department of Statistics, School of Mathematics, University of Leeds, Leeds LS2 9JT, UK
* Correspondence: mmjsa@leeds.ac.uk

Received: 30 January 2019; Accepted: 18 August 2019; Published: 1 01 September 2019

Abstract: Managing unemployment is one of the key issues in social policies. Unemployment insurance schemes are designed to cushion the financial and morale blow of loss of job but also to encourage the unemployed to seek new jobs more proactively due to the continuous reduction of benefit payments. In the present paper, a simple model of unemployment insurance is proposed with a focus on optimality of the individual's entry to the scheme. The corresponding optimal stopping problem is solved, and its similarity and differences with the perpetual American call option are discussed. Beyond a purely financial point of view, we argue that in the actuarial context the optimal decisions should take into account other possible preferences through a suitable utility function. Some examples in this direction are worked out.

Keywords: insurance; unemployment; optimal stopping; geometric Brownian motion; martingale; free boundary problem; American call option; utility

MSC: primary 97M30; secondary 60G40, 91B16, 91B30

---

1. Introduction

Assessing the risk in financial industries often aims at finding optimal choices in decision-making. In the insurance sector, optimality considerations are crucial primarily for the insurers, who have to address monetary issues (such as how to price the insurance policy so as not to run it at a loss but also to keep the product competitive) and time issues (e.g., when to release the product to the market). Less studied but also important are optimal decisions on behalf of the insured individuals, related to monetary issues (e.g., how profitable is taking up an insurance policy and the right portion of wealth to invest), consumption decisions (e.g., whether to maximize or optimize own consumption), or time-related decisions (such as when it is best to enter or exit an insurance scheme).

In this paper we focus on the particular type of products related to *unemployment insurance (UI)*, whereby an employed individual is covered against the risk of involuntary unemployment (e.g., due to redundancy). Various UI systems are designed to help cushion the financial (as well as morale) blow of loss of job and to encourage unemployed workers to find a new job as early as possible in view of the continued reduction of benefits. The protection is normally provided in the form of regular financial benefits (usually tax free) payable after the insured individual becomes unemployed and until a new job is found, but often only up to a certain maximum duration and with payments gradually decreasing over time. Many countries have UI schemes in place (Holmlund 1998; Kerr 1996), which are often run and funded by the governments, with contributions from employers and workers, but also by private insurance companies (GoCompare 2018). For example, the governmental UI systems administered in France and Belgium in the 1990s provided benefits decreasing with time according to a certain schedule; the amount of the benefit was determined by the age of the worker, their final wage/salary, the number of qualifying years in employment, family circumstances, etc.

In this work we introduce and analyze a simple UI model focusing on the optimal time for the individual to join the scheme. Before setting out the model formally, let us describe the situation in general terms. Consider an individual currently at work but who is concerned about possible loss of job, which may be a genuine potential threat due to the fluidity of the job market and the level of demand in this employment sector. To mitigate this risk, the employer or the social services have an unemployment insurance scheme in place, available to this person (perhaps after a certain qualifying period at work), which upon payment of a one-off entry premium would guarantee to the insured a certain benefit payment proportional to their final wage and determined by a specified declining benefit schedule, until a new job is found (see Figure 1).

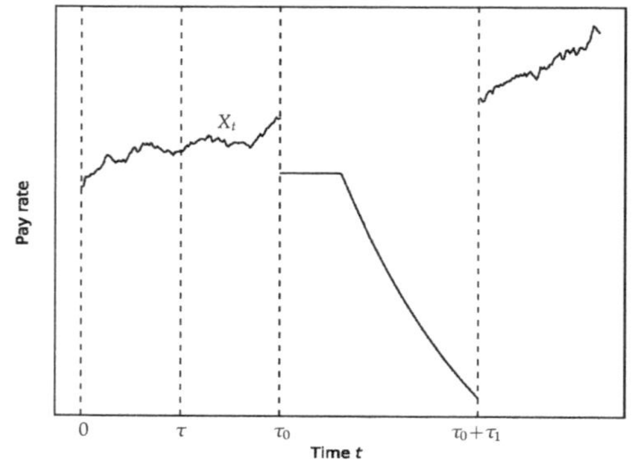

Figure 1. A time chart of the unemployment insurance scheme. The horizontal axis shows (continuous) time; the vertical axis indicates the pay rate (i.e., income receivable per unit time). The origin $t = 0$ indicates the start of employment. Two pieces of a random path X_t depict the dynamics of the individual's wage whilst in employment. The individual joins the UI scheme at entry time τ (by paying a premium P). When the current job ends (at time $\tau_0 > \tau$), a benefit proportional to the final wage X_{τ_0} is payable according to a predefined schedule (e.g., see Example 1), until a new job is found after the unemployment spell of duration τ_1.

The decision the individual is facing is *when* (rather than *if*) to join the scheme. What are the considerations being taken into account when contemplating such a decision? On the one hand, delaying the entry may be a good idea in view of the monetary inflation over time—since the entry premium is fixed, its actual value is decreasing with time. Also, it may be reasonably expected that the wage is likely to grow with time (e.g., due to inflation but also as a reward for improved skills and experience), which may have a potential to increase the total future benefit (which depends on the final wage). Last but not least, some savings may be needed before paying the entry premium becomes financially affordable. On the other hand, delaying the decision to join the insurance scheme is risky, as the individual remains unprotected against loss of job, with its financial as well as morale impact.

Thus, there is a scope for optimizing the decision about the entry time—probably not too early but also not too late. Apparently, such a decision should be based on the information available to date, which of course includes the inflation rate and also the unemployment and redeployment rates, all of which should, in principle, be available through the published statistical data. Another crucial input for the decision-making is the individual's wage as a function of time. We prefer to have the situation where this is modeled as a random process, the values of which may go up as well as down. This is the reason why we do not consider salaries (which are in practice piecewise constant and unlikely to decrease), and instead we are talking about *wages*, which are more responsive to supply and demand and are also subject to "real-wage" adjustments (e.g., through the consumer price index, CPI). Besides, loss of job is more likely in wage-based employments due to the fluidity of the job market. For simplicity, we model the wage dynamics using a diffusion process called *geometric Brownian motion*.[1]

To summarize, the optimization problem for our model aims to maximize the expected net present value of the UI scheme by choosing an optimal entry time τ^*. We will show that this problem can be solved exactly by using the well-developed optimal stopping theory (Peskir and Shiryaev 2006; Pham 2009; Shiryaev 1999). It turns out that the answer is provided by the hitting time of a suitable threshold b^*, that is, the first time τ_{b^*} when the wage process X_t will reach this level. Since the value of b^* is not known in advance, this leads to solving a free-boundary problem for the differential operator (generator) associated with the diffusion process (X_t). In fact, we first conjecture the aforementioned structure of the solution and find the value b^*, and then verify that this is indeed the true solution to the optimal stopping problem.

In the insurance literature, there has been much interest towards using optimality considerations, including optimal stopping problems. From the standpoint of insurer seeking to maximize their expected returns, the optimal stopping time may be interpreted as the time to suspend the current trading if the situation is unfavorable, and to recalculate premiums; see, e.g., Jensen (1997); Karpowicz and Szajowski (2007); Muciek (2002); and further references therein. Insurance research has also focused on optimality from the individual's perspective. One important direction relevant to the UI context was the investigation of the job seeking processes, especially when returning from the unemployed status (Boshuizen and Gouweleeuw 1995; McCall 1970; Wang and Wirjanto 2016). This was complemented by a more general research exploring ways to optimize and improve the efficacy of the UI systems (also in terms of reducing government expenditure), using incentives such as a decreasing benefit throughout the unemployment spell, in conjunction with sanctions and workfare; see Fredriksson and Holmlund (2006); Hairault et al. (2007); Hopenhayn and Nicolini (1997); Kolsrud et al. (2018); Landais et al. (2017), to cite but a few. A related strand of research is the study of optimal retirement strategies in the presence of involuntary unemployment risks and borrowing constraints (Choi and Shim 2006; De Angelis and Stabile 2019; Gerrard et al. 2012; Jang and Rhee 2013; Stabile 2006).

To the best of our knowledge, optimal stopping problems in the UI context (such as the optimal entry to/exit from a UI policy) have not received sufficient research attention. This issue is important, because knowing the optimal entry strategies is likely to enhance the motivation for individuals to join the UI scheme, thus ensuring better societal benefits through the UI policies; see analysis and discussion in Rebollo-Sanz and García-Pérez (2015). Knowledge of the optimal entry time for insured individuals, which has impact on the amount and duration of benefits to be claimed, will also help the insurers (both state and private) to optimize their financial practices; see a discussion in Landais and Spinnewijn (2017). Thus, our present work attempts to fill in the gap by addressing the question of the optimal timing to join the UI scheme.

It is interesting to point out that our optimal stopping problem and its solution have a lot in common with (but are not identical to) the well-known American call option in financial mathematics, where the option holder has the right to exercise it at any time (i.e., to buy a certain stock at an agreed price), and the problem is to determine the best time to do that, aiming to maximize the expected financial gain. However, unlike the American call option setting based on purely financial objectives, the optimal stopping solution obtained in our UI model is not entirely satisfactory from the individual's point of view, because the (optimal) waiting time τ_{b^*} may be infinite with positive probability (at least for some values of the parameters), and even if it is finite with probability one, the expected waiting time may be very long.

Motivated by this observation, we argue that certain elements of utility should be added to the analysis, aiming to quantify the individual's "impatience" as a measure of purpose and satisfaction.

---

[1] For technical convenience, we choose to work with continuous-time models, but our ideas can also be adapted to discrete time (which may be somewhat more natural, since the wage process is observed by the individual on a weekly time scale).

We suggest a few simple ideas of how utility might be accommodated in the UI optimal stopping framework. Despite the simplicity of such examples, in most cases they lead to much harder optimal stopping problems. Not attempting to solve these problems in full generality, we confine ourselves to exploring suboptimal solutions in the class of hitting times, which nonetheless provide useful insight into possible effects of inclusion of utility into the optimal stopping context.

The general concept of utility in economics was strongly advocated in the classical book by von Neumann and Morgenstern (1953), whose aim was in particular to overcome the idealistic assumption of a strictly rational behavior of market agents.[2] These ideas were quickly adopted in insurance, dating back to Borch (1961), and soon becoming part of the insurance mainstream, culminating in the Expected Utility Theory (see a recent book by Kaas et al. 2008) routinely used as a standard tool to price insurance products. In particular, examples of use of utility in the UI analysis are ubiquitous; see, e.g., Acemoglu and Shimer (2000); Baily (1978); Fredriksson and Holmlund (2006); Hairault et al. (2007); Holmlund (1998); Hopenhayn and Nicolini (1997); Kolsrud et al. (2018); Landais et al. (2017); Landais and Spinnewijn (2017). There have also been efforts to combine optimal stopping and utility (Chen et al. 2019; Choi and Shim 2006; Henderson and Hobson 2008; Karpowicz and Szajowski 2007; Muciek 2002; Wang and Wirjanto 2016). However, all such examples were limited to using utility functions to recalculate wealth, while other important objectives and preferences such as the desire to buy the policy or to reduce the waiting times have not been considered as yet, as far as we can tell.

The rest of the paper is organized as follows. In Section 2, our insurance model is specified and the optimization problem is set up. In Section 3, the optimal stopping problem is solved using a reduction to a suitable free boundary problem, including the identification of the critical threshold b^*. This is complemented in Section 4 by an elementary derivation using explicit information about the distribution of the hitting times for the geometric Brownian motion. Section 5 addresses various statistical issues and also provides a numerical example illustrating the optimality of the critical threshold b^*. In Section 6, we carry out the analysis of parametric dependence in our model upon two most significant exogenous parameters, the unemployment rate and the wage drift, and also give an economic interpretation thereof. In Section 7, we make a useful comparison of our problem and its solution with the classical American call option, which leads us to the discussion of the necessity of utility-based considerations in the optimal stopping context. Finally, Section 8 contains the summary discussion of our results, including suggestions for further work. Throughout the paper, we use the standard notation $a \wedge b := \min\{a,b\}$, $a \vee b := \max\{a,b\}$, and $a^+ := a \vee 0$.

2. Optimal Stopping Problem

2.1. The Model of Unemployment Insurance

Let us describe our model in more detail. Suppose that time $t \geq 0$ is continuous and is measured (in the units of weeks) starting from the beginning of the individual's employment. We assume without loss of generality that the unemployment insurance policy is available immediately (although in practice, a qualifying period at work would normally be required for eligibility). Let $X_t > 0$ denote the individual's wage (i.e., payment per week, paid in arrears) as a function of time $t \geq 0$, such that $X_0 = x$. We treat $X = (X_t,\, t \geq 0)$ as a random process defined on a filtered probability space $(\Omega, \mathcal{F}, (\mathcal{F}_t), \mathrm{P})$, where Ω is a suitable sample space (e.g., consisting of all possible paths of (X_t)), the filtration $(\mathcal{F}_t)$ is an increasing sequence of σ-algebras $\mathcal{F}_t \subset \mathcal{F}$, and P is a probability measure on the measurable space $(\Omega, \mathcal{F})$, which determines the distribution of various random inputs in the model, including (X_t). It is assumed that the process (X_t) is adapted to the filtration $(\mathcal{F}_t)$, that is, X_t is

[2] Impact of individualistic (not always rational) perception in economics and financial markets is the subject of the modern behavioral economics (see, e.g., a recent monograph by Dhami 2016).

$\mathcal{F}_t$-measurable for each $t \geq 0$. Intuitively, $\mathcal{F}_t$ is interpreted as the full information available up to time t, and measurability of X_t with respect to $\mathcal{F}_t$ means that this information includes knowledge of the values of the process X_t.

Furthermore, remembering that X_t is positive valued, we use for it a simple model of geometric Brownian motion driven by the stochastic differential equation

$$\frac{\mathrm{d}X_t}{X_t} = \mu\,\mathrm{d}t + \sigma\,\mathrm{d}B_t, \qquad X_0 = x, \tag{1}$$

where B_t is a standard Brownian motion (i.e., with mean zero, $\mathrm{E}(B_t) = 0$; variance, $\mathrm{Var}(B_t) = t$; and with continuous sample paths), and $\mu \in \mathbb{R}$ and $\sigma > 0$ are the drift and volatility rates, respectively. The Equation (1) is well known to have the explicit solution (Shiryaev 1999, chp. III, §3a, p. 237)

$$X_t = x \exp\left\{(\mu - \tfrac{1}{2}\sigma^2)\,t + \sigma B_t\right\} \quad (t \geq 0). \tag{2}$$

Note that

$$\mathrm{E}_x(X_t) = x\,\mathrm{e}^{\mu t}, \qquad \mathrm{Var}_x(X_t) = x^2\mathrm{e}^{2\mu t}\,(\mathrm{e}^{\sigma^2 t} - 1), \tag{3}$$

where E_x and Var_x denote expectation and variance with respect to the distribution of X_t given the initial value $X_0 = x$.

Let us now specify the unemployment insurance scheme. An individual who is currently employed may join the scheme by paying a fixed one-off premium $P > 0$ at the point of entry. If and when the current employment ends (say, at time instant τ_0), the benefit proportional to the final wage X_{τ_0} is payable according to the benefit schedule $h(s)$; that is, the payout at time $t \geq \tau_0$ is given by $X_{\tau_0} h(t - \tau_0)$. However, the payment stops when a new job is found after the unemployment spell of duration τ_1. For simplicity, we assume that both τ_0 and τ_1 have exponential distribution (with parameters λ_0 and λ_1, respectively); as mentioned in the Introduction, this guarantees a Markovian nature of the corresponding transitions. These random times are also assumed to be statistically independent of the process (X_t).

Possible transitions in the state space of our insurance model are presented in Figure 2, where symbols "0" and "1" encode the states of being employed and unemployed, respectively, whereas suffixes "+" and "–" indicate whether insurance is in place or not, respectively. Note that all transitions, except from 0– to 0+ (which is subject to optimal control based of observations over the wage process (X_t)), occur in a Markovian fashion; that is, the holding times are exponentially distributed (with parameters λ_0 if in states 0– and 0+, or λ_1 if in states 1– and 1+).

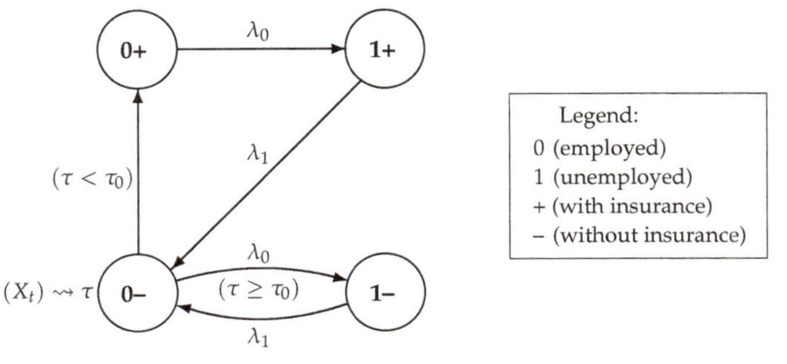

Figure 2. Schematic diagram of possible transitions in the unemployment insurance scheme. Here, τ_0 and τ_1 are the (exponential) holding times in states 0 and 1, with parameters λ_0 and λ_1, respectively, whereas τ is the entry time (i.e., from state 0– to state 0+), which is subject to optimal control based on observations over the wage process (X_t).

The individual's decision about a suitable time to join the scheme is based on the information available to date. In our model, this information encoded in the filtration $(\mathcal{F}_t)$ is provided by ongoing observations over the wage process (X_t). Thus, admissible strategies for choosing τ must be adapted to the filtration $(\mathcal{F}_t)$; namely, at any time instant, $t \ge 0$, it should be possible to determine whether τ has occurred or not yet, given all the information in $\mathcal{F}_t$. In mathematical terms, this means that τ is a *stopping time*, whereby for any $t \ge 0$ the event $\{\tau > t\}$ belongs to the σ-algebra $\mathcal{F}_t$ (see, e.g., Yeh 1995, chp. 1, §3, p. 25).

Remark 1. *In general, a stopping time τ is allowed to take values in $[0, \infty]$ including ∞, in which case waiting continues indefinitely and the decision to join the scheme is never taken. In practice, it is desirable that the stopping time τ be finite almost surely (a.s.) (i.e., $\mathrm{P}_x(\tau < \infty) = 1$), but this may not always be the case (see Section 4.1).*

2.2. Setting the Optimal Stopping Problem

As was explained informally in the introduction, there is a scope for optimizing the choice of the entry time τ, where optimality is measured by maximizing the expected financial gain from the scheme. Our next goal is to obtain an expression for the expected gain under the contract. First of all, conditional on the final wage X_{τ_0}, the expected future benefit to be received under this insurance contract is given by

$$X_{\tau_0}\, \mathrm{E}\left(\int_0^{\tau_1} \mathrm{e}^{-rs}\, h(s)\, \mathrm{d}s\right) = \beta\, X_{\tau_0}, \tag{4}$$

where r is the inflation rate and

$$\beta := \int_0^\infty \lambda_1 \mathrm{e}^{-\lambda_1 t} H(t)\, \mathrm{d}t, \qquad H(t) := \int_0^t \mathrm{e}^{-rs}\, h(s)\, \mathrm{d}s. \tag{5}$$

Note that the expectation in formula (4) is taken with respect to the (exponential) random waiting time τ_1 (with parameter λ_1), and that the expression inside integration involves discounting to the beginning of unemployment at time τ_0.

Example 1. *A specific example of the benefit schedule $h(s)$ is as follows,*

$$h(s) = \begin{cases} h_0, & 0 \le s \le s_0, \\ h_0\, \mathrm{e}^{-\delta(s - s_0)}, & s \ge s_0, \end{cases} \tag{6}$$

where $0 < h_0 \le 1$, $0 \le s_0 \le \infty$, and $\delta > 0$. Thus, the insured receives a certain fraction of their final wage (i.e., $h_0 X_{\tau_0}$) for a grace period s_0, after which the benefit is falling down exponentially with rate δ. This example is motivated by the declining unemployment compensation system in France (Kerr 1996).[3] Having specified the schedule function, all calculations can be done explicitly. In particular, the constant β in (4) is calculated from (5) as

$$\beta = \frac{h_0\,(1 - \mathrm{e}^{-(r+\lambda_1)s_0})}{r + \lambda_1} + \frac{h_0\, \mathrm{e}^{-(r+\lambda_1)s_0}}{r + \lambda_1 + \delta}.$$

---

[3] More specifically, according to the French UI system back in the 1990s (Kerr 1996, p. 8), a worker aged 50 or more, with eight months of insurable employment in the last twelve months, was entitled to full benefits equal to 57.4% of the final wage payable for the first eight months, thereafter declining by 15% every four months; however, the payments continued for no longer than 21 months overall. This leads to choosing the following numerical values in (6): $h_0 = 0.574$, $s_0 = 8\,(52/12) \doteq 34.7$ (weeks) and $\delta = -(3/52)\ln(1 - 0.15) \doteq 0.0094 = 0.94\%$ (per week). The restriction of the benefit term by $21\,(52/12) = 91$ weeks can be taken into account in our model by adjusting the parameter λ_1 from the condition $\mathrm{E}(\tau_1) = 91$, giving $\lambda_1 \doteq 0.0110$. A more conservative choice is to use a tail probability condition, for example, $\mathrm{P}(\tau_1 > 91) = 0.10$, yielding $\lambda_1 = -\ln(0.10)/91 \doteq 0.0253$ (with $\mathrm{E}(\tau_1) \doteq 39.5$).

In the extreme cases $s_0 = 0$ *or* $s_0 = \infty$, *this expression simplifies to*

$$\beta = \begin{cases} \dfrac{h_0}{\lambda_1}\left(1 - \dfrac{r+\delta}{r+\lambda_1+\delta}\right), & s_0 = 0, \\ \dfrac{h_0}{\lambda_1}\left(1 - \dfrac{r}{r+\lambda_1}\right), & s_0 = \infty. \end{cases}$$

Here, the first factor has a clear meaning as the product of pay per week (h_0) *and the mean duration of the benefit payment* ($\mathrm{E}(\tau_1) = 1/\lambda_1$), *whereas the second factor takes into account the discounting at rates* r *and* δ.

Returning to the general case, if the contract is entered immediately (subject to the payment of premium P), then the net expected benefit discounted to the entry time $t = 0$ is given by the gain function

$$g(x) := \mathrm{E}_x\big(\mathrm{e}^{-r\tau_0}\beta X_{\tau_0}\big) - P, \tag{7}$$

where $x = X_0$ is the starting wage and the symbol E_x now indicates expectation with respect to both τ_0 and X_{τ_0}. Recall that the random time τ_0 is independent of the process (X_t) and has the exponential distribution with parameter λ_0. Using the total expectation formula (Shiryaev 1996, §II.7, Definition 3, p. 214, and Property G*, p. 216) and substituting the expression (3), the expectation in (7) is computed as follows,

$$\begin{aligned} \mathrm{E}_x\big(\mathrm{e}^{-r\tau_0}X_{\tau_0}\big) &= \mathrm{E}_x\big(\mathrm{e}^{-r\tau_0}\,\mathrm{E}_x(X_{\tau_0}\,|\,\tau_0)\big) \\ &= \mathrm{E}_x\big(\mathrm{e}^{-r\tau_0}(x\,\mathrm{e}^{\mu\tau_0})\big) = x\int_0^\infty \mathrm{e}^{(\mu-r)t}\lambda_0\,\mathrm{e}^{-\lambda_0 t}\,\mathrm{d}t \\ &= \frac{\lambda_0 x}{r+\lambda_0-\mu}. \end{aligned} \tag{8}$$

Thus, substituting (8) into (7) and denoting

$$\tilde{r} := r + \lambda_0, \qquad \beta_1 := \frac{\beta\lambda_0}{\tilde{r}-\mu}, \tag{9}$$

the gain function is represented explicitly as

$$g(x) = \beta_1 x - P. \tag{10}$$

Of course, the computation in (8) is only meaningful as long as

$$\mu < r + \lambda_0 = \tilde{r}. \tag{11}$$

Assumption 1. *In what follows, we always assume that the condition* (11) *is satisfied.*

Remark 2. *In real-life applications, the wage growth rate* μ *is rather small* (*but may be either positive or negative*). *It is unlikely to exceed the inflation rate* r, *but even if it does, then it is hardly possible economically that it is greater than the combined inflation–unemployment rate* $\tilde{r} = r + \lambda_0$. *Thus, the condition* (11) *is absolutely realistic.*

To generalize the expression (10), consider a delayed entry time $\tau > 0$ (tacitly assuming that $\tau < \infty$). Discounting first to the entry time τ when the deduction of the premium P is activated, and then further down to the initial time moment $t = 0$, yields the expected net present value of the total gain as a function of the initial wage x,

$$\mathrm{eNPV}(x;\tau) := \mathrm{E}_x\big[\mathrm{e}^{-r\tau}\big(\mathrm{e}^{-r(\tau_0-\tau)}\beta X_{\tau_0} - P\big)\,\mathbb{1}_{\{\tau<\tau_0\}}\big], \tag{12}$$

where the expectation on the right now also includes averaging with respect to τ, which is a functional of the path (X_t). Note that the indicator function under the expectation specifies that the entry time τ must occur prior to τ_0, for otherwise there will be no gain.

Remark 3. *The notation (12) emphasizes that the expected net present value depends on the specific entry time τ. As was intuitively explained in the Introduction, there is a scope for optimizing the choice of τ, where optimality is measured by maximizing* $\mathrm{eNPV}(x;\tau)$.

Formula (12) indicates that the decision time τ has a finite (random) expiry date τ_0 (using the terminology of financial options). However, the expectation in (12) involves averaging with respect to τ_0. Moreover, taking advantage of exponential distribution of τ_0, the expression (12) can be rewritten without any expiry date (i.e., as a perpetual option).

Lemma 1. *The expected net present value defined by formula (12) can be expressed in the form*

$$\mathrm{eNPV}(x;\tau) = \mathrm{E}_x\Big[\mathrm{e}^{-\tilde{r}\tau} g(X_\tau)\, \mathbb{1}_{\{\tau<\infty\}}\Big], \tag{13}$$

where the function $g(\cdot)$ is defined in (7) and $\tilde{r} = r + \lambda_0$ (see (9)).

Proof. Since the distribution of τ_0 is exponential, the excess time $\tilde{\tau}_0 := \tau_0 - \tau$ conditioned on $\{\tau < \tau_0\}$ is again exponentially distributed (with the same parameter λ_0) and independent of τ. Hence, conditioning on τ (restricted to the event $\{\tau < \infty\}$) and using the total expectation formula as before, together with the (strong) Markov property of the process (X_t), we get from (12)

$$\begin{aligned}
\mathrm{eNPV}(x;\tau) &= \mathrm{E}_x\Big(\mathrm{E}_x\big[\mathrm{e}^{-r\tau}(\mathrm{e}^{-r(\tau_0-\tau)}\beta X_{\tau_0} - P)\, \mathbb{1}_{\{\tau_0>\tau\}} \,\big|\, \tau\big]\Big)\\
&= \mathrm{E}_x\Big(\mathrm{e}^{-r\tau}\mathrm{E}_x\big[(\mathrm{e}^{-r\tilde{\tau}_0}\beta X_{\tau+\tilde{\tau}_0} - P) \,|\, \tau\big] \cdot \mathrm{E}_x\big(\mathbb{1}_{\{\tau_0>\tau\}} \,\big|\, \tau\big)\Big)\\
&= \mathrm{E}_x\Big(\mathrm{e}^{-r\tau}\,\mathrm{E}_{X_\tau}(\mathrm{e}^{-r\tilde{\tau}_0}\beta \tilde{X}_{\tilde{\tau}_0} - P) \cdot \mathrm{P}_x(\tau_0 > \tau \,|\, \tau)\Big),
\end{aligned} \tag{14}$$

where $\tilde{X}_t := X_{\tau+t}$ $(t \ge 0)$ is a shifted wage process starting at $\tilde{X}_0 = X_\tau$. Substituting $\mathrm{P}_x(\tau_0 > \tau \,|\, \tau) = \mathrm{e}^{-\lambda_0\tau}$ and recalling notation (7), formula (14) is reduced to (13). □

Finally, without loss we can remove the indicator from the expression (13) by defining the value of the random variable under expectation to be zero on the event $\{\tau = \infty\}$. This definition is consistent with the limit at infinity. Indeed, observe using (2) and (8) that

$$\begin{aligned}
\mathrm{e}^{-\tilde{r}t} g(X_t) &= \mathrm{e}^{-\tilde{r}t}\left(\beta_1 x\, \mathrm{e}^{(\mu-\sigma^2/2)t+\sigma B_t} - P\right)\\
&= \beta_1 x \exp\left\{-t\,(\tilde{r} - \mu + \tfrac{1}{2}\sigma^2 + \sigma t^{-1} B_t)\right\} - P\mathrm{e}^{-\tilde{r}t}.
\end{aligned} \tag{15}$$

Due to the condition (11), $\tilde{r} - \mu + \frac{1}{2}\sigma^2 > \frac{1}{2}\sigma^2 > 0$. In addition, by the (strong) law of large numbers for the Brownian motion (see, e.g., Durrett 1999, Exercise 6.4, p. 265, or Shiryaev 1999, chp. III, §3b, p. 246),

$$\lim_{t\to\infty} t^{-1} B_t = 0 \quad (\mathrm{P}\text{-a.s.}).$$

Thus, the limit of (15) as $t \to \infty$ is zero (P_x-a.s.). Hence, the event $\{\tau = \infty\}$ does not contribute to the expectation (13), so that, substituting (8), we get

$$\mathrm{eNPV}(x;\tau) = \mathrm{E}_x\big(\mathrm{e}^{-\tilde{r}\tau} g(X_\tau)\big). \tag{16}$$

To summarize, identification of the optimal entry time $\tau = \tau^*$, in the sense of maximizing the expected net present value $\mathrm{eNPV}(x;\tau)$ as a function of strategy τ (see (16)), is reduced to solving the following optimal stopping problem,

$$v(x) = \sup_{\tau} \mathrm{E}_x\left(\mathrm{e}^{-\tilde{r}\tau} g(X_\tau)\right), \tag{17}$$

where the function $g(x)$ is given by (10) and the supremum is taken over the class of all admissible stopping times τ (i.e., adapted to the filtration $(\mathcal{F}_t)$). The supremum $v(x)$ in (17) is called the *value function* of the optimal stopping problem.

2.3. Allowing for Mortality

The simple model of unemployment insurance set out in Section 2.1 can be easily extended to include mortality. Following (Merton 1971, pp. 399–401), suppose that the individual who contemplates taking out the unemployment insurance policy may die (say, at a random time τ_2 from zero), independently of employment-related events and subject to a constant force of mortality λ_2. That is to say, given that the individual is alive at current age $t \ge 0$, the residual lifetime $\tau_2 - t$ is an independent random variable exponentially distributed with parameter λ_2,

$$\mathrm{P}(\tau_2 - t > s \,|\, \tau_2 > t) = \mathrm{e}^{-\lambda_2 s} \quad (s \ge 0).$$

The necessary modifications to the unemployment insurance model of Section 2.2 start by adjusting the formula for the expected future benefit (see (4)). Assuming that death does not occur prior to the time τ_0 of losing the job (i.e., $\tau_2 > \tau_0$, so that $\tilde{\tau}_2 := \tau_2 - \tau_0$ is exponentially distributed with parameter λ_2), the benefit payments cease at $\tau_1 \wedge \tilde{\tau}_2$ (i.e., when a new job is found or at death, whichever occurs first). Since τ_1 and $\tilde{\tau}_2$ are independent and both have exponential distributions, the random variable $\tau_1 \wedge \tilde{\tau}_2$ has the exponential distribution with parameter $\lambda_1 + \lambda_2$. Hence, the constant β from (5) is now written as

$$\beta = \int_0^\infty (\lambda_1 + \lambda_2)\,\mathrm{e}^{-(\lambda_1+\lambda_2)\,t} H(t)\,\mathrm{d}t.$$

Next, we need to take into account the effect of death in service, that is, if $\tau_2 \le \tau_0$. To be specific, it is reasonable to assume that the lump sum to be paid by the employer in this case is proportional to the final wage, say $a^\dagger X_{\tau_2}$. Then, separating the cases where death occurs after or prior to loss of job, it is easy to see that the definition (7) of the gain function (i.e., net expected benefit discounted to the policy entry time) takes the form

$$g(x) = \mathrm{E}_x\left(\mathrm{e}^{-r\tau_0} \beta X_{\tau_0} \mathbb{1}_{\{\tau_0 < \tau_2\}}\right) + \mathrm{E}_x\left(\mathrm{e}^{-r\tau_0} a^\dagger X_{\tau_2} \mathbb{1}_{\{\tau_2 \le \tau_0\}}\right) - P. \tag{18}$$

The first expectation in (18) is computed using conditioning on τ_0 and the total expectation formula (cf. (8)),

$$\begin{aligned}
\mathrm{E}_x\left(\mathrm{e}^{-r\tau_0} X_{\tau_0} \mathbb{1}_{\{\tau_0<\tau_2\}}\right) &= \mathrm{E}_x\left[\mathrm{e}^{-r\tau_0}\, \mathrm{E}_x\left(X_{\tau_0} \mathbb{1}_{\{\tau_0<\tau_2\}} \,|\, \tau_0\right)\right] \\
&= \mathrm{E}_x\left[\mathrm{e}^{-r\tau_0}\, \mathrm{E}_x(X_{\tau_0} \,|\, \tau_0) \cdot \mathrm{P}_x(\tau_2 > \tau_0 \,|\, \tau_0)\right] \\
&= \mathrm{E}_x\left(\mathrm{e}^{-r\tau_0}\, x \mathrm{e}^{\mu\tau_0}\, \mathrm{e}^{-\lambda_2\tau_0}\right) = x \int_0^\infty \mathrm{e}^{(\mu - r - \lambda_2)t}\, \lambda_0 \mathrm{e}^{-\lambda_0 t}\,\mathrm{d}t \\
&= \frac{\lambda_0 x}{r + \lambda_0 + \lambda_2 - \mu},
\end{aligned} \tag{19}$$

where in the second line we used conditional independence of X_{τ_0} and τ_2 given τ_0. Similarly, by conditioning on τ_2 the second expectation in (18) is represented as

$$\begin{aligned}\mathrm{E}_x\big(\mathrm{e}^{-r\tau_0}\,X_{\tau_2}\mathbb{1}_{\{\tau_2\le\tau_0\}}\big) &= \mathrm{E}_x\big[X_{\tau_2}\,\mathrm{E}_x\big(\mathrm{e}^{-r\tau_0}\mathbb{1}_{\{\tau_0\ge\tau_2\}}\,|\,\tau_2\big)\big]\\ &= \mathrm{E}_x\left[X_{\tau_2}\int_{\tau_2}^{\infty}\mathrm{e}^{-rt}\,\lambda_0\,\mathrm{e}^{-\lambda_0 t}\,\mathrm{d}t\right]\\ &= \frac{\lambda_0}{r+\lambda_0}\,\mathrm{E}_x\big(X_{\tau_2}\,\mathrm{e}^{-(r+\lambda_0)\tau_2}\big).\end{aligned} \tag{20}$$

Again conditioning on τ_2, the last expectation is computed as follows,

$$\begin{aligned}\mathrm{E}_x\big(X_{\tau_2}\,\mathrm{e}^{-(r+\lambda_0)\tau_2}\big) &= \mathrm{E}_x\big[\mathrm{e}^{-(r+\lambda_0)\tau_2}\,\mathrm{E}_x(X_{\tau_2}\,|\,\tau_2)\big]\\ &= \mathrm{E}_x\big(\mathrm{e}^{-(r+\lambda_0)\tau_2}\,x\,\mathrm{e}^{\mu\tau_2}\big)\\ &= x\int_0^{\infty}\mathrm{e}^{-(r+\lambda_0-\mu)t}\lambda_2\,\mathrm{e}^{-\lambda_2 t}\,\mathrm{d}t\\ &= \frac{\lambda_2 x}{r+\lambda_0+\lambda_2-\mu}.\end{aligned} \tag{21}$$

Finally, substituting the expressions (19)–(21) into the definition (18), we obtain explicitly

$$g(x) = \frac{\lambda_0\,x}{r+\lambda_0+\lambda_2-\mu}\left(\beta+\frac{\lambda_2\,a^{\dagger}}{r+\lambda_0}\right) - P.$$

This expression has the same form as (10) but with the parameters $\tilde{r}$ and β_1 redefined as follows (cf. (9)),

$$\tilde{r} := r+\lambda_0+\lambda_2, \qquad \beta_1 := \frac{\lambda_0}{\tilde{r}-\mu}\left(\beta+\frac{\lambda_2\,a^{\dagger}}{r+\lambda_0}\right).$$

In addition, the inequality (11) of Assumption 1 is updated accordingly. Subject to this reparameterization, all subsequent calculations leading to the optimal stopping problem (17) remain unchanged.

For the sake of clarity and in order not to distract the reader by unnecessary technicalities, in the rest of the paper we adhere to the original version of the model (i.e., with no mortality, $\lambda_2 = 0$); however, see the discussion at the end of Section 6.4 indicating an important regularizing role of mortality, helping to avoid undesirable inconsistencies of the model at small unemployment rates λ_0.

2.4. A Priori Properties of the Value Function

The next lemma shows that the optimal stopping problem (17) is well posed.

Lemma 2. *The value function $x \mapsto v(x)$ of the optimal stopping problem (17) has the following properties:*

(i) $v(0) = 0$ *and, moreover,* $v(x) \ge 0$ *for all* $x \ge 0$;
(ii) $v(x) < \infty$ *for all* $x \ge 0$.

Proof. (i) If $x = 0$ then, due to (2), $X_t \equiv 0$ (P_0-a.s.) and the stopping problem (17) is reduced to

$$v(0) = \sup_{\tau}\mathrm{E}_0(-P\,\mathrm{e}^{-\tilde{r}\tau}),$$

which has the obvious solution $\tau = \infty$ (P_0-a.s.), with the corresponding supremum value $v(0) = 0$. Furthermore, by considering $\tau = \infty$ (P_x-a.s.) it readily follows from (17) that $v(x) \ge 0$ for all $x \ge 0$.

(ii) Recalling that $\mu < \tilde{r}$ (see Assumption 1), observe that the process $\mathrm{e}^{-\tilde{r}t}X_t$ is a *supermartingale*; indeed, for $0 \le s \le t$ we have, using (2) and (3),

$$\begin{aligned}\mathrm{E}_x(\mathrm{e}^{-\tilde{r}t}X_t\,|\,\mathcal{F}_s) &= \mathrm{e}^{-\tilde{r}t}X_s\,\mathrm{E}\big(\mathrm{e}^{\sigma(B_t-B_s)+(\mu-\frac{1}{2}\sigma^2)(t-s)}\big)\\ &= \mathrm{e}^{-\tilde{r}t}X_s\,\mathrm{e}^{\mu(t-s)} \le \mathrm{e}^{-\tilde{r}s}X_s \quad (\mathrm{P}_x\text{-a.s.}).\end{aligned}$$

In particular,

$$E_x(e^{-\tilde{r}t}X_t) \le E_x(X_0) = x.$$

Hence, by Doob's optional sampling theorem for non-negative, right-continuous supermartingales (Yeh 1995, Theorem 8.18, pp. 140–41), we have

$$E_x(e^{-\tilde{r}\tau}X_\tau) \le E_x(X_0) = x,$$

and it follows that the supremum in (17) is finite. □

2.5. The Optimal Stopping Rule

For the wage process (X_t), consider the *hitting time* τ_b of a threshold $b \in \mathbb{R}$, defined by

$$\tau_b := \inf\{t \ge 0\colon X_t \ge b\} \in [0, \infty].$$

(As usual, we make a convention that $\inf \varnothing = \infty$.) Clearly, τ_b is a stopping time, that is, $\{\tau \le t\} \in \mathcal{F}_t$ for all $t \ge 0$. Since the process X_t has a.s.-continuous sample paths, on the event $\{\tau_b < \infty\}$ we have $X_{\tau_b} = b$ (P_x-a.s.).

As we will show, the optimal strategy for the optimal stopping problem (17) is to wait until the random process X_t hits a certain threshold b^* (see Figure 3). More precisely, the solution to (17) is provided by the following stopping rule,

$$\tau^* = \begin{cases} \tau_{b^*} & \text{if } x \in [0, b^*], \\ 0 & \text{if } x \in [b^*, \infty). \end{cases} \tag{22}$$

That is to say, if $x \ge b^*$ then one must stop and buy the policy immediately, or else wait until the hitting time $\tau_{b^*} \ge 0$ occurs and buy the policy then. (Of course, these two rules coincide when $x = b^*$.) However, if it happens so that $\tau_{b^*} = \infty$, then, according to the above rule, one must wait indefinitely, and therefore never buy the policy.

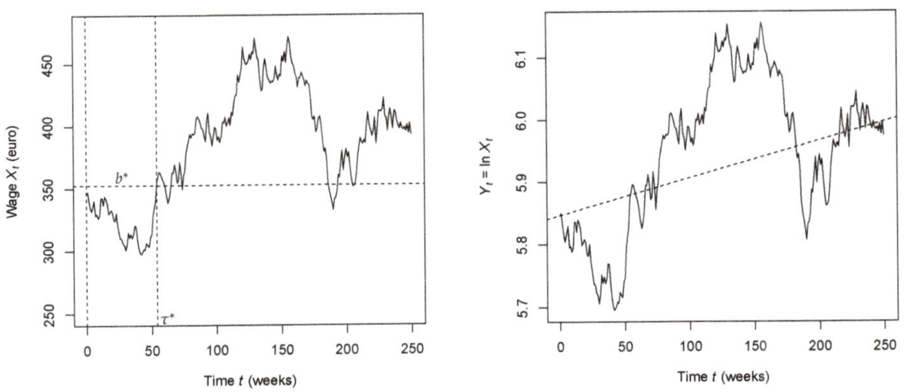

Figure 3. Simulated wage process X_t (left) and $Y_t = \ln X_t$ (right) according to the geometric Brownian motion model (2), with $X_0 = 346$ (euros) and parameters $\mu = 0.0004$ and $\sigma = 0.02$ (see Example 3). The dashed horizontal line in the left plot indicates the optimal threshold $b^* \doteq 352.37$ (euros) first attained in this simulation at $\tau^* = 54$ (weeks). The dashed line in the right plot shows the estimated drift of the log-transformed data (see Section 5.2).

The specific value of the critical threshold b^* is given by

$$b^* = \frac{Pq_*}{\beta_1(q_* - 1)}, \tag{23}$$

where

$$q_* = \frac{1}{\sigma^2}\left(-(\mu - \tfrac{1}{2}\sigma^2) + \sqrt{(\mu - \tfrac{1}{2}\sigma^2)^2 + 2\tilde{r}\sigma^2}\right). \tag{24}$$

It is straightforward to check, using condition (11), that $q_* > 1$ (see also Section 3.2). Finally, the corresponding value function (17) is specified as

$$v(x) = \begin{cases} (\beta_1 b^* - P)\left(\dfrac{x}{b^*}\right)^{q_*}, & x \in [0, b^*], \\ \beta_1 x - P, & x \in [b^*, \infty). \end{cases} \tag{25}$$

Equivalently, substituting the expression (23), formula (25) is explicitly rewritten as

$$v(x) = \begin{cases} \dfrac{P}{q_* - 1}\left(\dfrac{\beta_1(q_* - 1)x}{Pq_*}\right)^{q_*}, & 0 \le x \le \dfrac{Pq_*}{\beta_1(q_* - 1)}, \\ \beta_1 x - P, & x \ge \dfrac{Pq_*}{\beta_1(q_* - 1)}. \end{cases} \tag{26}$$

In particular, the function $x \mapsto v(x)$ is strictly increasing for $x \ge 0$, with $v(0) = 0$ (cf. Lemma 2).

These results will be proved in Section 3.

2.6. Deterministic Case

For orientation, it is useful to consider the simple baseline case $\sigma = 0$, where the random process X_t (see (2)) degenerates to the deterministic function

$$X_t = x\,\mathrm{e}^{\mu t} \quad (t \ge 0).$$

Hence, any stopping time τ is nonrandom, say $\tau = t$, and the optimal stopping problem (17) is reduced to

$$v(x) = \sup_{t \ge 0}\left[\mathrm{e}^{-\tilde{r}t}(\beta_1 x\,\mathrm{e}^{\mu t} - P)\right]. \tag{27}$$

The problem (27) is easily solved, with the maximizer t^* given by

$$t^* = \inf\{t \ge 0 \colon x\,\mathrm{e}^{\mu t} \ge b_0^*\} \in [0, \infty], \tag{28}$$

where

$$b_0^* = \begin{cases} \dfrac{P\tilde{r}}{\beta_1(\tilde{r} - \mu)}, & \mu > 0, \\ \dfrac{P}{\beta_1}, & \mu \le 0. \end{cases} \tag{29}$$

The expression (29) is consistent with the general formula (23), noting that, in the limit as $\sigma \downarrow 0$, the quantity (24) is reduced to (cf. (11))

$$q_* = \begin{cases} \dfrac{\tilde{r}}{\mu} > 1, & \mu > 0, \\ \infty, & \mu \le 0. \end{cases}$$

With this convention, it is easy to check that the value function (27) is given by the general formula (25). In particular, if $\mu \le 0$ and $x < b_0^*$, then, according to (28), $t^* = \infty$ and from (27) we get $v(x) = 0$;

indeed, the function $t \mapsto x\,\mathrm{e}^{\mu t}$ is nonincreasing, so it never attains the required threshold $b_0^* > x$. In contrast, if $x \geq b_0^*$, then by (28) $t^* = 0$ (for any μ), and (27) readily yields $v(x) = \beta_1 x - P$.

3. Solving the Optimal Stopping Problem

The optimal stopping problem (17) involves two tasks: (i) evaluating the value function $v(x)$ and (ii) identifying the maximizer $\tau = \tau^*$. A standard approach is to try and *guess* the solution and then to *verify* that it is correct.

3.1. Guessing the Solution

Let us look more closely at the nature of the value function $v(x)$ that we are trying to identify. Observe that by picking $\tau = 0$ in (17) yields the lower estimate

$$v(x) \geq g(x). \tag{30}$$

Clearly, if $v(x) > g(x)$ then we have not yet achieved the maximum payoff available, so we should continue to wait. On the other hand, if $v(x) = g(x)$ then the maximum has been attained and we should stop. This motivates the definition of the two regions, C (*continuation*) and S (*stopping*),

$$C := \{x \geq 0\colon v(x) > g(x)\}, \qquad S := \{x \geq 0\colon v(x) \leq g(x)\}.$$

By virtue of the Markov property of the process X_t, the same argument can be propagated to any time $t \geq 0$, provided that stopping has not yet occurred. Namely, if $X_t = x'$ (and $\tau \geq t$) then the problem (17) is updated with the new (residual) stopping time $\tau' = \tau - t$ and with the initial value x replaced by x'.

Thus, it is natural to expect that the optimal strategy prescribes to continue as long as the current wage value X_t belongs to the region C (i.e., $v(X_t) > g(X_t)$), but to stop when X_t first enters the region S (i.e., $v(X_t) \leq g(X_t)$). That is to say, the optimal stopping time should be given by[4]

$$\tau^* = \inf\{t \geq 0\colon X_t \in S\} = \inf\{t \geq 0\colon v(X_t) \leq g(X_t)\} \in [0, \infty]. \tag{31}$$

To clarify the plausible structure of the stopping set, S, recall (see the proof of Lemma 2(i)) that a zero value of the stopping problem (17) is achieved by simply using the strategy $\tau \equiv \infty$, that is, by never joining the scheme. Thus, if the initial wage $X_0 = x$ is small (e.g., such that $g(x) = \beta_1 x - P < 0$) then, in order to secure a positive payoff, we should wait for a sufficiently high wage X_t. This suggests that the stopping rule (31) is reduced to the first hitting time for a certain set on the plane $\{(t,x)\colon t \geq 0,\, x \geq 0\}$. Furthermore, noting that the definition (31) is time homogeneous, in that it does not change in the course of time t, we also hypothesize the simplest situation whereby the regions C and S are determined by a constant threshold $y = b^* > 0$,

$$C = [0, b^*), \qquad S = [b^*, \infty). \tag{32}$$

In other words, the conjectural hitting boundary does not depend on time.

Hence, we are led to the reduced optimal stopping problem over the subclass of hitting times,

$$u(x) = \sup_{b \geq 0} \mathrm{E}_x\big(\mathrm{e}^{-\tilde{r}\tau_b} g(X_{\tau_b})\big)\,. \tag{33}$$

---

[4] This conclusion is in accord with the general optimal stopping theory (Peskir and Shiryaev 2006, §2.2).

In particular, formula (31) specializes to

$$\tau_{b^*} = \inf\{t \geq 0\colon X_t \geq b^*\} = \inf\{t \geq 0\colon u(X_t) \leq g(X_t)\} \in [0, \infty]. \tag{34}$$

Our first task is to identify the value function $u(x)$ in (33) and the corresponding maximizer $b = b^*$ by solving the corresponding free-boundary problem (Section 3.2). After that, we will have to show that this solution is optimal in the general class of stopping times, that is, $u(x) = v(x)$ for all $x \geq 0$ (Section 3.3).

3.2. Free-Boundary Problem

According to general theory of optimal stopping (Peskir and Shiryaev 2006, chp. IV), in the continuation region $C = [0, b)$ (see (32)) the value function $u(x)$ from (33) must be *harmonic* with respect to the underlying process $\tilde{X}_t$ generated by X_t. More precisely, due to the discounting exponential factor in the optimal stopping problem (33), the process $\tilde{X}_t$ is obtained from X_t by independent *killing* (or discounting) with rate $\tilde{r}$ (Peskir and Shiryaev 2006, §§ 5.4, 6.3). Thus, if b is a suitable threshold and τ_b is the corresponding hitting time, then for any $x \geq 0$ the following condition must hold,

$$\mathrm{E}_x\big[\mathrm{e}^{-\tilde{r}(\tau_b \wedge t)} u(X_{\tau_b \wedge t})\big] = u(x) \quad (t \geq 0). \tag{35}$$

Note that the geometric Brownian motion X_t determined by the stochastic differential Equation (1) is a diffusion process with the infinitesimal generator

$$L := \mu x \frac{\mathrm{d}}{\mathrm{d}x} + \tfrac{1}{2}\sigma^2 x^2 \frac{\mathrm{d}^2}{\mathrm{d}x^2} \quad (x > 0). \tag{36}$$

The generator of the killed process $\tilde{X}_t$ is then given by (Peskir and Shiryaev 2006, § 6.3, p. 127)

$$\tilde{L} = L - \tilde{r} I, \tag{37}$$

where I is the identity operator. Then the harmonicity condition (35) can be reduced to the differential equation $\tilde{L}u = 0$, that is, $Lu - \tilde{r}u = 0$ (see (37)).

On the boundary $x = b$ of the set $C = [0, b)$, due to the stopping rule (34) we have $u(b) = g(b)$. Moreover, according to the *smooth fit principle* (Peskir and Shiryaev 2006, § 9.1), we must also satisfy the condition $u'(b) = g'(b)$. Finally, in view of the equality $v(0) = 0$ (see Lemma 2(i)), we add a Dirichlet boundary condition at zero, $u(0+) = \lim_{x \downarrow 0} u(x) = 0$. Thus, we arrive at the following *free-boundary problem*,

$$\begin{cases} Lu(x) - \tilde{r}u(x) = 0, & x \in (0, b), \\ u(b) = g(b), \\ u'(b) = g'(b), \\ u(0+) = 0, \end{cases} \tag{38}$$

where both $b > 0$ and $u(x)$ are unknown.

Substituting (10) and (36), the problem (38) is rewritten explicitly as

$$\begin{cases} \mu x\, u'(x) + \tfrac{1}{2}\sigma^2 x^2 u''(x) - \tilde{r}u(x) = 0, & x \in (0, b), \\ u(b) = \beta_1 b - P, \\ u'(b) = \beta_1, \\ u(0+) = 0. \end{cases} \tag{39}$$

Let us look for a solution of (39) in the form $u(x) = x^q$ $(x > 0)$, with a suitable parameter $q \in \mathbb{R}$. Then the differential equation in (39) yields

$$\tfrac{1}{2}\sigma^2 q(q-1) + \mu q - \tilde{r} = 0. \tag{40}$$

This quadratic equation has two distinct roots,

$$q_{1,2} = \frac{1}{\sigma^2}\left(-(\mu - \tfrac{1}{2}\sigma^2) \pm \sqrt{(\mu - \tfrac{1}{2}\sigma^2)^2 + 2\tilde{r}\sigma^2}\right),$$

where $q_2 < 0 < q_1 = q_*$ (see (24)). Also note that, due to the condition (11), the left-hand side of (40) is negative at $q = 1$, therefore $q_1 > 1$. Thus, the general solution of the differential Equation (39) is given by

$$u(x) = Ax^{q_1} + Bx^{q_2}, \quad x \in (0, b), \tag{41}$$

with arbitrary constants A and B. However, since $q_2 < 0$, the condition $u(0+) = 0$ implies that $B = 0$. Hence, (41) is reduced to $u(x) = Ax^{q_1} \equiv Ax^{q_*}$ $(0 < x < b)$. Furthermore, the boundary conditions in (39) yield

$$\begin{cases} Ab^{q_*} = \beta_1 b - P, \\ Aq_* b^{q_*-1} = \beta_1, \end{cases}$$

whence we find

$$A = \frac{\beta_1 b - P}{b^{q_*}}, \qquad b = \frac{Pq_*}{\beta_1(q_* - 1)}. \tag{42}$$

Thus, the required solution to (39) is given by

$$u(x) = \begin{cases} (\beta_1 b - P)\left(\dfrac{x}{b}\right)^{q_*}, & x \in [0, b], \\ \beta_1 x - P, & x \in [b, \infty) \end{cases} \tag{43}$$

where the threshold b is defined in (42) and $q_* > 1$ is the positive root of the Equation (40), given explicitly by formula (24).

3.3. *Verification of the Found Solution*

Using (42) and (43), it is easy to see that

$$\begin{aligned} u(x) &= g(x), \quad x \in [b, \infty), \\ u(x) &> g(x), \quad x \in [0, b), \end{aligned} \tag{44}$$

in accord with the heuristics outlined in Section 3.1 (see (32)). However, there is no need to check that the function $u(x)$ defined in (43) solves the reduced optimal stopping problem (33), because we can verify directly that $u(x)$ provides the solution to the original optimal stopping problem (17), that is, $u(x) = v(x)$ for all $x \geq 0$.

Remark 4. *Since* $u(0) = 0$ *by formula* (43) *and* $v(0) = 0$ *according to Lemma* 2(i), *in what follows it suffices to assume that* $x > 0$.

The proof of the claim above (commonly referred to as *verification theorem*) consists of two parts.

(i) Let us first show that $u(x) \geq v(x)$ $(x > 0)$. If the map $x \mapsto u(x)$ was a C^2-function (i.e., with continuous second derivative), then the classical *Itô formula* (Øksendal 2003, Theorem 4.1.2, p. 44) applied to $\mathrm{e}^{-\tilde{r}t}u(X_t)$ would yield, on account of (1) and (36),

$$\mathrm{e}^{-\tilde{r}t}u(X_t) = u(x) + \int_0^t \mathrm{e}^{-\tilde{r}s}\bigl(Lu(X_s) - \tilde{r}u(X_s)\bigr)\,\mathrm{d}s + M_t \quad (\mathrm{P}_x\text{-a.s.}), \tag{45}$$

where

$$M_t := \int_0^t \mathrm{e}^{-\tilde{r}s}u'(X_s)\,\sigma X_s\,\mathrm{d}B_s \quad (t \geq 0). \tag{46}$$

However, for the function $u(x)$ given by (43), its C^2-smoothness breaks down at the point $x = b$, where it is only C^1. However, $u(x)$ is strictly convex on $(0, b)$ (i.e., $u''(x) > 0$) and linear on (b, ∞), and we can define the action $Lu(x)$ at $x = b$ by using the one-sided second derivative, say,

$$u''(b-) = Pq_* b^{-2}. \tag{47}$$

In this situation, a generalization of the Itô formula holds, known as the *Itô–Meyer formula* (see (Shiryaev 1999, chp. VIII, §2a, p. 757)), which ensures that the representation (45) is still valid.

Recall that by construction (see the differential equation in (38)), we have

$$Lu(x) - \tilde{r}u(x) = 0, \quad x \in (0, b). \tag{48}$$

Moreover, it is easy to check using (47) that the equality (48) also extends to $x = b$. On the other hand, on account of the condition (11) and the definition of b in (42), for $x > b$ we get

$$\begin{aligned} Lu(x) - \tilde{r}u(x) &= \mu\beta_1 x - \tilde{r}(\beta_1 x - P) \\ &= \beta_1 x(\mu - \tilde{r}) + \tilde{r}P \\ &< \beta_1 b(\mu - \tilde{r}) + \tilde{r}P \\ &= \frac{P(\mu q_* - \tilde{r})}{q_* - 1} < 0, \end{aligned} \tag{49}$$

because, due to the Equation (40) and the inequality $q_* > 1$,

$$\mu q_* - \tilde{r} = -\tfrac{1}{2}\sigma^2 q_*(q_* - 1) < 0.$$

Thus, combining (48) and (49) we obtain

$$Lu(x) - \tilde{r}u(x) \le 0 \quad (x > 0). \tag{50}$$

Substituting the inequality (50) into formula (45), we conclude that, for any $x > 0$ and all $t \ge 0$,

$$u(x) + M_t \ge \mathrm{e}^{-\tilde{r}t} u(X_t) \quad (\mathrm{P}_x\text{-a.s.}). \tag{51}$$

According to formula (46), (M_t) is a continuous local martingale (Shiryaev 1999, chp. II, §1c, p. 101). Let (τ_n) be a localizing sequence of bounded stopping times, so that $\tau_n \uparrow \infty$ (P_x-a.s.) and the stopped process $(M_{\tau_n \wedge t})$ is a martingale, for each $n \in \mathbb{N}$.

Now, let τ be an arbitrary stopping time of (X_t). From (51) we get

$$\begin{aligned} u(x) + M_{\tau_n \wedge \tau} &\ge \mathrm{e}^{-\tilde{r}(\tau_n \wedge \tau)} u(X_{\tau_n \wedge \tau}) \\ &\ge \mathrm{e}^{-\tilde{r}(\tau_n \wedge \tau)} g(X_{\tau_n \wedge \tau}) \quad (\mathrm{P}_x\text{-a.s.}), \end{aligned} \tag{52}$$

using that $u(x) \ge g(x)$ for all $x \ge 0$ (see (44)). Taking expectation on both sides of the inequality (52) gives

$$u(x) \ge \mathrm{E}_x\big[\mathrm{e}^{-\tilde{r}(\tau_n \wedge \tau)} g(X_{\tau_n \wedge \tau})\big], \tag{53}$$

since by Doob's optional sampling theorem (Yeh 1995, Theorem 8.10, p. 131)

$$\mathrm{E}_x(M_{\tau_n \wedge \tau}) = \mathrm{E}_x(M_0) = 0.$$

By Fatou's lemma (Shiryaev 1996, §II.6, Theorem 2(a), p. 187), from (53) it follows

$$u(x) \geq \mathrm{E}_x\Big(\liminf_{n\to\infty} \mathrm{e}^{-\tilde{r}(\tau_n\wedge\tau)}\, g(X_{\tau_n\wedge\tau})\Big) = \mathrm{E}_x\big(\mathrm{e}^{-\tilde{r}\tau}\, g(X_\tau)\big)\,. \tag{54}$$

Finally, taking in (54) the supremum over all stopping times τ, we obtain

$$u(x) \geq \sup_\tau \mathrm{E}_x\big(\mathrm{e}^{-\tilde{r}\tau}\, g(X_\tau)\big) = v(x) \quad (x > 0),$$

as claimed.

(ii) Let us now prove the opposite inequality, $u(x) \leq v(x)$ $(x > 0)$. According to (30) and (44), we readily have $u(x) = g(x) \leq v(x)$ for $x \in [b, +\infty)$. Next, fix $x \in (0, b)$ and consider the representation (45) with t replaced by $\tau_n \wedge \tau_b$, where (τ_n) is the localizing sequence of stopping times for (M_t) as before. Then, by virtue of the identity (48) (which, as has been explained, is also true for $x = b$), it follows that

$$u(x) + M_{\tau_n\wedge\tau} = \mathrm{e}^{-\tilde{r}(\tau_n\wedge\tau_b)}\, u(X_{\tau_n\wedge\tau_b}) \quad (\mathrm{P}_x\text{-a.s.}). \tag{55}$$

Similarly as above, taking expectation on both sides of the equality (55) and again applying Doob's optional sampling theorem to the martingale $(M_{\tau_n\wedge t})$, we obtain

$$u(x) = \mathrm{E}_x\big[\mathrm{e}^{-\tilde{r}(\tau_n\wedge\tau_b)}\, u(X_{\tau_n\wedge\tau_b})\big]. \tag{56}$$

Note that, for $0 < x < b$, we have $0 \leq u(x) \leq u(b)$ and $0 \leq X_{\tau_n\wedge\tau_b} \leq b$ (P_x-a.s.), hence

$$0 \leq \mathrm{e}^{-\tilde{r}(\tau_n\wedge\tau_b)}\, u(X_{\tau_n\wedge\tau_b}) \leq u(b) \quad (\mathrm{P}_x\text{-a.s.}).$$

Using that $\tau_n \uparrow \infty$, observe that, P_x-a.s.,

$$\begin{aligned}\lim_{n\to\infty} \mathrm{e}^{-\tilde{r}(\tau_n\wedge\tau_b)}\, u(X_{\tau_n\wedge\tau_b}) &= \mathrm{e}^{-\tilde{r}\tau_b}\, u(X_{\tau_b})\, \mathbb{1}_{\{\tau_b<\infty\}} + \lim_{n\to\infty} \mathrm{e}^{-\tilde{r}\tau_n}\, u(X_{\tau_n})\, \mathbb{1}_{\{\tau_b=\infty\}} \\ &= \mathrm{e}^{-\tilde{r}\tau_b}\, u(b)\, \mathbb{1}_{\{\tau_b<\infty\}},\end{aligned} \tag{57}$$

because $X_{\tau_b} = b$ on the event $\{\tau < \infty\}$, while $0 \leq u(X_{\tau_n}) \leq u(b)$ on the event $\{\tau = \infty\}$. Hence, letting $n \to \infty$ in (56) and using the dominated convergence theorem (Shiryaev 1996, §II.6, Theorem 3, p. 187), we get, on account of (57),

$$\begin{aligned}u(x) &= \mathrm{E}_x\big(\mathrm{e}^{-\tilde{r}\tau_b}\, u(b)\, \mathbb{1}_{\{\tau_b<\infty\}}\big) \\ &= \mathrm{E}_x\big(\mathrm{e}^{-\tilde{r}\tau_b}\, g(b)\, \mathbb{1}_{\{\tau_b<\infty\}}\big) \\ &= \mathrm{E}_x\big(\mathrm{e}^{-\tilde{r}\tau_b}\, g(X_{\tau_b})\, \mathbb{1}_{\{\tau_b<\infty\}}\big) \\ &\leq v(x),\end{aligned}$$

according to (17). That is, we have proved that $u(x) \leq v(x)$ for all $0 < x < b$, as required.

Thus, the proof of the verification theorem is complete.

4. Elementary Solution of the Reduced Problem

4.1. Distribution of the Hitting Time

In view of the formula (2), the hitting problem for the process X_t is reduced to that for the Brownian motion with drift,

$$\tau_b := \inf\{t \geq 0\colon X_t = b\} \equiv \inf\{t \geq 0\colon B_t + \tilde{\mu} t = \tilde{b}\}, \tag{58}$$

where

$$\tilde{\mu} = \frac{\mu - \frac{1}{2}\sigma^2}{\sigma}, \qquad \tilde{b} = \frac{1}{\sigma}\ln\frac{b}{x}. \tag{59}$$

Suppose that $x \le b$, so that $\tilde{b} \ge 0$. The explicit expression for the Laplace transform of the hitting time (58) is well known (see, e.g., Durrett 1999, Exercises 6.29 and 6.31, p. 268, or Etheridge 2002, Proposition 3.3.5, p. 61).

Proposition 1. *For $x \le b$ and any $\theta > 0$, set*

$$\Phi_{x,b}(\theta) := \mathrm{E}_x(\mathrm{e}^{-\theta\tau_b}) \equiv \mathrm{E}_x\left(\mathrm{e}^{-\theta\tau_b}\mathbb{1}_{\{\tau_b<\infty\}}\right). \tag{60}$$

Then

$$\Phi_{x,b}(\theta) = \exp\left\{-\tilde{b}\left(\sqrt{\tilde{\mu}^2 + 2\theta} - \tilde{\mu}\right)\right\}, \quad \theta > 0, \tag{61}$$

where $\tilde{\mu}$ and $\tilde{b}$ are defined in (59).

Substituting the expressions (59), the formula (61) is rewritten as

$$\Phi_{x,b}(\theta) = \left(\frac{x}{b}\right)^{q_1(\theta)}, \quad \theta > 0, \tag{62}$$

where $q_1(\theta)$ is given by (cf. (24))

$$q_1(\theta) = \frac{1}{\sigma^2}\left(-(\mu - \tfrac{1}{2}\sigma^2) + \sqrt{(\mu - \tfrac{1}{2}\sigma^2)^2 + 2\theta\sigma^2}\right). \tag{63}$$

As usual, it is straightforward to extract from the Laplace transform (60) some explicit information about the distribution of the hitting time τ_b. First, by the monotone convergence theorem (Shiryaev 1996, §II.6, Theorem 1(a), p. 186) we have

$$\lim_{\theta\downarrow 0}\Phi_{x,b}(\theta) = \mathrm{E}_x(\mathbb{1}_{\{\tau_b<\infty\}}) = \mathrm{P}_x(\tau_b < \infty).$$

Hence, noting from (63) that

$$q_1(0) = \begin{cases} 0 & \text{if } \mu - \frac{1}{2}\sigma^2 \ge 0, \\ 1 - \dfrac{2\mu}{\sigma^2} & \text{if } \mu - \frac{1}{2}\sigma^2 < 0, \end{cases} \tag{64}$$

we obtain

$$\mathrm{P}_x(\tau_b < \infty) = \left(\frac{x}{b}\right)^{q_1(0)} = \begin{cases} 1, & \mu - \frac{1}{2}\sigma^2 \ge 0, \\ \left(\dfrac{x}{b}\right)^{1-2\mu/\sigma^2}, & \mu - \frac{1}{2}\sigma^2 < 0. \end{cases} \tag{65}$$

Remark 5. *The result* (65) *shows that hitting the critical threshold $b = b^*$, as required by the stopping rule, is only certain when the wage growth rate is large enough, $\mu \ge \frac{1}{2}\sigma^2$. Thus, the "dangerous" case is when $\mu < \frac{1}{2}\sigma^2$, whereby relying only on the optimal stopping recipe may not be practical. This observation may serve as a germ of the idea to connect the optimality problem in the insurance context with the notion of* utility *(cf. the discussion in Section* 7.1 *below).*

Via the Laplace transform $\Phi_{x,b}(\theta)$, we can also obtain the mean hitting time $\mathrm{E}_x(\tau_b)$ in the case $\mu \ge \frac{1}{2}\sigma^2$, where $\tau_b < \infty$ (P_x-a.s.). Namely, again using the monotone convergence theorem we have

$$\lim_{\theta\downarrow 0}\frac{\partial\Phi_{x,b}(\theta)}{\partial\theta} = -\lim_{\theta\downarrow 0}\mathrm{E}_x(\tau_b\,\mathrm{e}^{-\theta\tau_b}) = -\mathrm{E}_x(\tau_b).$$

Hence, differentiating formula (62) at $\theta = 0$ and noting from (63) that $q_1(0) = 0$ (cf. (64)) and

$$q_1'(0) = \begin{cases} \infty, & \mu = \frac{1}{2}\sigma^2, \\ \dfrac{1}{\mu - \frac{1}{2}\sigma^2}, & \mu > \frac{1}{2}\sigma^2, \end{cases}$$

we get

$$\mathrm{E}_x(\tau_b) = -\ln\left(\frac{x}{b}\right)\left(\frac{x}{b}\right)^{q_1(0)} q_1'(0) = \begin{cases} \infty, & \mu = \frac{1}{2}\sigma^2, \\ \dfrac{\ln(b/x)}{\mu - \frac{1}{2}\sigma^2}, & \mu > \frac{1}{2}\sigma^2. \end{cases} \tag{66}$$

4.2. Alternative Derivation

An alternative (and more direct) method to derive the formulas (65) and (66) is based on general theory of Markov processes by solving the suitable boundary value problems (Øksendal 2003, §9). Namely, the hitting probability $\pi(x) := \mathrm{P}_x(\tau_b < \infty)$ as a function of $x > 0$ satisfies the Dirichlet problem (Øksendal 2003, §9.2)

$$\begin{cases} L\pi(x) = 0 & (0 < x < b), \\ \pi(b) = 1. \end{cases} \tag{67}$$

The differential equation in (67) reads

$$\tfrac{1}{2}\sigma^2 x^2 \pi''(x) + \mu x \pi'(x) = 0 \quad (0 < x < b),$$

which is easily solved to give

$$\pi(x) = c_1 x^{1-2\mu/\sigma^2} + c_2.$$

If $1 - 2\mu/\sigma^2 < 0$ (i.e., $\mu - \frac{1}{2}\sigma^2 > 0$) then $c_1 = 0$ (since $\pi(x)$ is bounded), and due to the boundary condition $\pi(b) = 1$ it follows that $c_2 = 1$ and $\pi(x) \equiv 1$. A similar argument shows that $\pi(x) \equiv 1$ in the case $1 - 2\mu/\sigma^2 = 0$. Finally, if $1 - 2\mu/\sigma^2 > 0$ then, noting that $\pi(0) = 0$, we conclude that $c_2 = 0$ and, due to the boundary condition, $c_1 = b^{-1+2\mu/\sigma^2}$. Thus, formula (65) is proved.

Similarly, the mean hitting time $m(x) := \mathrm{E}_x(\tau_b)$ (with $\mu - \frac{1}{2}\sigma^2 > 0$) satisfies the Poisson problem (Øksendal 2003, §9.3)

$$\begin{cases} Lm(x) = -1 & (0 < x < b), \\ m(b) = 0. \end{cases} \tag{68}$$

As usual, to solve the problem (68), it is convenient to approximate it with a two-sided boundary problem by adding an auxiliary Neumann (reflection) condition at $\varepsilon > 0$,

$$\begin{cases} Lm_\varepsilon(x) = -1 & (\varepsilon < x < b), \\ m_\varepsilon(b) = 0, \\ m_\varepsilon'(\varepsilon) = 0, \end{cases} \tag{69}$$

and then taking the limit of $m_\varepsilon(x)$ as $\varepsilon \downarrow 0$. This procedure will produce the correct solution $m(x)$ since $\lim_{\varepsilon\downarrow 0} \mathrm{P}_x(\tau_\varepsilon < \infty) = \mathrm{P}_x(\tau_0 < \infty) = 0$ (for any $x > 0$).

A particular solution to the inhomogeneous differential equation

$$\tfrac{1}{2}\sigma^2 x^2 m_\varepsilon''(x) + \mu x m_\varepsilon'(x) = -1 \quad (\varepsilon < x < b)$$

can be sought in the form $m_0(x) = c_0 \ln x$, which gives $c_0 = -1/(\mu - \frac{1}{2}\sigma^2)$. Thus, the general solution of (69) can be expressed as

$$m_\varepsilon(x) = -\frac{\ln x}{\mu - \frac{1}{2}\sigma^2} + c_1 x^{1-2\mu/\sigma^2} + c_2. \tag{70}$$

Now, using the boundary conditions in (69) it is straightforward to check that

$$\lim_{\varepsilon\downarrow 0} c_1 = 0, \qquad \lim_{\varepsilon\downarrow 0} c_2 = \frac{\ln b}{\mu - \frac{1}{2}\sigma^2}.$$

Hence, from (70) we get

$$m(x) = \lim_{\varepsilon\downarrow 0} m_\varepsilon(x) = \frac{\ln(b/x)}{\mu - \frac{1}{2}\sigma^2},$$

which retrieves the result (66).

Remark 6. *The same method applied to the killed process $\tilde{X}_t$ with generator $\tilde{L} = L - \tilde{r}I$ (see (37)) provides a neat interpretation of the value function $u(x)$ as given by (43). Namely, rewrite the expectation in (33) (i.e., $\mathrm{eNPV}(x;\tau_b)$) in the form $\tilde{\mathrm{E}}_x(g(\tilde{X}_{\tau_b}))$, where $\tilde{\mathrm{E}}_x$ denotes expectation with respect to the killed process $(\tilde{X}_t)$, and note that, for $b \ge 0$,*

$$\tilde{\mathrm{E}}_x(g(\tilde{X}_{\tau_b})) = \begin{cases} g(b)\,\tilde{\mathrm{P}}_x(\tau_b < \infty), & x \in [0,b], \\ g(x), & x \in [b,\infty). \end{cases}$$

In turn, the hitting probability $\tilde{\pi}(x) := \tilde{\mathrm{P}}_x(\tau_b < \infty)$ can be easily found by solving the corresponding Dirichlet problem (cf. (67)),

$$\begin{cases} \tilde{L}\tilde{\pi}(x) = 0 \quad (0 < x < b), \\ \tilde{\pi}(b) = 1. \end{cases}$$

Indeed, repeating the calculations in Section 3.2, it is straightforward to get $\tilde{\pi}(x) = (x/b)^{q^*}$.

4.3. Direct Maximization

Using the results of the previous sections, we can easily solve the optimal stopping problem (17), at least in the subclass of hitting times $\tau = \tau_b$ (see (33)),

$$u(x) = \sup_{b\ge 0} \mathrm{eNPV}(x;\tau_b) = \sup_{b\ge 0} \mathrm{E}_x\big(\mathrm{e}^{-\tilde{r}\tau_b}(\beta_1 X_{\tau_b} - P)\big). \tag{71}$$

Observe that if $x \ge b$ then $\tau_b = 0$ and $X_{\tau_b} = x$ (P_x-a.s.), so that $\mathrm{eNPV}(x;\tau_b) \equiv \beta_1 x - P$ for all $b \in [0,x]$. Let now $b \in [x,\infty)$. As already noted, on the event $\{\tau_b < \infty\}$ we have $X_{\tau_b} = b$ (P_x-a.s.), hence, according to (17) and (62),

$$\mathrm{eNPV}(x;\tau_b) = (\beta_1 b - P)\,\mathrm{E}_x(\mathrm{e}^{-\tilde{r}\tau_b}) = (\beta_1 b - P)\left(\frac{x}{b}\right)^{q_*} \quad (b \ge x), \tag{72}$$

where $q_* = q_1(\theta)|_{\theta=\tilde{r}}$ (cf. (24) and (63)). It is straightforward to find the maximizer for the function (72). Indeed, the condition $(\partial/\partial b)\,\mathrm{eNPV}(x;\tau_b) \ge 0$, equivalent to

$$\beta_1 b^{-q_*} - q_*(\beta_1 b - P)\,b^{-q_*-1} \ge 0,$$

holds for all $b \in [0, b^*]$, where

$$b^* = \frac{Pq_*}{\beta_1(q_* - 1)}, \tag{73}$$

which is the same optimal threshold as before (cf. (23)). Thus, the supremum of $\mathrm{eNPV}(x;\tau_b)$ over $b \ge x$ is attained at $b = b^*$ if $x \le b^*$ or at $b = x$ if $x \ge b^*$.

The corresponding value function $u(x)$ is then calculated as (cf. (25))

$$u(x) = \begin{cases} (\beta_1 b^* - P)\left(\dfrac{x}{b^*}\right)^{q_*}, & x \in [0, b^*], \\ \beta_1 x - P, & x \in [b^*, \infty). \end{cases} \tag{74}$$

Finally, substituting (73) into (74), we obtain explicitly (cf. (26))

$$u(x) = \begin{cases} \dfrac{P}{q_* - 1}\left(\dfrac{\beta_1 (q_* - 1)x}{Pq_*}\right)^{q_*}, & 0 \le x \le \dfrac{Pq_*}{\beta_1(q_* - 1)}, \\ \beta_1 x - P, & x \ge \dfrac{Pq_*}{\beta_1(q_* - 1)}. \end{cases} \tag{75}$$

5. Statistical Issues and Numerical Illustration

5.1. Specifying the Model Parameters

From the practical point of view, in order to exercise the stopping rule (22), the individual concerned needs to be able to compute the critical threshold b^* expressed in (23), for which the knowledge is required about β_1 (defined in (9)) and therefore about the parameters r, λ_0, μ and β (see (5)); furthermore, to evaluate the quantity q_* defined in (24), one needs to estimate $\mu - \frac{1}{2}\sigma^2$ and σ^2 itself. Specifically,

- The loss of job rate λ_0 can be extracted from the publicly available data about the mean length at work, which is theoretically given by $\mathrm{E}(\tau_0) = 1/\lambda_0$.
- Likewise, the inflation rate r is also in the public domain.
- To specify the wage growth rate μ, a simple approach is just to set $\mu = r$ as a crude version of a "tracking" rule. However, it may be possible that the individual's wage growth rate μ is, to some extent, stipulated by the job contract—for example, that it must not exceed the inflation rate r by more than 1% per annum (applicable, e.g., to civil servants) or, by contrast, that it must be no less than r minus 0.5% per annum (more realistic in the private sector). In practical terms, this would often mean that the actual growth rate μ is kept on the lowest predefined level.
- More generally, the wage growth rate μ can be estimated by observing the wage process X_t. This can be implemented by first using regression analysis on $Y_t = \ln X_t$ and estimating the regression line slope $\mu - \frac{1}{2}\sigma^2$ (see (2)). In addition, the volatility σ^2 can be estimated by using a suitable quadratic functional of the sample path (Y_t).
- Finally, knowing the benefit schedule (which should be available through the insurance policy's terms and conditions), it is in principle possible to calculate, or at least estimate the value β.

To summarize, certain estimation procedures need to be carried out along with the online observation of the sample path (X_t). More details (most of which are quite standard) are provided in the next two subsections.

5.2. Estimating the Drift and Volatility

Denote for short $a := \mu - \frac{1}{2}\sigma^2$. According to the geometric Brownian motion model (2), we have

$$Y_t := \ln X_t = \ln x + \sigma B_t + at, \qquad Y_0 = \ln x.$$

Suppose the process X_t is observed over the time interval $t \in [0, T]$ on a discrete-time grid $t_i = iT/n$ ($i = 0, \ldots, n$), and consider the consecutive increments

$$Z_i := Y_{t_i} - Y_{t_{i-1}} = \sigma(B_{t_i} - B_{t_{i-1}}) + a\,(t_i - t_{i-1}) \quad (i = 1, \ldots, n). \tag{76}$$

Note that the increments of the Brownian motion in (76) are mutually independent and have normal distribution with zero mean and variance $t_i - t_{i-1} = T/n$, respectively. Therefore, (Z_i) is an independent random sample with normal marginal distributions,

$$Z_i \sim \mathcal{N}\left(\frac{aT}{n}, \frac{\sigma^2 T}{n}\right) \qquad (i = 1, \ldots, n).$$

Then, it is standard to estimate the parameters via the sample mean and sample variance,

$$\hat{a}_n := \frac{n}{T} \cdot \bar{Z} = \frac{Z_1 + \cdots + Z_n}{T} = \frac{Y_T - Y_0}{T}, \tag{77}$$

$$\hat{\sigma}_n^2 := \frac{n}{T} \cdot \frac{1}{n-1} \sum_{i=1}^{n} (Z_i - \bar{Z})^2. \tag{78}$$

These estimators are unbiased,

$$\mathrm{E}(\hat{a}_n) = a = \mu - \tfrac{1}{2}\sigma^2, \qquad \mathrm{E}(\hat{\sigma_n}^2) = \sigma^2,$$

with mean square errors

$$\mathrm{Var}(\hat{a}_n) = \frac{\sigma^2}{T}, \qquad \mathrm{Var}(\hat{\sigma}_n^2) = \frac{2\sigma^4}{n-1}.$$

In turn, the parameter μ is estimated by

$$\hat{\mu}_n = \hat{a}_n + \tfrac{1}{2}\hat{\sigma}_n^2,$$

with mean $\mathrm{E}(\hat{\mu}_n) = \mathrm{E}(\hat{a}_n) + \frac{1}{2}\mathrm{E}(\hat{\sigma}_n^2) = a + \frac{1}{2}\sigma^2 = \mu$ and mean square error

$$\mathrm{Var}(\hat{\mu}_n) = \mathrm{Var}(\hat{a}_n) + \tfrac{1}{4}\mathrm{Var}(\hat{\sigma}_n^2) = \frac{\sigma^2}{T} + \frac{\sigma^4}{2(n-1)}$$

(due to independence of the estimators $\hat{a}_n$ and $\hat{\sigma}_n^2$).

Note that the estimator $\hat{a}_n$ in (77) only employs the last observed value, Y_T; in particular, its mean square error is not sensitive to the grid size $\Delta t_i = T/n$, and only tends to zero with increasing observational horizon, $T \to \infty$. This makes the estimation of the drift parameter a difficult in the sense that very long observations over Y_t are required to achieve an acceptable precision (Ekström and Lu 2011, Example 2.1, p. 3). For instance, let $\mu = 0.004$ and $\sigma = 0.02$ (per week), then $a = 0.0038$; if $T = 25$ (weeks) then the 95%-confidence bounds for a are given by $\hat{a} \pm 1.96\,\sigma/\sqrt{T} = \hat{a} \pm 0.00784$, so the margin of error is about twice as big as the value of a itself. To reduce it, say to $0.5a$, one needs $T \approx 425$ (weeks), which exemplifies slow convergence.

In contrast, the mean square error of the estimator $\hat{\sigma}_n^2$ in (78) tends to zero as $n \to \infty$, with T fixed. Thus, estimation of the parameter σ^2 can be made asymptotically precise.

A numerical example illustrating the estimation of μ and σ^2 using simulated data will be given at the end of Section 5.4. A brief discussion of practical choices of μ, based on sensitivity analysis, is provided at the end of Section 6.3.

5.3. Hypothesis Testing

In view of the drawback in the general solution of the optimal stopping problem in that the stopping time τ_{b^*} may be infinite, that is, $\mathrm{P}_x(\tau_{b^*} = \infty) > 0$, which occurs when $a = \mu - \frac{1}{2}\sigma^2 < 0$ (see Section 4.1), a reasonable pragmatic approach to decision-making in our model may be based on testing the null hypothesis $H_0\colon a \geq 0$ versus the alternative $H_1: a < 0$ (at some intuitively acceptable significance level, e.g., $\alpha = 0.05$). Namely, as long as H_0 remains tenable, one keeps waiting for the hitting time τ_{b^*} to occur, but once H_0 has been rejected, it is reasonable to terminate waiting and buy the policy immediately.

The corresponding test is specified as follows. Again, suppose that the process Y_t is observed on a discrete time grid $t_i = iT/n$, and set $Z_i = Y_{t_i} - Y_{t_{i-1}}$ $(i = 1, \dots, n)$. Let $z(\alpha)$ be the upper α-quantile of the standard normal distribution $\mathcal{N}(0,1)$, that is, $1 - \Phi(z(\alpha)) = \alpha$, where $\Phi(x) = \frac{1}{\sqrt{2\pi}} \int_{-\infty}^{x} \mathrm{e}^{-u^2/2}\,\mathrm{d}u$. Then the null hypothesis $H_0\colon a \geq 0$ is to be rejected at significance level α whenever

$$Z_1 + \cdots + Z_n \leq \inf_{a \geq 0} \left\{ aT - z(\alpha)\sigma\sqrt{T} \right\},$$

that is,

$$Y_T - Y_0 \leq -z(\alpha)\sigma\sqrt{T}. \tag{79}$$

This test is uniformly most powerful among all tests with probability of error of type I not exceeding α, that is, $\mathrm{P}(\text{reject } H_0 \mid H_0 \text{ true}) \leq \alpha$.

The normal test (79) assumes that the variance σ^2 is known. As mentioned before, this presents no real restriction if the process Y_t is observable continuously (i.e., if the grid (t_i) can be refined indefinitely). If this is not the case (e.g., because the wage process can only be observed on the weekly basis) then the test (79) is replaced by the t-test,

$$Y_T - Y_0 \leq -t_{n-1}(\alpha)\hat{\sigma}\sqrt{T},$$

where $\hat{\sigma}^2$ is the sample variance (see (78)) and $t_{n-1}(\alpha)$ is the upper α-quantile of the t-distribution with $n-1$ degrees of freedom.

In practice, the hypothesis testing is carried out sequentially (e.g., weekly) as the observational horizon T increases. The advantage of this approach is that the resulting stopping time is finite with probability one (i.e., P_x-a.s.); indeed, it is the minimum between the optimal stopping time τ_{b^*} (which is finite P_x-a.s. under the null hypothesis $H_0\colon a \geq 0$) and the first time of rejecting H_0 (which is finite P_x-a.s. if H_0 is false).

5.4. Numerical Examples

To be specific, we use euro as the monetary unit. First of all, the value of the constant β, which encapsulates information about the benefit schedule as well as the rate λ_1 of finding new job (see (5)), is chosen to be

$$\beta = 30.$$

Thus, the overall expected benefit payable over the lifetime of the policy (and projected to the beginning of unemployment) is taken to be equal to 30 weekly wages; that is, if the final wage is 400 (euro per week) then the total to be received is

$$400.00 \times 30 = 12\,000.00 \text{ (euro)}.$$

Further, we set

$$\lambda_0 = 0.01, \qquad r = 0.0004.$$

This means that the expected time until loss of job is $1/\lambda_0 = 100$ (weeks), that is, about 1 year and 11 months, whereas the annual inflation rate is

$$\mathrm{e}^{(365/7)\cdot 0.0004} - 1 = 0.02107617 \approx 2.11\%,$$

which is quite realistic.

Next, we need to specify the premium P and the parameters of the wage process X_t, First, choose the initial value $x = X_0$ as

$$x = 346.00 \text{ (euro)}.$$

This is motivated by the French labour legislation, whereby the current minimum pay rate is set as 9.88 euro per hour (WageIndicator 2018), with a 35-hour workweek (Estevão and Sá 2008; Gubian et al. 2004), giving

$$9.88 \times 35 = 345.80 \text{ (euro per week)}.$$

As for the premium, it is set at the value

$$P = 9\,000.00 \text{ (euro)},$$

which equates to about 26 minimum weekly wages (i.e., income over about half a year). For simplicity, we also choose

$$\mu = r = 0.0004, \tag{80}$$

so that the wage growth rate is the same as inflation r (in reality, it could be slightly less). Then from (9), using (80), we get

$$\beta_1 = \frac{\lambda_0 \beta}{\tilde{r} - \mu} = \beta = 30.$$

For the volatility σ, we will illustrate two opposite cases, $\mu < \frac{1}{2}\sigma^2$ and $\mu > \frac{1}{2}\sigma^2$.

Example 2. *Set $\sigma = 0.04$, then $\mu - \frac{1}{2}\sigma^2 = -0.0004 < 0$. From (24) we calculate $q_* = 3.864208$, then (42) yields*

$$b^* = 404.7410 = 404.74 \text{ (euro)}.$$

Using (65), the hitting probability is calculated as

$$\mathrm{P}_x(\tau_{b^*} < \infty) = 0.9245906.$$

Finally, using (43), we obtain the value of this contract,

$$v(346) = 1714.2780 = 1714.28 \text{ (euro)}.$$

Example 3. *Now, set $\sigma = 0.02$, then $\mu - \frac{1}{2}\sigma^2 = 0.0002 > 0$. Furthermore, using (24) we calculate $q_* = 6.728416$, and from (42)*

$$b^* = 352.3705 = 352.37 \text{ (euro)}.$$

Hence, using (66), the expected hitting time is found to be

$$\mathrm{E}(\tau_{b^*}) = 91.22197 = 91.2 \text{ (weeks)}.$$

Finally, according to formula (25), the value of this contract is calculated as

$$v(346) = 1\,389.6190 = 1\,389.62 \text{ (euro)}.$$

In the simulation of the process X_t shown in Figure 3, the drift $a = \mu - \frac{1}{2}\sigma^2$ is estimated using formula (77) as $\hat{a} \doteq 0.0005994$. Estimation of the variance σ^2 according to formula (78) (on a weekly time grid) gives $\hat{\sigma}^2 \doteq 0.0003723$, while the true value is $\sigma^2 = 0.0004$. Hence, the parameter μ is estimated by $\hat{\mu} \doteq 0.0007855$; recall that the true value is $\mu = 0.0004$.

6. Parametric Dependencies

In this section, we aim to explore the parametric dependencies of the solution of our insurance problem, that is, of the optimal threshold b^* given by (23) and the value function $v = v(x)$ given by (25). In particular, it is helpful to analyze different asymptotic regimes as well as (the sign of) appropriate partial derivatives, so as to ascertain the direction of changes under small perturbations and to understand their economic meaning. This is a key ingredient of sensitivity analysis and of the so-called *comparative statics* (Merton 1969, Section VII).

In what follows, we confine ourselves to a discussion of the two most important exogenous parameters—the wage drift μ and the unemployment rate λ_0. The constraint (11) implies that the range of the parameters μ and λ_0 is specified as follows,

$$-\infty < \mu < \tilde{r} = r + \lambda_0, \qquad 0 \vee (\mu - r) < \lambda_0 < \infty.$$

Remark 7. *The next two technical subsections are elementary but rather tedious, and the reader wishing to grasp the results quickly may just inspect the plots in Figures 4 and 5.*

6.1. Monotonicity

By virtue of the quadratic Equation (40), the formula (23) can be conveniently rewritten as

$$b^* = \frac{P(\frac{1}{2}\sigma^2 q_* + \tilde{r})}{\beta\lambda_0}. \tag{81}$$

First, fix λ_0 and consider the function $\mu \mapsto b^*$. Differentiating the Equation (23) and then again using (23) to eliminate μ, we obtain

$$\frac{\partial q_*}{\partial \mu} = -\frac{q_*}{\frac{1}{2}\sigma^2(2q_* - 1) + \mu} = -\frac{q_*^2}{\frac{1}{2}\sigma^2 q_*^2 + \tilde{r}} < 0. \tag{82}$$

Hence, using (81) and (82),

$$\frac{\mathrm{d}b^*}{\mathrm{d}\mu} = \frac{\partial b^*}{\partial \mu} + \frac{\partial b^*}{\partial q_*} \cdot \frac{\partial q_*}{\partial \mu} = -\frac{P(\frac{1}{2}\sigma^2 q_*^2)}{\beta\lambda_0(\frac{1}{2}\sigma^2 q_*^2 + \tilde{r})} < 0. \tag{83}$$

and, therefore, b^* is a decreasing function of μ (see Figure 4a).

Similarly, the Equation (40) yields

$$\frac{\partial q_*}{\partial \lambda_0} = \frac{1}{\frac{1}{2}\sigma^2(2q_* - 1) + \mu} = \frac{q_*}{\frac{1}{2}\sigma^2 q_*^2 + r + \lambda_0} > 0. \tag{84}$$

From (81) and (84), after some rearrangements we obtain

$$\begin{aligned}\frac{\mathrm{d}b^*}{\mathrm{d}\lambda_0} &= \frac{\partial b^*}{\partial \lambda_0} + \frac{\partial b^*}{\partial q_*} \cdot \frac{\partial q_*}{\partial \lambda_0}\\ &= -\frac{P(\frac{1}{2}\sigma^2 q_* + r)}{\beta\lambda_0^2} + \frac{P(\frac{1}{2}\sigma^2 q_*)}{\beta\lambda_0(\frac{1}{2}\sigma^2 q_*^2 + r + \lambda_0)}\\ &= -\frac{P\left[(\frac{1}{2}\sigma^2 q_* + r)(\frac{1}{2}\sigma^2 q_*^2 + r) + \lambda_0 r\right]}{\beta\lambda_0^2(\frac{1}{2}\sigma^2 q_*^2 + r + \lambda_0)} < 0,\end{aligned} \tag{85}$$

and it follows that the function $\lambda_0 \mapsto b^*$ is decreasing (see Figure 4b).

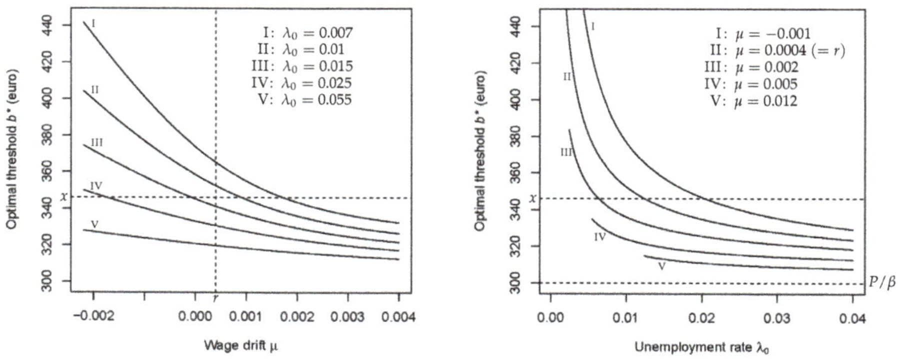

(a) $\mu \mapsto b^*$ (b) $\lambda_0 \mapsto b^*$

Figure 4. Graphs illustrating parametric dependencies of the optimal threshold (23): (**a**) on the wage drift $\mu < \tilde{r}$ and (**b**) on the unemployment rate $\lambda_0 > 0 \vee (\mu - r)$, for selected values of λ_0 and μ, respectively. The values of other model parameters used throughout are as in Example 3: $r = 0.0004$, $P = 9\,000$, $\beta = 30$, and $\sigma = 0.02$. The dashed horizontal line in both plots indicates the initial wage $x = 346$. The dashed vertical line in (**a**) indicates $\mu = r$. The lower dashed horizontal line in (**b**)

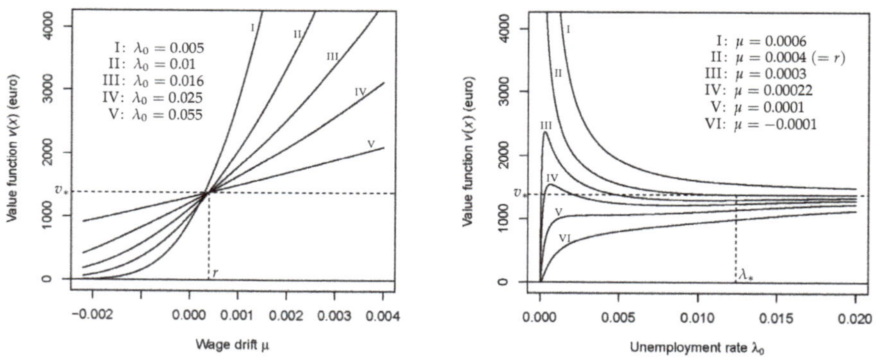

(a) $\mu \mapsto v(x)$ (b) $\lambda_0 \mapsto v(x)$

Figure 5. Graphs illustrating parametric dependencies of the value function (25): (**a**) on the wage drift $\mu < \tilde{r}$ and (**b**) on the unemployment rate $\lambda_0 > 0 \vee (\mu - r)$, for selected values of λ_0 and μ, respectively. The values of other model parameters used throughout are as in Example 3: $r = 0.0004$, $P = 9000$, $\beta = 30$, $\sigma = 0.02$, and $x = 346$. The dashed horizontal lines in both plots correspond to the value $v_* := \beta x - P = 1\,380$. The dashed vertical line in (**a**) indicates $\mu = r$; in this case, shown as curve II in plot (**b**), $v(x) \equiv v_*$ for all $\lambda_0 \geq \lambda_* \doteq 0.012420$ (see (92)). That is why curves III, IV and V in plot (**a**) all intersect at $\mu = r$.

Let us now turn to the value function $v = v(x)$. First, consider v as a function of μ, thus keeping λ_0 fixed. Using the expression (23), we can rewrite the first line of the formula (25) (i.e., for $x \leq b^*$) as

$$v = \frac{P}{q_* - 1} \left(\frac{x}{b^*} \right)^{q_*}. \tag{86}$$

Differentiating (86), we get

$$\frac{\partial v}{\partial q_*} = -\frac{P}{(q_*-1)^2}\left(\frac{x}{b^*}\right)^{q_*}\left(1+(q_*-1)\ln\left(\frac{b^*}{x}\right)\right) < 0, \tag{87}$$

$$\frac{\partial v}{\partial b^*} = -\frac{Pq_*}{(q_*-1)\,b^*}\left(\frac{x}{b^*}\right)^{q_*} < 0. \tag{88}$$

Hence, on account of the inequalities (82), (84), (87) and (88),

$$\frac{\mathrm{d}v}{\mathrm{d}\mu} = \frac{\partial v}{\partial \mu} + \frac{\partial v}{\partial q_*}\cdot\frac{\partial q_*}{\partial \mu} + \frac{\partial v}{\partial b^*}\cdot\frac{\mathrm{d}b^*}{\mathrm{d}\mu} > 0. \tag{89}$$

If $x \ge b^*$, then from the second line of (25) we readily obtain

$$\frac{\mathrm{d}v}{\mathrm{d}\mu} = \frac{\beta\lambda_0 x}{(\tilde{r}-\mu)^2} > 0. \tag{90}$$

Thus, in all cases $\mathrm{d}v/\mathrm{d}\mu > 0$, which implies that the function $\mu \mapsto v$ is increasing (see Figure 5a).

Finally, fix μ and consider the function $\lambda_0 \mapsto v$. If $x \ge b^*$, then v is given by the second line of (25), that is,

$$v = \frac{\beta\lambda_0 x}{\lambda_0 + r - \mu} - P. \tag{91}$$

In particular, if $\mu = r$, then (91) is reduced to $v \equiv v_* := \beta x - P$. From (91) it follows that

$$\frac{\mathrm{d}v}{\mathrm{d}\lambda_0} = \frac{\beta x(r-\mu)}{(\lambda_0+r-\mu)^2}\begin{cases} < 0, & \mu > r, \\ = 0, & \mu = r, \\ > 0, & \mu < r. \end{cases}$$

Due to monotonicity of the function $\lambda_0 \mapsto b^*$ (see (85)), v is given by (91) as long as $\lambda_0 \ge \lambda_*$, for some critical value $\lambda_* \equiv \lambda_*(\mu) \le \infty$. It will be shown below (see (99)) that $\lim_{\lambda_0\to\infty} b_* = P/\beta$, so $\lambda_* < \infty$ if and only $x > P/\beta$. Clearly, λ_* is determined by the condition $b^* = x$ (see (23)) together with the Equation (40). In the special case $\mu = r$ (assuming that $x > P/\beta$), these equations can be solved to yield

$$\lambda_* = \frac{P}{\beta x}\left(\frac{\frac{1}{2}\sigma^2\beta x}{\beta x - P} + r\right). \tag{92}$$

In particular, in Example 3 this gives $\lambda_* \doteq 0.012420$. From the consideration above, it also follows that if $x > P/\beta$, then (see (91))

$$\lim_{\lambda_0\to\infty} v = v_* = \beta x - P. \tag{93}$$

In the case $x \le b^*$, we use formula (86). Similarly to (89),

$$\frac{\mathrm{d}v}{\mathrm{d}\lambda_0} = \frac{\partial v}{\partial \lambda_0} + \frac{\partial v}{\partial q_*}\cdot\frac{\partial q_*}{\partial \lambda_0} + \frac{\partial v}{\partial b^*}\cdot\frac{\mathrm{d}b^*}{\mathrm{d}\lambda_0}. \tag{94}$$

Substituting the expressions (82), (84), (87), and (88) into (94), canceling immaterial factors and recalling formula (81), the condition $\mathrm{d}v/\mathrm{d}\lambda_0 < 0$ is reduced to

$$\left(\frac{1}{2}\sigma^2 q_* + r\right)\left(\frac{1}{2}\sigma^2 q_*^2 + r\right) + \lambda_0 r < \left(\frac{1}{q_*-1} + \ln\left(\frac{b^*}{x}\right)\right)\left(\frac{1}{2}\sigma^2 q_*^2 + r + \lambda_0\right). \tag{95}$$

It can proved that if $\mu \ge r$, then the inequality (95) holds for all $\lambda_0 < \lambda_*$, but the analysis becomes difficult for $\mu < r$. Numerical plots (see Figure 5b) suggest that in the latter case the function $\lambda_0 \mapsto v$ may be non-monotonic, with the derivative $\mathrm{d}v/\mathrm{d}\lambda_0$ possibly vanishing in up to two points, provided that $r - \varepsilon < \mu < r$ with $\varepsilon > 0$ small enough. To be more specific, the plots in Figure 5b illustrate the case $x > P/\beta$, with the common asymptote (93). For $x \leq P/\beta$, the plots look similar (not shown here) but with $\lim_{\lambda_0 \to \infty} v = 0$ (see (102) below), so the derivative $\mathrm{d}v/\mathrm{d}\lambda_0$ may vanish in at most one point.

6.2. Limiting Values

Let us investigate the functions b^* and v in the limits (i) $\mu \to -\infty$ or $\mu \uparrow \tilde{r}$, and (ii) $\lambda_0 \to \infty$ or $\lambda_0 \downarrow 0$ ($\mu < r$), $\lambda_0 \downarrow \mu - r$ ($\mu \geq r$). Start by observing, using Equation (40), that

$$\lim_{\mu \to -\infty} q_* = \infty, \qquad \lim_{\mu \uparrow \tilde{r}} q_* = 1, \tag{96}$$

and moreover,

$$q_* - 1 \sim \frac{\tilde{r} - \mu}{\frac{1}{2}\sigma^2 + \tilde{r}} \qquad (\mu \uparrow \tilde{r}). \tag{97}$$

Similarly, $\lim_{\lambda_0 \to \infty} q_* = \infty$; on the other hand, if $\mu < r$ then $\lim_{\lambda_0 \downarrow 0} q_* = q_*|_{\lambda_0 = 0} > 1$, while if $\mu \geq r$ then

$$q_* - 1 \sim \frac{\lambda_0 - (\mu - r)}{\frac{1}{2}\sigma^2 + \mu} \qquad (\lambda_0 \downarrow \mu - r). \tag{98}$$

Hence, from (81) and (96) it readily follows that $b^* \to \infty$ ($\mu \to -\infty$) and

$$b^* \to \frac{P(\frac{1}{2}\sigma^2 + \tilde{r})}{\beta\lambda_0} \qquad (\mu \uparrow \tilde{r}).$$

Also, using that $q_* \to \infty$ ($\lambda_0 \to \infty$), from (23) we get

$$b^* \to \frac{P}{\beta} \qquad (\lambda_0 \to \infty). \tag{99}$$

In the opposite limit, if $\mu > r$ then, according to (81) and (98),

$$b^* \to \frac{P(\frac{1}{2}\sigma^2 + \mu)}{\beta(\mu - r)} \qquad (\lambda_0 \downarrow \mu - r), \tag{100}$$

while if $\mu \leq r$ then $\lim_{\lambda_0 \downarrow 0} b^* = \infty$; in particular, for $\mu = r$

$$b^* \sim \frac{P(\frac{1}{2}\sigma^2 + r)}{\beta\lambda_0} \qquad (\lambda_0 \downarrow 0). \tag{101}$$

For the value function $v = v(x)$, from formula (86) we get, using (96) and (97),

$$\lim_{\mu \to -\infty} v = 0, \qquad \lim_{\mu \uparrow \tilde{r}} v = \infty.$$

Furthermore, according to (93), if $x > P/\beta$, then $v \to v_* = \beta x - P$ as $\lambda_0 \to \infty$. In the opposite case, due to monotonicity of b^* (see (85)) and the limit (99) we have $b^* > P/\beta \geq x$, so using formula (86) and recalling that $q_* \to \infty$, we get

$$v \leq \frac{P}{q_* - 1} \to 0 \qquad (\lambda_0 \to \infty). \tag{102}$$

Now, consider the limit of v as λ_0 approaches the lower edge of its range. If $\mu < r$ then (86) implies that $\lim_{\lambda \downarrow 0} v = 0$, since $b^* \to \infty$ and $q_* \to q_*|_{\lambda_0 = 0} > 1$. If $\mu = r$ then, using (98) and (101) (with $\mu = r$), we obtain

$$v \sim \beta x \lambda_0^{q_* - 1} = \beta x \exp\{(q_* - 1)\ln \lambda_0\} \to \beta x \qquad (\lambda_0 \downarrow 0). \tag{103}$$

Finally, if $\mu > r$, then from (86) it readily follows, according to (98) and (100),

$$v \sim \frac{\beta x(\mu - r)}{\lambda - (\mu - r)} \to \infty \qquad (\lambda_0 \downarrow \mu - r). \tag{104}$$

6.3. Comparative Statics and Sensitivity Analysis

The goal of comparative statics is to understand how varying values of exogenous parameters affect a target function of interest. For instance, consider the optimal threshold b^* as a function of both unemployment rate λ_0 and wage drift μ. Rather then fixing one of these parameters and then plotting b^* against the remaining parameter (as was done in Figure 4), it is useful to plot a family of comparative statics plots showing the *isolines* (or *level curves*) for different values (levels) of the function, that is, $b^*(\lambda_0, \mu) = \text{const}$ (see Figure 6a). As may be expected from Figure 4, the plots of the function $\lambda_0 = \lambda_0(\mu)$ (determined implicitly by the level condition) behave as monotone decreasing graphs. Analogous plots for the value function are presented in Figure 6b; the plots become non-monotonic for v large enough. If λ_0 is fixed then the value v grows with μ, in agreement with (89) and (90). Similarly, if $\mu > r$ is fixed then v decreases with λ_0, converging to the limit $v_* = \beta x - P$ as $\lambda_0 \to \infty$ (see (93)), represented by curve II in Figure 5b. If $v > v_*$ then there are up to two different values of λ_0 (and common μ) producing the same value v, while for v smaller than but close enough to v_*, the number of su ssi

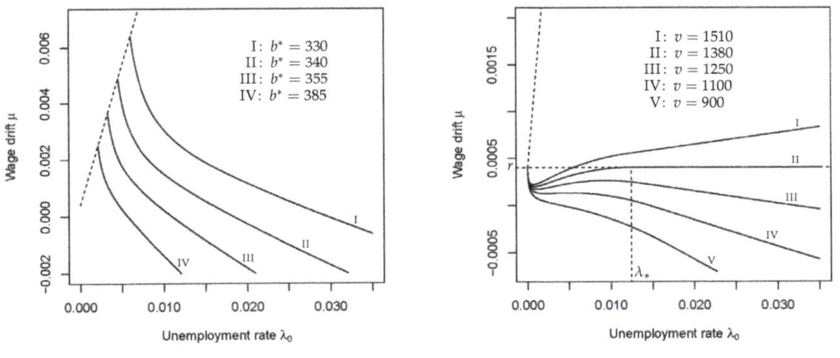

(a) Isolines of b^* (b) Isolines of $v = v(x)$

Figure 6. Isolines (level curves) of the optimal stopping problem solution on the (λ_0, μ)-plane: (**a**) $b^*(\lambda_0, \mu) = \text{const}$ (optimal threshold (23)); (**b**) $v(\lambda_0, \mu) = \text{const}$ (value function (25)). The values of other parameters used throughout are as in Example 3: $r = 0.0004$, $P = 9\,000$, $\beta = 30$, $\sigma = 0.02$, and $x = 346$. The slanted dashed lines in both plots show the boundary $\mu = \lambda_0 + r$ (see (11)). In plot b, the horizontal dashed line indicates $\mu = r$ and the vertical dashed line shows $\lambda_* \doteq 0.012420$ (cf. Figure 5b).

Let us also comment on the sensitivity of our numerical examples presented in Section 5.4. The question here is, how much the output values (say, the optimal threshold b^* and the value v) would change under a small variation of one of the background parameters. In the linear approximation, the change factor is given by the corresponding partial derivative. As in the previous sections, we address the sensitivity with regard to the wage drift μ (around the set value $\mu = 0.0004$) and the unemployment rate λ_0 (around $\lambda_0 = 0.01$). Other model parameters are fixed as in Section 5.4, that is, $r = 0.0004$, $P = 9\,000$, $\beta = 30$, and $x = 346$. As for the volatility parameter σ, it is set to be $\sigma = 0.04$ as in Example 2 or $\sigma = 0.02$ as in Example 3. The required partial derivatives of b^* and v can be computed using the formulas derived in Section 6.1; the results are presented in Table 1a.

Table 1. Sensitivity check of numerical results for the functions b^* and v in Examples 2 and 3: (**a**) parametric derivatives and (**b**) increments in response to a 1%-change in the background parameters.

(a) Derivatives		
Derivative	**Example 2**	**Example 3**
$db^*/d\mu$	−16 037.57	−13 962.43
$dv/d\mu$	842 062.30	993 991.20
$db^*/d\lambda_0$	−6 323.813	−3 161.906
$dv/d\lambda_0$	−46 485.530	−8 768.435
(b) Increments (euro)		
Increment	**Example 2**	**Example 3**
Δb^* (μ)	−0.06415	−0.05585
Δv (μ)	3.36825	3.97597
Δb^* (λ_0)	−0.63238	−0.31619
Δv (λ_0)	−4.64855	−0.87684

Numerical values in Table 1a may seem quite big, but they should be offset by small background values of the parameters, $\mu = 0.0004$ and $\lambda_0 = 0.01$. If we increase them by a small amount, say by 1%, then the absolute increments would be

$$\Delta\mu = 0.0004/100 = 4 \cdot 10^{-6}, \qquad \Delta\lambda_0 = 0.01/100 = 10^{-4}.$$

Hence, using Table 1a, we obtain the corresponding approximate increments of the target functions b^* and v (see Table 1b), which look more palatable. One interesting observation is that the value v reacts about 5 times stronger to the change of the unemployment rate λ_0 when the volatility σ gets 2 times bigger (from $\sigma = 0.02$ in Example 3 to $\sigma = 0.04$ in Example 2); in contrast, the change of v in response to an increase of the wage drift is much less pronounced. This highlights the primary significance of the unemployment rate, which is of course only natural.

Sensitivity analysis with regard to the wage drift μ is also useful in the light of the difficulty in estimation of μ from the data, mentioned in Section 5.2. The results in Table 1b suggest that a reasonably small error in selecting μ has only a minor effect on the identification of the optimal threshold b^* and the value v; for instance, overestimating it by 1% will decrease b^* by just 0.01 euro, while the value v will be up by about 0.60 euro. Thus, an individual using a moderately inflated value of their wage rate would take a slightly overoptimistic view about the timing of joining the insurance scheme and its expected benefit. On the other hand, a risk-averse individual may take a more conservative view and prefer to underestimate their wage drift μ, which will raise the threshold b^* resulting in a longer waiting time. For the insurance company though, it may be reasonable to try and avoid underestimation of the wage drift of potential customers, so as to reduce the risk of overpaying the benefits.

6.4. Economic Interpretation

Monotonic decay of the optimal threshold b^* with an increase of the unemployment rate λ_0 (see (85) and Figure 4b) has a clear economic appeal: a bigger unemployment rate λ_0 means a higher risk of losing the job, which demands a lower target threshold b^* in order to expedite joining the insurance scheme. The economic rationale for the monotonicity of b^* as a function of μ (see (83) and Figure 4a) is different—a bigger wage drift μ makes it more likely to reach a higher final wage X_{τ_0} by the time of loss of job, so lowering the threshold b^* adds incentive to an earlier entry.

Monotonic growth of the value v as a function of the wage drift μ (see (89), (90), and Figure 5a) is also meaningful—indeed, when the wage drift μ gets bigger, there is more potential to reach a higher final wage X_{τ_0} by the time of loss of job, which increases the expected benefit β_1 (see (9)) and, therefore, the value $v = v(x)$ of the insurance policy.

The behavior of the value function $v = v(x)$ in response to a varying unemployment rate λ_0 is more interesting, as indicated by the plots in Figure 5b. In the case $\mu < r$, it is satisfactory to see that the value v, vanishing in the limit as $\lambda_0 \downarrow 0$, starts growing with λ_0, thus reflecting a good efficiency of the insurance policy against an increasing risk of unemployment. On the other side of the policy, this may present a growing risk for the insurance company which will have to finance an increasing number of claims. But with the unemployment rate λ_0 getting ever bigger, the value v should stay bounded, so must converge to a limit as $\lambda_0 \to \infty$, given by $v_* = \beta x - P$ if $x > P/\beta$ (see (93)) or $v_* = 0$ otherwise (see (102)). In particular, Figure 5b shows that, for a certain range of μ, the value v achieves its maximum at some λ_0. However, the graphs also reveal that if μ keeps increasing then the value plots may have a more complicated non-monotonic behavior, which is harder to interpret economically.

On the other hand, as is evident from Figure 5b, in the case $\mu \geq r$ our model produces a counter-intuitive increase of the value v as λ_0 approaches the left edge of its range—it is hard to believe that the value may grow as the risk of unemployment falls. Moreover, as was computed in (104), for $\mu > r$ the corresponding limit of v is infinite! But perhaps the most striking example emerges in the borderline case $\mu = r$, whereby formally setting $\lambda_0 = 0$ we would get, according to (101), that the threshold b^* is infinite (unlike the case $\mu > r$, see (101)), so that the wage process (X_t) never reaches it; therefore, we never buy the insurance policy (understandably so, as there is no risk of losing the job), and nonetheless its value is positive in this limit (see (93)). The explanation of this paradox lies in the way how the optimal stopping is exercised for small $\lambda_0 > 0$: here, the threshold b^* is high and there is only a very small probability that it is ever reached; before this happens, we stay idle, but if and when the threshold is hit then the expected payoff is rather big, which contributes enough to the expected net present value to keep it positive in the limit $\lambda_0 \downarrow 0$ (see (103)).

Thus, the artefacts in our model as indicated above are caused by not putting any constraint on the waiting times. This can be rectified, for example, by introducing *mortality*, as was sketched in Section 2.3; in particular, such a regularization should restore a zero limit of v at the lower edge of λ_0.

7. Including Utility Considerations

7.1. Perpetual American Call Option

Our model (and its solution) resembles that of the optimal stopping problem for the *(perpetual) American call option* (see a detailed discussion in Shiryaev 1999, chp. VIII, §2a). More specifically, the holder of a call option may exercise the right to buy an asset (e.g., one unit of stock) at any time for a predetermined strike price K, where the decision is based on observations over the random process of stock prices (S_t), assumed to follow a geometric Brownian motion model. The term *perpetual* is used to indicate that there is no expiration date, so the right to buy extends indefinitely.

The optimal time instant $\tau = \tau^*$ to buy, bearing in mind a purely financial target of maximizing the profit $S_\tau - K$, is the solution of the following optimal stopping problem,

$$V(x) = \sup_\tau \mathrm{E}_x\big(\mathrm{e}^{-r\tau}(S_\tau - K)^+\big), \tag{105}$$

where S_t is a geometric Brownian motion with parameters $\mu < r$ and $\sigma > 0$, the supremum is taken over all stopping times τ adapted to the filtration associated with (S_t). The positive truncation $(\cdot)^+$ corresponds to the constraint that the option holder is not in a position to buy at the price K higher than the current spot price S_t. The solution to (105) is well known (Shiryaev 1999, chp. VIII, §2a) to be given by the hitting time $\tau^* = \tau_{b^*}$, with the optimal threshold

$$b^* = \frac{Kq^*}{q^* - 1},$$

where q^* is given by formula (24) but with $\tilde{r} = r + \lambda_0$ replaced by r. The corresponding value function is given by

$$V(x) = \begin{cases} (b^* - K)\left(\dfrac{x}{b^*}\right)^{q_*}, & x \in [0, b^*], \\ x - K, & x \in [b^*, \infty). \end{cases}$$

Observe that our optimal stopping problem (17) can be rewritten as

$$v(x) = \beta_1 \sup_{\tau} \mathrm{E}_x\left(\mathrm{e}^{-\tilde{r}\tau}(X_\tau - \tilde{K})\right), \qquad \tilde{K} := P/\beta_1, \tag{106}$$

which makes it look very similar to the perpetual American call option problem (105). However, there are several important differences. Firstly, unlike the gain function in the American call option problem (105), no truncation is applied in (106), because the financial gain is not the sole priority in this context and therefore the individual is prepared to tolerate negative values of $\beta_1 X_\tau - P$ (despite the fact that, under the optimal strategy, the value function $v(x)$ is always non-negative, see Lemma 2(i) and formula (25)).[5] In addition, as was mentioned in Remark 5 and in Section 5.3, the hitting time τ_{b^*} may be infinite with a positive probability (i.e., when $\mu < \frac{1}{2}\sigma^2$), which may be deemed impractical in the insurance context, but is considered to be acceptable for exercising the American call option. This simple observation helps to realize the fundamental conceptual difference between the two problems; indeed, the insurance optimal stopping does not focus only on the financial gain, but also places an ultimate priority on acquiring an insurance cover *per se*. Hence, a more realistic formulation of the optimal stopping problem in the UI model should involve a certain *utility*, which specifies the individual's weighted preferences for satisfaction; for example, impatience against waiting for too long before joining the UI scheme.

7.2. Heuristic Optimal Stopping Models with Utility

Here, we present a few informal thoughts about the possible inclusion of utility in the optimality analysis. As already mentioned, in the case $\mu < \frac{1}{2}\sigma^2$ the probability of hitting the critical threshold b^* is less than 1, so there is a probability that the individual will never join the insurance scheme if the optimal stopping rule is strictly followed. This is of course not desirable, as the individual puts high priority on getting insured at some point in time (hopefully, prior to loss of job).

One simple way to take these additional requirements into account is to extend the optimal stopping problem (17) as follows:

$$\begin{aligned} v^{\dagger}(x) &= \sup_{\tau}\left[\kappa \mathrm{P}_x(\tau < \infty) + \mathrm{eNPV}(x;\tau)\right] \\ &= \sup_{\tau} \mathrm{E}_x\left(\kappa \mathbb{1}_{\{\tau<\infty\}} + \mathrm{e}^{-\tilde{r}\tau} g(X_\tau)\right), \end{aligned} \tag{107}$$

where the supremum is again taken over all stopping times τ adapted to the process (X_t), and the coefficient $\kappa \geq 0$ is a predefined weight representing the individual's personal attitude (preference) towards the two contributing terms. If $\mathrm{P}_x(\tau < \infty) = 1$ then the first term in (107) is reduced to a constant (κ), leading to a pure optimal stopping problem as before; however, if $\mathrm{P}_x(\tau < \infty) < 1$ then the first term enhances the role of candidate stopping times τ that are less likely to be infinite.

The problem (107) can be rewritten in a more standard form by pulling out the common discounting factor under expectation,

$$v^{\dagger}(x) = \sup_{\tau} \mathrm{E}_x\left(\mathrm{e}^{-\tilde{r}\tau} G(\tau, X_\tau)\right), \tag{108}$$

---

[5] The equivalence of the problems (105) and (106), which we have established directly, is not a coincidence: it is known (Villeneuve 2007, Proposition 3.1, p. 185) that, under mild assumptions, the solution of the general optimal stopping problem $v(x) = \sup_\tau \mathrm{E}_x(\mathrm{e}^{-r\tau} g(X_\tau))$ does not change with the positive truncation of $g(\cdot)$.

with

$$G(t,x) := \kappa\, e^{\tilde{r}t} + g(x), \quad (t,x) \in [0,\infty] \times [0,\infty). \tag{109}$$

Unfortunately, the optimal stopping problem (108) is not amenable to an exact solution as before, because the gain function (109) depends also on the time variable (Peskir and Shiryaev 2006, chp. IV). In this case, the problem (108) may again be reduced to a suitable (but more complex) free-boundary problem, but the hitting boundary (of a certain set on the (t,x)-plane) is no longer a straight line.

More generally, our optimal stopping problem can be modified by replacing the indicator in (107) with the expression $e^{-\rho\tau}$ ($\rho > 0$),

$$v^{\dagger}(x) = \sup_{\tau} \mathrm{E}_x\big(\kappa\, e^{-\rho\tau} + e^{-\tilde{r}\tau} g(X_\tau)\big), \tag{110}$$

which retains the flavour of progressively penalizing larger values of τ, including $\tau = \infty$. Here, the gain function (109) takes the form

$$G(t,x) = \kappa\, e^{(\tilde{r}-\rho)t} + g(x).$$

In particular, by choosing $\rho = \tilde{r}$ the problem (110) is transformed into

$$v^{\dagger} = \sup_{\tau} \mathrm{E}_x\big(e^{-\tilde{r}\tau}(\beta_1 X_\tau + \kappa - P)\big),$$

which is the same problem as (17) but with the premium P replaced by $P - \kappa$.

Another, more drastic approach to amending the standard optimal stopping problem (17) stems from the observation that even if $\tau < \infty$ (P_x-a.s.), it may take long to wait for τ to happen—for instance, if $\mathrm{E}_x(\tau) = \infty$. In other words, it is reasonable to take into account the expected value of τ, leading to the combined optimal stopping problem

$$v^{\dagger}(x) = \sup_{\tau} \big[\kappa\, \mathrm{P}_x(\tau < \infty) + \kappa \exp\{-\mathrm{E}_x(\tau)\} + \mathrm{eNPV}(x;\tau)\big]. \tag{111}$$

If $\mathrm{P}_x(\tau < \infty) < 1$ then $\mathrm{E}_x(\tau) = \infty$ and the problem (111) is reduced to (107), whereas if $\mathrm{P}_x(\tau < \infty) = 1$ then, effectively, only the term with the expectation remains in (111). However, a disadvantage of the formulation (111) is that it cannot be expressed in the form (108). Trying to amend this would take us back to the version (110).

It is interesting to look at how the value function depends on the preference parameter κ. The next property is intuitively obvious.

Proposition 2. *For each $x > 0$, the value function $v^{\dagger}(x)$ of the optimal stopping problem (110) is a strictly increasing function of κ. The same is true for the problem (111).*

Proof. We use the notation $v^{\dagger}(x;\kappa)$ to indicate the dependence of the value function on the parameter κ. For $\kappa_1 < \kappa_2$ and any stopping time $\tau \not\equiv \infty$, we have

$$\mathrm{E}_x\big(\kappa_1 e^{-\rho\tau} + e^{-\tilde{r}\tau} g(X_\tau)\big) < \mathrm{E}_x\big(\kappa_2 e^{-\rho\tau} + e^{-\tilde{r}\tau} g(X_\tau)\big) \le v^{\dagger}(x;\kappa_2). \tag{112}$$

Suppose that τ_* is a maximizer for the optimal stopping problem (110) with $\kappa = \kappa_1$. Then, according to (112),

$$v^{\dagger}(x;\kappa_1) = \mathrm{E}_x\big(\kappa_1 e^{-\rho\tau_*} + e^{-\tilde{r}\tau_*} g(X_{\tau_*})\big) < v^{\dagger}(x;\kappa_2),$$

that is, $v^{\dagger}(x;\kappa_1) < v^{\dagger}(x;\kappa_2)$ as claimed. Similar arguments apply to the problem (111). □

7.3. Suboptimal Solutions

As already mentioned, the optimal stopping problems outlined in Section 7.2 are difficult to solve in full generality. To gain some insight about the qualitative effects of the added utility-type terms, it may be reasonable to restrict our attention to solutions in the subclass of hitting times τ_b. Despite such solutions will only be suboptimal, the advantage is that the reduced problems can be solved using that all the ingredients are available explicitly (see Section 4.1).

For example, the original problem (107) is replaced by

$$u^{\dagger}(x) = \sup_{b\ge 0} \left[\kappa\, \mathrm{P}_x(\tau_b < \infty) + \mathrm{eNPV}(x;\tau_b)\right]. \tag{113}$$

Similarly as in Section 4.3, we only need to maximize the functional in (113) over $b \ge x$. Indeed, if $b \le x$ then $\tau_b = 0$ (P_x-a.s.) and, according to (7) and (16),

$$\sup_{b\le x} \left[\kappa\, \mathrm{P}_x(\tau_b < \infty) + \mathrm{eNPV}(x;\tau_b)\right] = \kappa + \mathrm{eNPV}(x;0) = \kappa + \beta_1 x - P,$$

whereas

$$\begin{aligned}\sup_{b\ge x} \left[\kappa\, \mathrm{P}_x(\tau_b < \infty) + \mathrm{eNPV}(x;\tau_b)\right] &\ge \left[\kappa\, \mathrm{P}_x(\tau_b < \infty) + \mathrm{eNPV}(x;\tau_b)\right]_{b=x} \\ &= \kappa + \beta_1 x - P.\end{aligned}$$

Assume that $\mu - \frac{1}{2}\sigma^2 < 0$ (for otherwise $\mathrm{P}_x(\tau_b < \infty) = 1$, thus leading to the same optimal stopping problem as before). Then, according to (65), the probability $\mathrm{P}_x(\tau_b < \infty)$ becomes a strictly decreasing function of $b \in [x,\infty)$, and so the maximum in (113) is achieved by a different stopping strategy, with a lower optimal threshold $b^{\dagger}$. More precisely, by virtue of formulas (65) and (72), the problem (113) is explicitly rewritten as

$$u^{\dagger}(x) = \sup_{b\ge x} \left[\kappa \left(\frac{x}{b}\right)^{1-2\mu/\sigma^2} + (\beta_1 b - P)\left(\frac{x}{b}\right)^{q_*}\right], \tag{114}$$

where $q_* > 1$ is defined in (24). Differentiating with respect to b, it is easy to check that the maximizer for the problem (114) is given by

$$b^{\dagger} = \min\left\{ b \ge x\colon\ a\kappa \left(\frac{b}{x}\right)^{q_*-a} + (q_*-1)\beta_1 b \ge P q_* \right\},$$

where $a := 1 - 2\mu/\sigma^2 < 1 < q_*$.

The following (slightly artificial) version of the utility keeps the spirit of (113) but is amenable to the exact analysis:

$$u^{\dagger}(x) = \sup_{b\ge 0} \left[\kappa \{\mathrm{P}_x(\tau_b < \infty)\}^{q_*/(1-2\mu/\sigma^2)} + \mathrm{eNPV}(x;\tau_b)\right]. \tag{115}$$

Indeed, using the same substitutions (65) and (72) as before, (115) is reduced to (cf. (114))

$$u^{\dagger}(x) = \sup_{b\ge x} \left[(\beta_1 b + \kappa - P)\left(\frac{x}{b}\right)^{q_*}\right], \tag{116}$$

which is the same problem as (71) but with P replaced by $P - \kappa$ (cf. (72)). Therefore, from (73) we immediately obtain the maximizer

$$b^{\dagger} = \frac{(P-\kappa)\,q_*}{\beta_1(q_*-1)} = b^* - \frac{\kappa q_*}{\beta_1(q_*-1)} \le b^*. \tag{117}$$

This is a strictly decreasing (linear) function of κ; in particular, $b^\dagger = b^*$ if $\kappa = 0$ and $b^\dagger = 0$ if $\kappa = P$. The corresponding value function is given by (cf. (74))

$$u^\dagger(x) = \begin{cases} (\beta_1 b^\dagger + \kappa - P)\left(\dfrac{x}{b^\dagger}\right)^{q_*}, & x \in [0, b^\dagger], \\ \beta_1 x + \kappa - P, & x \in [b^\dagger, \infty), \end{cases} \tag{118}$$

or more explicitly (cf. (75))

$$u^\dagger(x) = \begin{cases} \dfrac{P-\kappa}{q_*-1}\left(\dfrac{\beta_1(q_*-1)x}{(P-\kappa)\,q_*}\right)^{q_*}, & 0 \le x \le \dfrac{(P-\kappa)\,q_*}{\beta_1(q_*-1)}, \\ \beta_1 x + \kappa - P, & x \ge \dfrac{(P-\kappa)\,q_*}{\beta_1(q_*-1)}. \end{cases} \tag{119}$$

If x is fixed then the problem value $u^\dagger$, as a function of κ, is given by the first or the second line in (119) according as $\kappa \in [0, \kappa^\dagger]$ or $\kappa \in [\kappa^\dagger, \infty)$, respectively, where

$$\kappa^\dagger := P - \frac{\beta_1(q_*-1)x}{q_*}. \tag{120}$$

The dependence of $b^\dagger$ and $u^\dagger(x)$ upon the utility parameter $\kappa \in [0, P]$ is illustrated in Figure 7, while Figure 8 demonstrates the functional dependence of the hitting probability $\mathrm{P}_x(\tau_b < \infty)$ and the mean hitting time $\mathrm{E}_x(\tau_b)$ upon the variable threshold $b \ge 0$, along with the corresponding plots of the e

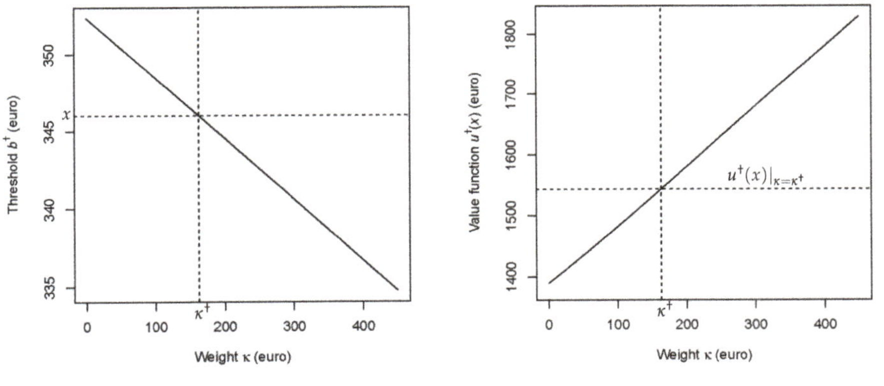

(a) $\kappa \mapsto b^\dagger$ (b) $\kappa \mapsto u^\dagger(x)$

Figure 7. Functional dependence on the preference weight κ in the reduced optimal stopping problem (115): (**a**) the optimal threshold $b^\dagger$ (see (117)) and (**b**) the value function $u^\dagger(x)$ (see (119)). Numerical values of the parameters used are as in Example 3: $r = \mu = 0.0004$, $P = 9\,000$, $\beta = 30$, $\sigma = 0.02$, and $x = 346$. In particular, if $\kappa = 0$ then $b^\dagger$ coincides with $b^* \doteq 352.3705$ and $u^\dagger(x)$ coincides with $v(x) \doteq 1389.6190$. The dashed vertical lines on both plots indicate the value $\kappa^\dagger \doteq 162.7108$ (see (120)) separating different regimes for $u^\dagger(x)$ according to (119). When $\kappa = \kappa^\dagger$, we have $b^\dagger = x = 346$, shown as a dashed horizontal line in plot a; the corresponding value function is given by $u^\dagger(x) = \beta_1 x + \kappa^\dagger - P \doteq 1542.7110$ (see (118)), shown as a dashed horizontal line in plot b. Note that the graph of $u^\dagger(x)$ in plot b looks almost linear for $\kappa \in [0, \kappa^\dagger]$, because the ratio κ/P is quite small, $0 \le \kappa/P \le \kappa^\dagger/P \doteq 0.01808$; the slope here is approximately $v(x)(q_*-1)/P \doteq 0.88448$, as compared to slope 1 of the linear graph for $\kappa \ge \kappa^\dagger$.

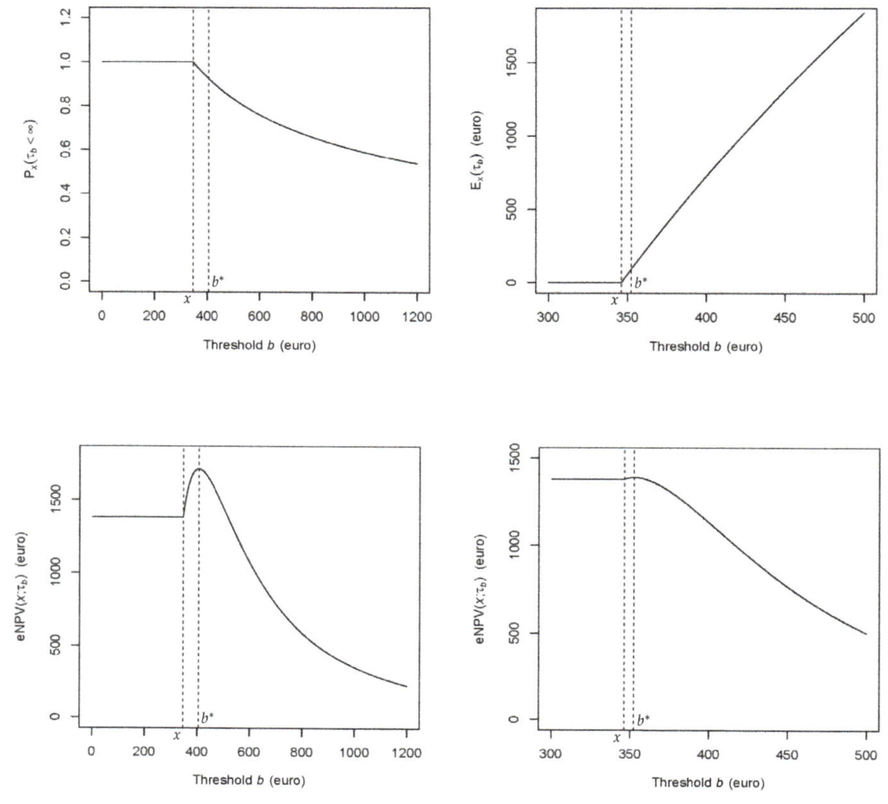

(c) $b \mapsto \mathrm{eNPV}(x;\tau_b)$ $(\mu < \frac{1}{2}\sigma^2)$ (d) $b \mapsto \mathrm{eNPV}(x;\tau_b)$ $(\mu > \frac{1}{2}\sigma^2)$

Figure 8. Theoretical graphs for functionals of the hitting time τ_b versus threshold $b \geq 0$. Upper row: (**a**) the hitting probability $\mathrm{P}_x(\tau_b < \infty)$ (see (65)) and (**b**) the mean hitting time $\mathrm{E}_x(\tau_b)$ (see (66)). Bottom row: the expected net present value $\mathrm{eNPV}(x;\tau_b)$ (see (72)) with $\mu < \frac{1}{2}\sigma^2$ (**c**) or $\mu > \frac{1}{2}\sigma^2$ (**d**). The values of parameters used throughout are as in Section 5.4: $x = 346$, $P = 9\,000$, $\beta_1 = 30$, $\mu = 0.0004$, and $\sigma = 0.04$ (left) or $\sigma = 0.02$ (right). The dashed vertical lines in each plot indicate x and $b^* \doteq 404.7410$ (left) (see Example 2) or $b^* \doteq 352.3705$ (right) (see Example 3).

Remark 8. *Note that $u^{\dagger}(x)$ is a strictly increasing function of $\kappa \in [0, P]$, in accord with Proposition 2. In particular, $u^{\dagger}(x)$ coincides with the original value function $u(x)$ given by (75), but with the premium P replaced by $P - \kappa$. This can be interpreted as the individual's consent to convert additional satisfaction, gained by virtue of pursuing the optimal stopping problem (115) instead of (17), into a higher premium, $P^{\dagger} = P + \kappa$. Such an effect is characteristic of the use of risk-averse utility functions under the Expected Utility Theory (Kaas et al. 2008); see also a discussion below in Section 7.4.*

In the case $\mu > \frac{1}{2}\sigma^2$, instead of (111) we may consider the simplified problem

$$u^{\dagger}(x) = \sup_{b \geq 0} \left[\kappa \exp\{-\mathrm{E}_x(\tau_b)\} + \mathrm{eNPV}(x;\tau_b)\right]. \tag{121}$$

Upon the substitution of formulas (66) and (72), it is rewritten in the form (cf. (114))

$$u^{\dagger}(x) = \sup_{b \geq x} \left[\kappa \, \frac{\ln(b/x)}{\mu - \frac{1}{2}\sigma^2} + (\beta_1 b - P) \left(\frac{x}{b}\right)^{q_*}\right]. \tag{122}$$

Again, the maximization problem (122) can be solved (at least, numerically). For an analytic solution, it is convenient to modify the problem (121) as follows,

$$u^{\dagger}(x) = \sup_{b \geq 0} \left[\kappa \exp\left(-\frac{q_*}{\mu - \frac{1}{2}\sigma^2} \mathrm{E}_x(\tau_b) \right) + \mathrm{eNPV}(x; \tau_b) \right].$$

Similarly to (122), this leads to the maximization problem that coincides with (116) and, therefore, has the same solution (117) and (118) (or, equivalently, (119)).

7.4. Connections to Expected Utility Theory

The considerations above can be linked to the standard Expected Utility Theory (Kaas et al. 2008). In the usual setting, it is assumed that an individual uses (perhaps, subconsciously) a certain utility $U(w)$, as a function of financial wealth w, to assess losses, gains and the resulting satisfaction. Generically, given the current wealth w and some random future loss Y, the expected loss (measured via utility $U(\cdot)$) may be expressed as $\mathrm{E}\big[U(w-Y)\big]$. The individual is inclined to pay a premium P and buy the insurance policy as long as the expected utility without insurance is no more than $U(w-P)$,

$$\mathrm{E}\,[U(w-Y)] \leq U(w-P). \tag{123}$$

The balance condition

$$\mathrm{E}\,[U(w-Y)] = U(w-P) \tag{124}$$

determines the maximum premium $P_{\max}$ the customer is prepared to pay (in fact, at this point it makes no difference whether to buy the insurance or not).

In the baseline case with $U(w) \equiv w$, the conditions (123) and (124) are reduced to

$$P \leq P_{\max} = \mathrm{E}(Y). \tag{125}$$

However, choosing a different utility function may well change this threshold. For instance, if the random loss Y has exponential distribution with parameter $\theta = 0.001$, then according to (125) we have $P_{\max} = \mathrm{E}(Y) = 1/\theta = 1\,000$. In contrast, let the utility function be chosen as $U(w) = 1 - \exp(-\frac{1}{2}\theta w)$. Here, the utility is between 0 and 1 if the wealth w is positive, but it becomes increasingly negative for a negative wealth; that is, strong weight is placed against negative wealth, which may be characteristic of a risk-averse individual. In this case, it is easy to check that

$$P_{\max} = \frac{2 \ln 2}{\theta} = 1386.294 > 1\,000.$$

Thus, the individual is happy to pay more than before to protect themselves from the perceived risk of significant losses. That is to say, an additional amount of satisfaction is convertible into an extra premium.

In our case, if the UI was to be entered immediately, at time $t = 0$, then the value of this decision would be $\mathrm{eNPV}(x;0) = \beta_1 x - P$ (see (8) and (16)). Clearly, in order for this to be non-negative, the premium P must satisfy the condition

$$P \leq P_{\max} = \beta_1 x.$$

For instance, in the setting of the numerical example in Section 5.4, we get $P_{\max} = 30 \times 346 = 10\,380$, while the set premium is $P = 9\,000$.

Similarly, if the decision was taken at a stopping time τ, then, conditional on the wage X_τ, the maximum premium payable would be given by $P_{\max} = \beta_1 X_\tau$. Thus, the value of $P_{\max}$ goes up or down together with the current wage. However, in our setting the entry time is not decided in advance, being subject to the stopping rule based on observations over (X_t). As a result, the value function $v(x)$

($x > 0$) of the optimal stopping problem is always positive for any premium P, no matter how high (see formula (26)). Apparently, this is manufactured by selecting the threshold b^* high enough, which guarantees that, in the (rare) event of hitting it, the mean value of this strategy will be positive.

This may not be satisfactory from the standpoint of the Expected Utility Theory; however, there is no contradiction, because in its standard version this theory does not allow for an optional stopping. Adding utility terms to the gain function in the spirit of Sections 7.2 and 7.3 helps to amend the situation (see Remark 8), but the maximum premium payable still remains indeterminate.

The explanation of this paradox lies in the simple fact that the gain function in the optimal stopping problems considered so far does not include any losses. A simple way to account for such losses is to include *consumption* in the model. Namely, suppose for simplicity that the consumption rate c is constant; for instance, the net present value of consumption over time interval $[0, t]$ is given by

$$\int_0^t \mathrm{e}^{-rs} c \,\mathrm{d}s = \frac{c\,(1-\mathrm{e}^{-rt})}{r}.$$

It is natural to assume that the wage X_t is sufficient to finance the consumption, so that $\mathrm{E}_x(X_t) = x\,\mathrm{e}^{\mu t} \geq c$ for all $t \geq 0$ (see (3)). In turn, for this to hold it suffices to assume that $X_0 = x \geq c$ and $\mu \geq 0$. Hence, we need to take into account consumption only over the unemployment spell $[\tau_0, \tau_0 + \tau_1]$, where the wage is replaced by the UI benefit. The expected net present value of this consumption is given by

$$\begin{aligned}\gamma := \mathrm{E}\left(\mathrm{e}^{-r\tau_0}\int_0^{\tau_1} \mathrm{e}^{-rs} c\,\mathrm{d}s\right) &= \mathrm{E}(\mathrm{e}^{-r\tau_0}) \cdot \mathrm{E}\left(\frac{c\,(1-\mathrm{e}^{-r\tau_1})}{r}\right)\\ &= \frac{\lambda_0 c}{(r+\lambda_0)(r+\lambda_1)},\end{aligned}$$

using independence of τ_0 and τ_1 and their exponential distributions (with parameters λ_0 and λ_1, respectively). Thus, our basic optimal stopping problem (17) is modified to

$$v^{\ddagger}(x) = \sup_{\tau} \mathrm{E}_x\left([\mathrm{e}^{-\tilde{r}\tau} g(X_\tau) - \gamma\right),$$

which has the same solution as before (see Section 2.5) but with the new value function $v^{\ddagger}(x) = v(x) - \gamma$, that is (cf. (25)),

$$v^{\ddagger}(x) = \begin{cases} (\beta_1 b^* - P)\left(\dfrac{x}{b^*}\right)^{q_*} - \gamma, & x \in [0, b^*],\\ \beta_1 x - P - \gamma, & x \in [b^*, \infty).\end{cases}$$

Now, the inequality $v^{\ddagger}(x) \geq 0$ can be easily solved for P to yield

$$P \leq P^{\ddagger}_{\max} := \begin{cases} \beta_1 b^* - \gamma\left(\dfrac{b^*}{x}\right)^{q_*}, & x \in [0, b^*],\\ \beta_1 x - \gamma, & x \in [b^*, \infty).\end{cases} \tag{126}$$

Note that $P^{\ddagger}_{\max}$ in (126) is a decreasing function of γ, but an increasing function of x. Thus, as could be expected, the maximum affordable premium gets lower with the increase of consumption, but becomes higher with the increase of the wage.

Remark 9. *Of course, consumption can also be incorporated into the optimal stopping models involving utility (see Sections 6.3 and 7.2), but we omit technical details.*

8. Concluding Remarks

In this paper, we have set up and solved an optimal stopping problem in a stylized UI model. The model and its solution are useful by illustrating approaches to optimal strategy of an individual seeking to get insured. By including consumption in the model, we have also demonstrated how a fair premium can be calculated, which makes our UI model usable also from the insurer's perspective.

An explicit closed-form solution of the corresponding optimal stopping problem was possible due to some simplifying assumptions—in particular, exponential distribution of time τ_0 to loss of job and constant inflation rate r. The analysis also strongly relied on the simplest model for the wage process (X_t), that is, geometric Brownian motion with constant drift μ and volatility σ^2.

Let us indicate a few directions of making our UI model more realistic. Firstly, indefinite term of UI insurance could be replaced by a finite expiration term for the benefit schedule (akin to American call option with finite horizon), which would lead to a harder (time-dependent) optimal stopping problem (cf. Peskir and Shiryaev 2006, §25.2). Also, the assumption of exponential distribution of τ_0 needs to be tested on the basis of real unemployment data. Note, however, that fitting a different distribution for τ_0 will invalidate the expression (13) for the expected net present value $\mathrm{eNPV}(x;\tau)$ and, therefore, will change the gain function in the optimal stopping problem (17), making it more difficult to solve.

The parameters of the model may also need to be made time-dependent, causing obvious complications to the model. On the other hand, the implicit assumption of passive waiting for a new job during the unemployment spell may not be realistic, or at least not desirable as individuals would rather be expected to seek jobs more proactively. Thus, it may be interesting to combine our UI model with job-seeking models such as in Boshuizen and Gouweleeuw (1995).

The inclusion of utility terms in the optimal setting is novel in this context, and illuminates significant changes in the individual's behavior when driven by utility considerations. In particular, the value of the optimal stopping problem (110) is an increasing function of the preference coefficient κ (see Proposition 2). This result is intuitively appealing, as it conforms with the usual impact of utility function (under the Expected Utility Theory), allowing one to convert extra satisfaction into extra premium. This is confirmed by our analysis of suboptimal solutions in Section 7.3 (see Figure 7). Finally, it would be interesting to study the optimal stopping problem (110) in more detail.

Author Contributions: J.S.A. and L.V.B. have both contributed to this paper.

Funding: J.S.A. was supported by a Leeds Anniversary Research Scholarship (LARS) from the University of Leeds.

Acknowledgments: Both authors have greatly benefited from many useful discussions with Tiziano De Angelis, who has also contributed to the design of this study. J.S.A. is grateful to Elena Issoglio for helpful comments. We thank the three anonymous reviewers for their useful feedback. In particular, Reviewer #1 proposed an extension of our insurance model by inclusion of constant force of mortality and pointed out the classical paper by Merton (1971); Reviewer #2 commented on positive truncation in optimal stopping and brought to our attention a paper by Villeneuve (2007); and Reviewer #3 offered advice on the sensitivity analysis and economic interpretation.

Conflicts of Interest: The authors declare no conflicts of interest.

References

Acemoglu, Daron, and Robert Shimer. 2000. Productivity gains from unemployment insurance. *European Economic Review* 44: 1195–224. [CrossRef]

Baily, Martin Neil. 1978. Some aspects of optimal unemployment insurance. *Journal of Public Economics* 10: 379–402. [CrossRef]

Borch, Karl. 1961. The utility concept applied to the theory of insurance. *ASTIN Bulletin* 1: 245–55. [CrossRef]

Boshuizen, Frans A., and José M. Gouweleeuw. 1995. A continuous-time job search model: General renewal processes. *Communications in Statistics. Stochastic Models* 11: 349–69. [CrossRef]

Chen, Xiaoshan, Xun Li, and Fahuai Yi. 2019. Optimal stopping investment with non-smooth utility over an infinite time horizon. *Journal of Industrial and Management Optimization* 15: 81–96. [CrossRef]

Choi, Kyoung Jin, and Gyoocheol Shim. 2006. Disutility, optimal retirement, and portfolio selection. *Mathematical Finance* 16: 443–67. [CrossRef]

De Angelis, Tiziano, and Gabriele Stabile. 2019. On the free boundary of an annuity purchase. *Finance and Stochastics* 23: 97–137. [CrossRef]

Dhami, Sanjit. 2016. *The Foundations of Behavioral Economic Analysis*. Oxford: Oxford University Press.

Durrett, Rick. 1999. *Essentials of Stochastic Processes*, 1st ed. Springer Texts in Statistics. New York: Springer.

Ekström, Erik, and Bing Lu. 2011. Optimal selling of an asset under incomplete information. *International Journal of Stochastic Analysis* 2011: 543590. [CrossRef]

Estevão, Marcello, and Filipa Sá. 2008. The 35-hour workweek in France: Straightjacket or welfare improvement? (with comments by Barbara Petrongolo and panel discussion). *Economic Policy* 23: 417–63. [CrossRef]

Etheridge, Alison. 2002. *A Course in Financial Calculus*. Cambridge: Cambridge University Press. [CrossRef]

Fredriksson, Peter, and Bertil Holmlund. 2006. Optimal unemployment insurance design: Time limits, monitoring, or workfare? *International Tax and Public Finance* 13: 565–85. [CrossRef]

Gerrard, Russell, Bjarne Højgaard, and Elena Vigna. 2012. Choosing the optimal annuitization time post-retirement. *Quantitative Finance* 12: 1143–59. [CrossRef]

GoCompare. 2018. Unemployment Protection Insurance (Search & Comparison Web Site). Available online: www.gocompare.com/unemployment-protection (accessed on 22 August 2019).

Gubian, Alain, Stéphane Jugnot, Frédéric Lerais, and Vladimir Passeron. 2004. Les effets de la RTT sur l'emploi: Des estimations *ex ante* aux évaluations *ex post* (French). [The effects of the shorter working week on employment: From *ex-ante* simulations to *ex-post* evaluations.] *Économie et Statistique* 376–377: 25–54. Available online: www.persee.fr/doc/estat_0336-1454_2004_num_376_1_7233 (accessed on 22 August 2019). [CrossRef]

Hairault, Jean-Olivier, François Langot, Sébastien Ménard, and Thepthida Sopraseuth. 2007. Optimal unemployment insurance in a life cycle model. *Society for Economic Dynamics Meeting Papers*, Paper 422, 25p. Available online: https://economicdynamics.org/meetpapers/2007/paper_422.pdf (accessed on 22 August 2019).

Henderson, Vicky, and David Hobson. 2008. An explicit solution for an optimal stopping/optimal control problem which models an asset sale. *Annals of Applied Probability* 18: 1681–705. [CrossRef]

Holmlund, Bertil. 1998. Unemployment insurance in theory and practice. *Scandinavian Journal of Economics* 100: 113–41. [CrossRef]

Hopenhayn, Hugo A., and Juan Pablo Nicolini. 1997. Optimal unemployment insurance. *Journal of Political Economy* 105: 412–38. [CrossRef]

Jang, Bong-Gyu, Seyoung Park, and Yuna Rhee. 2013. Optimal retirement with unemployment risks. *Journal of Banking and Finance* 37: 3585–604. [CrossRef]

Jensen, Uwe. 1997. An optimal stopping problem in risk theory. *Scandinavian Actuarial Journal* 1997: 149–59. [CrossRef]

Kaas, Rob, Marc Goovaerts, Jan Dhaene, and Michel Denuit. 2008. *Modern Actuarial Risk Theory Using R*, 2nd ed. Berlin: Springer. [CrossRef]

Karpowicz, Anna, and Krzysztof Szajowski. 2007. Double optimal stopping of a risk process. *Stochastics* 79: 155–67. [CrossRef]

Kerr, Kevin B. 1996. Unemployment compensation systems and reforms in selected OECD countries. Background Paper BP-415E, Library of Parliament, Parliamentary Research Branch. Government of Canada Publications, Ottawa, 22p. Available online: http://publications.gc.ca/collections/Collection-R/LoPBdP/BP-e/bp415-e.pdf (accessed on 22 August 2019).

Kolsrud, Jonas, Camille Landais, Peter Nilsson, and Johannes Spinnewijn. 2018. The optimal timing of unemployment benefits: Theory and evidence from Sweden. *American Economic Review* 108: 985–1033. [CrossRef]

Landais, Camille, Arash Nekoei, Peter Nilsson, David Seim, and Johannes Spinnewijn. 2017. Risk-based selection in unemployment insurance: Evidence and implications. IFS Working Paper W17/22, Institute for Fiscal Studies, London, 69p. [CrossRef]

Landais, Camille, and Johannes Spinnewijn. 2017. The value of unemployment insurance. CEPR Discussion Paper No. DP13624, Centre for Economic Policy Research (CEPR), London, 70p. Available online: https://cepr.org/active/publications/discussion_papers/dp.php?dpno=12364 (accessed on 22 August 2019).

McCall, John J. 1970. Economics of information and job search. *The Quarterly Journal of Economics* 84: 113–26. [CrossRef]

Merton, Robert C. 1969. Lifetime portfolio selection under uncertainty: The continuous-time case. *The Review of Economics and Statistics* 51: 247–57. [CrossRef]

Merton, Robert C. 1971. Optimum consumption and portfolio rules in a continuous-time model. *Journal of Economic Theory* 3: 373–413. [CrossRef]

Muciek, Bogdan Krzysztof. 2002. Optimal stopping of a risk process: Model with interest rates. *Journal of Applied Probability* 39: 261–70. [CrossRef]

Neumann, John von, and Oskar Morgenstern. 1953. *Theory of Games and Economic Behavior*, 3rd ed. Princeton: Princeton University Press.

Øksendal, Bernt. 2003. *Stochastic Differential Equations: An Introduction with Applications*, 6th ed. Universitext. Berlin: Springer. [CrossRef]

Peskir, Goran, and Albert Shiryaev. 2006. *Optimal Stopping and Free-Boundary Problems*. Lectures in Mathematics, ETH Zürich. Basel: Birkhäuser. [CrossRef]

Pham, Huyên. 2009. *Continuous-Time Stochastic Control and Optimization with Financial Applications*. Stochastic Modelling and Applied Probability. Berlin: Springer, vol. 61. [CrossRef]

Rebollo-Sanz, Yolanda F., and J. Ignacio García-Pérez. 2015. Are unemployment benefits harmful to the stability of working careers? The case of Spain. *SERIEs* 6: 1–41. [CrossRef]

Shiryaev, Albert N. 1996. *Probability*, 2nd ed. Graduate Texts in Mathematics. New York: Springer, vol. 95. [CrossRef]

Shiryaev, Albert N. 1999. *Essentials of Stochastic Finance: Facts, Models, Theory*. Advanced Series on Statistical Science & Applied Probability. Singapore: World Scientific, vol. 3. [CrossRef]

Stabile, Gabriele. 2006. Optimal timing of the annuity purchase: Combined stochastic control and optimal stopping problem. *International Journal of Theoretical and Applied Finance* 9: 151–70. [CrossRef]

Villeneuve, Stéphane. 2007. On threshold strategies and the smooth-fit principle for optimal stopping problems. *Journal of Applied Probability* 44: 181–98. [CrossRef]

WageIndicator. 2018. Minimum Wages in France with effect from 01-01-2018 to 31-12-2018. Available online: https://wageindicator.org/salary/minimum-wage/france/archive/minimum-wages-in-france-with-effect-from-01-01-2018-to-31-12-2018 (accessed on 22 August 2019).

Wang, Tan, and Tony S. Wirjanto. 2016. Risk aversion, uncertainty, unemployment insurance benefit and duration of "wait" unemployment. *Annals of Economics and Finance* 7: 1–34. Available online: http://aeconf.com/Articles/May2016/aef170101.pdf (accessed on 22 August 2019).

Yeh, James. 1995. *Martingales and Stochastic Analysis*. Series on Multivariate Analysis. Singapore: World Scientific, vol. 1. [CrossRef]

© 2019 by the authors. Licensee MDPI, Basel, Switzerland. This article is an open access article distributed under the terms and conditions of the Creative Commons Attribution (CC BY) license (http://creativecommons.org/licenses/by/4.0/).

risks

MDPI

Article

American Options on High Dividend Securities: A Numerical Investigation

Francesco Rotondi

Department of Finance, Bocconi University, 20136 Milan, Italy; rotondi.francesco@unibocconi.it

Received: 28 February 2019; Accepted: 15 May 2019; Published: 21 May 2019

Abstract: I document a sizeable bias that might arise when valuing out of the money American options via the Least Square Method proposed by Longstaff and Schwartz (2001). The key point of this algorithm is the regression-based estimate of the continuation value of an American option. If this regression is ill-posed, the procedure might deliver biased results. The price of the American option might even fall below the price of its European counterpart. For call options, this is likely to occur when the dividend yield of the underlying is high. This distortion is documented within the standard Black–Scholes–Merton model as well as within its most common extensions (the jump-diffusion, the stochastic volatility and the stochastic interest rates models). Finally, I propose two easy and effective workarounds that fix this distortion.

Keywords: American options; least square method; derivatives pricing; binomial tree; stochastic interest rates; quadrinomial tree

JEL Classification: G13

---

1. Introduction

Whereas most of the exchange-traded options on global financial indexes can be exercised only at maturity, thus being European-style options, the vast majority of equity options are American-style, as they can be exercised at any time up to their maturity. Evaluation of American-style options is, therefore, of crucial relevance in the financial industry.[1]

The fair pricing of this kind of claims is tricky even within simple market models due to their embedded optimization problem. In fact, since the holder of an American option has the right to exercise it at any time up to maturity, she will do so at the moment in which the expected payoff of the option is maximum. Therefore, virtually at each instant in time, she has to compare what she would get by the immediate exercise of the option to what she would get in the future if she waits and exercises the option later on. In turns, what she would get in the future depends on her future decisions: this recursive structure of the decision problem makes the evaluation of American claims quite complicated. See, e.g., Detemple (2014) for an extensive review of the main pricing methods of American-style derivatives.

Longstaff and Schwartz (2001) proposed the Least Square Methods (LSM henceforth), an interesting, fast and flexible Monte Carlo-based algorithm to price American options. The key point of the LMS is a regression-based approximation of the continuation value for the American option, which overcomes the well known issue of recursively estimating the conditional expectation of future optimal exercises.

---

[1] See, e.g., the *CBOE Market Statistics* annual report released by the Chicago Board Options Exchange, the largest trading market for derivatives. In 2016, the overall dollar value of all the equity options traded at the CBOE was roughly equal to $66 billion with an average of 1.35 million equity options traded daily corresponding to 205 million call options and 135 million put through the year.

At maturity, the option is exercised whenever in the money. Then, the optimal policy is retrieved going backward by comparing the immediate exercise payoff with the continuation value, which is approximated by the fitted values of a pathwise regression of all future payoffs on the immediate payoff. Since this regression is run on the paths along which the option is in the money, if there are too few of them, the regression is ill-posed and produces biased estimates of the continuation value. This propagates recursively and the final estimate of the price of the American option might be biased. Such bias might be so large that the American option price falls below the price of its European counterpart, delivering a price that violates the no arbitrage assumption as American options are always worth more than their European counterparts due to the early exercise premium.

If the option starts even mildly out of the money, the probability that the underlying reverts back to the in the money region depends on the drift of the risky asset. This drift depends in turns on the risk-free interest rate, on the dividend yield and on the volatility of the equity. Under realistic combinations of these parameters, the probability that initially out of the money option ends up in the in the money region is quite low. This damages the regression-based estimation of the continuation value of the American option thus altering (usually lowering) the final price. As an example, a high dividend yield relative to a low risk-free interest rate depresses the drift of a lognormal risky asset and, therefore, the stock is expected to decrease. In this case, the evaluation of an American option on this stock through the LSM, would most likely deliver a biased result.

My analysis builds on the large literature about the weaknesses and the related improvements of the Monte Carlo-regression based methods for pricing American options. Among others, García (2003) and Kan and Reesor (2012) analysed and corrected the biases of the algorithm due to suboptimal exercise decisions whereas, as an example, Belomestny et al. (2015) and Fabozzi et al. (2017) proposed further improvements of the original LSM.

Out of the money options play a key role in hedging strategies to protect investors against sudden drop/peak of the equity. Furthermore, Carr and Madan (2001) showed how to replicate any derivative whose payoff is a smooth function of the underlying at maturity with fixed positions in the bond, the stock itself and out of the money European call and put options. As European options on equity are quite illiquid, American ones are used in practice (delivering a small deviation from the perfect replication). Therefore, the correct evaluation of American out of the money options is relevant as well.

The remaining of the paper is organized as follows. Section 2 analyses the aforementioned flaw of the LSM in the standard diffusive framework of Black–Scholes–Merton. The following three sections address this issue within the three most common extensions of the standard diffusive framework. Section 3 deals with the jump-diffusion model, Section 4 with the stochastic interest rate framework and, finally, Section 5 with the stochastic volatility one. Section 6 concludes.

2. American Equity Options, Constant Interest Rates

I first analyse the LSM in a simple diffusive framework, as the one of Black and Scholes (1973) and Merton (1973). The risk-free interest rate is assumed to be deterministic. In Section 2.1, I first review the LSM and I highlight the possible flaws that might arise when valuing out of the money American option. Then, I propose a possible workaround to overcome them. In Section 2.2, I propose some numerical example to quantify the size of the flaws and to show how the workaround delivers correct results.

2.1. Theoretical Framework

2.1.1. The Primary Assets

Assume that the market is arbitrage-free and let $r \in (-1, +\infty)$ be the constant prevailing risk-free interest rate[2]. The risk-free interest rate is capitalized through a traded bond with price $B(t) = e^{rt}$. Consider a traded lognormal risky security S whose price dynamics under the[3] risk-neutral probability measure $\mathbb{Q}$ solve the following stochastic differential equation (SDE henceforth):

$$dS(t) = (r-q)S(t)dt + \sigma S(t)dW(t), \quad S(0) = S_0 \tag{1}$$

with $t \in \mathbb{R}^+$, where W is a $\mathbb{Q}$-Brownian motion, $\sigma \in \mathbb{R}^+$ is the constant volatility of the security, q its continuous dividend yield and $S_0 \in \mathbb{R}^+$ is its current price at $t = 0$. It is well known that the solution to Equation (1) delivers the following explicit expression for the price of the risky security

$$S(t) = S_0 \exp\left[\left(r - q - \frac{\sigma^2}{2}\right)t + \sigma W(t)\right], \quad t \geq 0. \tag{2}$$

Notice that the continuously compounded rate of return over $[0, t]$ on S,

$$\ln \frac{S(t)}{S_0} = \left(r - q - \frac{\sigma^2}{2}\right)t + \sigma W(t)$$

has two contributions: the first one is deterministic and depends on the drift $\mu^{\mathbb{Q}} := r - q - \sigma^2/2$ of the security; the second one is normally distributed with zero mean and variance equal to $\sigma^2 t$. Globally, the expected rate of return over $[0, t]$ is therefore normally distributed with mean $\mu^{\mathbb{Q}}t$ and variance $\sigma^2 t$. Furthermore, as time goes by, the deterministic component $\mu^{\mathbb{Q}}t$ prevails over the random one $\sigma W(t)$[4]. Therefore, the investor expects the security to appreciate as time goes by proportionally to the constant drift $\mu^{\mathbb{Q}}$.

2.1.2. The Derivatives

Let $f(S)$, $S \in \mathbb{R}^+$, be the payoff of a derivative written on $S(t)$. For a thorough analysis of many derivatives in this diffusion framework, see, e.g., Björk (2009). I restrict my investigation only to plain vanilla options; these are derivatives whose payoff can be cashed in by investors if (and only if) it is positive and that depends only on the current value of the underlying. The two instances of these options I will investigate are the call options, with $f(S) = (S - K)^+$, and the put options, with $f(S) = (K - S)^+$, where in both cases K, the strike price of the option, is the constant quantity specified on the contract at which the holder of the option has the right to buy or to sell, respectively, the underlying[5].

---

2 I advisedly allow for $r \in [-1, 0]$ in order to possibly replicate also the current situation of the Eurozone where "risk-free" government bonds, such as German ones, display negative yield up to few years maturities.

3 Under these assumptions, the market is actually also complete; therefore, the risk-neutral measure $\mathbb{Q}$ is unique.

4 It holds true (see, e.g., Revuz and Yor (2001)) that $\limsup_{t \to +\infty} \frac{W(t)}{\sqrt{2t \log_2 t}} = 1$ and $\liminf_{t \to +\infty} \frac{W(t)}{\sqrt{2t \log_2 t}} = -1$ almost surely; as $\pm\sqrt{2t \log_2 t} = o(t)$, $\limsup_{t \to +\infty} \frac{\mu^{\mathbb{Q}}t + \sigma W(t)}{\mu^{\mathbb{Q}}t} = 1$.

5 $(x)^* := \max\{0, x\}$ denotes the positive part. The holder of an option will exercise it if and only if it delivers a positive payoff; if this is not the case, the option will not be exercised and its payoff is floored at zero.

European-style options can be exercised only at maturity $T \in \mathbb{R}^+$. As their payoff at maturity is $f(S(T))$, the fundamental no-arbitrage pricing equation gives the value of these options at any time t, from inception, $t = 0$, up to maturity T

$$\pi_f^E(t) = \mathbb{E}^{\mathbb{Q}}\left[f(S(T))\frac{B(t)}{B(T)} \middle| \mathcal{F}_t \right] = \mathbb{E}^{\mathbb{Q}}\left[f(S(T))e^{-r(T-t)} \middle| \mathcal{F}_t \right]. \tag{3}$$

For call and put options, $\pi_f(t)$ admits a closed form solution, the celebrated Black–Scholes–Merton formula first derived by Black and Scholes (1973) and Merton (1973).

American-style options can be exercised at any time up to their maturity $T \in \mathbb{R}^+$. If exercised at $t \in [0, T]$, their payoff is $f(S(t))$. Clearly, a rational investor would exercise an American option when the payoff it delivers is the greatest possible. Therefore, the value of an American option at any time t is

$$\pi_f^A(t) = \operatorname*{ess\ sup}_{\tau \in [t,T]} \mathbb{E}^{\mathbb{Q}}\left[f(S(\tau))e^{-r(\tau-t)} \middle| \mathcal{F}_t \right], \tag{4}$$

where the essential supremum accounts for the fact that the sup is taken on an (uncountable) family of random variables defined up to zero-probability sets. In other words, the value of the American option is determined by the optimal stopping time τ that maximizes the discounted payoff. It is well known that $\pi_f^A(t)$ admits closed form expressions for neither call nor put options.

The evaluation of American options has, therefore, to rely on numerical techniques. As greatly summed up by Detemple (2014), there are broadly three valuation approaches to tackle this issue:

- the variational inequality approach, which generalizes the Black-Scholes PDE and translates into a free boundary problem;
- the lattice approach, inspired by the seminal work of Cox et al. (1979), who discretized the evolution of the underlying asset S and evaluated the American option backward along this discretization; and
- the least square method, first introduced by Longstaff and Schwartz (2001), who exploited a Monte Carlo simulation to recursively estimate the expected future payoff of the American option.

The present work focuses on the last approach, the LSM, as it is widely used thanks to the simplicity and the flexibility of its algorithm. Nevertheless, I show that, when implemented without few shrewdnesses, the LSM might deliver biased results under some realistic combinations of assets' parameters.

2.1.3. The LSM

The general LSM is effectively illustrated in Section 2 of Longstaff and Schwartz (2001). For ease of reading, I briefly recall here its working flow.

First, the LSM considers a uniform discretization of the investment window $[0, T]$ and evaluates a Bermudan-style option that can be exercised at any discrete monitoring date of the time partition. Then, a large number of sample paths of the security S is simulated; each of them is monitored at every possible exercise date.

The LSM runs backward in time. At maturity T, the option is exercised only along the paths in which it ends up in the money. Therefore, the optimal exercise policy at T is known along all the paths and simply prescribes to exercise the option when it is in the money. At any intermediate monitoring date t_i, the holder of the option considers the immediate payoff she would get by the early exercise of the option, $f(S(t_i))$. Along all the paths in which the immediate exercise is positive[6], the holder of the option has to decide whether she is better off by exercising it right at t_i or by waiting and

---

[6] If the payoff from the immediate exercise at t_i of the option is zero, a rational investor would not exercise it and she would surely hold it on waiting for a positive payoff later on.

exercising it later on. In other words, she has to compare the immediate exercise value of the option to its continuation value. This continuation value is the discounted expected value of the option as if it were optimally exercised from t_{i+1} on and can be expressed by a conditional expected value as follows

$$\mathbb{E}^{\mathbb{Q}}\left[\pi_f^A(t_{i+1})e^{-r(t_{i+1}-t_i)}\middle|\mathcal{F}_{t_i}\right]. \tag{5}$$

In this discrete time backward recursion, the optimal exercise policy has been found along all the paths from T to t_{i+1}; consequently, the value of the American option along all the paths is known as well at t_{i+1}. As the key point of the algorithm, the LSM regresses pathwise the discounted values of the American option at t_{i+1} on some polynomials in the immediate exercises values $f(S(t_i)) \in \mathcal{F}_{t_i}$[7]. In other words, it is assumed that

$$\mathbb{E}^{\mathbb{Q}}\left[\pi_f^A(t_{i+1})e^{-r(t_{i+1}-t_i)}\middle|\mathcal{F}_{t_i}\right] = \sum_{m\in\mathbb{N}} \beta_m L_m\left(f(S(t_i))\right), \tag{6}$$

where $\{L_m(\cdot)\}_{m\in\mathbb{N}}$ is an orthonormal basis of $\mathcal{L}^2$.

The intuition here is that the variation across the paths in which the option is in the money at t_i conveys some information about the value of the option after a "short" time has passed. The continuation values along all the paths are then obtained as the fitted values of the regression in Equation (6). Once the continuation value of the option is known along all the paths, it can be compared to the immediate exercise and the optimal exercise policy is updated for all the paths. As the optimal exercise policy is now known from t_i to T, the algorithm moves backward considering the choice the option holder faces at t_{i-1}.

Once the optimal policy has been derived also at $t = 0$, the value of the Bermudan–American option is obtained by the average of the discounted cashflows (which may occur at different instants in time depending on the particular path of S) across all the paths.

The LSM method is as powerful as flexible. Its implementation is indeed quite straightforward, requires few lines of code and is reasonably fast in delivering the results. The scope of the LSM is almost unbounded: as it works pathwise, the investor just needs to be able to simulate path by path the relevant processes in order to exploit it. This is why it is important to avoid all the possible flaws that come with it.

2.1.4. Possible Flaws of the LSM

As already pointed out, the key point of the algorithm is the regression-based approximation of the continuation value that overcomes the well known issue of the recursive estimation of the conditional expectation of future optimal exercises.

If the regression in Equation (6) is ill-posed[8], there might be severe consequences in the estimation of the continuation value of the option and, consequently, on the updating of the optimal exercise policy and, ultimately, on the value of the option at $t = 0$.

I investigate two issues that might affect negatively the regression in Equation (6) at some t_i:

1. there are fewer in the money paths than the number M of the polynomial taken from the orthonormal basis of $\mathcal{L}^2$; and
2. the paths along which the option is in the money deliver very low immediate exercise values that translate into a rank-deficient matrix of regressors, especially when high order polynomials are considered.

---

7 Notice that, if the conditional expectation of two random variables, $\mathbb{E}[Y|X]$, is an element of the $\mathcal{L}^2$ space, since $\mathcal{L}^2$ is an Hilbert space, $\mathbb{E}[Y|X]$ can be represented as a linear combination of the elements of an orthonormal basis of the space.

8 See, e.g., Wooldridge (2013), Section 2.2, for a careful explanation of the linear regression model and of the related necessary assumptions for its unbiased and efficient estimation.

Consider the linear model $Y = X\beta + \varepsilon$ with $Y, \varepsilon \in \mathbb{R}^{N\times 1}$, $X \in \mathbb{R}^{N\times M}$, $\beta \in \mathbb{R}^{M\times 1}$ where M is the number of regressors, namely the explanatory variables, N is the number of observations and β is the vector of parameters one is interested in. One crucial assumption for the least square estimator of β, $\hat{\beta} = (X'X)^{-1}X'Y$, to be efficient is that $rank(X) = M$, namely that all the regressors are linearly independent. As, by definition, $rank(X) \leq \min\{M, N\}$, if there are not enough observation, namely if $N < M$, the aforementioned hypothesis cannot hold true by construction and the estimate $\hat{\beta}$ one gets might display quite large variances and be far from the true value.

In the LSM, at each time step t_i, N represents the number of the in the money paths and M is the number of polynomials included. If the number of the in the money paths is less than the number of polynomials included, the estimates of the continuation values are not reliable. This might happen when the option starts out of the money. As concretely shown in the following subsection, when the maturity of the option is short and the time step small, there are few in the money paths at the first monitoring dates. The option is clearly not optimally exercised at these monitoring dates. Nevertheless, the imprecise estimate of β one gets at these dates might distort the continuation value and make it even negative. If this were the case, the algorithm would prescribe to exercise the option immediately as a seemingly null payoff is still better than a negative one. Clearly, this would drastically affect the final value of the Bermudan–American option.

The very same dramatic outcome can be reached if, at any t_i, there are enough in the money paths but the immediate exercise values along them is too close to zero. If this was the case, the matrix of the regressors can still have no full rank as the high grade polynomials[9] get closer and closer to zero. This would make one or more regressor equal to the null vector which gives no contribution to the rank of the matrix of regressors, which, in turns, would become rank deficient delivering the problems outlined above.

These issues are not explicitly debated in Longstaff and Schwartz (2001) probably because of the few possible exercise dates, 50 per year, they allow and the few basis functions, the first three Laguerre polynomials, they exploit in the regressions.

As Clément et al. (2002) proved, the value of the Bermudan option obtained through the LSM converges to the no-arbitrage price of the related American option as the following three quantities jointly tend to infinity: the number of time steps, n, the number of simulated paths, $NSim$, and the number of basis, m, exploited in the regression in Equation (6). When implementing the LSM, one has to choose finite values of the three aforementioned parameters for sake of feasibility.

As can be seen in Figure 1 top, for the evaluation of American option in the standard diffusive framework, the LSM needs at least $NSim \geq 10^4$ and $n/T \geq 125$ in order to obtain relative errors smaller than a percentage point. Interestingly, as can be seen in Figure 1 bottom, it also turn out that adding more basis function does not improve the estimate of the continuation value but it rather slows the algorithm and increases the probability that one of the two pitfalls described above manifests.[10]

2.1.5. Fixing of the Possible Flaws of the LSM

To fix the issues described above, I propose two workarounds: the first is finance-based whereas the second is econometric-based[11].

The first one prescribes to estimate the continuation values along all the paths as the original LSM algorithm says, namely as the fitted values of the (possibly ill-posed) regression, and then to floor these estimates pathwise with the current value of the European option obtained by the Black–Scholes–Merton formula. This can be seen as a financial sanity check: the expected payoff that

---

[9] For all the possible choices of basis functions $\{L_m(X)\}_{m\in\mathbb{N}}$, it holds that $\lim_{m\to+\infty, X\to 0} L_m(X) = 0$; see Chapter 22 of Abramowitz and Stegun (1970) for a comprehensive review of the basis functions of $\mathcal{L}^2$.

[10] The same analysis can be carried out within any of the three extensions to the standard diffusive model: No relevant differences arise though.

[11] I'm grateful to an anonymous referee for suggesting this extremely simple and effective econometric-based workaround.

the holder of the American option considers in her exercise decision cannot be lower than the one she would get by exercising the option at maturity.

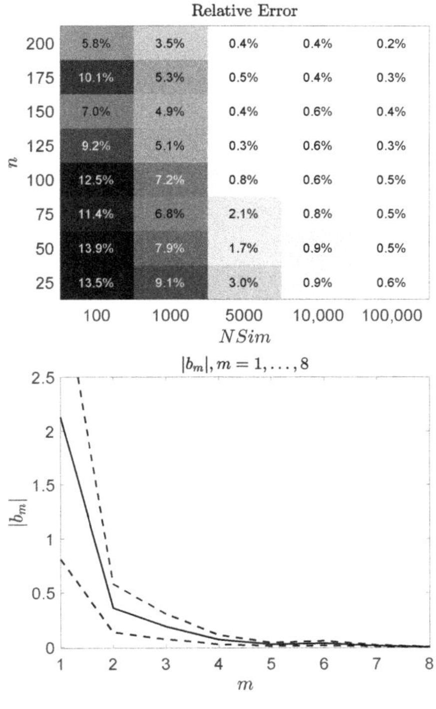

Figure 1. (**Top panel**): Relative pricing errors with respect to the binomial tree of an American call option in the standard Black–Scholes–Merton model with $S_0 = 100$, $K/S_0 = 105$, $r = 3\%$, $q = 4\%$, $T = 1$, $m = 6$; the darker the cell, the higher the relative error; (**Bottom panel**): absolute value of the average of the first 8 betas of the regression in Equation (6) for the evaluation of the previous American call option. Twenty independent Monte Carlo (MC henceforth) simulations were run.

The second one prescribes to run a constrained regression where the continuation value is forced to be non-negative. Since the flaws of the LSM are likely to arise when the early exercise of the option is never optimal, preventing the continuation value from being negative is enough to correctly postpone the exercise of the American option.

Both e workarounds fully solve the issue pointed out above. The following subsection shows it by means of multiple numerical examples.

2.2. Numerical Investigation

As pointed out in the previous subsection, the issues with the LSM are more likely to arise when the option is out of the money.

I focus my numerical investigation on the two most traded options: the American call and the American put option. Besides the level of the initial moneyness at which the option is written, also the particular choice of the other parameters plays a role in the determining whether the underlying is expected to move towards the in the money/out of the money region.

The call option, namely when $f(S) = (S - K)^+$, is out of the money at t if $S(t) < K$. Conversely, the put option, with $f(S) = (K - S)^+$, is out of the money at t if $S(t) > K$. Notice that, if the options share the same parameters, these two events are clearly complementary: the call option is out of the money if and only if the related put option is in the money. As it can be directly derived by Equation (2), the unconditional risk-neutral probability evaluated at $t = 0$ that the call option is out of the money at a given $t \in (0, T]$ is

$$\mathbb{Q}\left(S(t) < K\right) = N\left(\frac{\ln\frac{K}{S(0)} - \left(r - q - \frac{\sigma^2}{2}\right)t}{\sigma\sqrt{t}}\right) =: N(-d_2), \tag{7}$$

where $N(\cdot) : \mathbb{R} \to (0,1)$ is the cumulative distribution function of a 0–1 normal random variable and $d_2 := \frac{\ln\frac{S(0)}{K} + \left(r-q-\frac{\sigma^2}{2}\right)t}{\sigma\sqrt{t}} = \frac{\ln\frac{S(0)}{K} + \mu^{\mathbb{Q}}t}{\sigma\sqrt{t}}$ varies with t. Analogously, the unconditional risk-neutral probability evaluated at $t = 0$ that the put option is out of the money at a given is $N(d_2)$. Table 1 shows the sensitivities of these two probabilities to the parameters of the model.

Table 1. Sensitivities of $N(-d_2)/N(d_2)$, the risk-neutral initial probability that the call/put option ends out of the money at t, to the parameters of the model. $+$ (resp. $-$) indicates a positive (resp. negative) sensitivity of the probability to the parameter under investigation. ? indicates that the sign of sensitivity of the probability to the parameter is not unique and might change. S_0 is always kept constant.

	K	r	q	σ
$N(-d_2)$	$+$	$-$	$+$	?
$N(d_2)$	$-$	$+$	$-$	?

The probability in Equation (7) and its complementary one are of great interest in investigating whether the pitfalls described in the previous subsection are likely to arise or not.

Consider the call option and fix a monitoring date t_i. If at the first step of the LSM one simulates $NSim$ paths of the underlying, then the call option is expected to be in the money at t_i along $NSim \cdot N(d_2)$ paths. If $NSim \cdot N(d_2) < M$, where M is the number of the basis polynomials included in the regression, or $NSim \cdot N(d_2) > M$ but along these very few paths the option is mildly in the money, the issues described above may arise. If the call option starts even a little bit out of the money, the number of in the money paths expected at the first monitoring dates is extremely low; this worsens for security with high dividend yield q and if the prevailing risk-free interest rate r is low.

Figure 2 shows the impact of the moneyness S_0/K on the probability that a call option is in the money at the first monitoring dates. As can be seen, few paths are expected to be in the money when the option has a moneyness roughly larger than 1.04.

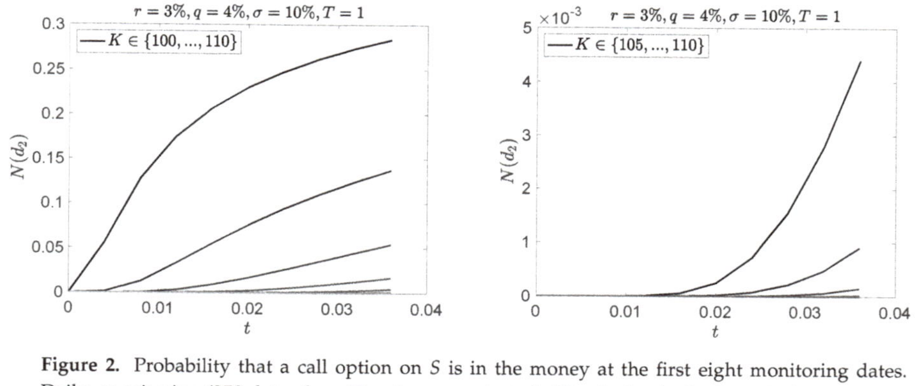

Figure 2. Probability that a call option on S is in the money at the first eight monitoring dates. Daily monitoring (250 dates for a $T = 1$ year maturity). The darker is the line, the higher is the strike price K. The panel on the right zooms in the one on the left focusing on more out of the money call options.

Figure 3 shows the same probability that a call option on S that starts mildly out of the money ($K/S_0 = 105\%$) reaches the in the money region at the first monitoring dates for different (and realistic) values of r and q. As an example, if one million paths are generated ($NSim = 10^6$), none of them is expected to be in the money at the first three monitoring dates when $r = 3\%$ and $q = 4\%$; only three paths are expected to be in the money at the fourth monitoring date and, since usually $M \approx 6$ basis functions are exploited in the regression, one would introduce four times a bias in the estimate of the continuation value.

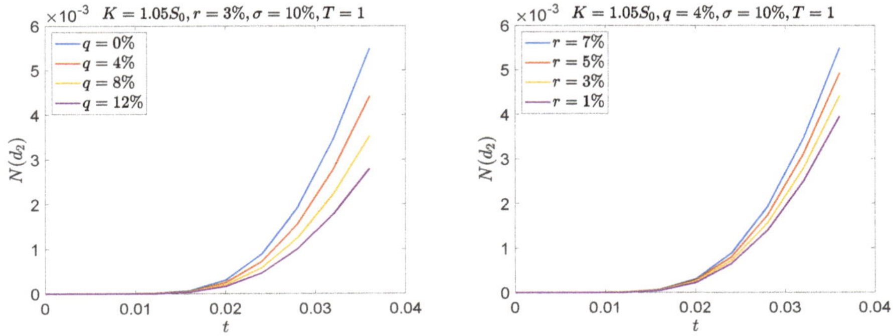

Figure 3. Probability that a call option on S is in the money at the first eight monitoring dates. Daily monitoring (250 dates for a $T = 1$ year maturity).

Table 2 shows some numerical examples. Three levels of moneyness are considered. In the first case, $K/S_0 = 1.02$, the LSM provides good results even without any correction, but in the case large dividend yield: nevertheless, the distortion here is quite small and the price of the American option is much larger than its European counterpart and quite close to the benchmark. However, the correction of the LSM fixes this issue and delivers coherent results. In the other two levels of moneyness, when the option starts a little bit more out of the money, the LSM without correction heavily underprices the American call delivering also large standard errors.

When any of the corrections to the LSM is implemented instead, the results basically coincide with the ones derived in the binomial model of Cox et al. (1979), which, for the large number of the steps considered, can be assumed as a benchmark. Numerical imprecisions appear also when early exercise is never optimal ($r \approx q$) and, therefore, the price of the European option and of the American are roughly the same. In this case, the tiny difference between the two is much smaller than the confidence interval of the LSM's estimates and such approach delivers unreliable results.

Completely analogous (and symmetric) results are obtained for out of the money put options, especially when the dividend yield q is low and the risk-free interest rate r is high. See, e.g., Carr and Chesney (1997); Detemple (2001) for a throughout discussion on the put-call symmetry for American-style options.

Table 2. Numerical results, Black–Scholes–Merton model. $S_0 = 100$, $T = 1$, $\sigma = 10\%$, 150 possible exercise dates per year. $\pi^E_{BS}(0)$: initial price of the European call option computed with the Black–Scholes–Merton formula. $\pi^A_{CRR}(0)$: initial price of the American call option computed with the Cox–Ross–Rubinstein binomial tree (average of the price obtained with 250 and 251 steps). $\pi^A_{\text{LSM}}(0)^*$ ($\pi^A_{\text{LSM}}(0)$): initial price of the American call option computed with the LSM not corrected (corrected) for the pitfalls previously described; the first six Laguerre polynomials are used for the regression: $L_m(x) = \frac{e^{\frac{x}{2}}}{m!}\frac{\mathrm{d}^m}{\mathrm{d}x^m}(x^m e^{-x})$, with $m = 0, \cdots, 6$; $NSim = 10^5$, standard errors obtained by 20 independent MC simulations. MC estimates that do not include the benchmark value within the confidence interval are denoted by $\star$.

K/S_0	r	q	$\pi^E_{BS}(0)$	$\pi^A_{CRR}(0)$	$\pi^A_{\text{LSM}}(0)^*$	s.e.	$\pi^A_{\text{LSM}}(0)$	s.e.
102%	5%	4%	3.3955	3.3965	3.3953	(0.0031)	3.3942	(0.0026)
		6%	2.5558	2.6513	2.6504	(0.0023)	2.6489	(0.0035)
		8%	1.8765	2.1129	2.1133	(0.0034)	2.0134	(0.0021)
	3%	4%	2.6074	2.6881	2.6879	(0.0035)	2.6900	(0.0043)
		6%	1.9144	2.1376	2.1369	(0.0027)	2.1384	(0.0018)
		8%	1.3694	1.7149	1.7096 $\star$	(0.0049)	1.7118	(0.0032)
	1%	4%	1.9531	2.1628	2.1602	(0.0032)	2.1609	(0.0040)
		6%	1.3971	1.7324	1.7343	(0.0025)	1.7248	(0.0041)
		8%	0.9724	1.3973	1.3896 $\star$	(0.0052)	1.3976	(0.0027)
105%	5%	4%	2.2971	2.2983	1.7515 $\star$	(0.3618)	2.2988	(0.0036)
		6%	1.6672	1.7209	1.4135 $\star$	(0.4398)	1.7193	(0.0019)
		8%	1.1782	1.3048	0.9535 $\star$	(0.3175)	1.3045	(0.0024)
	3%	4%	1.7009	1.7468	1.0236 $\star$	(0.3757)	1.7494	(0.0057)
		6%	1.2020	1.3222	0.9634 $\star$	(0.2135)	1.3204	(0.0025)
		8%	0.8262	1.0018	0.7122 $\star$	(0.2588)	1.0093	(0.0029)
	1%	4%	1.2263	1.3399	0.8669 $\star$	(0.2495)	1.3375	(0.0038)
		6%	0.8429	1.0140	0.7095 $\star$	(0.2236)	1.0124	(0.0028)
		8%	0.5629	0.7667	0.3622 $\star$	(0.2486)	0.7415	(0.0032)
108%	5%	4%	1.4930	1.4930	1.1524 $\star$	(0.2163)	1.4921	(0.0037)
		6%	1.0433	1.0719	0.8451 $\star$	(0.2461)	1.0695	(0.0039)
		8%	0.7088	0.7741	0.5428 $\star$	(0.1856)	0.7745	(0.0026)
	3%	4%	1.0644	1.0890	0.6342 $\star$	(0.3154)	1.0894	(0.0032)
		6%	0.7231	0.7853	0.5526 $\star$	(0.2866)	0.7841	(0.0019)
		8%	0.4771	0.5635	0.3623 $\star$	(0.1849)	0.5626	(0.0032)
	1%	4%	0.7377	0.7968	0.4255 $\star$	(0.2121)	0.7965	(0.0025)
		6%	0.4868	0.5711	0.3574 $\star$	(0.1937)	0.5723	(0.0021)
		8%	0.3117	0.4066	0.2114 $\star$	(0.0984)	0.4073	(0.0024)

3. American Equity Options, Jump-Diffusion Model

In this Section, I propose a first variation of the standard Black–Scholes market. More specifically, I allow for stock price process to jump at random dates and with an idiosyncratic intensity. For the sake of simplicity, the risk-free interest rate is kept constant. The result is the well known jump-diffusion model first introduced by Merton (1976), which can be seen as the first generalization of the standard Black–Scholes–Merton model.

As in the previous section, Section 3.1 describes the theoretical aspects of the analysis, whereas Section 3.2 contains the related numerical examples.

3.1. Theoretical Framework: The Primary Assets and the Derivatives

Assume that the market is arbitrage free. Two assets are traded: the usual riskless bond $B(t) = e^{rt}$ and a risky asset S. To match some features of real market data like high peaks and heavy tails, it is convenient to relax the continuity hypothesis of the risky stock's price and allow it to jump at random times. This introduces a new source risk in the market: The jump risk. Following the seminal work of Merton (1976) and as greatly explained by Glasserman (2003), I postulate that, since jumps are assumed to be independent of each other and of the stock's level, the jump risk can be diversified away by investing in many difference stocks. Hence, the investors require no jump risk premium. This hypothesis being made, the risk-neutral measure $\mathbb{Q}$ becomes unique and derivatives on S can be priced uniquely.

Under $\mathbb{Q}$, the price process of S solves

$$\mathrm{d}S(t) = S(t^-)\left((r-q)\mathrm{d}t + \sigma \mathrm{d}W^{\mathbb{Q}}(t) + \mathrm{d}J(t)\right), \quad S(0) = S_0, \tag{8}$$

where $J(t) = \sum_{j=1}^{N(t)}(Y_j - 1)$ is a jump process, Y_js are i.i.d. positive random variables and $N(t)$ is a Poisson process with intensity $\lambda > 0$ that counts how many jumps occurred before t included (with the convention $N(0) = 0$). As outlined before, $W^{\mathbb{Q}}$, the Y_js and N are assumed to be independent of each other. Jumps arrive at random instants and the waiting time before to consecutive jumps is exponentially distributed with parameter λ. Furthermore, it is convenient to assume that the jumps Y_js are $\mathbb{Q}$-lognormally distributed with mean a and volatility b^2.

Under all of these assumptions and setting $m := \mathbb{E}^{\mathbb{Q}}\left[Y_j - 1\right] = e^{a+b^2/2} - 1$, the explicit solution of $S(t)$ in Equation (8) is

$$S(t) = S_0 \exp\left[\left(r - q - \lambda m - \frac{\sigma^2}{2}\right)t + \sigma W^{\mathbb{Q}}(t)\right]\prod_{j=1}^{N(t)} Y_j$$

and, conditioning on n jumps having occurred before t, namely, conditioning on $N(t) = n$,

$$S(t)|_{N(t)=n} = S_0 \exp\left[\left(r - q - \lambda m - \frac{\sigma^2}{2}\right)t + \sigma W^{\mathbb{Q}}(t) + an + b\sqrt{n}Z\right],$$

where Z is standard normal random variable independent of $W^{\mathbb{Q}}(t)$. It also holds true in distribution

$$S(t)|_{N(t)=n} = S_0 \exp\left[\left(r_n(t) - q - \frac{\sigma_n^2(t)}{2}\right)t + \sigma_n(t) W^{\mathbb{Q}}(t)\right] \tag{9}$$

with $r_n(t) := r - m\lambda + \frac{n}{t}\left(a + \frac{b^2}{2}\right)$ and $\sigma_n^2(t) := \sigma^2 + \frac{n}{t}b^2$. The deterministic drift of $S(t)|_{N(t)=n}$ here is $\mu^{\mathbb{Q}} = r - m\lambda + na/t - q - \sigma^2/2$, strictly lower than in the standard model when $a \geq 0$.

The price at t of European and American derivatives within the present jump-diffusion model are still given by the risk-neutral expected values in Equations (3) and (4). For the European call, with $f(S(T)) = (S(T) - K)^+$ and suppressing the argument of $r_n(t)$ and $\sigma_n^2(t)$, it holds

$$\pi_{JD}^E(t) = \sum_{n=0}^{\infty} e^{-\lambda'(T-t)}\frac{(\lambda'(T-t))^n}{n!}\pi_{BS}^E(t; r_n, \sigma_n) \tag{10}$$

with $\lambda' := \lambda(1+m)$, $\pi_{BS}^E(t; r_n, \sigma_n) = S(t)e^{-q(T-t)}N(d_n) - Ke^{-r(T-t)}N(d_n - \sigma_n\sqrt{T-t})$ and

$$d_n := \frac{1}{\sigma_n\sqrt{T-t}}\left[\ln\frac{S(t)}{K} + \left(r_n - q + \frac{\sigma_n^2}{2}\right)(T-t)\right]. \tag{11}$$

As usual, the pricing formula for a European put option can be retrieved by put-call parity.

The pricing of American options within the jump-diffusion model has to rely on numerical techniques instead, based on extensions of the celebrated Black–Scholes partial differential equation (see, e.g., Kinderlehrer and Stampacchia (2000) for a complete analysis on how to price American options through variational inequalities and Friedman (1982) for general solving schemes for PDEs and free boundary problems). Zhang (1997) provided an extremely useful characterization of a finite difference scheme to price American options in the jump-diffusion model.

3.2. Numerical Investigation

With the very same technique exploited to derive $\pi_{JD}^{E}(t)$ and starting from Equation (9), it can be shown that the risk-neutral probability that a call option on S is in the money at $t \in (0, T]$ is

$$\mathbb{Q}\left(S(t) > K\right) = \sum_{n=0}^{\infty} e^{-\lambda t} \frac{(\lambda t)^{n}}{n!} N(d_n - \sigma_n \sqrt{t}). \tag{12}$$

This probability is again increasing in r and decreasing in q, as Figure 4 shows. Nevertheless, as the drift of the underlying is now smaller due to the non negligible probability of a downward jump, this probability is slightly larger than the same one in the standard diffusive model.

This implies a lower expected growth of S that translates into smaller call option prices, as it can be seen comparing Tables 2 and 3 that share the same parameters.

As can be seen from the numerical examples in Table 3, the LSM works almost fine also at an intermediate level of out of moneyness, but when the dividend rate is too large.

Table 3. Numerical results, jump-diffusion. $S_0 = 100$, $T = 1$, $\sigma = 10\%$, $a = 0$, $b = 1\%$, $\lambda = 1$; 150 possible exercise dates per year. $\pi_{JD}^{E}(0)$: initial price of the European call option computed with Equation (10). $\pi_{FD}^{A}(0)$: initial price of the American call option computed solving the free boundary problem by finite differences. $\pi_{\text{LSM}}^{A}(0)^{*}$ ($\pi_{\text{LSM}}^{A}(0)$): initial price of the American call option computed with the LSM not corrected (corrected) for the pitfalls previously described; the regression involves the first six Laguerre polynomials for the values of the immediate exercise payoff; $NSim = 10^5$, standard errors obtained by 20 independent MC simulations. MC estimates that do not include the benchmark value within the confidence interval are denoted by $\star$.

K/S_0	r	q	$\pi_{JD}^{E}(0)$	$\pi_{FD}^{A}(0)$	$\pi_{\text{LSM}}^{A}(0)^{*}$	s.e.	$\pi_{\text{LSM}}^{A}(0)$	s.e.
102%	5%	4%	2.7297	2.7321	2.7301	(0.0025)	2.7312	(0.0031)
		6%	2.1466	2.2184	2.2158	(0.0034)	2.2175	(0.0062)
		8%	1.6861	1.9121	1.9134	(0.0028)	1.9103	(0.0043)
	3%	4%	2.1900	2.2448	2.2442	(0.0033)	2.2456	(0.0037)
		6%	1.7201	1.9289	1.9293	(0.0024)	1.9301	(0.0024)
		8%	1.3339	1.7143	1.6887 $\star$	(0.0206)	1.7142	(0.0026)
	1%	4%	1.7549	1.9461	1.9436	(0.0025)	1.9458	(0.0019)
		6%	1.3608	1.7283	1.7274	(0.0031)	1.7296	(0.0032)
		8%	1.0425	1.5446	1.5101 $\star$	(0.0329)	1.5439	(0.0027)
105%	5%	4%	1.9863	1.9878	1.9857	(0.0034)	1.9885	(0.0024)
		6%	1.5511	1.5982	1.5998	(0.0026)	1.5997	(0.0036)
		8%	1.1962	1.3516	1.3519	(0.0012)	1.3489	(0.0042)
	3%	4%	1.5824	1.6182	1.6189	(0.0032)	1.6168	(0.0037)
		6%	1.2204	1.3640	1.3625	(0.0048)	1.3638	(0.0031)
		8%	0.9304	1.1968	1.1789 $\star$	(0.0107)	1.1999	(0.0048)
	1%	4%	1.2450	1.3766	1.3739	(0.0027)	1.3748	(0.0028)
		6%	0.9492	1.2068	1.2041	(0.0029)	1.2045	(0.0026)
		8%	0.7162	1.0671	0.6845 $\star$	(0.0714)	1.0701	(0.0052)
108%	5%	4%	1.4367	1.4376	1.1214 $\star$	(0.4147)	1.4369	(0.0028)
		6%	1.1027	1.1332	0.8427 $\star$	(0.2845)	1.1327	(0.0014)
		8%	0.8370	0.9414	0.6854 $\star$	(0.2656)	0.9402	(0.0023)
	3%	4%	1.1249	1.1480	0.9697 $\star$	(0.3274)	1.1459	(0.0043)
		6%	0.8539	0.9503	0.6369 $\star$	(0.1667)	0.9489	(0.0034)
		8%	0.6419	0.8234	0.4214 $\star$	(0.2546)	0.8251	(0.0037)
	1%	4%	0.8711	0.9595	0.6214 $\star$	(0.2652)	0.9602	(0.0026)
		6%	0.6549	0.8306	0.4886 $\star$	(0.2145)	0.8295	(0.0028)
		8%	0.4882	0.7265	0.3215 $\star$	(0.1341)	0.7255	(0.0017)

This is coherent with the numerical figures of the previous section. Again, when the early exercise is almost never optimal, the price of the European option falls inside the confidence interval of the Monte Carlo estimate for the American price, making it not really reliable.

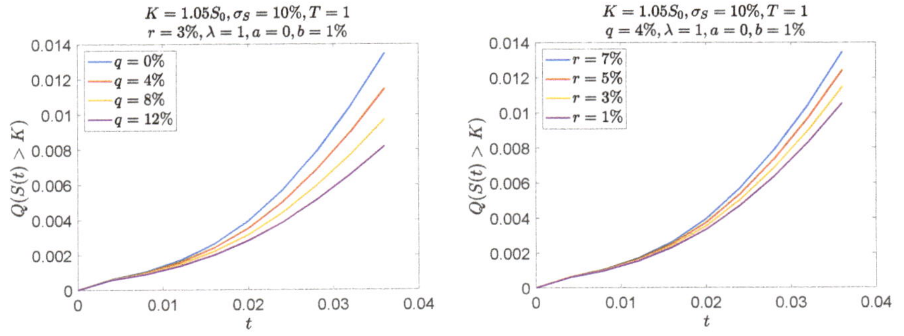

Figure 4. Probability that a call option on S in jump-diffusion framework is in the money at the first eight monitoring dates. Daily monitoring (250 dates for a $T = 1$ year maturity).

4. American Equity Options, Stochastic Interest Rates

In this section, I propose a second generalized market where the short-term risk free interest rate is stochastic. More specifically, I assume that the interest rate follows a mean-reverting stochastic process, as described first by the seminal work of Vasicek (1977). For the sake of simplicity, the volatilities of both the stock price process and of the locally risk-free interest rate are assumed to be constant. As in Sections 2 and 3, Section 4.1 describes the theoretical aspects of the analysis, whereas Section 4.2 contains the related numerical examples.

4.1. Theoretical Framework: The Primary Assets and the Derivatives

Assume that the market is arbitrage-free. The locally risk-free interest rate r follows an Ornstein–Uhlenbeck process. The locally risk-free rate is capitalized through a bond whose price at t is $B(t) = e^{\int_0^t r(s)\mathrm{d}s}$. A zero-coupon bond is traded in market as well. It pays out 1 at maturity T and its price at t is labeled by $p(t,T)$. As in the previous Section, this markets involves two sources of uncertainty: The standard diffusive market risk and the interest rate one. Nevertheless, since the investor can hedge from both through S and the T-bond, the market is complete and all the derivatives can be uniquely priced. The explicit formula for the price of the zero-coupon bond $p(t,T)$ can be found, for example, in Brigo and Mercurio (2007). Finally, a lognormal risky security S is traded. I allow for a non-zero correlation between the two processes. Under the risk-neutral measure $\mathbb{Q}$, the two solve the following SDEs:

$$\begin{aligned} \mathrm{d}S(t) &= S(t)\left((r(t)-q)\mathrm{d}t + \sigma_S \mathrm{d}W_S^{\mathbb{Q}}(t)\right), \quad S(0) = S_0 \\ \mathrm{d}r(t) &= \kappa\left(\theta - r(t)\right)\mathrm{d}t + \sigma_r \mathrm{d}W_r^{\mathbb{Q}}(t), \quad r(0) = r_0 \end{aligned} \tag{13}$$

with $\langle \mathrm{d}W_S^{\mathbb{Q}}(t), \mathrm{d}W_r^{\mathbb{Q}}(t)\rangle = \rho \mathrm{d}t$. According to standard notation, the new parameters in Equation (13) represent: $\sigma_S > 0$ the volatility of the risky asset, κ the speed of mean-reversion of the short-term interest rate, θ its long-run mean, $\sigma_r > 0$ the volatility of the short-term interest rate and $\rho \in [-1,1]$ the correlation between the Brownian shocks on S and r. The explicit solution to the SDEs in Equation (13) is

$$\begin{aligned} S(t) &= S_0 \exp\left[\int_0^t r(s)\mathrm{d}s - \left(q + \frac{\sigma_S^2}{2}\right)t + \sigma_S W_S(t)\right], \\ r(t) &= r_0 e^{-\kappa t} + \theta(1 - e^{-\kappa t}) + \sigma_r \int_0^t e^{-\kappa(t-s)}\mathrm{d}W_r(s). \end{aligned} \tag{14}$$

As before, the contribution of the drift of S, $\int_0^t r(s)\mathrm{d}s - \left(q + \frac{\sigma_S^2}{2}\right) t$, prevails over its volatility part $\sigma_S W_S(t)$. Therefore, the expected behaviour of the paths of S depends mostly on the drift.

The pricing formulas for European and American derivatives with maturity $T \in \mathbb{R}^+$ and payoff $f(S(\cdot))$ closely recall Equations (3) and (4):

$$\pi_f^E(t) = \mathbb{E}^{\mathbb{Q}}\left[f(S(T))\frac{B(t)}{B(T)}\middle| \mathcal{F}_t\right] = \mathbb{E}^{\mathbb{Q}}\left[f(S(T))e^{-\int_t^T r(s)\mathrm{d}s}\middle| \mathcal{F}_t\right]$$
$$\pi_f^A(t) = \operatorname*{ess\ sup}_{\tau\in[t,T]} \mathbb{E}^{\mathbb{Q}}\left[f(S(\tau))e^{-\int_t^\tau r(s)\mathrm{d}s}\middle| \mathcal{F}_t\right].$$

For European call and put options, the pricing formulas depart slightly from the standard Black–Scholes–Merton ones as now the variability of the locally risk-free interest rate has to be accounted for. The full derivation of the modified formulas can be found in the Appendix of Battauz and Rotondi (2019). For the European call option, $f(S(T)) = (S(T) - K)^+$ and it holds

$$\pi_f^E(t) = S(t)e^{-q(T-t)}N(\tilde{d}_1) - Kp(t,T)N(\tilde{d}_2) \tag{15}$$

with

$$\begin{aligned}
\tilde{d}_1 &= \frac{1}{\sqrt{\Sigma_{t,T}^2}}\left(\ln\frac{S(t)}{Kp(t,T)} + \frac{1}{2}\Sigma_{t,T}^2 - q(T-t)\right),\\
\tilde{d}_2 &= \tilde{d}_1 - \sqrt{\Sigma_{t,T}^2},\\
\Sigma_{t,T}^2 &= \sigma_S^2(T-t) + 2\sigma_S\sigma_r\rho\left(\frac{-1+e^{-\kappa(T-t)}+\kappa(T-t)}{k^2}\right) + \\
&\quad -\sigma_r^2\left(\frac{3+e^{-2\kappa(T-t)}-4e^{-\kappa(T-t)}-2\kappa(T-t)}{2k^3}\right),
\end{aligned} \tag{16}$$

whereas the related formula for the European put option can be retrieved by put-call parity.

The extension of the pricing to American options is less trivial. The variational inequality approach can be generalized including the new state variable r but it becomes quite tricky. On the contrary, the generalization of the binomial tree of Cox et al. (1979) is less involved: Battauz and Rotondi (2019) proposed a quadrinomial tree that models the joint evolution of S and r within a lattice structure. This allows for a relatively simple and fast evaluation of American claims.

Longstaff and Schwartz (2001) already allowed in their original work for a stochastic interest rate, which actually changes a little the LSM described in the previous Section. Nevertheless, the valuation algorithm suffers from the same drawbacks of the constant interest rate framework as the following subsection shows.

4.2. Numerical Investigation

Since the core of the LSM is unchanged, the drawback spotted out in the previous section might affect the pricing exercise also in this framework. The risk-neutral probability that the option is in the money is still pivotal. Going through the proof of Equation (15), it turns out that, in the present framework, the risk-neutral probability evaluated at $t = 0$ that a call option is in the money at a given $t \in (0, T]$ is

$$\mathbb{Q}(S(t) > K) = N\left(\frac{1}{\sqrt{\Sigma_{0,t}^2}}\left(\ln\frac{S_0}{Kp(0,t)} + \frac{1}{2}\Sigma_{0,t}^2 - qt\right)\right) = N(\tilde{d}_2), \tag{17}$$

where $\Sigma_{0,t}^2$ is defined in Equation (16). At the first steps of the LSM, this probability is again extremely low if the option starts even a little bit out of the money.

Figure 5 shows that also when the short-term interest rate is stochastic, very few paths of a simulation are expected to be in the money at the first monitoring dates. Without the numerical correction proposed at the end of Section 2.1, the LSM is likely to provide again wrong estimates.

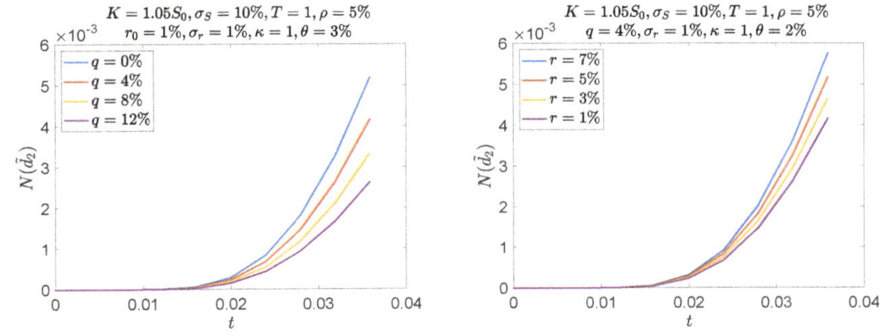

Figure 5. Probability that a call option on S in a stochastic interest rate framework is in the money at the first eight monitoring dates. Daily monitoring (250 dates for a $T = 1$ year maturity).

Table 4 shows some numerical examples that match the ones of Table 2.

Table 4. Numerical results, Vasicek model. $S_0 = 100$, $T = 1$, $\sigma = 10\%$, $\sigma_r = 1\%$, $\kappa = 1$, $\theta = 3\%$; 150 possible exercise dates per year. $\pi^{E}_{\widetilde{BS}}(0)$: initial price of the European call option computed with Equation (15). $\pi^{A}_{\widetilde{BR}}(0)$: initial price of the American call option computed with the quadrinomial tree of Battauz and Rotondi (2019) (average of the price obtained with 150 and 151 steps). $\pi^{A}_{\widetilde{LSM}}(0)^*$ ($\pi^{A}_{\widetilde{LSM}}(0)$): initial price of the American call option computed with the LSM not corrected (corrected) for the pitfalls previously described; the regression involves the first four Laguerre polynomials for the values of the immediate exercise payoff and the first four Laguerre polynomials for the current value of r; $NSim = 10^5$, standard errors obtained by 20 independent MC simulations. MC estimates that do not include the benchmark value within the confidence interval are denoted by *.

K/S_0	r_0	q	$\pi^{E}_{\widetilde{BS}}(0)$	$\pi^{A}_{\widetilde{BR}}(0)$	$\pi^{A}_{\widetilde{LSM}}(0)^*$	s.e.	$\pi^{A}_{\widetilde{LSM}}(0)$	s.e.
102%	5%	4%	3.1074	3.1424	3.1433	(0.0021)	3.1412	(0.0036)
		6%	2.3141	2.4910	2.4901	(0.0025)	2.4896	(0.0032)
		8%	1.6847	1.9970	1.9958	(0.0036)	1.9982	(0.0023)
	3%	4%	2.6170	2.7026	2.7011	(0.0029)	2.7028	(0.0017)
		6%	1.9232	2.1473	2.1452	(0.0039)	2.1464	(0.0026)
		8%	1.3772	1.7213	1.7195	(0.0036)	1.7215	(0.0019)
	1%	4%	2.1930	2.3223	2.3205	(0.0027)	2.3231	(0.0030)
		6%	1.5858	1.8467	1.8452	(0.0031)	1.8450	(0.0022)
		8%	1.1160	1.4803	1.4764 *	(0.0032)	1.4816	(0.0020)
105%	5%	4%	2.0746	2.0950	1.4113 *	(0.1999)	2.0941	(0.0030)
		6%	1.4935	1.5882	1.0263 *	(0.2665)	1.5896	(0.0035)
		8%	1.0461	1.2088	0.7596 *	(0.2133)	1.2092	(0.0031)
	3%	4%	1.7116	1.7553	1.2524 *	(0.2932)	1.7569	(0.0051)
		6%	1.2111	1.3275	0.8142 *	(0.3120)	1.3288	(0.0036)
		8%	0.8331	1.0053	0.6368 *	(0.2743)	1.0033	(0.0042)
	1%	4%	1.3966	1.4653	0.9235 *	(0.2293)	1.4658	(0.0036)
		6%	0.9709	1.1037	0.8097 *	(0.1773)	1.1015	(0.0027)
		8%	0.6557	0.8312	0.4521 *	(0.1884)	0.8323	(0.0017)
108%	5%	4%	1.3303	1.3430	0.9593 *	(0.2273)	1.3411	(0.0027)
		6%	0.9213	0.9747	0.6695 *	(0.2874)	0.9749	(0.0020)
		8%	0.6211	0.7055	0.4241 *	(0.2132)	0.7063	(0.0031)
	3%	4%	1.0723	1.0966	0.7946 *	(0.1537)	1.0967	(0.0037)
		6%	0.7297	0.7910	0.4215 *	(0.1632)	0.7923	(0.0021)
		8%	0.4821	0.5675	0.2559 *	(0.1241)	0.5670	(0.0023)
	1%	4%	0.8538	0.8903	0.4178 *	(0.1896)	0.8914	(0.0025)
		6%	0.5703	0.6371	0.3558 *	(0.1181)	0.6352	(0.0028)
		8%	0.3695	0.4528	0.2036 *	(0.1087)	0.4531	(0.0012)

First, it is interesting to notice that prices do not vary much when $r_0 = 3\%$ with respect to the ones obtained with a deterministic interest rate $r = 3\%$. This is due to the fact that, in the stochastic interest rate case, the long-run value is exactly $\theta = r_0$; therefore, r is simply expected to oscillate around $r_0 = \theta$ in a symmetric (and thus not very relevant) way. Prices are a little bit higher in the stochastic rate framework to account for the variability in the interest rate itself. This variability is relevant when r_0 is significantly different from θ. When $r_0 > \theta$, r is expected to decrease towards θ: This implies a lower expected drift of S and a smaller call option's price with respect to the standard case with a deterministic $r = r_0$. The converse holds true when $r_0 < \theta$, thus delivering a larger call option's price with respect to the standard model. If the pitfalls of the LSM are not corrected as proposed, the prices of the American call options fall constantly below their European counterpart. If the correction is made, instead, the LSM produces results that are comparable to the benchmark.

5. American Equity Options, Stochastic Volatility

Finally, in this section, I propose a third generalization of the standard Black–Scholes market. More specifically, I allow for the volatility of the stock price process to be stochastic while setting, for the sake of simplicity, the risk-free interest rate to be constant. The result is the celebrated model of stochastic volatility first introduced by the seminal work of Heston (1993).

As in the previous sections, Section 5.1 describes the theoretical aspects of the analysis, whereas Section 5.2 contains the related numerical examples.

5.1. Theoretical Framework: The Primary Assets and the Derivatives

Assume that the market is arbitrage-free. The instantaneous variance ν of the stock process S follows a Cox-Ingersoll-Ross (CIR henceforth) process, namely, a mean-reverting, non-negative[12] stochastic process first introduced by Cox et al. (1985). In this setting, the market involves two state variables: the risky asset's price and the volatility level. Consequently, there are two types of risks: the standard diffusive risk associated to S and the new volatility risk associated to ν. Since only the risky stock S and the riskless bond $B(t) = e^{rt}$ are traded, the market is not complete as the investor cannot hedge from the volatility risk. Therefore, the risk neutral measure $\mathbb{Q}$ is not unique. Nevertheless, uniqueness of contingent claims' prices in this incomplete market is still attainable by making an assumption on the price of volatility risk. As proposed by Heston (1993), I assume that the price of volatility risk is proportional to the instantaneous volatility itself and I denote the constant of proportionality by λ_ν, which becomes another exogenous parameter of the model. Thanks to this assumption, the risk-neutral measure $\mathbb{Q}$ is unique and the processes that drive the markets solve the following SDEs

$$\begin{aligned} \mathrm{d}S(t) &= (r-q)S(t)\mathrm{d}t + \sqrt{\nu(t)}S(t)\mathrm{d}W_S^{\mathbb{Q}}(t), && S(0) = S_0 \\ \mathrm{d}\nu(t) &= \left[\kappa\left(\nu_\infty - \nu(t)\right) - \lambda_\nu \nu(t)\right]\mathrm{d}t + \xi\sqrt{\nu(t)}\mathrm{d}W_\nu^{\mathbb{Q}}(t), && \nu(0) = \nu_0 \end{aligned} \tag{18}$$

with $\langle \mathrm{d}W_S^{\mathbb{Q}}, W_\nu^{\mathbb{Q}} \rangle = \rho \mathrm{d}t$. According to standard notation, the new parameters in Equation (18) represent: κ the speed of mean-reversion on the volatility, ν_∞ its long-run mean, ξ the volatility of the volatility process (the so called "vol of vol"), and $\rho \in [-1, 1]$ the correlation between the Brownian shocks on S and ν. Although $\nu(t)$ admits no explicit solution[13], the one for $S(t)$ in Equation (18) is

$$S(t) = S_0 \exp\left[\left(r - q - \frac{\nu(t)}{2}\right)t + \sqrt{\nu(t)}W_S^{\mathbb{Q}}(t)\right], \quad t \geq 0. \tag{19}$$

---

[12] With respect to the specification of $\nu(t)$ in Equation (18), if the so-called Feller condition holds true, namely if $2\kappa\theta > \xi^2$, $\nu(t)$ is also strictly positive almost surely.

[13] As effectively explained in Subsection 3.4 of Glasserman (2003), a CIR process is not explicitly solvable; nevertheless, it can be shown that it is distributed, up to a scale factor, as a non-central chi-squared random variable.

As before, the contribution of the drift of S, $\left(r - q - \frac{\nu(t)}{2}\right)t$ prevails over its diffusive part $\sqrt{\nu(t)}W_S^{\mathbb{Q}}(t)$ and it is still the main driver of its expected future behaviour.

The price at t of European and American options are still given by the risk-neutral expected values in Equation (3) and (4), where now the dynamics of S is shown by Equation (19).

For European options, the closed-form pricing formula are derived in the first section of Heston (1993). For the European call option, namely when the payoff function is $f(S(T)) = (S(T) - K)^+$, it holds at any $t \in [0, T]$

$$\pi_H^E(t) = S(t)e^{-q(T-t)}P_1 - Ke^{-r(T-t)}P_2 \tag{20}$$

with

$$P_j = \frac{1}{2} + \frac{1}{\pi}\int_0^{+\infty} \mathrm{Re}\left[\frac{1}{ix}\exp\left(ix\left(S(t) - \ln(K)\right) + C_j(T-t,x) + D_j(T-t,x)\nu(t)\right)\right]\mathrm{d}x, \quad j = 1,2, \tag{21}$$

where i is the imaginary unit, $\mathrm{Re}[\cdot]$ the real part operator and, for $j = 1,2$,

$$\begin{aligned}
C_j(\tau,x) &= (r-q)xi\tau + \frac{\kappa\nu_\infty}{\xi^2}\left[(b_j - \rho\xi xi + d_j(x))\tau - 2ln\left(\frac{1 - g_j(x)e^{d_j(x)\tau}}{1 - g_j(x)}\right)\right],\\
D_j(\tau,x) &= \frac{b_j - \rho\xi xi + d_j(x)}{\xi^2},\\
g_j(x) &= \frac{b_j - \rho\xi xi + d_j(x)}{b_j - \rho\xi xi - d_j(x)},\\
d_j(x) &= \sqrt{(\rho\xi xi - b_j)^2 - \xi^2(2u_j xi - x^2)},
\end{aligned}$$

$$u_1 = 0.5, \quad u_2 = -0.5, \quad b_1 = \kappa + \lambda_\nu\nu - \rho\xi, \quad b_2 = \kappa + \lambda.$$

The analogous formula for the European put option can be retrieved by put-call parity.

The pricing of American option within this stochastic volatility framework is quite challenging. This is precisely one of the cases in which the LSM is of great help as, on the contrary, one can easily simulate the paths of Equation (18). The benchmark I will compare the performance of the modified LSM to is a finite difference approach to the free boundary problem for the American call option (see, e.g., Pascucci (2008) on this approach). The following numerical investigation focuses on the American call option in the Heston model; analogous results can be retrieved by the put–call symmetry for American options within the Heston model described by Battauz et al. (2014).

5.2. Numerical Investigation

By analogy with the standard Black–Scholes–Merton formula and as carefully described by Heston (1993), P_2 in Equation (20) represents the risk-neutral probability that an European call option on S closes in the money. As in the previous cases, this probability depends heavily on the drift of S, $\left(r - q - \frac{\nu(t)}{2}\right)t$, and it is increasing with respect to the risk-free interest rate and decreasing with respect to the dividend yield.

Figure 6 provides a graphical illustration of this intuition. Notice that, as in the previous cases, at the first monitoring dates, very few paths are expected to be in the money if the option is even mildly out of the money at inception. As before, this worsens when the drift of the underlying becomes negative.

Table 5 shows some numerical examples in the spirit of the previous sections. First, prices of the options are a little bit larger here with respect to the standard model due to the positive volatility risk premium. Then, the LSM fails in providing correct estimates in the very same cases of the standard model. Nevertheless, the correction is still effective.

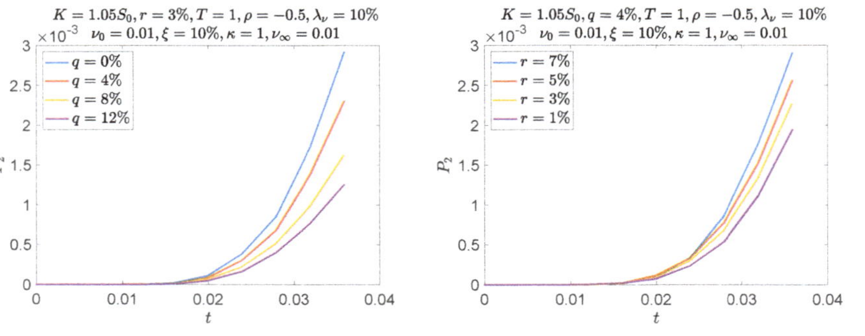

Figure 6. Probability that a call option on S in within the Heston model is in the money at the first eight monitoring dates. Daily monitoring (250 dates for a $T = 1$ year maturity).

Table 5. Numerical results, Heston model. $S_0 = 100$, $T = 1$, $\nu_0 = 0.01$, $\xi = 10\%$, $\kappa = 1$, $\nu_\infty = 0.01$, $\lambda_\nu = 10\%$; 150 possible exercise dates per year. $\pi_H^E(0)$: initial price of the European call option computed with Equation (20). $\pi_{BR}^A(0)$: initial price of the American call option computed solving the free boundary problem by finite differences. $\pi_{\text{LSM}}^A(0)^*$ ($\pi_{\text{L}\tilde{\text{S}}\text{M}}^A(0)$): initial price of the American call option computed with the LSM not corrected (corrected) for the pitfalls previously described; the regression involves the first four Laguerre polynomials for the values of the immediate exercise payoff and the first four Laguerre polynomials for the current value of ν; $NSim = 10^5$, standard errors obtained by 20 independent MC simulations. MC estimates that do not include the benchmark value within the confidence interval are denoted by *.

K/S_0	r	q	$\pi_H^E(0)$	$\pi_{FD}^A(0)$	$\pi_{\text{LSM}}^A(0)^*$	s.e.	$\pi_{\text{L}\tilde{\text{S}}\text{M}}^A(0)$	s.e.
102%	5%	4%	3.2587	3.2588	3.2530	(0.0065)	3.2580	(0.0036)
		6%	2.3580	2.4389	2.4401	(0.0042)	2.4405	(0.0039)
		8%	1.6416	1.8626	1.8601	(0.0028)	1.8647	(0.0038)
	3%	4%	2.4057	2.4741	2.4809	(0.0070)	2.4762	(0.0024)
		6%	1.6748	1.8841	1.8802	(0.0045)	1.8890	(0.0040)
		8%	1.1198	1.4607	$1.4572^\star$	(0.0021)	1.4589	(0.0047)
	1%	4%	1.7087	1.9062	1.9063	(0.0023)	1.9058	(0.0036)
		6%	1.1424	1.4746	1.4736	(0.0013)	1.4759	(0.0028)
		8%	0.7326	1.1628	$1.1604^\star$	(0.0017)	1.1597	(0.0053)
105%	5%	4%	2.0737	2.0738	$1.4938^\star$	(0.3181)	2.0744	(0.0029)
		6%	1.4186	1.4820	$0.6268^\star$	(0.2667)	1.4835	(0.0032)
		8%	0.9316	1.0361	$0.5911^\star$	(0.1911)	1.0395	(0.0039)
	3%	4%	1.4473	1.4820	$0.6037^\star$	(0.2722)	1.4796	(0.0035)
		6%	0.9504	1.0500	$0.5094^\star$	(0.1900)	1.0524	(0.0027)
		8%	0.5976	0.7486	$0.4932^\star$	(0.1214)	0.7471	(0.0024)
	1%	4%	0.9697	1.0643	$0.5353^\star$	(0.1909)	1.0644	(0.0023)
		6%	0.6107	0.7574	$0.5181^\star$	(0.1281)	0.7568	(0.0017)
		8%	0.3686	0.5440	$0.2180^\star$	(0.1039)	0.5436	(0.0021)
108%	5%	4%	1.2346	1.2347	$0.3744^\star$	(0.1680)	1.2336	(0.0029)
		6%	0.7975	0.8168	$0.2408^\star$	(0.1277)	0.8176	(0.0035)
		8%	0.4940	0.5408	$0.2372^\star$	(0.0880)	0.5400	(0.0024)
	3%	4%	0.8136	0.8304	$0.2964^\star$	(0.1243)	0.8329	(0,0027)
		6%	0.5040	0.5488	$0.2497^\star$	(0.0823)	0.5508	(0.0028)
		8%	0.2992	0.3616	$0.1409^\star$	(0.0534)	0.3638	(0.0020)
	1%	4%	0.5142	0.5570	$0.4261^\star$	(0.1136)	0.5544	(0.0023)
		6%	0.3053	0.3664	$0.2439^\star$	(0.0935)	0.3691	(0.0018)
		8%	0.1736	0.2410	$0.1273^\star$	(0.0636)	0.2399	(0.0015)

6. Conclusions

The Least Square Methods proposed by Longstaff and Schwartz (2001) is one of the most widely used algorithms to price American equity options. I quantified and corrected a sizeable bias that could arise if the regression exploited for the approximation of the continuation value of the option is ill-posed. I showed that this might happen when the option is even mildly out of the money at inception and when the underlying is not likely to go back into the in the money region. For American call options, this is likely to happen when the risk-free interest rate is low and the dividend yield is higher within the all the most commons financial market models.

Funding: This research received no external funding.

Acknowledgments: I thank Anna Battauz for insightful discussions and precious comments on the present work; all the remaining errors are my own.

Conflicts of Interest: The author declares no conflict of interest.

References

Abramowitz, Milton, and Irene A. Stegun. 1970. *Handbook of Mathematical Functions*. Mineola: Dover Publications.

Battauz, Anna, and Francesco Rotondi. 2019. American Options and Stochastic Interest Rates. Available online: http://didattica.unibocconi.it/mypage/index.php?IdUte=49395&idr=6877&lingua=ita (accessed on 21 March 2019).

Battauz, Anna, Marzia De Donno and Alessandro Sbuelz. 2014. The put-call symmetry for American options in the Heston stochastic volatility model. *Mathematical Finance Letters* 7: 1–8.

Belomestny, Denis, Fabian Dickmann, and Tigran Nagapetyan. 2015. Pricing Bermudan options via multilevel approximation methods. *SIAM Journal on Financial Mathematics* 6: 448–66. [CrossRef]

Björk, Tomas. 2009. *Arbitrage Theory in Continuous Time*, 3rd ed. Hong Kong: Oxford Finance.

Black, Fischer, and Myron Scholes. 1973. The pricing of options and corporate liabilities. *Journal of Political Economy* 81: 637–54. [CrossRef]

Brigo, Damiano, and Fabio Mercurio. 2017. *Interest Rate Models-Theory and Practice: With Smile, Inflation and Credit*. Berlin: Springer Science & Business Media.

Carr, Peter, and Marc Chesney. 1997. American Put Call Symmetry. Available online: https://pdfs.semanticscholar.org/fed1/b276f01b0ddb787cfcc9d0d2b8953fcd03dc.pdf (accessed on 21 March 2019).

Carr, Peter, and Dilip Madan. 2001. Optimal positioning in derivative securities. *Quantitative Finance* 1: 19–77. [CrossRef]

Clément, Emmanuelle, Damien Lamberton, and Philip Protter. 2002. An analysis of a least squared regression method for American option pricing. *Finance and Stochastics* 6: 449–71. [CrossRef]

Cox, John C., Jonathan E. Ingersoll, and Stephen A. Ross. 1985. A theory of the term structure of interest rates. *Econometrica* 53: 385–407. [CrossRef]

Cox, John C., Stephen A. Ross, and Mark Rubinstein. 1979. Option pricing: A simplified approach. *Journal of Financial Economics* 7: 229–63. [CrossRef]

Detemple, Jerome. 2001. American options: Symmetry properties. In *Handbooks in Mathematical Finance*. Cambridge: Cambridge University Press, pp. 67–104.

Detemple, Jerome. 2014. Optimal exercise for derivative securities. *Annual Review of Financial Economics* 6: 459–87. [CrossRef]

Fabozzi, Frank J., Tommaso Paletta, and Radu Tunaru. 2017. An improved least squares Monte Carlo valuation method based on heteroscedasticity. *European Journal of Operational Research* 263: 698–706. [CrossRef]

Friedman, Avner. 1982. *Variational Principles and Free Boundary Problems, Pure and Applied Mathematics*. Hoboken: Wiley.

García, Diego. 2003. Convergence and biases of Monte Carlo estimates of American option prices using a parametric exercise rule. *Journal of Economics and Control* 27: 1855–79. [CrossRef]

Glasserman, Paul. 2003. *Monte Carlo Methods in Financial Engineering*. Berlin: Springer.

Heston, Steven L. 1993. A closed-form solution for options with stochastic volatility with applications to bond and currency options. *The Review of Financial Studies* 6: 327–43. [CrossRef]

Kan, Kin Hung, and R. Mark Reesor. 2012. Bias reduction for pricing American options by least-squares Monte Carlo. *Applied Mathematical Finance* 19: 195–217. [CrossRef]

Kinderlehrer, David, and Guido Stampacchia. 2000. An introduction to variational inequalities and their applications. Classics in Applied Mathematics. In *Society for Industrial and Applied Mathematics*. University City: SIAM, vol. 31.

Longstaff, Francis A., and Eduardo S. Schwartz. 2001. Valuing American options by simulation: A simple least-square approach. *The Review of Financial Studies* 14: 113–47. [CrossRef]

Merton, Robert C. 1976. Option pricing when underlying stock returns are discontinuous. *Journal of Financial Economics* 3: 125–44. [CrossRef]

Merton, Robert C. 1973. Theory of rational option pricing. *Bell Journal of Economics and Management Science* 4: 141–83. [CrossRef]

Pascucci, Andrea. 2008. Free boundary and optimal stopping problems for American Asian options. *Finance and Stochastics* 12: 21–41. [CrossRef]

Revuz, Daniel, and Marc Yor. 2001. *Continuous Martingales and Brownian Motion*, 3rd ed. Berlin: Springer.

Vasicek, Oldrich. 1977. An equilibrium characterization of the term structure. *Journal of Financial Economics* 5: 177–88. [CrossRef]

Wooldridge, Jeffrey M. 2013. *Introductory Econometrics: A Modern Approach*, 5th ed. South Western: Cengage Learning.

Zhang, Xiao Lan. 1997. Numerical analysis of American option pricing in a jump-diffusion model. *Mathematics of Operations Research* 22: 668–90. [CrossRef]

© 2019 by the authors. Licensee MDPI, Basel, Switzerland. This article is an open access article distributed under the terms and conditions of the Creative Commons Attribution (CC BY) license (http://creativecommons.org/licenses/by/4.0/).

risks

MDPI

Article

Optimal Excess-of-Loss Reinsurance for Stochastic Factor Risk Models

Matteo Brachetta *,†,‡ **and Claudia Ceci** †,‡

Department of Economics, University of Chieti-Pescara, 42-65127 Pescara, Italy; c.ceci@unich.it
* Correspondence: matteo.brachetta@unich.it
† Current address: Viale Pindaro, 42-65127 Pescara, Italy.
‡ These authors contributed equally to this work.

Received: 31 January 2019; Accepted: 26 April 2019; Published: 1 May 2019

Abstract: We study the optimal excess-of-loss reinsurance problem when both the intensity of the claims arrival process and the claim size distribution are influenced by an exogenous stochastic factor. We assume that the insurer's surplus is governed by a marked point process with dual-predictable projection affected by an environmental factor and that the insurance company can borrow and invest money at a constant real-valued risk-free interest rate r. Our model allows for stochastic risk premia, which take into account risk fluctuations. Using stochastic control theory based on the Hamilton-Jacobi-Bellman equation, we analyze the optimal reinsurance strategy under the criterion of maximizing the expected exponential utility of the terminal wealth. A verification theorem for the value function in terms of classical solutions of a backward partial differential equation is provided. Finally, some numerical results are discussed.

Keywords: optimal reinsurance; excess-of-loss reinsurance; Hamilton-Jacobi-Bellman equation; stochastic factor model; stochastic control

MSC: 93E20; 91B30; 60G57; 60J75

JEL Classification: G220; C610

1. Introduction

In this paper, we analyze the optimal excess-of-loss reinsurance problem from the insurer's point of view, under the criterion of maximizing the expected utility of the terminal wealth. It is well known that the reinsurance policies are very effective tools for risk management. In fact, by means of a risk sharing agreement, they allow the insurer to reduce unexpected losses, to stabilize operating results, to increase business capacity and so on. Among the most common arrangements, the proportional and the excess-of-loss contracts are of great interest. The former was intensively studied in Irgens and Paulsen (2004); Liu and Ma (2009); Liang et al. (2011); Liang and Bayraktar (2014); Zhu et al. (2015); Brachetta and Ceci (2019) and references therein. The latter was investigated in these articles: in Zhang et al. (2007) and Meng and Zhang (2010), the authors proved the optimality of the excess-of-loss policy under the criterion of minimizing the ruin probability, with the surplus process described by a Brownian motion with drift; in Zhao et al. (2013) the Cramér-Lundberg model is used for the surplus process, with the possibility of investing in a financial market represented by the Heston model; in Sheng et al. (2014) and Li and Gu (2013) the risky asset is described by a Constant Elasticity of Variance (CEV) model, while the surplus is modelled by the Cramér-Lundberg model and its diffusion approximation, respectively; finally, in Li et al. (2018) the authors studied a robust optimal strategy under the diffusion approximation of the surplus process.

The common ground of the cited works is the underlying risk model, which is the Cramér-Lundberg model (or its diffusion approximation)[1]. In the actuarial literature it is of great importance, because it is simple enough to perform calculations. In fact, the claims arrival process is described by a Poisson process with constant intensity (or a Brownian motion, in the diffusion model). Nevertheless, as noticed by many authors (e.g., Grandell (1991); Hipp (2004)), it needs generalization in order to take into account the so called *size fluctuations* and *risk fluctuations*, i.e., variations of the number of policyholders and modifications of the underlying risk, respectively.

The main goal of our work is to extend the classical risk model by modelling the claims arrival process as a marked point process with dual-predictable projection affected by an exogenous stochastic process Y. More precisely, both the intensity of the claims arrival process and the claim size distribution are influenced by Y. Thanks to this environmental factor, we achieve a reasonably realistic description of any risk movement. For example, in automobile insurance Y may describe weather conditions, road conditions, traffic volume and so on. All these factors usually influence the accident probability as well as the damage size.

Some noteworthy attempts in that direction can be found in Liang and Bayraktar (2014) and Brachetta and Ceci (2019), where the authors studied the optimal proportional reinsurance. In the former, the authors considered a Markov-modulated compound Poisson process, with the (unobservable) stochastic factor described by a finite state Markov chain. In the latter, the stochastic factor follows a general diffusion. In addition, in Brachetta and Ceci (2019) the insurance and the reinsurance premia are not evaluated by premium calculation principles (see Young (2006)), because they are stochastic processes depending on Y. In our paper, we extend further the risk model, because the claim size distribution is influenced by the stochastic factor, which is described by a diffusion-type stochastic differential equation (SDE). In addition, we study a different reinsurance contract, which is the excess-of-loss agreement.

To the best of our knowledge stochastic risk factor models in insurance have not been considered so far. This is in contrast with financial literature where risky asset dynamics affected by exogenous stochastic factors have been largely considered, see for instance Ceci (2009); Ceci and Gerardi (2009); Ceci and Gerardi (2010); Zariphopoulou (2009) and Ceci (2012).

In our model the insurer is also allowed to lend or borrow money at a given interest rate r. During recent years, negative interest rates drew the attention of many authors. For example, since June 2016 the European Central Bank (ECB) fixed a negative Deposit facility rate, which is the interest banks receive for depositing money within the ECB overnight. Presently, it is -0.4%. As a consequence, in our framework $r \in \mathbb{R}$. We point out that there is no loss of generality due to the absence of a risky asset, because as long as the insurance and the financial markets are independent (which is a standard hypothesis in non-life insurance), the optimal reinsurance strategy turns out to depend only on the risk-free asset (see Brachetta and Ceci (2019) and references therein). As a consequence, the optimal investment strategy can be eventually obtained using existing results in the literature.

The paper is organized as follows: in Section 2, we formulate the model assumptions and describe the maximization problem; in Section 3 we derive the Hamilton-Jacobi-Bellman (HJB) equation; in Section 4, we investigate the candidate optimal strategy, which is suggested by the HJB derivation; in Section 5, we provide the verification argument with a probabilistic representation of the value function; finally, in Section 6 we perform some numerical simulations.

2. Model Formulation

Let $(\Omega, \mathcal{F}, \mathbb{P}, \{\mathcal{F}_t\}_{t\in[0,T]})$ be a complete probability space endowed with a filtration which satisfies the usual conditions, where $T > 0$ is the insurer's time horizon. We model the insurance losses through a marked point process $\{(T_n, Z_n)\}_{n\geq 1}$ with local characteristics influenced by an environment

[1] See Lundberg (1903); Schmidli (2018).

stochastic factor $Y \doteq \{Y_t\}_{t\in[0,T]}$. Here, the sequence $\{T_n\}_{n\geq 1}$ describes the claim arrival process and $\{Z_n\}_{n\geq 1}$ the corresponding claim sizes. Precisely, T_n, $n = 1, \ldots,$ are $\{\mathcal{F}_t\}_{t\in[0,T]}$ stopping times such that $T_n < T_{n+1}$ a.s. and Z_n, $n = 1, \ldots,$ are $(0, +\infty)$-random variables such that $\forall n = 1, \ldots, Z_n$ is $\mathcal{F}_{T_n}$-measurable.

The stochastic factor Y is defined as the unique strong solution to the following SDE:

$$dY_t = b(t, Y_t)\,dt + \gamma(t, Y_t)\,dW_t^{(Y)}, \qquad Y_0 \in \mathbb{R}, \tag{1}$$

where $\{W_t^{(Y)}\}_{t\in[0,T]}$ is a standard Brownian motion on $(\Omega, \mathcal{F}, \mathbb{P}, \{\mathcal{F}_t\}_{t\in[0,T]})$. We assume that the following conditions hold true:

$$\mathbb{E}\left[\int_0^T |b(t, Y_t)|\,dt + \int_0^T \gamma(t, Y_t)^2\,dt\right] < +\infty, \tag{2}$$

$$\sup_{t\in[0,T]} \mathbb{E}[|Y_t|^2] < +\infty. \tag{3}$$

We will denote by $\{\mathcal{F}_t^Y\}_{t\in[0,T]}$ the natural filtration generated by the process Y.

The random measure corresponding to the losses process $\{(T_n, Z_n)\}_{n\geq 1}$ is given by

$$m(dt, dz) \doteq \sum_{n\geq 1} \delta_{(T_n, Z_n)(dt,dz)} \mathbb{1}_{\{T_n \leq T\}}, \tag{4}$$

where $\delta_{(t,x)}$ denotes the Dirac measure located at point (t, x). We assume that its $\{\mathcal{F}_t\}_{t\in[0,T]}$-dual predictable projection $\nu(dt, dz)$ has the form

$$\nu(dt, dz) = dF(z, Y_t)\lambda(t, Y_t)\,dt, \tag{5}$$

where

- $F(z, y) : [0, +\infty) \times \mathbb{R} \to [0, 1]$ is such that $\forall y \in \mathbb{R}$, $F(\cdot, y)$ is a distribution function, with $F(0, y) = 0$;
- $\lambda(t, y) : [0, T] \times \mathbb{R} \to (0, +\infty)$ is a strictly positive measurable function.

In the sequel, we will assume the following integrability conditions:

$$\mathbb{E}\left[\int_0^T \int_0^{+\infty} \nu(dt, dz)\right] = \mathbb{E}\left[\int_0^T \lambda(t, Y_t)\,dt\right] < +\infty, \tag{6}$$

and

$$\mathbb{E}\left[\int_0^T \int_0^{+\infty} z^2\,\lambda(t, Y_t)dF(z, Y_t)\,dt\right] < +\infty. \tag{7}$$

According to the definition of dual predictable projection, for every nonnegative, $\{\mathcal{F}_t\}_{t\in[0,T]}$-predictable and $[0, +\infty)$-indexed process $\{H(t, z)\}_{t\in[0,T]}$ we have that[2]

$$\mathbb{E}\left[\int_0^T \int_0^{+\infty} H(t, z)\,m(dt, dz)\right] = \mathbb{E}\left[\int_0^T \int_0^{+\infty} H(t, z)\,\lambda(t, Y_t)dF(z, Y_t)\,dt\right]. \tag{8}$$

In particular, choosing $H(t, z) = H_t$ with $\{H_t\}_{t\in[0,T]}$ any nonnegative $\{\mathcal{F}_t\}_{t\in[0,T]}$-predictable process

$$\mathbb{E}\left[\int_0^T \int_0^{+\infty} H(t)\,m(dt, dz)\right] = \mathbb{E}\left[\int_0^T H(t)\,dN_t\right] = \mathbb{E}\left[\int_0^T H_t\,\lambda(t, Y_t)\,dt\right], \tag{9}$$

---

2 For details on marked point processes theory, see Brémaud (1981).

i.e., the claims arrival process $N_t = m((0,t] \times [0,+\infty)) = \sum_{n\geq 1} \mathbb{1}_{\{T_n \leq t\}}$ is a point process with stochastic intensity $\{\lambda(t, Y_t)\}_{t\in[0,T]}$.

Now we give the interpretation of $F(z, Y_t)$ as conditional distribution of the claim sizes[3].

Proposition 1. *$\forall n = 1,\dots$ and $\forall A \in \mathcal{B}([0,+\infty))$ the following equality holds:*

$$\mathbb{P}[Z_n \in A \mid \mathcal{F}_{T_n^-}] = \mathbb{P}[Z_n \in A \mid \mathcal{F}^Y_{T_n}] = \int_A dF(z, Y_{T_n}) \qquad \mathbb{P}\text{-a.s.},$$

where $\mathcal{F}_{T_n^-}$ is the strict past of the σ-algebra generated by the stopping time T_n:

$$\mathcal{F}_{T_n^-} := \sigma\{A \cap \{t < \tau_n\}, A \in \mathcal{F}_t, t \in [0,T]\}.$$

Proof. See Appendix A. □

This means that in our model both the claim arrival intensity and the claim size distribution are affected by the stochastic factor Y. This is a reasonable assumption; for example, in automobile insurance Y may describe weather, road conditions, traffic volume, and so on. For a detailed discussion of this topic see also Brachetta and Ceci (2019).

Remark 1. *Let us observe that for any $\{\mathcal{F}_t\}_{t\in[0,T]}$-predictable and $[0,+\infty)$-indexed process $\{H(t,z)\}_{t\in[0,T]}$ such that*

$$\mathbb{E}\left[\int_0^T \int_0^{+\infty} |H(t,z)|\, \lambda(t, Y_t) dF(z, Y_t)\, dt\right] < +\infty,$$

the process

$$M_t = \int_0^t \int_0^{+\infty} H(s,z)\, \big(m(ds,dz) - \nu(ds,dz)\big), \qquad t \in [0,T]$$

turns out to be an $\{\mathcal{F}_t\}_{t\in[0,T]}$-martingale. If in addition

$$\mathbb{E}\left[\int_0^T \int_0^{+\infty} |H(t,z)|^2\, \lambda(t, Y_t) dF(z, Y_t)\, dt\right] < +\infty,$$

then $\{M_t\}_{t\in[0,T]}$ is a square integrable $\{\mathcal{F}_t\}_{t\in[0,T]}$-martingale and

$$\mathbb{E}[M_t^2] = \mathbb{E}\left[\int_0^t \int_0^{+\infty} |H(s,z)|^2\, \lambda(s, Y_s) dF(z, Y_s)\, ds\right] \qquad \forall t \in [0,T].$$

Moreover, the predictable covariation process of $\{M_t\}_{t\in[0,T]}$ is given by

$$\langle M \rangle_t = \int_0^t \int_0^{+\infty} |H(s,z)|^2\, \lambda(s, Y_s) dF(z, Y_s)\, ds,$$

that is $\{M_t^2 - \langle M \rangle_t\}_{t\in[0,T]}$ is an $\{\mathcal{F}_t\}_{t\in[0,T]}$-martingale[4].

In this framework we define the cumulative claims up to time $t \in [0,T]$ as follows

$$C_t = \sum_{n\geq 1} Z_n \mathbb{1}_{\{T_n \leq t\}} = \int_0^t \int_0^{+\infty} z\, m(ds,dz),$$

[3] This result is an extension of Proposition 2.4 in Ceci and Gerardi (2006).
[4] For these results and other related topics see e.g., Bass (2004).

and the insurer's reserve process is described by

$$R_t = R_0 + \int_0^t c_s ds - C_t,$$

where $R_0 > 0$ is the initial wealth and $\{c_t\}_{t\in[0,T]}$ is a nonnegative $\{\mathcal{F}_t\}_{t\in[0,T]}$-adapted process representing the gross insurance risk premium. In the sequel we assume $c_t = c(t, Y_t)$, for a suitable function $c(t,y)$ such that $\mathbb{E}\left[\int_0^T c(t,Y_t)dt\right] < +\infty$. Let us notice that Equation (7) implies that

$$\mathbb{E}[C_T] = \mathbb{E}\left[\int_0^T \int_0^{+\infty} zm(dt,dz)\right] = \mathbb{E}\left[\int_0^T \int_0^{+\infty} z\,\lambda(t,Y_t)dF(z,Y_t)\,dt\right] < +\infty.$$

Now we allow the insurer to buy an excess-of-loss reinsurance contract. By means of this agreement, the insurer chooses a retention level $\alpha \in [0,+\infty)$ and for any future claim the reinsurer is responsible for all the amount which exceeds that threshold α (e.g., $\alpha = 0$ means full reinsurance). For any dynamic reinsurance strategy $\{\alpha_t\}_{t\in[0,T]}$, the insurer's surplus process is given by

$$R_t^\alpha = R_0 + \int_0^t (c_s - q_s^\alpha)\,ds - \int_0^t \int_0^{+\infty} (z \wedge \alpha_s)\,m(ds,dz),$$

where $\{q_t^\alpha\}_{t\in[0,T]}$ is a nonnegative $\{\mathcal{F}_t\}_{t\in[0,T]}$-adapted process representing the reinsurance premium rate. In addition, we suppose that the following assumption holds true.

Assumption 1. *(Excess-of-loss reinsurance premium) Let us assume that for any reinsurance strategy $\{\alpha_t\}_{t\in[0,T]}$ the corresponding reinsurance premium process $\{q_t^\alpha\}_{t\in[0,T]}$ admits the following representation:*

$$q_t^\alpha = q(t, Y_t, \alpha_t) \qquad \forall t \in [0,T],$$

where $q(t,y,\alpha) : [0,T] \times \mathbb{R} \times [0,+\infty) \to [0,+\infty)$ is a continuous function in α, with continuous partial derivatives $\frac{\partial q(t,y,\alpha)}{\partial \alpha}$, $\frac{\partial^2 q(t,y,\alpha)}{\partial \alpha^2}$ in $\alpha \in [0,+\infty)$, such that

1. *$\frac{\partial q(t,y,\alpha)}{\partial \alpha} \le 0$ for all $(t,y,\alpha) \in [0,T] \times \mathbb{R} \times [0,+\infty)$, since the premium is increasing with respect to the protection level;*
2. *$q(t,y,0) > c(t,y)$ $\forall (t,y) \in [0,T] \times \mathbb{R}$, because the cedant is not allowed to gain a profit without risk.*

In the rest of the paper, $\frac{\partial q(t,y,0)}{\partial \alpha}$ should be intended as a right derivative. Moreover, we assume that

$$\mathbb{E}\left[\int_0^T q(t,Y_t,0)\,dt\right] < +\infty.$$

Assumption 1 formalizes the minimal requirements for a process $\{q_t^\alpha\}_{t\in[0,T]}$ to be a reinsurance premium. In the next examples we briefly recall the most famous premium calculation principles, because they are widely used in optimal reinsurance problems solving. In Appendix B the reader can find a rigorous derivation of the formulas (10) and (11) below.

Example 1. *The most famous premium calculation principle is the expected value principle (abbr. EVP)[5]. The underlying conjecture is that the reinsurer evaluates her premium in order to cover the expected losses plus a load which depends on the expected losses. In our framework, under the EVP the reinsurance premium is given by the following expression:*

$$q(t,y,\alpha) = (1+\theta)\lambda(t,y) \int_0^{+\infty} (z - z \wedge \alpha)\,dF(z,y), \tag{10}$$

[5] See Young (2006).

for some safety loading $\theta > 0$.

Example 2. *Another important premium calculation principle is the variance premium principle (abbr. VP). In this case, the reinsurer's loading is proportional to the variance of the losses. More formally, the reinsurance premium admits the following representation:*

$$q(t,y,\alpha) = \lambda(t,y)\int_0^{+\infty}(z - z\wedge\alpha)\,dF(z,y) + \theta\lambda(t,y)\int_0^{+\infty}(z - z\wedge\alpha)^2\,dF(z,y), \tag{11}$$

for some safety loading $\theta > 0$.

Furthermore, the insurer can lend or borrow money at a fixed interest rate $r \in \mathbb{R}$. More precisely, every time the surplus is positive, the insurer lends it and earns interest income if $r > 0$ (or pays interest expense if $r < 0$); on the contrary, when the surplus becomes negative, the insurer borrows money and pays interest expense (or gains interest income if $r < 0$).

Under these assumptions, the total wealth dynamic associated with a given strategy α is described by the following SDE:

$$dX_t^\alpha = dR_t^\alpha + rX_t^\alpha\,dt, \qquad X_0^\alpha = R_0. \tag{12}$$

It can be verified that the solution to (12) is given by the following expression:

$$X_t^\alpha = R_0e^{rt} + \int_0^t e^{r(t-s)}\left[c(s,Y_s) - q(s,Y_s,\alpha_s)\right]ds - \int_0^t\int_0^{+\infty} e^{r(t-s)}(z\wedge\alpha_s)\,m(ds,dz). \tag{13}$$

Remark 2. *Let us define*

$$K \doteq \max\{e^{rT},1\}. \tag{14}$$

We have that

$$\mathbb{E}[\sup_{t\in[0,T]}|X_t^\alpha|] \le K\mathbb{E}\left[R_0 + \int_0^T c_t\,dt + \int_0^T q(t,Y_t,0)\,dt + C_T\right] < +\infty. \tag{15}$$

Our aim is to find the optimal strategy α in order to maximize the expected exponential utility of the terminal wealth, that is

$$\sup_{\alpha\in\mathcal{A}}\mathbb{E}\left[1 - e^{-\eta X_T^\alpha}\right] = 1 - \inf_{\alpha\in\mathcal{A}}\mathbb{E}\left[e^{-\eta X_T^\alpha}\right],$$

where $\eta > 0$ is the risk-aversion parameter and $\mathcal{A}$ is the set of all admissible strategies as defined below.

Definition 1. *We denote by $\mathcal{A}$ the set of all admissible strategies, that is the class of all nonnegative $\{\mathcal{F}_t\}_{t\in[0,T]}$-predictable processes $\{\alpha_t\}_{t\in[0,T]}$. With the notation $\mathcal{A}_t$ we refer to the same class, restricted to the strategies starting from $t \in [0,T]$.*

Remark 3. *We need additional integrability conditions in order to ensure that under $\alpha = 0$ (full reinsurance) and $\alpha = +\infty$ (null reinsurance) the expected utility is finite. Precisely, under condition*

$$\mathbb{E}\left[e^{\eta\int_0^T e^{r(T-s)}q(s,Y_s,0)\,ds}\right] < +\infty, \tag{16}$$

we get that

$$\mathbb{E}\left[e^{-\eta X_T^0}\right] = \mathbb{E}\left[e^{-\eta R_0e^{rT} - \eta\int_0^T e^{r(T-s)}\left[c(s,Y_s) - q(s,Y_s,0)\right]ds}\right] < +\infty$$

and under

$$\mathbb{E}\left[e^{\eta K C_T}\right] < +\infty, \tag{17}$$

with K given in (14), *we have that*

$$\mathbb{E}\left[e^{-\eta X_T^\infty}\right] = \mathbb{E}\left[e^{-\eta R_0 e^{rT} - \eta \int_0^T e^{r(T-s)} c(s,Y_s)\, ds + \eta \int_0^T \int_0^{+\infty} e^{r(T-s)} z\, m(ds,dz)}\right] \leq \mathbb{E}\left[e^{\eta K C_T}\right] < +\infty.$$

In the next proposition we give a sufficient condition for Equation (17).

Proposition 2. *Assume that there exists an integrable function $\Phi : [0,T] \to (0,+\infty)$ such that*

$$\int_0^{+\infty} (e^{\eta K z} - 1)\lambda(t,y) dF(z,y) \leq \Phi(t) \qquad \forall (t,y) \in [0,T] \times \mathbb{R}, \tag{18}$$

where the constant K is given in (14). *Then Equation* (17) *is fulfilled.*

Proof. Since $\{C_t\}_{t\in[0,T]}$ is a pure-jump process, we have that

$$\begin{aligned} e^{\eta K C_t} &= e^{\eta K C_0} + \sum_{s\leq t} \left(e^{\eta K C_s} - e^{\eta K C_{s-}} \right) \\ &= 1 + \sum_{s\leq t} e^{\eta K C_{s-}} \left(e^{\eta K \Delta C_s} - 1 \right) \\ &= 1 + \int_0^t e^{\eta K C_{s-}} \int_0^{+\infty} \left(e^{\eta K z} - 1 \right) m(ds,dz). \end{aligned}$$

Taking the expectation, by Equation (8) we get that

$$\begin{aligned} \mathbb{E}[e^{\eta K C_t}] &= 1 + \mathbb{E}\left[\int_0^t e^{\eta K C_{s-}} \int_0^{+\infty} \left(e^{\eta K z} - 1 \right) \lambda(s,Y_s) dF(z,Y_s)\, ds \right] \\ &\leq 1 + \int_0^t \mathbb{E}\left[e^{\eta K C_s}\right] \Phi(s)\, ds. \end{aligned}$$

Applying Gronwall's lemma we obtain that

$$\mathbb{E}[e^{\eta K C_t}] \leq e^{\int_0^t \Phi(s) ds} \qquad \forall t \in [0,T].$$

□

As usual in stochastic control problems, we focus on the corresponding dynamic problem:

$$\operatorname*{ess\,inf}_{\alpha\in\mathcal{A}_t} \mathbb{E}\left[e^{-\eta X_{t,x}^\alpha(T)} \mid \mathcal{F}_t\right], \qquad t \in [0,T], \tag{19}$$

where $X_{t,x}^\alpha(T)$ denotes the insurer's wealth process starting from $(t,x) \in [0,T] \times \mathbb{R}$ evaluated at time T.

3. HJB Formulation

In order to solve the optimization problem (19), we introduce the *value function* $v : [0,T] \times \mathbb{R}^2 \to [0,+\infty)$ associated with it, that is

$$v(t,x,y) \doteq \inf_{\alpha\in\mathcal{A}_t} \mathbb{E}\left[e^{-\eta X_{t,x}^\alpha(T)} \mid Y_t = y\right]. \tag{20}$$

This function, if sufficiently regular, is expected to solve the Hamilton-Jacobi-Bellman (HJB) equation:

$$\begin{cases} \inf_{\alpha \in [0,+\infty)} \mathcal{L}^{\alpha} v(t,x,y) = 0 & \forall (t,x,y) \in [0,T] \times \mathbb{R}^2 \\ v(T,x,y) = e^{-\eta x} & \forall (x,y) \in \mathbb{R}^2, \end{cases} \tag{21}$$

where $\mathcal{L}^{\alpha}$ denotes the Markov generator of the couple (X_t^{α}, Y_t) associated with a constant control α. In what follows, we denote by $\mathcal{C}_b^{1,2}$ the class of all bounded functions $f(t, x_1, \ldots, x_n)$, with $n \geq 1$, with bounded first order derivatives $\frac{\partial f}{\partial t}, \frac{\partial f}{\partial x_1}, \ldots, \frac{\partial f}{\partial x_n}$ and bounded second order derivatives with respect to the spatial variables $\frac{\partial^2 f}{\partial x_1^2}, \ldots, \frac{\partial f}{\partial x_n^2}$.

Lemma 1. *Let $f : [0,T] \times \mathbb{R}^2 \to \mathbb{R}$ be a function in $\mathcal{C}_b^{1,2}$. The Markov generator of the stochastic process (X_t^{α}, Y_t) for all constant strategies $\alpha \in [0,+\infty)$ is given by the following expression:*

$$\begin{aligned} \mathcal{L}^{\alpha} f(t,x,y) = {} & \frac{\partial f}{\partial t}(t,x,y) + \frac{\partial f}{\partial x}(t,x,y)\left[rx + c(t,y) - q(t,y,\alpha)\right] + b(t,y)\frac{\partial f}{\partial y}(t,x,y) \\ & + \frac{1}{2}\gamma(t,y)^2 \frac{\partial^2 f}{\partial y^2}(t,x,y) + \int_0^{+\infty} \Big[f(t, x - z \wedge \alpha, y) - f(t,x,y) \Big] \lambda(t,y)\, dF(z,y). \end{aligned} \tag{22}$$

Proof. For any $f \in \mathcal{C}_b^{1,2}$, applying Itô's formula to the stochastic process $f(t, X_t^{\alpha}, Y_t)$, we get the following expression:

$$f(t, X_t^{\alpha}, Y_t) = f(0, X_0^{\alpha}, Y_0) + \int_0^t \mathcal{L}^{\alpha} f(s, X_s^{\alpha}, Y_s)\, ds + M_t,$$

where $\mathcal{L}^{\alpha}$ is defined in (22) and

$$\begin{aligned} M_t = {} & \int_0^t \gamma(s, Y_s) \frac{\partial f}{\partial y}(s, X_s^{\alpha}, Y_s)\, dW_s^{(Y)} \\ & + \int_0^t \int_0^{+\infty} \Big(f(s, X_s^{\alpha} - z \wedge \alpha, Y_s) - f(s, X_s^{\alpha}, Y_s) \Big) \big(m(ds,dz) - \nu(ds,dz) \big). \end{aligned}$$

In order to complete the proof, we have to show that $\{M_t\}_{t\in[0,T]}$ is an $\{\mathcal{F}_t\}_{t\in[0,T]}$-martingale. For the first term, we observe that

$$\mathbb{E}\left[\int_0^t \gamma(s, Y_s)^2 \left(\frac{\partial f}{\partial y}(s, X_s^{\alpha}, Y_s) \right)^2 ds \right] < +\infty,$$

because the partial derivative is bounded and using the assumption (2). For the second term, it is sufficient to use the boundedness of f and the condition (6). □

Remark 4. *Since the couple (X_t^{α}, Y_t) is a Markov process, any Markovian control is of the form $\alpha_t = \alpha(t, X_t^{\alpha}, Y_t)$, where $\alpha(t,x,y)$ denotes a suitable function. The generator $\mathcal{L}^{\alpha} f(t,x,y)$ associated with a general Markovian strategy can be easily obtained by replacing α with $\alpha(t,x,y)$ in (22).*

In order to simplify our optimization problem, we present a preliminary result.

Remark 5. *Let $g : \mathbb{R} \mapsto [0,+\infty)$ be an integrable function such that $g(0) = 0$. For any $\alpha \in [0,+\infty)$, the following equation holds true:*

$$\int_0^{+\infty} g(z \wedge \alpha)\, dF(z,y) = \int_0^{\alpha} g'(z) \bar{F}(z,y)\, dz \qquad \forall y \in \mathbb{R},$$

where $\bar{F}(z,y) \doteq 1 - F(z,y)$. In fact, by integration by parts we get that

$$
\begin{aligned}
\int_0^{+\infty} g(z \wedge \alpha)\, dF(z,y) &= \int_0^{\alpha} g(z)\, dF(z,y) + \int_\alpha^{+\infty} g(\alpha)\, dF(z,y) \\
&= g(\alpha)F(\alpha,y) - g(0)F(0,y) - \int_0^{\alpha} g'(z)F(z,y)\, dz + g(\alpha)[1 - F(\alpha,y)] \\
&= -\int_0^{\alpha} g'(z)F(z,y)\, dz + \int_0^{\alpha} g'(z)\, dz \\
&= \int_0^{\alpha} g'(z)(1 - F(z,y))\, dz.
\end{aligned} \tag{23}
$$

Now let us consider the ansatz $v(t,x,y) = e^{-\eta x e^{r(T-t)}}\varphi(t,y)$, which is motivated by the following proposition.

Proposition 3. *Let us suppose that there exists a function $\varphi : [0,T] \times \mathbb{R} \to (0,+\infty)$ solution to the following Cauchy problem:*

$$
\begin{aligned}
\frac{\partial \varphi}{\partial t}(t,y) &+ b(t,y)\frac{\partial \varphi}{\partial y}(t,y) + \frac{1}{2}\gamma(t,y)^2 \frac{\partial^2 \varphi}{\partial y^2}(t,y) \\
&+ \eta e^{r(T-t)}\varphi(t,y)\big[-c(t,y) + \inf_{\alpha \in [0,+\infty)} \Psi^\alpha(t,y)\big] = 0,
\end{aligned} \tag{24}
$$

with final condition $\varphi(T,y) = 1$, $\forall y \in \mathbb{R}$, where

$$
\Psi^\alpha(t,y) \doteq q(t,y,\alpha) + \lambda(t,y) \int_0^{\alpha} e^{\eta z e^{r(T-t)}} \bar{F}(z,y)\, dz, \qquad \alpha \in [0,+\infty). \tag{25}
$$

Then the function

$$
v(t,x,y) = e^{-\eta x e^{r(T-t)}}\varphi(t,y) \tag{26}
$$

solves the HJB problem given in (21).

Proof. From the expression (26) we can easily verify that

$$
\begin{aligned}
e^{\eta x e^{r(T-t)}} \mathcal{L}^\alpha v(t,x,y) &= \frac{\partial \varphi}{\partial t}(t,y) - \eta e^{r(T-t)}\varphi(t,y)\big[c(t,y) - q(t,y,\alpha)\big] \\
&+ b(t,y)\frac{\partial \varphi}{\partial y}(t,y) + \frac{1}{2}\gamma(t,y)^2 \frac{\partial^2 \varphi}{\partial y^2}(t,y) \\
&+ \int_0^{+\infty} \Big[e^{\eta (z\wedge\alpha) e^{r(T-t)}}\varphi(t,y) - \varphi(t,y)\Big]\lambda(t,y)\, dF(z,y).
\end{aligned}
$$

By Remark 5, taking $g(z) = e^{\eta z e^{r(T-t)}} - 1$, we can rewrite the last integral in this more convenient way:

$$
\varphi(t,y)\lambda(t,y) \int_0^{+\infty} \Big[e^{\eta (z\wedge\alpha) e^{r(T-t)}} - 1\Big]\, dF(z,y) = \varphi(t,y)\lambda(t,y) \int_0^{\alpha} \eta e^{r(T-t)} e^{\eta z e^{r(T-t)}}\, \bar{F}(z,y)\, dz.
$$

Now we define $\Psi^\alpha(t,y)$ by means of the Equation (25), obtaining the following equivalent expression:

$$
\begin{aligned}
e^{\eta x e^{r(T-t)}} \mathcal{L}^\alpha v(t,x,y) &= \frac{\partial \varphi}{\partial t}(t,y) - \eta e^{r(T-t)}\varphi(t,y)c(t,y) \\
&+ b(t,y)\frac{\partial \varphi}{\partial y}(t,y) + \frac{1}{2}\gamma(t,y)^2 \frac{\partial^2 \varphi}{\partial y^2}(t,y) + \eta e^{r(T-t)}\varphi(t,y)\Psi^\alpha(t,y).
\end{aligned}
$$

Taking the infimum over $\alpha \in [0,+\infty)$, by (24) we find out the PDE in (21). The terminal condition in (21) immediately follows by definition. □

The previous result suggests to focus on the minimization of the function (25), that is the aim of the next section.

4. Optimal Reinsurance Strategy

In this section, we study the following minimization problem:

$$\inf_{\alpha\in[0,+\infty)} \Psi^{\alpha}(t,y), \tag{27}$$

where $\Psi^{\alpha}(t,y) : [0,T]\times\mathbb{R}\to(0,+\infty)$ is defined in (25).

In particular, we provide a complete characterization of the optimal reinsurance strategy. In the sequel we assume $0 \leq F(z,y) < 1\ \forall(z,y)\in[0,+\infty)\times\mathbb{R}$.

Proposition 4. *Let us suppose that $\Psi^{\alpha}(t,y)$ is strictly convex in $\alpha \in [0,+\infty)$ and let us define the set $A_0 \subseteq [0,T]\times\mathbb{R}$ as follows:*

$$A_0 \doteq \left\{ (t,y)\in[0,T]\times\mathbb{R} \mid -\frac{\partial q(t,y,0)}{\partial\alpha} \leq \lambda(t,y) \right\}. \tag{28}$$

If the equation

$$-\frac{\partial q(t,y,\alpha)}{\partial\alpha} = \lambda(t,y)e^{\eta\alpha e^{r(T-t)}}\bar{F}(\alpha,y) \tag{29}$$

admits at least one solution in $(0,+\infty)$ for any $(t,y)\in[0,T]\times\mathbb{R}\setminus A_0$, denoted by $\hat{\alpha}(t,y)$, then the minimization problem (27) admits a unique solution $\alpha^*(t,y)\in[0,+\infty)$ given by

$$\alpha^*(t,y) = \begin{cases} 0 & (t,y)\in A_0 \\ \hat{\alpha}(t,y) & (t,y)\in[0,T]\times\mathbb{R}\setminus A_0. \end{cases} \tag{30}$$

Proof. The function $\Psi^{\alpha}(t,y)$ is continuous in $\alpha\in[0,+\infty)$ by definition (see Assumption 1) and for any $(t,y)\in[0,T]\times\mathbb{R}$ its derivative is given by the following expression:

$$\frac{\partial\Psi^{\alpha}(t,y)}{\partial\alpha} = \frac{\partial q(t,y,\alpha)}{\partial\alpha} + \lambda(t,y)e^{\eta\alpha e^{r(T-t)}}\bar{F}(\alpha,y). \tag{31}$$

Since $\Psi^{\alpha}(t,y)$ is convex in $\alpha\in[0,+\infty)$ by hypothesis, if $(t,y)\in A_0$ then $\frac{\partial\Psi^{0}(t,y)}{\partial\alpha}\geq 0$, and $\alpha^*(t,y)=0$, because the derivative $\frac{\partial\Psi^{\alpha}(t,y)}{\partial\alpha}$ is increasing in α and there is no stationary point in $(0,+\infty)$. Else, if $(t,y)\in[0,T]\times\mathbb{R}\setminus A_0$ then $\frac{\partial\Psi^{0}(t,y)}{\partial\alpha}<0$, and $\alpha^*(t,y)$ coincides with the unique stationary point of $\Psi^{\alpha}(t,y)$, which is $\hat{\alpha}(t,y)\in(0,+\infty)$. Let us notice that it exists by hypothesis and it is unique because $\Psi^{\alpha}(t,y)$ is strictly convex. □

By the previous proposition, we observe that $\lambda(t,y)$ is an important threshold for the insurer: as long as the marginal cost of the full reinsurance falls in the interval $(0,\lambda(t,y)]$, the optimal choice is full reinsurance.

Unfortunately, it is not always easy to check whether $\Psi^{\alpha}(t,y)$ is strictly convex in $\alpha\in[0,+\infty)$ or not. In the next result such an hypothesis is relaxed, while the uniqueness of the solution to (29) is required.

Proposition 5. *Suppose that Equation (29) admits a unique solution $\hat{\alpha}(t,y) \in (0,+\infty)$ for any $(t,y) \in [0,T] \times \mathbb{R} \setminus A_0$. Moreover, let us assume that*

$$\frac{\partial^2 q(t,y,\hat{\alpha}(t,y))}{\partial \alpha^2} > -\lambda(t,y) e^{\eta \hat{\alpha}(t,y) e^{r(T-t)}} \frac{\partial \bar{F}(\hat{\alpha}(t,y),y)}{\partial z} \quad \forall (t,y) \in [0,T] \times \mathbb{R} \setminus A_0. \tag{32}$$

Then the minimization problem (27) admits a unique solution $\alpha^*(t,y) \in [0,+\infty)$ given by (30).

Proof. Recalling the proof of Proposition 4, if $(t,y) \in A_0$ then $\frac{\partial \Psi^0(t,y)}{\partial \alpha} \geq 0$ and $\alpha^*(t,y) = 0$. For any $(t,y) \in [0,T] \times \mathbb{R} \setminus A_0$, by hypothesis there exists a unique stationary point $\hat{\alpha}(t,y) \in (0,+\infty)$. By simple calculations, using (32) we notice that

$$\frac{\partial^2 \Psi^{\hat{\alpha}}(t,y)}{\partial \alpha^2} > 0,$$

hence $\hat{\alpha}(t,y)$ is the unique minimizer and this completes the proof. □

The next result deals with the existence of a solution to (29). In particular, it is sufficient to require that the claim size distribution is heavy-tailed, which is a relevant case in non-life insurance (see Rolski et al. (1999), chp. 2), plus a technical condition for the reinsurance premium.

Proposition 6. *Let us assume that the reinsurance premium $q(t,y,\alpha)$ is such that*[6]

$$\lim_{\alpha \to +\infty} \frac{\partial q(t,y,\alpha)}{\partial \alpha} = l \in \mathbb{R}$$

and the claim size distribution is heavy-tailed in this sense:

$$\int_0^{+\infty} e^{kz} \, dF(z,y) = +\infty \qquad \forall k > 0, y \in \mathbb{R}.$$

Then, for any $(t,y) \in [0,T] \times \mathbb{R} \setminus A_0$, the Equation (29) admits at least one solution in $(0,+\infty)$.

Proof. The following property of heavy-tailed distributions is a well known implication of our assumption:

$$\lim_{z \to +\infty} e^{kz} \bar{F}(z,y) = +\infty \qquad \forall k > 0, y \in \mathbb{R}.$$

Hence, by Equation (31), for any $(t,y) \in [0,T] \times \mathbb{R} \setminus A_0$

$$\lim_{\alpha \to +\infty} \frac{\partial \Psi^{\alpha}(t,y)}{\partial \alpha} = \lim_{\alpha \to +\infty} \left[\frac{\partial q(t,y,\alpha)}{\partial \alpha} + \lambda(t,y) e^{\eta \alpha e^{r(T-t)}} \bar{F}(\alpha,y) \right] = +\infty.$$

On the other hand, we know that

$$\frac{\partial \Psi^0(t,y)}{\partial \alpha} < 0 \qquad \forall (t,y) \in [0,T] \times \mathbb{R} \setminus A_0.$$

As a consequence, $\frac{\partial \Psi^{\alpha}(t,y)}{\partial \alpha}$ being continuous in $\alpha \in [0,+\infty)$, there exists $\hat{\alpha}(t,y) \in (0,+\infty)$ such that $\frac{\partial \Psi^{\hat{\alpha}}(t,y)}{\partial \alpha} = 0$. □

Now we turn the attention to the other crucial hypothesis of Proposition 4, which is the convexity of $\Psi^{\alpha}(t,y)$. The reader can easily observe that the reinsurance premium convexity plays a central role.

[6] E.g., if q is convex in α.

Proposition 7. *Suppose that the reinsurance premium $q(t,y,\alpha)$ is convex in $\alpha \in [0,+\infty)$ and $F(z,y) = (1-e^{-\zeta(y)z})\mathbb{1}_{\{z>0\}}$ for some function $\zeta(y)$ such that $0 < \zeta(y) < \eta \min\{e^{rT},1\}$ $\forall y \in \mathbb{R}$. Then the function $\Psi^{\alpha}(t,y)$ defined in (25) is strictly convex in $\alpha \in [0,+\infty)$.*

Proof. Recalling the expression (25), it is sufficient to prove the convexity of the following term:

$$\int_0^{\alpha} e^{\eta z e^{r(T-t)}} \bar{F}(z,y)\, dz.$$

For this purpose, let us evaluate its second order derivative:

$$e^{\eta \alpha e^{r(T-t)}} \left(\eta e^{r(T-t)} \bar{F}(\alpha,y) + \frac{\partial \bar{F}(\alpha,y)}{\partial z} \right).$$

Now the term in brackets is

$$\eta e^{r(T-t)} e^{-\zeta(y)\alpha} - \zeta(y) e^{-\zeta(y)\alpha} > 0 \qquad \forall t \in [0,T].$$

The proof is complete. □

By Proposition 1, the hypothesis on the claim sizes distribution above may be read as assuming that the claims are exponentially distributed conditionally to Y.

4.1. Expected Value Principle

Now we investigate the special case of the expected value principle introduced in Example 1.

Proposition 8. *Under the EVP (see Equation (10)), the optimal reinsurance strategy $\alpha^*(t) \in [0,+\infty)$ is given by*

$$\alpha^*(t) = e^{-r(T-t)} \frac{\log(1+\theta)}{\eta}, \qquad t \in [0,T]. \tag{33}$$

Proof. Using Remark 5, we can rewrite the Equation (10) as follows:

$$q(t,y,\alpha) = (1+\theta)\lambda(t,y) \left[\int_0^{+\infty} z\, dF(z,y) - \int_0^{\alpha} \bar{F}(z,y)\, dz \right].$$

As a consequence, we have that

$$\frac{\partial q(t,y,\alpha)}{\partial \alpha} = -(1+\theta)\lambda(t,y)\bar{F}(\alpha,y) \qquad \forall \alpha \in [0,+\infty).$$

For $\alpha = 0$, we have that

$$\frac{\partial \Psi^0(t,y)}{\partial \alpha} = \frac{\partial q(t,y,0)}{\partial \alpha} + \lambda(t,y) < 0 \qquad \forall (t,y) \in [0,T] \times \mathbb{R},$$

hence $A_0 = \emptyset$ and by Proposition 4 the minimizer belongs to $(0,+\infty)$. Now we look for the stationary points, i.e., the solutions to the Equation (29), that in this case reads as follows:

$$(1+\theta)\lambda(t,y)\bar{F}(\alpha,y) = \lambda(t,y) e^{\eta \alpha e^{r(T-t)}} \bar{F}(\alpha,y). \tag{34}$$

Solving this equation, we obtain the unique solution given by (33). In order to prove that it coincides with the unique minimizer to (27), it is sufficient to show that

$$\frac{\partial^2 \Psi^{\alpha^*(t)}(t,y)}{\partial \alpha^2} > 0.$$

For this purpose, observe that

$$\begin{aligned}\frac{\partial^2 \Psi^{\alpha^*(t)}(t,y)}{\partial \alpha^2} &= \frac{\partial^2 q(t,y,\alpha^*(t))}{\partial \alpha^2} + \lambda(t,y) e^{\eta \alpha^*(t) e^{r(T-t)}} \left(\eta e^{r(T-t)} \bar{F}(\alpha^*(t),y) + \frac{\partial \bar{F}(\alpha^*(t),y)}{\partial z} \right) \\ &> -(1+\theta)\lambda(t,y) \frac{\partial \bar{F}(\alpha^*(t),y)}{\partial z} + \lambda(t,y) e^{\eta \alpha^*(t) e^{r(T-t)}} \frac{\partial \bar{F}(\alpha^*(t),y)}{\partial z} \\ &= 0.\end{aligned}$$

The proof is complete. □

Remark 6. *Formula (33) was found by Zhao et al. (2013) (see eq. 3.31, p. 508). We point out that it is a completely deterministic strategy. This fact is crucially related to the use of the EVP rather than the underlying model; in fact, in Zhao et al. (2013) the authors considered the Cramér-Lundberg model under the EVP*[7].

From the economic point of view, by Equation (33) it is easy to show that the optimal retention level is decreasing with respect to the interest rate and the risk-aversion; on the contrary, it is increasing with respect to the reinsurer's safety loading. In addition, the sensitivity with respect to the time-to-maturity depends on the sign of r.

Another relevant aspect of (33) is that it is independent of the claim size distribution. To the authors this result seems quite unrealistic. In fact, any subscriber of an excess-of-loss contract is strongly worried about possibly extreme events, hence the claims distribution is expected to play an important role.

4.2. Variance Premium Principle

This subsection is devoted to derive an optimal strategy under the variance premium principle (see Example 2).

Proposition 9. *Let us suppose that $\Psi^{\alpha}(t,y)$ is strictly convex in $\alpha \in [0,+\infty)$ and*

$$\lim_{z \to +\infty} e^{\eta \min\{e^{rT},1\} z} \bar{F}(z,y) = l, \tag{35}$$

for some $l > 0$ (eventually $l = +\infty$).

Under the VP (see Equation (11)) the optimal reinsurance strategy $\alpha^*(t,y)$ is the unique solution to the following equation:

$$\left(e^{\eta \alpha e^{r(T-t)}} + 2\theta\alpha - 1\right)\bar{F}(\alpha,y) = 2\theta \int_{\alpha}^{+\infty} z\, dF(z,y). \tag{36}$$

Proof. The proof is based on Proposition (4). By Equation (11) we get its derivative:

$$\frac{\partial q(t,y,\alpha)}{\partial \alpha} = \lambda(t,y)\bar{F}(\alpha,y)(2\theta\alpha - 1) - 2\theta\lambda(t,y) \int_{\alpha}^{+\infty} z\, dF(z,y).$$

It is clear that the set A_0 defined in (28) is empty, because for any $(t,y) \in [0,T] \times \mathbb{R}$

$$-\frac{\partial q(t,y,0)}{\partial \alpha} = \lambda(t,y)\bar{F}(0,y) + 2\theta\lambda(t,y) \int_{0}^{+\infty} z\, dF(z,y) > \lambda(t,y).$$

[7] It is not surprising, in fact in Brachetta and Ceci (2019) and references therein also the optimal proportional reinsurance under EVP turns out to be deterministic.

Hence the minimizer should coincide with the unique stationary point of $\Psi^\alpha(t,y)$, i.e., the solution to (36). In order to prove it, we need to ensure the existence of a solution to (36). For this purpose, we notice that on the one hand

$$\frac{\partial \Psi^0(t,y)}{\partial \alpha} = -2\theta\lambda(t,y)\int_0^{+\infty} z\,dF(z,y) < 0.$$

On the other hand, for $\alpha \to +\infty$, by (35) we get

$$\lim_{\alpha\to+\infty} \frac{\partial \Psi^\alpha(t,y)}{\partial \alpha} = \lambda(t,y)\lim_{\alpha\to+\infty}\left[(e^{\eta\alpha e^{r(T-t)}} + 2\theta\alpha - 1)\bar{F}(\alpha,y) - 2\theta\int_\alpha^{+\infty} z\,dF(z,y)\right] > 0.$$

As a consequence, by the continuity of $\Psi^\alpha(t,y)$ there exists a point $\alpha^* \in (0,+\infty)$ such that $\frac{\partial \Psi^{\alpha^*}(t,y)}{\partial \alpha} = 0$. Such a solution is unique because $\Psi^\alpha(t,y)$ is strictly convex by hypothesis. □

Conversely to Proposition 8, the optimal retention level given in Proposition 9 is still dependent on the stochastic factor Y. Such a dependence is spread through the claim size distribution.

Remark 7. *We observe that any heavy-tailed distribution (see the proof of Proposition 6) satisfies the condition (35) with $l = +\infty$.*

Now we specialize the variance premium principle to conditionally exponentially distributed claims.

Proposition 10. *Under the VP, suppose that $F(z,y) = (1 - e^{-\zeta(y)z})\mathbb{1}_{\{z>0\}}$ for some function $\zeta(y)$ such that $\zeta(y) > 0\ \forall y \in \mathbb{R}$. The optimal reinsurance strategy is given by*

$$\alpha^*(t,y) = e^{-r(T-t)}\frac{\log\left(1 + \frac{2\theta}{\zeta(y)}\right)}{\eta}, \qquad (t,y) \in [0,T]\times\mathbb{R}. \tag{37}$$

Proof. By the proof of Proposition 9, we know that under VP $A_0 = \emptyset$. Now, under our hypotheses, by Equation (31) we readily get

$$\begin{aligned}
\frac{\partial \Psi^\alpha(t,y)}{\partial \alpha} &= \lambda(t,y)\left[(e^{\eta\alpha e^{r(T-t)}} + 2\theta\alpha - 1)\bar{F}(\alpha,y) - 2\theta\int_\alpha^{+\infty} z\,dF(z,y)\right] \\
&= \lambda(t,y)\left[(e^{\eta\alpha e^{r(T-t)}} + 2\theta\alpha - 1)e^{-\zeta(y)\alpha} - 2\theta e^{-\zeta(y)\alpha}\left(\alpha + \frac{1}{\zeta(y)}\right)\right] \\
&= \lambda(t,y)e^{-\zeta(y)\alpha}\left[e^{\eta\alpha e^{r(T-t)}} - 1 - \frac{2\theta}{\zeta(y)}\right].
\end{aligned}$$

The equation $\frac{\partial \Psi^\alpha(t,y)}{\partial \alpha} = 0$ admits a unique solution, given by Equation (37). At this point $\alpha^*(t,y)$, the function $\Psi^\alpha(t,y)$ is strictly convex, because

$$\begin{aligned}
\frac{\partial \Psi^{\alpha^*}(t,y)}{\partial \alpha} &= -\zeta(y)\frac{\partial \Psi^{\alpha^*}(t,y)}{\partial \alpha} + \lambda(t,y)e^{-\zeta(y)\alpha^*}\eta e^{r(T-t)}e^{\eta\alpha^* e^{r(T-t)}} \\
&= \lambda(t,y)e^{-\zeta(y)\alpha^*}\eta e^{r(T-t)}e^{\eta\alpha^* e^{r(T-t)}} > 0.
\end{aligned}$$

It follows that $\alpha^*(t,y)$ is the unique minimizer by Proposition 30. □

Contrary to Equation (33), the explicit formula (37) keeps the dependence on the stochastic factor Y. In addition, the following result holds true.

Remark 8. *Suppose that $F(z,y) = (1 - e^{-\zeta(y)z})\mathbb{1}_{\{z>0\}}$ for some function $\zeta(y)$ such that $\zeta(y) > 0\ \forall y \in \mathbb{R}$. We consider two different reinsurance safety loadings $\theta_{EVP}, \theta_{VP} > 0$, referring to the EVP and VP, respectively. Moreover, let us denote by $\alpha^*_{EVP}(t)$ and $\alpha^*_{VP}(t,y)$ the optimal retention level under the EVP and VP, given in Equations (33) and (37), respectively. It is easy to show that $\forall t \in [0,T]$*

$$\alpha^*_{VP}(t,y) \begin{cases} > \alpha^*_{EVP}(t) & \forall y : \zeta(y) < \frac{2\theta_{VP}}{\theta_{EVP}} \\ \leq \alpha^*_{EVP}(t) & \text{otherwise.} \end{cases}$$

From the practical point of view, as long as the stochastic factor fluctuations result in a rate parameter $\zeta(y)$ higher than the threshold $\frac{2\theta_{VP}}{\theta_{EVP}}$, the optimal retention level evaluated through the expected value principle turns out to be larger than the variance principle.

5. Verification Theorem

Theorem 1 (Verification Theorem). *Let us suppose that Equation (18) holds good and $\varphi : [0,T] \times \mathbb{R} \to (0,+\infty)$ is a bounded classical solution $\varphi \in \mathcal{C}^{1,2}((0,T) \times \mathbb{R}) \cap \mathcal{C}([0,T] \times \mathbb{R})$ to the Cauchy problem (24), such that*

$$\left| \frac{\partial \varphi}{\partial y}(t,y) \right| \leq C(1 + |y|^{\beta}) \qquad \forall (t,y) \in [0,T] \times \mathbb{R}, \tag{38}$$

for some constants $\beta, C > 0$. Then the function $v(t,x,y) = e^{-\eta x e^{r(T-t)}}\varphi(t,y)$ is the value function in Equation (20). As a byproduct, the strategy $\alpha^*_t \doteq \alpha^*(t, Y_t)$ described in Proposition 4 is an optimal control.

Proof. By Proposition 3, the function $v(t,x,y)$ defined in Equation (26) solves the HJB problem (21). Hence for any $(t,x,y) \in [0,T] \times \mathbb{R}^2$

$$\mathcal{L}^{\alpha} v(s, X^{\alpha}_{t,x}(s), Y_{t,y}(s)) \geq 0 \qquad \forall s \in [t,T], \alpha \in \mathcal{A}_t,$$

where $\{X^{\alpha}_{t,x}(s)\}_{s\in[t,T]}$ and $\{Y_{t,y}(s)\}_{s\in[t,T]}$ denote the solutions to (12) and (1) at time $s \in [t,T]$, starting from $(t,x) \in [0,T] \times \mathbb{R}$ and $(t,y) \in [0,T] \times \mathbb{R}$, respectively.
From Itô's formula we get

$$v(T, X^{\alpha}_{t,x}(T), Y_{t,y}(T)) = v(t,x,y) + \int_t^T \mathcal{L}^{\alpha} v(s, X^{\alpha}_{t,x}(s), Y_s)\, ds + M_T - M_t, \tag{39}$$

with $\{M_r\}_{r\in[t,T]}$ defined by

$$\begin{aligned} M_r = &\int_t^r \gamma(s, Y_s) \frac{\partial v}{\partial y}(s, X^{\alpha}_{t,x}(s), Y_s)\, dW^{(Y)}_s \\ &+ \int_t^r \int_0^{+\infty} \Big(v(s, X^{\alpha}_{t,x}(s) - z \wedge \alpha, Y_s) - v(s, X^{\alpha}_{t,x}(s), Y_s) \Big) \big(m(ds,dz) - \nu(ds,dz)\big). \end{aligned} \tag{40}$$

In order to show that $\{M_r\}_{r\in[t,T]}$ is an $\{\mathcal{F}_t\}_{t\in[0,T]}$-local-martingale, we use a localization argument, taking

$$\tau_n \doteq \inf\{s \in [t,T] \mid X^{\alpha}_{t,x}(s) < -n \vee |Y_s| > n\}, \qquad n \in \mathbb{N}.$$

The reader can easily check that $\{\tau_n\}_{n\in\mathbb{N}}$ is a non decreasing sequence of stopping time such that $\lim_{n\to+\infty} \tau_n = +\infty$ (see Equations (15) and (3)). For the diffusion term of M_r, using the assumptions (38) and (2), we notice that

$$
\begin{aligned}
&\mathbb{E}\left[\int_t^{T\wedge\tau_n} \gamma(s,Y_s)^2 \left(\frac{\partial v}{\partial y}(s,X^{\alpha}_{t,x}(s),Y_s)\right)^2 ds\right] \\
&= \mathbb{E}\left[\int_t^{T\wedge\tau_n} \gamma(s,Y_s)^2 e^{-2\eta X^{\alpha}_{t,x}(s)e^{r(T-t)}} \left(\frac{\partial \varphi}{\partial y}(s,Y_s)\right)^2 ds\right] \\
&\leq C_n\,\mathbb{E}\left[\int_t^{T\wedge\tau_n} \gamma(s,Y_s)^2\, ds\right] < +\infty \qquad \forall n \in \mathbb{N},
\end{aligned}
$$

where $C_n > 0$ is a constant depending on n. For the jump term, by the condition (18) and Remark 1, we get

$$
\begin{aligned}
&\mathbb{E}\left[\int_t^{T\wedge\tau_n}\int_0^{+\infty} |v(s,X^{\alpha}_{t,x}(s)-z\wedge\alpha,Y_s)-v(s,X^{\alpha}_{t,x}(s),Y_s)|\nu(ds,dz)\right] \\
&\leq \mathbb{E}\left[\int_t^{T\wedge\tau_n}\int_0^{+\infty} \left|e^{-\eta K X^{\alpha}_{t,x}(s)}(e^{\eta K(z\wedge\alpha)}-1)\varphi(s,Y_s)\right|\nu(ds,dz)\right] \\
&\leq \tilde{C}_n\,\mathbb{E}\left[\int_t^{T\wedge\tau_n}\int_0^{+\infty} (e^{\eta K z}-1)\lambda(s,Y_s)dF(z,Y_s)\,ds\right] < +\infty,
\end{aligned}
$$

with $\tilde{C}_n$ denoting a positive constant dependent on n. Thus $\{M_r\}_{r\in[t,T]}$ turns out to be an $\{\mathcal{F}_t\}_{t\in[0,T]}$-local-martingale and $\{\tau_n\}_{n\in\mathbb{N}}$ is a localizing sequence for it. Now, taking the conditional expectation of (39) with $T\wedge\tau_n$ in place of T, we obtain that

$$
\mathbb{E}[v(T\wedge\tau_n, X^{\alpha}_{t,x}(T\wedge\tau_n), Y_{t,y}(T\wedge\tau_n)) \mid \mathcal{F}_t] \geq v(t,x,y) \quad \forall (t,x,y)\in[0,\wedge\tau_n]\times\mathbb{R}^2, \alpha\in\mathcal{A}_t, n\in\mathbb{N}.
$$

Let us notice that

$$
\mathbb{E}[v(T\wedge\tau_n, X^{\alpha}_{t,x}(T\wedge\tau_n), Y_{t,y}(T\wedge\tau_n))^2] \leq \tilde{C}e^{-2\eta n e^{r(T-t)}} \leq \tilde{C},
$$

where $\tilde{C} > 0$ is a constant. As a consequence, $\{v(T\wedge\tau_n, X^{\alpha}_{t,x}(T\wedge\tau_n), Y_{t,y}(T\wedge\tau_n))\}_{n\in\mathbb{N}}$ is a sequence of uniformly integrable random variables. By classical results in probability theory, it converges almost surely. Using the monotonicity and the boundedness of $\{\tau_n\}_{n\in\mathbb{N}}$, together with the non explosion of $\{X^{\alpha}_{t,x}(s)\}_{s\in[t,T]}$ and $\{Y_{t,y}(s)\}_{s\in[t,T]}$ (see (15) and (3)), taking the limit for $n\to+\infty$ we conclude that

$$
\begin{aligned}
\mathbb{E}[v(T, X^{\alpha}_{t,x}(T), Y_{t,y}(T)) \mid \mathcal{F}_t] &= \lim_{n\to+\infty}\mathbb{E}[v(T\wedge\tau_n, X^{\alpha}_{t,x}(T\wedge\tau_n), Y_{t,y}(T\wedge\tau_n)) \mid \mathcal{F}_t] \\
&\geq v(t,x,y) \qquad \forall t\in[0,T], \alpha\in\mathcal{A}_t.
\end{aligned}
$$

As a byproduct, since $\alpha^*(t,y)$ given in Proposition 4 realizes the infimum in (27), we have that $\mathcal{L}^{\alpha^*}v(t,x,y) = 0$ and, replicating the calculations above, we obtain the equality

$$
\mathbb{E}\left[e^{-\eta X^{\alpha^*}_{t,x}(T)} \mid Y_t = y\right] = \inf_{\alpha\in\mathcal{A}_t}\mathbb{E}\left[e^{-\eta X^{\alpha}_{t,x}(T)} \mid Y_t = y\right] = v(t,x,y),
$$

i.e., $\alpha^*_t \doteq \alpha^*(t,Y_t)$ is an optimal control. □

By Theorem 1, the value function (20) can be characterized as a transformation of the solution to the partial differential equation (PDE) (24). Nevertheless, an explicit expression is not available, except for very special cases. The following result provides a probabilistic representation by means of the Feynman-Kac theorem.

Proposition 11. *Under the same assumptions of Theorem 1, the value function (20) admits the following representation:*

$$v(t,x,y) = e^{-\eta x e^{r(T-t)}}\, \mathbb{E}\left[e^{\int_t^T \eta e^{r(T-s)} \left(\inf_{\alpha \in [0,+\infty)} \Psi^\alpha(s,Y_s) - c(s,Y_s)\right) ds} \mid Y_t = y \right], \tag{41}$$

where $\Psi^\alpha(t,y)$ *is the function defined in* (25).

Proof. The thesis immediately follows by Theorem 1 and the Feynman-Kac representation of $\varphi(t,y)$. □

Remark 9. *We refer to* Heath and Schweizer (2000) *for existence and uniqueness of a solution to the PDE* (24).

6. Numerical Results

In this section, we show some numerical results, mostly based on Propositions 8 and 10. We assumed the following dynamic of the stochastic factor Y for performing simulations:

$$dY_t = 0.3\, dt + 0.3\, dW_t^{(Y)}, \qquad Y_0 = 1.$$

The $\{\mathcal{F}_t\}_{t\in[0,T]}$-dual predictable projection $\nu(dt,dz)$ (see Equation (5)) is determined by these functions:

$$\lambda(t,y) = \lambda_0 e^{\frac{1}{2}y}, \qquad \lambda_0 = 0.1,$$
$$F(z,y) = (1 - e^{-\zeta(y)z})\mathbb{1}_{\{z>0\}}, \quad \text{with } \zeta(y) = e^y + 1.$$

The parameters are set according to Table 1 below.

Table 1. Simulation parameters.

Parameter	Value
c	1
T	5 Y
η	0.5
θ	0.1
r	5%
N	500
M	5000

The SDEs are approximated through a classical Euler's scheme with steps length $\frac{T}{N}$, while the expectations are evaluated by means of Monte Carlo simulations with parameter M.

In Figure 1 we show the dynamic strategies under EVP and VP, computed by the Equations (33) and (37), respectively.

In Figure 2 we start the sensitivity analysis investigating the effect of the risk aversion parameter on the optimal strategy at time $t = 0$. As expected, there is an inverse relationship. Notice that for high values of η the two strategies tend to the same level.

Figure 3 refers to the sensitivity analysis with respect to the reinsurance safety loading θ. When $\theta = 0$ the strategies coincide (because the premia coincide), then they diverge for increasing values of θ.

In Figure 4 we observe that the distance between the retention levels in the two cases is larger when $r < 0$ and it decreases as long as r increases. Nevertheless, even for positive values of the risk-free interest rate the distance is not negligible (see the pictures above, with $r = 0.05$).

In Figure 5 we study the response of the optimal strategy to variations of the time horizon. The two cases exhibit the same behavior, which is strongly influenced by the sign of the interest rate. In fact, if $r < 0$ the retention level increases with the time horizon, while if $r > 0$ the optimal strategy decreases with T.

Finally, thanks to Proposition 11 we are able to numerically approximate the value function by simulating the trajectories of Y. The graphical result (under VP) is shown in Figure 6 below.

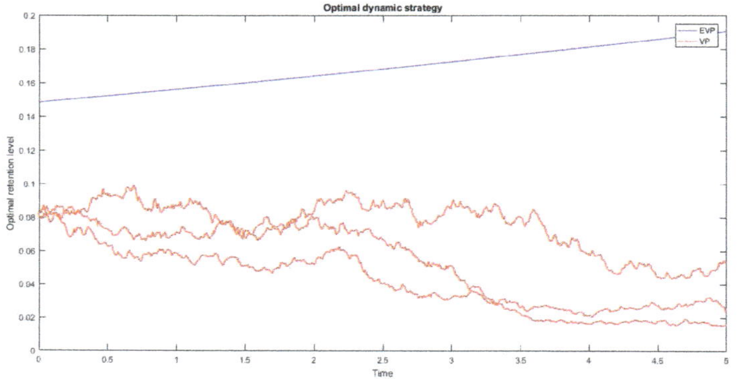

Figure 1. The dynamics of the optimal strategies under EVP (red) and VP (blue).

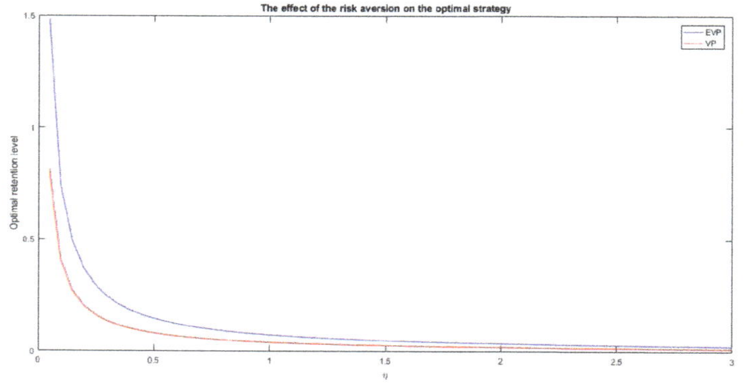

Figure 2. The effect of the risk aversion on the optimal strategy under EVP (red) and VP (blue).

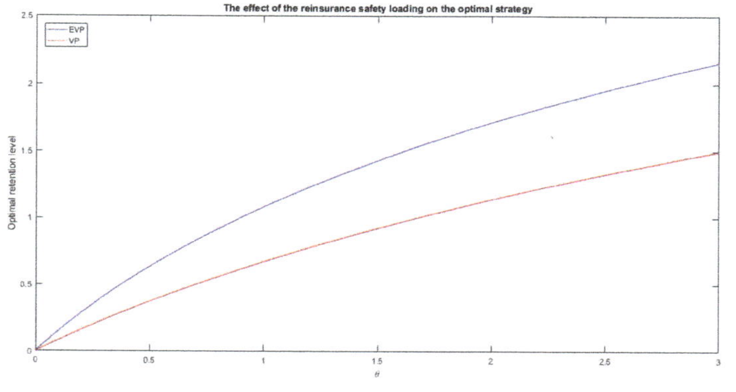

Figure 3. The effect of the reinsurer's safety loading on the optimal strategy under EVP (red) and VP (blue).

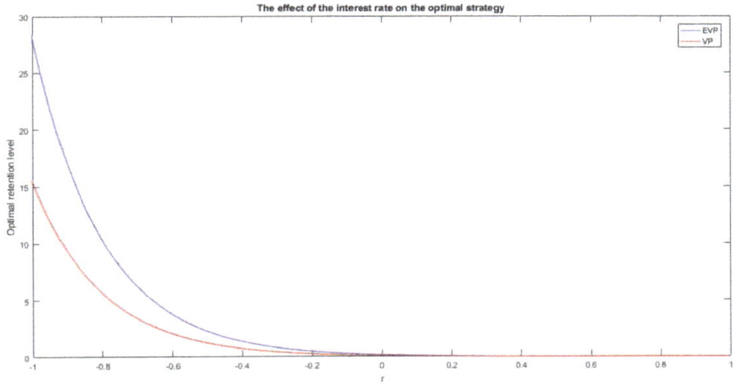

Figure 4. The effect of the risk-free interest rate on the optimal strategy under EVP (red) and VP (blue).

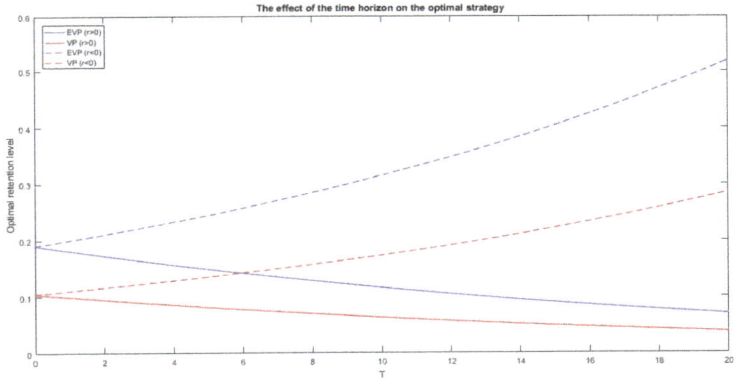

Figure 5. The effect of the time horizon on the optimal strategy under EVP (red) and VP (blue).

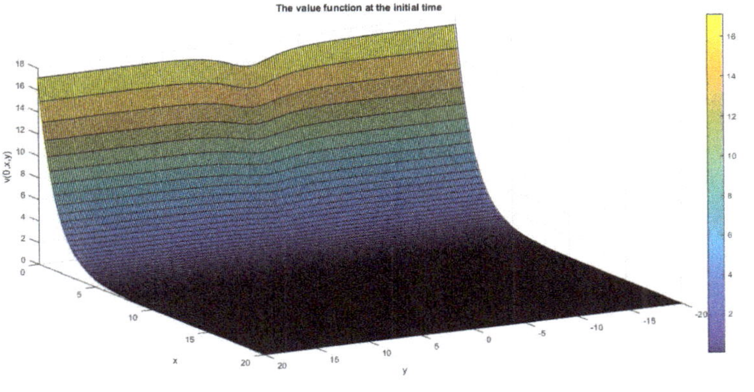

Figure 6. The value function $v(0, x, y)$ at the initial time.

Author Contributions: The authors contributed equally to the work.

Funding: This research received no external funding.

Acknowledgments: The authors are grateful to both the anonymous reviewers for their interesting comments and important suggestions. The authors are members of the Gruppo Nazionale per l'Analisi Matematica, la Probabilità e le loro Applicazioni (GNAMPA) of the Istituto Nazionale di Alta Matematica (INdAM).

Conflicts of Interest: The authors declare no conflict of interest.

Abbreviations

The following abbreviations are used in this manuscript:

CEV	Constant Elasticity of Variance
SDE	Stochastic Differential Equation
ECB	European Central Bank
HJB	Hamilton-Jacobi-Bellman
EVP	Expected value principle
VP	Variance premium principle
PDE	Partial Differential Equation

Appendix A

Proof of Proposition 1. Let us consider $H(s,z) = H_s \mathbb{1}_A(z)$, with $\{H_s\}_{s\in[0,T]}$ any nonnegative $\{\mathcal{F}_s\}_{s\in[0,T]}$-predictable process and $A \in \mathcal{B}([0,+\infty))$. By Equation (8) we get $\forall t \in [0,T]$

$$\mathbb{E}\left[\int_0^t \int_0^{+\infty} H_s \mathbb{1}_A(z) m(ds,dz)\right] = \mathbb{E}\left[\sum_{n\geq 1} H_{T_n} \mathbb{1}_{\{Z_n\in A\}} \mathbb{1}_{\{T_n\leq t\}}\right] = \mathbb{E}\left[\int_0^t H_s \lambda(s,Y_s) \int_A dF(z,Y_s) ds\right].$$

By Equation (9) we can rewrite this quantity as follows:

$$\mathbb{E}\left[\int_0^t H_s \int_A dF(z,Y_s) dN_s\right] = \mathbb{E}\left[\sum_{n\geq 1} H_{T_n} \mathbb{1}_{\{T_n\leq t\}} F(A,Y_{T_n})\right],$$

with the notation $F(A,y) \doteq \int_A dF(z,y)$.

On the other hand, since $H_{T_n} \mathbb{1}_{\{T_n\leq t\}}$ is an $\mathcal{F}_{T_n^-}$-measurable random variable (see Appendix 2, T4 in Brémaud (1981)), we have that

$$\mathbb{E}\left[\sum_{n\geq 1} H_{T_n} \mathbb{1}_{\{Z_n\in A\}} \mathbb{1}_{\{T_n\leq t\}}\right] = \mathbb{E}\left[\sum_{n\geq 1} H_{T_n} \mathbb{1}_{\{T_n\leq t\}} \mathbb{P}[Z_n \in A \mid \mathcal{F}_{T_n^-}]\right].$$

Hence

$$\mathbb{E}\left[\sum_{n\geq 1} H_{T_n} \mathbb{1}_{\{T_n\leq t\}} \mathbb{P}[Z_n \in A \mid \mathcal{F}_{T_n^-}]\right] = \mathbb{E}\left[\sum_{n\geq 1} H_{T_n} \mathbb{1}_{\{T_n\leq t\}} F(A,Y_{T_n})\right]. \tag{A1}$$

By the arbitrariness of t we can choose $t = T \wedge T_1$. In this case, Equation (A1) reads as

$$\mathbb{E}\left[H_{T_1} \mathbb{1}_{\{T_1\leq T\}} \mathbb{P}[Z_1 \in A \mid \mathcal{F}_{T_1^-}]\right] = \mathbb{E}\left[H_{T_1} \mathbb{1}_{\{T_1\leq T\}} F(A,Y_{T_1})\right].$$

By the arbitrariness of $\{H_s\}_{s\in[0,T]}$ we deduce the thesis for $n=1$. Now let us choose $t = T\wedge T_2$. Equation (A1) becomes

$$\mathbb{E}\left[H_{T_1} \mathbb{1}_{\{T_1\leq T\}} \mathbb{P}[Z_1 \in A \mid \mathcal{F}_{T_1^-}] + H_{T_2} \mathbb{1}_{\{T_2\leq T\}} \mathbb{P}[Z_2 \in A \mid \mathcal{F}_{T_2^-}]\right]$$
$$= \mathbb{E}\left[H_{T_1} \mathbb{1}_{\{T_1\leq T\}} F(A,Y_{T_1}) + H_{T_2} \mathbb{1}_{\{T_2\leq T\}} F(A,Y_{T_2})\right].$$

In view of the preceding equation, we obtain the desired equality for $n = 2$. Repeating the same argument for $n = 3, 4, \ldots$ we complete the thesis. $\square$

Appendix B

In this section we motivate formulas (10) and (11). Let us denote by $\{C_t^\alpha\}_{t\in[0,T]}$ the reinsurer's cumulative losses at time t:

$$C_t^\alpha = \int_0^t \int_0^{+\infty} (z - z \wedge \alpha_s)\, m(ds, dz), \qquad t \in [0, T].$$

Recalling (5), by Equation (10) in Example 1 we readily check that for any strategy $\{\alpha_t\}_{t\in[0,T]}$ under the EVP

$$\begin{aligned}
\mathbb{E}\left[\int_0^t q(s, Y_s, \alpha_s)\, ds\right] &= (1+\theta)\mathbb{E}\left[\int_0^t \int_0^{+\infty} (z - z \wedge \alpha_s)\, \lambda(s, Y_s)\, dF(z, Y_s)\, ds\right] \\
&= (1+\theta)\mathbb{E}\left[\int_0^t \int_0^{+\infty} (z - z \wedge \alpha_s)\, m(ds, dz)\right] \\
&= (1+\theta)\mathbb{E}[C_t^\alpha],
\end{aligned}$$

for some safety loading $\theta > 0$, i.e., for any time $t \in [0, T]$ the expected premium covers the expected losses plus an additional (proportional) term, which is the expected net income.

Now let us focus on Example 2. Under the VP the reinsurance premium should satisfy the following equation:

$$\mathbb{E}\left[\int_0^t q(s, Y_s, \alpha_s)\, ds\right] = \mathbb{E}[C_t^\alpha] + \theta\, \mathrm{var}[C_t^\alpha], \tag{A2}$$

for some safety loading $\theta > 0$. We need to evaluate the variance term. Let us introduce the following stochastic process:

$$M_t^\alpha = \int_0^t \int_0^{+\infty} (z - \alpha_s)_+ \big(m(ds, dz) - \nu(ds, dz)\big), \qquad t \in [0, T],$$

denoting $(x - y)_+ = x - x \wedge y$. We have that

$$\begin{aligned}
\mathrm{var}[C_t^\alpha] &= \mathbb{E}[(C_t^\alpha)^2] - \mathbb{E}[C_t^\alpha]^2 \\
&= \mathbb{E}[|M_t^\alpha|^2] + \mathbb{E}\left[\left(\int_0^t \int_0^{+\infty} (z - \alpha_s)_+ \lambda(s, Y_s) dF(z, Y_s)\, ds\right)^2\right] \\
&\quad + 2\mathbb{E}\left[M_t^\alpha \int_0^t \int_0^{+\infty} (z - \alpha_s)_+ \lambda(s, Y_s) dF(z, Y_s)\, ds\right] - \mathbb{E}[C_t^\alpha]^2.
\end{aligned}$$

Denoting by $\langle M^\alpha \rangle_t$ the predictable covariance process of M_t^α, using Remark 1 we finally obtain

$$\begin{aligned}
\mathrm{var}[C_t^\alpha] &= \mathbb{E}[\langle M^\alpha \rangle_t] + \mathrm{var}\left[\int_0^t \int_0^{+\infty} (z - \alpha_s)_+ \lambda(s, Y_s) dF(z, Y_s)\, ds\right] \\
&\quad + 2\mathbb{E}\left[M_t^\alpha \int_0^t \int_0^{+\infty} (z - \alpha_s)_+ \lambda(s, Y_s) dF(z, Y_s)\, ds\right] \\
&= \mathbb{E}\left[\int_0^t \int_0^{+\infty} (z - \alpha_s)_+^2\, \lambda(s, Y_s) dF(z, Y_s)\, ds\right] + \mathrm{var}\left[\int_0^t \int_0^{+\infty} (z - \alpha_s)_+ \lambda(s, Y_s) dF(z, Y_s)\, ds\right] \\
&\quad + 2\mathbb{E}\left[M_t^\alpha \int_0^t \int_0^{+\infty} (z - \alpha_s)_+ \lambda(s, Y_s) dF(z, Y_s)\, ds\right].
\end{aligned}$$

Under the special case $\lambda(t,y) = \lambda(t)$ and $F(z,y) = F(z)$ (e.g., under the Cramér-Lundberg model), for any constant strategy $\alpha \in [0, +\infty)$ the previous equation reduces to

$$\mathrm{var}[C_t^\alpha] = \int_0^t \int_0^{+\infty} (z-\alpha)_+^2 \, \lambda(s) dF(z) \, ds.$$

Extending this formula to the model formulated in Section 2, we obtain the expression (11). Of course, there will be an approximation error, because in our general model the intensity and the claim size distribution depend on the stochastic factor. Nevertheless, this is a common procedure in the actuarial literature.

References

Bass, Richard F. 2004. Stochastic differential equations with jumps. *Probability Surveys* 1: 1–19. [CrossRef]

Brachetta, Matteo, and Claudia Ceci. 2019. Optimal proportional reinsurance and investment for stochastic factor models. *Insurance: Mathematics and Economics* 87: 15–33. [CrossRef]

Brémaud, Pierre. 1981. *Point Processes and Queues. Martingale Dynamics*. Berlin and Heidelberg: Springer.

Ceci, Claudia. 2009. An HJB approach to exponential utility maximisation for jump processes. *International Journal of Risk Assessment and Management* 11: 104–21. [CrossRef]

Ceci, Claudia. 2012. Utility maximization with intermediate consumption under restricted information for jump market models. *International Journal of Theoretical and Applied Finance (IJTAF)* 15: 1–34. [CrossRef]

Ceci, Claudia, and Anna Gerardi. 2006. A model for high frequency data under partial information: A filtering approach. *International Journal of Theoretical and applied Finance* 9: 555–76. [CrossRef]

Ceci, Claudia, and Anna Gerardi. 2009. Utility-based hedging and pricing with a nontraded asset for jump processes. *Nonlinear Analysis: Theory, Methods & Applications* 71: e1953–69.

Ceci, Claudia, and Anna Gerardi. 2010. Wealth optimization and dual problems for jump stock dynamics with stochastic factor. *Stochastics: An International Journal of Probability and Stochastic Processes* 82: 403–25. [CrossRef]

Grandell, Jan. 1991. *Aspects of Risk Theory*. Berlin and Heidelberg: Springer.

Heath, David, and Martin Schweizer. 2000. Martingales versus pdes in finance: An equivalence result with examples. *Journal of Applied Probability* 37: 947–57. [CrossRef]

Hipp, Christian. 2004. Stochastic control with applications in insurance. In *Stochastic Methods in Finance*. Berlin and Heidelberg: Springer, chp. 3, pp. 127–64.

Irgens, Christian, and Jostein Paulsen. 2004. Optimal control of risk exposure, reinsurance and investments for insurance portfolios. *Insurance: Mathematics and Economics* 35: 21–51. [CrossRef]

Li, Danping, Yan Zeng, and Hailiang Yang. 2018. Robust optimal excess-of-loss reinsurance and investment strategy for an insurer in a model with jumps. *Scandinavian Actuarial Journal* 2: 145–71. [CrossRef]

Li, Qicai, and Mengdi Gu. 2013. Optimization problems of excess-of-loss reinsurance and investment under the cev model. *ISRN Mathematical Analysis* 2013: 383265. [CrossRef]

Liang, Zhibin, and Erhan Bayraktar. 2014. Optimal reinsurance and investment with unobservable claim size and intensity. *Insurance: Mathematics and Economics* 55: 156–66. [CrossRef]

Liang, Zhibin, Kam Chuen Yuen, and Junyi Guo 2011. Optimal proportional reinsurance and investment in a stock market with ornstein–uhlenbeck process. *Insurance: Mathematics and Economics* 49: 207–15. [CrossRef]

Liu, Yuping, and Jin Ma. 2009. Optimal reinsurance/investment problems for general insurance models. *The Annals of Applied Probability* 19: 1495–528. [CrossRef]

Lundberg, Fillip. 1903. Approximerad Framställning av Sannolikehetsfunktionen, Terförsäkering av Kollektivrisker. Ph.D. dissertation, Almqvist and Wiksell, Uppsala, Sweden.

Meng, Hui, and Xin Zhang. 2010. Optimal risk control for the excess of loss reinsurance policies. *ASTIN Bulletin* 40: 179–97. [CrossRef]

Rolski, Tomasz, Hanspeter Schmidli, Volker Schmidt, and Jozef L. Teugels. 1999. *Stochastic Processes for Insurance and Finance*. Hoboken: Wiley.

Schmidli, Hanspeter. 2018. *Risk Theory*. Springer Actuarial. Cham: Springer International Publishing.

Sheng, De-Lei, Ximin Rong, and Hui Zhao. 2014. Optimal control of investment-reinsurance problem for an insurer with jump-diffusion risk process: Independence of brownian motions. *Abstract and Applied Analysis* 2014: 194962. [CrossRef]

Young, Virginia R. 2006. Premium principles. In *Encyclopedia of Actuarial Science*. Atlanta: American Cancer Society, vol. 3.

Zariphopoulou, Thaleia. 2009. Optimal asset allocation in a stochastic factor model—An overview and open problems. In *Advanced Financial Modelling, Radon Series in Computational and Applied Mathematics*. Berlin: De Gruyter, vol. 8, pp. 427–53.

Zhang, Xin, Ming Zhou, and Junyi Guo. 2007. Optimal combinational quota-share and excess-of-loss reinsurance policies in a dynamic setting. *Applied Stochastic Models in Business and Industry* 23: 63–71. [CrossRef]

Zhao, Hui, Ximin Rong, and Yonggan Zhao. 2013. Optimal excess-of-loss reinsurance and investment problem for an insurer with jump–diffusion risk process under the heston model. *Insurance: Mathematics and Economics* 53: 504–14. [CrossRef]

Zhu, Huiming, Chao Deng, Shengjie Yue, and Yingchun Deng. 2015. Optimal reinsurance and investment problem for an insurer with counterparty risk. *Insurance: Mathematics and Economics* 61: 242–54. [CrossRef]

© 2019 by the authors. Licensee MDPI, Basel, Switzerland. This article is an open access article distributed under the terms and conditions of the Creative Commons Attribution (CC BY) license (http://creativecommons.org/licenses/by/4.0/).

risks

MDPI

Article

Imbalance Market Real Options and the Valuation of Storage in Future Energy Systems

John Moriarty [1] and Jan Palczewski [2,*]

[1] School of Mathematical Sciences, Queen Mary University of London, London E1 4NS, UK; j.moriarty@qmul.ac.uk
[2] School of Mathematics, University of Leeds, Leeds LS2 9JT, UK
* Correspondence: J.Palczewski@leeds.ac.uk; Tel.: +44-113-3435180

Received: 13 December 2018; Accepted: 28 March 2019; Published: 11 April 2019

Abstract: As decarbonisation progresses and conventional thermal generation gradually gives way to other technologies including intermittent renewables, there is an increasing requirement for system balancing from new and also fast-acting sources such as battery storage. In the deregulated context, this raises questions of market design and operational optimisation. In this paper, we assess the real option value of an arrangement under which an autonomous energy-limited storage unit sells incremental balancing reserve. The arrangement is akin to a perpetual American swing put option with random refraction times, where a single incremental balancing reserve action is sold at each exercise. The power used is bought in an energy imbalance market (EIM), whose price we take as a general regular one-dimensional diffusion. The storage operator's strategy and its real option value are derived in this framework by solving the twin timing problems of when to buy power and when to sell reserve. Our results are illustrated with an operational and economic analysis using data from the German Amprion EIM.

Keywords: multiple optimal stopping; general diffusion; real option analysis; energy imbalance market

1. Introduction

In today's electric grids, power system security is managed in real time by the system operator, who coordinates electricity supply and demand in a manner that avoids fluctuations in frequency or disruption of supply (see, for example, New Zealand Electricity Authority 2016). In addition, the system operator carries out planning work to ensure that supply can meet demand, including the procurement of non-energy or ancillary services such as operating reserve, the capacity to make near real-time adjustments to supply and demand. These services are provided principally by network solutions such as the control of large-scale generation, although from a technical perspective they can also be provided by smaller, distributed resources such as demand response or energy storage (National Grid ESO 2019a; Xu et al. 2016). Such resources have strongly differing operating characteristics: when compared to thermal generation, for example, energy storage is energy limited but can respond much more quickly. Storage also has important time linkages, since each discharge necessitates a corresponding recharge at a later time.

The coming decades are expected to bring a period of "energy transition" in which markets for ancillary services will evolve, among other highly significant changes to generation, consumption and network operation. The UK government, for example, has an ambition that *"new solutions such as storage or demand-side response can compete directly with more traditional network solutions"* (UK Office of Gas and Electricity Markets 2017, p. 29). In harmony, the UK System Operator National Grid has recently declared its intention to *"create a marketplace for balancing that encourages new and existing providers, and all new technology types"* (National Grid ESO 2019b). In anticipation of changes such as these, we will examine the participation of autonomous energy storage in a future marketplace for balancing.

Operating reserve is typically procured via a two-price mechanism, with a reservation payment plus an additional utilisation payment each time the reserve is called for (Ghaffari and Venkatesh 2013; Just and Weber 2008). Since the incentivisation and efficient use of operating reserve for system balancing is of increasing importance with growing penetration of variable renewable generation (King et al. 2011), several system operators have recently introduced real-time energy imbalance markets (EIMs) in which operating reserve is pooled, including in Germany (Ocker and Ehrhart 2017) and California (Lenhart et al. 2016; Western EIM 2019). Such markets typically involve the submission of bids and offers from several providers for reserves running across multiple time periods, which are then accepted, independently in each period, in price order until the real-time balancing requirement is met. As one provider can potentially be called upon over multiple consecutive periods, this reserve procurement mechanism is not well suited to energy-limited reserves such as energy storage. However, storage-oriented solutions are being pioneered in a number of countries including a recent tender by the National Grid in the UK (National Grid ESO 2019a) and various trials by state system operators in the US (Xu et al. 2016).

This paper considers operating reserve contracts for energy limited storage devices such as batteries. In contrast to previous work on the pricing and hedging of energy options where settlement is financial (see, for example, Benth et al. (2008) and references therein), we take account of the physical settlement required in system balancing, considering also the limited energy and time linkages of storage. The potential physical feedback effects of such contracts are investigated by studying the operational policy of the storage or battery operator. To address the limited nature of storage, the considered reserve contract is for a fixed quantity of energy. In this way, each contract written can be physically covered with the appropriate amount of stored energy. We consider a simple arrangement where the system operator sets the contract parameters, namely the premia (the reservation and utilisation payments) plus an EIM price level x^* at which the energy is delivered. That is, rather than being the outcome of a price formation process, these parameters are set administratively. Our analysis thus focuses exclusively on the timing of the battery operator's actions. This dynamic modelling contrasts with previous economic studies of operating reserve in the literature, which have largely been static (Just and Weber 2008).

To quantify the economic opportunity for the storage operator, we use real options analysis. Real Options analysis is the application of option pricing techniques to the valuation of non-financial or 'real' investments with flexibility (Borison 2005; Dixit and Pindyck 1994). Here, the energy storage unit is the real asset, and is coupled with the timing flexibility of the battery operator, who observes the EIM price in real time. The arrangement may be viewed as providing the battery operator with a real perpetual American put option on the reserve contract described above. This option is either of swing type (called the lifetime problem in this paper) or of single exercise type (the single problem). The feature that sets it apart from the existing literature on swing options is the random refraction time (cf. Carmona and Touzi 2008).

A key question in Real Options analyses is the specification of the driving randomness (Borison 2005). In this paper, we model the EIM price to resemble the historical statistical dynamics of imbalance prices. In common with electricity spot prices and commodity prices more generally but unlike the prices of financial assets, imbalance prices typically exhibit significant mean reversion (Ghaffari and Venkatesh 2013; Pflug and Broussev 2009).

To avoid trivial cases, we impose the following, mild, sustainability conditions on the arrangement:

S1. The battery operator has a positive expected profit from the arrangement.
S2. The reserve contract cannot lead to a certain financial loss for the system operator.

Condition **S1** is also known as the individual rationality or participation condition (Fudenberg et al. 1991). While the battery operator is assumed to be a profit maximiser, the system operator may engage in the arrangement for wider reasons than profit maximisation. To acknowledge the potential additional benefits provided by batteries, for example in providing response quickly and without direct emissions, condition **S2** is less strict than individual rationality.

By considering reserve contracts for incremental capacity (defined as an increase in generation or equivalently a decrease in load), we are able to provide complete solutions whose numerical evaluation is straightforward. Contracts for a decrease in generation, or an increase in load, lead to a fundamentally different set of optimisation problems which have been partially solved by Szabó and Martyr (2017).

This study extends earlier work (Moriarty and Palczewski 2017) with two important differences. Firstly, the dynamics of the imbalance price is described there by an exponential Brownian motion. In the present paper, by employing a different methodological approach, we obtain explicit results for mean-reverting processes (and also other general diffusions) which better describe the statistical properties of imbalance prices (Ghaffari and Venkatesh 2013; Pflug and Broussev 2009). Secondly, the present paper takes into account deterioration of the store. Without this feature, it was found that the value of storage is either very small (corresponding roughly to writing a single reserve contract) or infinite.

Through a benchmark case study, we obtain the following economic recommendations. Firstly, investments in battery storage to provide reserve will be profitable on average for a wide range of the contract parameters. Secondly, the EIM price level x^* at which energy is delivered is an important consideration. This is because, as x^* increases, the EIM price reaches x^* significantly less frequently and the reserve contract starts to provide cover for rare events, resulting in infrequent power delivery and low utilisation of the battery, which may make the business case unattractive. These observations suggest that the contractual arrangement studied in this paper is more suitable for the frequent balancing of less severe imbalance.

1.1. Objectives

Given the model parameters x^*, $p_c \geq 0$ and $K_c \geq 0$, we wish to analyse the actions A1–A3 below (a graphical description of this sequence of actions is provided in Figure 1):

A1 The battery operator selects a time to purchase a unit of energy on the EIM and stores it.

A2 With this physical cover in place, the battery operator then chooses a later time to sell the incremental reserve contract to the system operator in exchange for the initial premium p_c.

A3 The system operator requests delivery of power when the EIM price X first lies above the level x^* and immediately receives the contracted unit of energy in return for the utilisation payment K_c.

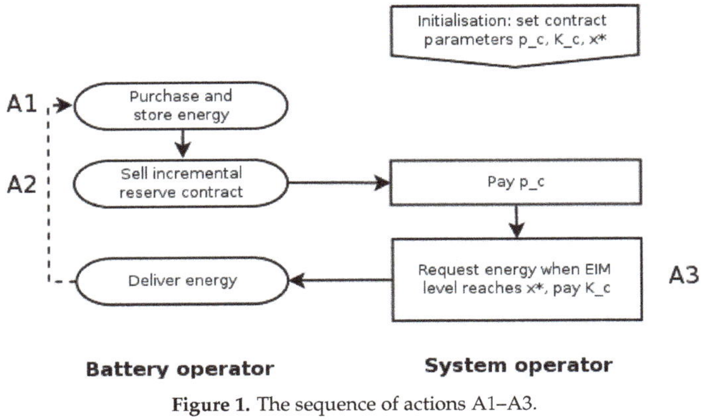

Figure 1. The sequence of actions A1–A3.

Thus, the system operator obtains incremental reserve from the arrangement in preference to using the EIM, when the EIM price is higher than the level x^* specified by the system operator. When the sequence A1–A3 is carried out once, we refer to this as the single problem; when it is repeated indefinitely back-to-back, we refer to it as the lifetime problem.

In the lifetime problem, because storage is energy limited, action A3 must be completed before the sequence A1–A3 can begin again. Thus, if the arrangement is considered as a real swing put option, the time between A2 and A3 is a random refraction period during which no exercise is possible. Note that, after action A3, the battery operator will perform action A1 again when the EIM price has fallen sufficiently. Mathematically, therefore, we have the following objectives:

M1 For the single and lifetime problems, find the highest EIM price $\check{x}$ at which the battery operator may buy energy when acting optimally.

M2 For the single and lifetime problems, find the expected value of the total discounted cash flows (value function) for the battery operator corresponding to each initial EIM price $x \geq \check{x}$.

We also aim to provide a straightforward numerical procedure to explicitly calculate $\check{x}$ and the value function (for $x \geq \check{x}$) in the lifetime problem.

1.2. Approach and Related Work

We take the EIM price to be a continuous time stochastic process $(X_t)_{t \geq 0}$. Since markets operate in discrete time, this is an approximation, made for analytical tractability. Nevertheless, it is consistent with the physical fact that the system operator's system balancing challenge is both real-time and continuous.

Mathematically, the problem is one of choosing two optimal stopping times corresponding to the two actions A1 and A2, based on the evolution of the stochastic process X (The reader is refered to Peskir and Shiryaev (2006, chp. 1) for a thorough presentation of optimal stopping problems). We centre our solution techniques around ideas of Beibel and Lerche (2000), who characterise optimal stopping times using the Laplace transforms of first hitting times for the process X (see, for example, Borodin and Salminen (2012, sec. 1.10)). Methods and results from the single problem are then combined with a fixed point argument for the lifetime analysis.

Our methodological results feed into a growing body of research on timing problems in trading. In a financial context, Zervos et al. (2013) optimise the performance of "buy low, sell high" strategies, using the same Laplace transforms to provide a candidate value function, which is later verified as a solution to certain quasi-variational inequalities. An analogous strategy in an electricity market using hydroelectric storage is studied in Carmona and Ludkovski (2010) where the authors use Regression Monte Carlo methods to approximately solve the dynamic programming equations for a related optimal switching problem. Our results differ from the above papers in two aspects. Our analysis is purely probabilistic, leading to arguments that do not refer to the theory of PDEs and quasi-variational inequalities. Secondly, our characterisation of the value function and the optimal policy is explicit up to a single, one-dimensional nonlinear optimisation, which, as we demonstrate in an empirical experiment, can be performed in milliseconds using standard scientific software. Related to our lifetime analysis, Carmona and Dayanik (2008) apply probabilistic techniques to study the optimal multiple-stopping problem for a general linear regular diffusion process and reward function. However, the latter work deals with a finite number of option exercises in contrast to our lifetime analysis which addresses an infinite sequence of exercises via a fixed point argument. Our work thus yields results with a significantly simpler and more convenient structure.

The contracts we consider have features in common with the reliability options used in Colombia, Ireland and the ISO New England market and currently being introduced in Italy (Mastropietro et al. 2018). Reliability options pay an initial premium to a generator, usually require physical cover, and have a reference market price and a strike price that plays a similar role to x^*. Typically, the strike price is set at the variable cost of the technology used to satisfy demand peaks, and the generator is contracted to pay back the difference between the market price and the strike price in periods when energy is delivered and the market price is higher. However, instead of being designed for system balancing, the purpose of reliability options is to ensure sufficient investment in generation capacity.

The remainder of the paper is organised as follows. The mathematical formulation and main tools are developed in Section 2. In the results of Section 3, we show that, for a range of price processes X incorporating mean reversion, solutions for all initial values x can be obtained. Furthermore, an empirical illustration using data from the German Amprion system operator is provided and qualitative implications are drawn, while Section 5 presents the conclusions. Auxiliary results are collected in the appendices.

2. Methodology

2.1. Formulation and Preliminary Results

In this section, we characterise the real option value in the single and lifetime problems using the theory of regular one-dimensional diffusions. Denoting by $(W_t)_{t\geq 0}$ a standard Brownian motion, let $X = (X_t)_{t\geq 0}$ be a (weak) solution of the stochastic differential equation:

$$dX_t = \mu(X_t)dt + \sigma(X_t)dW_t, \tag{1}$$

with boundaries $a \in \mathbb{R} \cup \{-\infty\}$ and $b \in \mathbb{R} \cup \{\infty\}$. The solution of this equation with the initial condition $X_0 = x$ defines a probability measure $\mathbb{P}^x$ and the related expectation operator $\mathbb{E}^x$. We assume that the boundaries are natural or entrance-not-exit, i.e., the process cannot reach them in finite time, and that X is a regular diffusion process, meaning that the state space $I := (a, b)$ cannot be decomposed into smaller sets from which X cannot exit. The existence and uniqueness of such an X is guaranteed if the functions μ and σ are Borel measurable in I with $\sigma^2 > 0$, and

$$\forall\, y \in I,\ \exists\, \varepsilon > 0 \text{ such that } \int_{y-\varepsilon}^{y+\varepsilon} \frac{1+|\mu(\xi)|}{\sigma^2(\xi)}\, d\xi < +\infty \tag{2}$$

(see Karatzas and Shreve (1991, Theorem 5.5.15); condition (2) holds if, for example, μ is locally bounded and σ is locally bounded away from zero). Necessary and sufficient conditions for the boundaries a and b to be non-exit points, i.e., natural or entrance-not-exit, are formulated in Karatzas and Shreve (1991, Theorem 5.5.29). In particular, it is sufficient that the scale function

$$p(x) := \int_c^x \exp\left(-2\int_c^z \frac{\mu(u)}{\sigma^2(u)}du\right) dz, \quad x \in I \tag{3}$$

converges to $-\infty$ when x approaches a and to $+\infty$ when x approaches b. (Here, $c \in I$ is arbitrary and the condition stated above does not depend on its choice.) These conditions are mild, in the sense that they are satisfied by all common diffusion models for commodity prices, including those in Section 3.

Denote by τ_x the first time that the process X reaches $x \in I$:

$$\tau_x = \inf\{t \geq 0 : X_t = x\}. \tag{4}$$

For $r > 0$, define

$$\psi_r(x) = \begin{cases} \mathbb{E}^x\{e^{-r\tau_c}\}, & x \leq c, \\ 1/\mathbb{E}^c\{e^{-r\tau_x}\}, & x > c, \end{cases} \qquad \phi_r(x) = \begin{cases} 1/\mathbb{E}^c\{e^{-r\tau_x}\}, & x \leq c, \\ \mathbb{E}^x\{e^{-r\tau_c}\}, & x > c, \end{cases} \tag{5}$$

for any fixed $c \in I$ (different choices of c merely result in a scaling of the above functions). It can be verified directly that function $\phi_r(x)$ is strictly decreasing in x while $\psi_r(x)$ is strictly increasing, and, for $x, y \in I$, we have

$$\mathbb{E}^x\{e^{-r\tau_y}\} = \begin{cases} \psi_r(x)/\psi_r(y), & x < y, \\ \phi_r(x)/\phi_r(y), & x \geq y. \end{cases} \tag{6}$$

Since the boundaries a, b are natural or entrance-not-exit, we have $\psi_r(a+) \geq 0$, $\phi_r(b-) \geq 0$ and $\psi_r(b-) = \phi_r(a+) = \infty$ (Borodin and Salminen 2012, Sec. II.1).

2.1.1. Optimal Stopping Problems and Solution Technique

The class of optimal stopping problems which we use in this paper is

$$v(x) = \sup_{\tau} \mathbb{E}^x\{e^{-r\tau}\vartheta(X_\tau)\mathbf{1}_{\tau<\infty}\}, \tag{7}$$

where the supremum is taken over the set of all (possibly infinite) stopping times. Here, ϑ is the payoff function and v is the value function. If a stopping time τ^* exists which attains the supremum in (7), we call this an optimal stopping time. In addition, if v and ϑ are continuous, then the set

$$\Gamma := \{x \in I : v(x) = \vartheta(x)\} \tag{8}$$

is a closed subset of I. Under general conditions (Peskir and Shiryaev 2006, chp. 1), which are satisfied by all stopping problems studied in this paper, $\tau^* = \inf\{t \geq 0 : \ X_t \in \Gamma\}$ is the smallest optimal stopping time and the set Γ is then called the stopping set.

Appendix A contains three lemmas providing a classification of solutions to the stopping problem (7) which will be used below.

2.1.2. Single Problem

Let $(X_t)_{t\geq 0}$ denote the EIM price. We will develop a mathematical representation of actions A1–A3 (see Section 1.1) when only one reserve contract is traded. Considering A3, the time of power delivery is the first time that the EIM price exceeds a predetermined level x^*:

$$\hat{\tau}_e = \inf\{t \geq 0 : X_t \geq x^*\}.$$

Given the present level x of the EIM price, the expected net present value of the utilisation payment exchanged at time $\hat{\tau}_e$ can be expressed as follows thanks to (6):

$$h_c(x) = E^x\{e^{-r\hat{\tau}_e}K_c\} = \begin{cases} K_c, & x \geq x^*, \\ K_c\frac{\psi(x)}{\psi(x^*)}, & x < x^*. \end{cases} \tag{9}$$

Therefore, the optimal timing of action A2 corresponds to solving the following optimal stopping problem:

$$\sup_{\tau} \mathbb{E}^x\{e^{-r\tau}(p_c + h_c(X_\tau))\mathbf{1}_{\tau<\infty}\}.$$

Since the utilisation payment K_c obtained when the EIM price exceeds x^* is positive and constant, as is the initial premium p_c, it is best to obtain these cashflows as soon as possible. The solution of the above stopping problem is therefore trivial: the contract should be sold immediately after completing action A1, i.e., immediately after providing physical cover for the reserve contract. Optimally timing the simultaneous actions A1 and A2, the purchase of energy and sale of the incremental reserve contract, is therefore the core optimisation task. It corresponds to solving the following optimal stopping problem:

$$V_c(x) = \sup_{\tau} E^x\{e^{-r\tau}(-X_\tau + p_c + h_c(X_\tau))\mathbf{1}_{\tau<\infty}\} = \sup_{\tau} E^x\{e^{-r\tau}h(X_\tau)\mathbf{1}_{\tau<\infty}\}, \tag{10}$$

where the payoff

$$h(x) = -x + p_c + h_c(x) \tag{11}$$

is non-smooth since h_c is non-smooth. The function $V_c(x)$ is the real option value in the single problem.

2.1.3. Lifetime Problem Formulation and Notation

In addition, to having a design life of multiple decades, thermal power stations have the primary purpose of generating energy rather than providing ancillary services. In contrast, electricity storage technologies such as batteries have a design life of years and may be dedicated to providing ancillary services. In this paper, we take into account the potentially limited lifespan of electricity storage by modelling a multiplicative degradation of their storage capacity: each charge–discharge cycle reduces the capacity by a factor $A \in (0,1)$.

We now turn to the lifetime problem. To this end, suppose that a nonnegative continuation value $\zeta(x,\alpha)$ is also received at the same time as action A3. It is a function of the capacity of the store $\alpha \in (0,1)$ and the EIM price x, and represents the future proceeds from the arrangement.

The expected net present value of action A3 is now

$$h^{\zeta}(x,\alpha) := E^x\{e^{-r\hat{\tau}_e}(\alpha K_c + \zeta(X_{\hat{\tau}_e}, A\alpha))\} = \begin{cases} (\alpha K_c + \zeta(x^*, A\alpha))\frac{\psi(x)}{\psi(x^*)}, & x < x^*, \\ \alpha K_c + \zeta(x, A\alpha), & x \geq x^*, \end{cases} \tag{12}$$

where $A \in (0,1)$ is the multiplicative decrease of storage capacity per cycle. Here, the optimal timing of action A2 may be non trivial due to the continuation value $\zeta(x,\alpha)$. We will show, however, that, for the functions ζ of interest in this paper, it is optimal to sell the reserve contract immediately after action A1, identically as in the single problem. The timing of action A1 requires the solution of the optimal stopping problem

$$\mathcal{T}\zeta(x,\alpha) := \sup_{\tau} E^x\{e^{-r\tau}(-\alpha X_\tau + \alpha p_c + h^{\zeta}(X_\tau,\alpha))\mathbf{1}_{\tau<\infty}\}. \tag{13}$$

The optimal stopping operator $\mathcal{T}$ makes the dependence on ζ explicit: it maps ζ onto the real option value of a selling a single reserve contract followed by continuation according to ζ. We define the lifetime value function $\widehat{V}$ as the limit

$$\widehat{V}(x) = \lim_{n\to\infty}(\mathcal{T}^n\mathbf{0})(x,1) \tag{14}$$

(if the limit exists), where $\mathcal{T}^n$ denotes the n-fold iteration of the operator $\mathcal{T}$ and $\mathbf{0}$ is the function identically equal to 0. Thus,, $\mathcal{T}^n\mathbf{0}$ is the real option value of selling at most n reserve contracts under the arrangement. (Note that a priori it may not be optimal to sell all n contracts in this case, since it is possible to offer fewer contracts and refrain from trading afterwards by choosing $\tau = \infty$.)

Calculation of the lifetime value function requires the analysis of a two-argument function. We will show now that this computation may be reduced to a function of the single argument x. Define $\zeta_0(x,\alpha) = 0$ and $\zeta_{n+1}(x,\alpha) = \mathcal{T}\zeta_n(x,\alpha)$. We interpret $\zeta_n(x,\alpha)$ as the maximum expected wealth accumulated over at most n cycles of the actions A1–A3 when the initial capacity of the store is α.

Lemma 1. *We have* $\zeta_n(x,\alpha) = \alpha\hat{\zeta}_n(x)$, *where* $\hat{\zeta}_n(x) = \zeta_n(x,1)$. *Moreover,* $\hat{\zeta}_n(x) = \hat{\mathcal{T}}^n\mathbf{0}(x)$, *where*

$$\hat{\mathcal{T}}\hat{\zeta}(x) = \sup_\tau \mathbb{E}^x\{e^{-r\tau}\big(-X_\tau + p_c + \hat{h}^{\hat{\zeta}}(X_\tau)\big)\mathbf{1}_{\tau<\infty}\}, \tag{15}$$

and

$$\hat{h}^{\hat{\zeta}}(x) = \begin{cases} \big(K_c + A\hat{\zeta}(x^*)\big)\frac{\psi(x)}{\psi(x^*)}, & x < x^*, \\ K_c + A\hat{\zeta}(x), & x \geq x^*. \end{cases} \tag{16}$$

Proof. The proof is by induction. Clearly, the statement is true for $n = 0$. Assume it is true for $n \geq 0$. Then,

$$\zeta_{n+1}(x,\alpha) = \mathcal{T}\zeta_n(x,\alpha) = \alpha \sup_\tau \mathbb{E}^x\{e^{-r\tau}\big(-X_\tau + p_c + \frac{1}{\alpha}h^{\zeta_n}(X_\tau,\alpha)\big)\mathbf{1}_{\tau<\infty}\},$$

and

$$\frac{1}{\alpha}h^{\zeta_n}(x,\alpha) = E^x\{e^{-r\hat{\tau}_e}(K_c + \frac{1}{\alpha}\zeta_n(X_{\hat{\tau}_e}, A\alpha))\} = E^x\{e^{-r\hat{\tau}_e}(K_c + A\hat{\zeta}_n(X_{\hat{\tau}_e}))\}.$$

Hence, $\zeta_{n+1}(x,\alpha) = \alpha\hat{\mathcal{T}}\hat{\zeta}_n(x) = \alpha\zeta_{n+1}(x,1)$. Consequently, $\hat{\zeta}_n = \hat{\mathcal{T}}^n\mathbf{0}$. □

Assume that $\zeta_n(x,\alpha)$ converges to $\zeta(x,\alpha)$ as $n \to \infty$. Then, clearly, $\hat{\zeta}_n$ converges to $\hat{\zeta}(x) = \zeta(x,1)$. It is also clear that ζ is a fixed point of $\mathcal{T}$ if and only if $\hat{\zeta}$ is a fixed point of $\hat{\mathcal{T}}$. Therefore, we have simplified the problem to that of finding a limit of $\hat{\mathcal{T}}^n\mathbf{0}(x)$. The stopping problem $\hat{\mathcal{T}}\hat{\zeta}$ will be called the normalised stopping problem and its payoff denoted by

$$\hat{h}(x,\hat{\zeta}) = \begin{cases} -x + p_c + \frac{\psi_r(x)}{\psi_r(x^*)}\big(K_c + A\hat{\zeta}(x^*)\big), & x < x^*, \\ -x + p_c + K_c + A\hat{\zeta}(x), & x \geq x^*. \end{cases} \tag{17}$$

In particular, $\hat{\mathcal{T}}\mathbf{0}$ coincides with the single problem's value function V_c.

Notation. In the remainder of this paper, a caret (hat) will be used over symbols relating to the normalised lifetime problem:

$$\widehat{V}(x) = \lim_{n\to\infty} \hat{\mathcal{T}}^n\mathbf{0}(x).$$

2.1.4. Sustainability Conditions Revisited

The sustainability conditions **S1** and **S2** introduced in Section 1 are our standing economic assumptions. The next lemma, proved in the appendices, expresses them quantitatively. This makes way for their use in the mathematical considerations below.

Lemma 2. *When taken together, the sustainability conditions* **S1** *and* **S2** *are equivalent to the following quantitative conditions:*

S1*: $\sup_{x\in(a,b)} h(x) > 0$, *and*
S2*: $p_c + K_c < x^*$.

Notice that **S1*** is always satisfied when $a \leq 0$.

2.2. Three Exhaustive Regimes in the Single Problem

In this section, we consider the single problem. Recall that the sustainability assumptions, or equivalently assumptions **S1*** and **S2***, are in force. For completeness, the notation and general optimal stopping theory used below is presented in Appendix A.

Since the boundary a is not-exit, we have $\phi_r(a+) = \infty$. When h is given by (11), the limit L of (A3) is then

$$L_c := \limsup_{x\to a} \frac{-x}{\phi_r(x)}. \tag{18}$$

It can also be verified that the analogous constant R defined in (A4) in the appendices satisfies $R < \infty$ since, by **S2***, h is negative on $[x^*, \infty)$. The following theorem completes our aim **M2**.

Theorem 1. *(Single problem) Assume that conditions* **S1*** *and* **S2*** *hold. With the definition (18), there are three exclusive cases:*

(A) $L_c \leq \frac{h(x)}{\phi_r(x)}$ *for some* $x \implies$ *there is* $\hat{x} < x^*$ *that maximises* $\frac{h(x)}{\phi_r(x)}$*, and then, for* $x \geq \hat{x}$*,* $\tau_{\hat{x}}$ *is optimal, and*

$$V_c(x) = \phi_r(x)\frac{h(\hat{x})}{\phi_r(\hat{x})}, \qquad x \geq \hat{x}. \tag{19}$$

(B) $\infty > L_c > \frac{h(x)}{\phi_r(x)}$ *for all* $x \implies V_c(x) = L_c\,\phi_r(x)$ *and there is no optimal stopping time.*

(C) $L_c = \infty \implies V_c(x) = \infty$ *and there is no optimal stopping time.*

Moreover, in cases A and B, the value function V_c *is continuous.*

Proof. By condition **S1***, $h(y)$ is positive for some $y \in I$ and the value function $V_c(x) > 0$. For case A, note first that the function h is negative on $[x^*, b)$ by **S2***, see (9) and (11). Therefore, the supremum of $\frac{h}{\phi_r}$ is positive and must be attained at some (not necessarily unique) $\hat{x} \in (a, x^*)$. The optimality of $\tau_{\hat{x}}$ for $x \geq \hat{x}$ then follows from Lemma A1. Case B follows from Lemma A2 and the fact that $L_c > 0$. Lemma A2 proves case C. The continuity of V_c follows from Lemma A3. □

The optimal strategy in case A is of a threshold type. When an arbitrary threshold strategy $\tau_{\tilde{x}}$ is used, the resulting expected value for $x \geq \tilde{x}$ is given by $\phi_r(x)h(\tilde{x})/\phi_r(\tilde{x})$. Figure 2 (whose problem data fall into case A) shows the potentially high sensitivity of the expected value of discounted cash flows for the single problem with respect to the level of the threshold $\tilde{x}$. It is therefore important in general to identify the optimal threshold accurately.

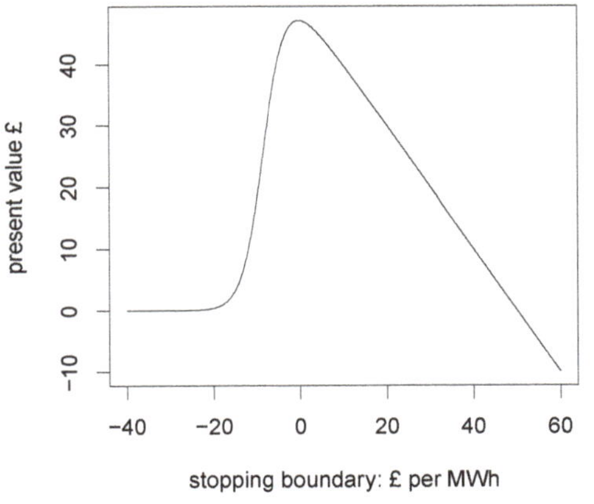

Figure 2. Sensitivity of the expected value in the single problem with respect to the stopping boundary. The EIM price is modelled as an Ornstein-Uhlenbeck process $dX_t = 3.42(47.66 - X_t)dt + 30.65dW_t$ (time measured in days, fitted to Elexon Balancing Mechanism price half-hourly data from July 2011 to March 2014). The interest rate $r = 0.03$, power delivery level $x^* = 60$, the initial premium $p_c = 10$, and the utilisation payment $K_c = 40$. The initial price is X_0 is set equal to x^*.

We now show that, for commonly used diffusion price models, it is case A in the above theorem which is of principal interest. This is due to the mild sufficient conditions established in the following lemma which are satisfied, for example, by the examples in Section 3. Although condition 2(b) in Lemma 3 is rather implicit, it may be interpreted as requiring that the process X does not 'escape relatively quickly to $-\infty$' (see Appendix D for a further discussion and examples) and it is satisfied, for example, by the Ornstein-Uhlenbeck process.

Lemma 3. *If condition* **S1*** *holds, then:*

1. *The equality $L_c = 0$ implies case A of Theorem 1.*
2. *Any of the following conditions is sufficient for $L_c = 0$:*
   (a) $a > -\infty$,
   (b) $a = -\infty$ *and* $\lim_{x\to-\infty} \frac{x}{\phi_r(x)} = 0$.

Proof. Condition **S1*** ensures that h takes positive values. Hence, the ratio $\frac{h(x)}{\phi_r(x)} > 0 = L_c$ for some x. For assertion 2(a), recall from Section 2 that $\phi_r(a+) = \infty$ since the boundary a is not-exit. Then, we have $L_c = \limsup_{x\to a}(-x)/\phi_r(x) = 0$ as $a > -\infty$. In 2(b), the equality $L_c = 0$ is immediate from the definition of L_c. □

Turning now to aim **M1**, we have

Corollary 1. *In the setting of Theorem 1 for the single problem, either*

(a) *the quantity*

$$\check{x} := \max\left\{ x \in I : \frac{h(x)}{\phi_r(x)} = \sup_{y\in I} \frac{h(y)}{\phi_r(y)} \right\} \tag{20}$$

is well-defined, i.e., the set is non-empty. Then, $\check{x}$ is the highest price at which the battery operator may buy energy when acting optimally, and we have $\check{x} < x^*$ (this is case A); or

(b) *there is no price at which it is optimal for the battery operator to purchase energy. In this case, the single problem's value function may either be infinite (case C) or finite (case B).*

Proof. (a) Since the maximiser $\hat{x}$ in case A of Theorem 1 is not necessarily unique, the set in (20) may contain more than one point. Since h and ϕ_r are continuous and all maximisers lie to the left of x^*, this set is closed and bounded from above, so $\check{x}$ is well-defined and a maximiser in case A. For any stopping time τ with $\mathbb{P}^x\{X_\tau > \check{x}\} > 0$, it is immediate from assertion 3 of Lemma A1 that τ is not optimal for the problem $V_c(x)$, $x \geq \check{x}$. Part (b) follows directly from cases B and C of Theorem 1. □

Corollary 1 confirms that it is optimal for the battery operator to buy energy only when the EIM price is strictly lower than the price x^* which would trigger immediate power delivery to the system operator. Thus, the battery operator (when acting optimally) does not directly conflict with the system operator's balancing actions.

2.3. Two Exhaustive Regimes in the Lifetime Problem

Turning to the lifetime problem, we begin by letting $\hat{\zeta}(x)$ in definition (16) be a general nonnegative continuation value depending only on the EIM price x, and studying the normalised stopping problem (15) in this case (the payoff $\hat{h}$ is therefore defined as in (17)).

We now wish to study the value of n cycles A1–A3, and hence the lifetime value, by iterating the operator $\hat{\mathcal{T}}$. To justify this approach, it is necessary to check the timing of action A2 in the lifetime problem. With the actions A1–A3 defined as in Section 1.1, recall that the timing of action A2 is trivial in the single problem: after A1 it is optimal to perform A2 immediately. Lemma A5, which may be found in Appendix B, confirms that the same property holds in the lifetime problem.

We may now provide the following answer to objective **M1** for the lifetime problem.

Corollary 2. *Assume that conditions* **S1*** *and* **S2*** *hold. In the lifetime problem with $\hat{\zeta} = \widehat{V}$, either:*

(a) *the quantity*

$$\check{x} := \max\left\{x \in I : \frac{\hat{h}(x,\hat{\zeta})}{\phi_r(x)} = \sup_{y \in I} \frac{\hat{h}(y,\hat{\zeta})}{\phi_r(y)}\right\} \tag{21}$$

is well-defined, i.e., the set is non-empty. Then, $\check{x}$ is the highest price at which the battery operator can buy energy when acting optimally in the lifetime problem, and we have $\check{x} < x^*$ (cases 1 and 2a in Lemma A4 in Appendix B); or

(b) *there is no price at which it is optimal for the battery operator to purchase energy. In this case, the lifetime value function may either be infinite (case 3) or finite (case 2b in Lemma A4 in Appendix B).*

Proof. The proof proceeds exactly as that of Corollary 1 with the exception of showing that $\check{x} < x^*$ (this is because Lemma A4 in the appendices, which characterises the possible solution types in the lifetime problem, does not guarantee the strict inequality $\check{x} < x^*$). Assume then $\check{x} = x^*$. At the EIM price $X_t = \check{x} = x^*$, the power delivery to the system operator is immediately followed by the purchase of energy by the battery operator and this cycle can be repeated instantaneously, arbitrarily many times. However, since each such cycle is loss making for the battery operator by condition **S2***, this strategy would lead to unbounded losses almost surely in the lifetime problem started at EIM price x^* leading to $\widehat{V}(x^*) = -\infty$. This would contradict the fact that $\widehat{V} > 0$, so we conclude that $\check{x} < x^*$. □

Pursuing aim **M2**, we will show now that there are two regimes in the lifetime problem: either the lifetime value function is strictly greater than the single problem's value function (and the cycle A1–A3 is repeated infinitely many times), or the lifetime value equals the single problem's value. Although the latter case appears counterintuitive, it is explained by the fact that the lifetime problem's value is then attained only in the limit when the purchase of energy (action A1) is made at a decreasing sequence of prices converging to a, the left boundary of the process (X_t). In this limit, the benefit of future payoffs becomes negligible, equating the lifetime value to the single problem's value.[1]

Theorem 2. *There are two exclusive regimes:*

(α) *$\widehat{V}(x) > V_c(x)$ for all $x \geq x^*$,*

(β) *$\widehat{V}(x) = V_c(x)$ for all $x \geq x^*$ (or both are infinite for all x).*

Moreover, in regime (α), an optimal stopping time exists when the continuation value is $\hat{\zeta} = \hat{\zeta}_n = \widehat{\mathcal{T}}^n\mathbf{0}$ for $n > 0$ (that is, for a finite number of reserve contracts), and when $\hat{\zeta} = \widehat{V}$ (for the lifetime value function).

Proof. We take the continuation value $\hat{\zeta} = V_c$ in Lemma A4 from Appendix B and consider separately its cases 1, 2a, 2b and 3. Firstly, in case 3, we have $V_c = \infty$, implying that also $\widehat{V} = \infty$ and we have regime (β).

Case 2 of Lemma A4 corresponds to case B of Theorem 1, when there is no optimal stopping time in the single problem and $V_c(x) = L_c\phi_r(x)$ for all $x \in I$. Considering first case 2b and defining $\hat{\zeta}_n$ as in Lemma A6 in Appendix B, it follows that $\hat{\zeta}_2(x) = L_c\phi_r(x) = V_c(x)$ for $x \in I$ and consequently $\widehat{V} = V_c$, which again corresponds to regime (β).

In case 2a of Lemma A4, suppose first that the maximiser $\hat{x} \leq x^*$ is such that $\frac{\hat{h}(\hat{x},\hat{\zeta}_1)}{\phi_r(\hat{x})} = L_c$. Then, for $x \geq x^* \geq \hat{x}$, we have $\hat{\zeta}_2(x) = \phi_r(x)\frac{\hat{h}(\hat{x},\hat{\zeta}_1)}{\phi_r(\hat{x})} = L_c\phi_r(x)$, which also yields regime (β). On the other hand, when $\frac{\hat{h}(\hat{x},\hat{\zeta}_1)}{\phi_r(\hat{x})} > L_c$, we have for $x \geq x^* \geq \hat{x}$ that $\hat{\zeta}_2(x) = \phi_r(x)\frac{\hat{h}(\hat{x},\hat{\zeta}_1)}{\phi_r(\hat{x})} > L_c\phi_r(x) = \hat{\zeta}_1(x)$, and so regime ($\alpha$) applies by the monotonicity of the operator $\widehat{\mathcal{T}}$. From the definition of $\hat{h}$ in (17), and holding the point $\hat{x} \leq x^*$ constant, this monotonicity implies that $\frac{\hat{h}(\hat{x},\hat{\zeta}_n)}{\phi_r(\hat{x})} > L_c$ for all $n > 1$ and that $\frac{\hat{h}(\hat{x},\widehat{V})}{\phi_r(\hat{x})} > L_c$.

1 If the lifetime value is infinite then so is the single problem's value and they are equal in this sense. When the lifetime value is zero then it is optimal not to enter the contract, and so the single problem's value is also zero.

We conclude that case 2a of Lemma A4 applies (rather than case 2b) for a finite number of reserve contracts and also in the lifetime problem.

Considering now the maximiser $\hat{x}$ defined in case 1 of Lemma A4, we have for $x \geq x^* \geq \hat{x}$ that

$$\hat{\zeta}_2(x) = \phi_r(x)\frac{\hat{h}(\hat{x},\hat{\zeta}_1)}{\phi_r(\hat{x})} \geq \frac{\hat{h}(\hat{x}_0,\hat{\zeta}_1)}{\phi_r(\hat{x}_0)} > \frac{\hat{h}(\hat{x}_0,\mathbf{0})}{\phi_r(\hat{x}_0)} = \hat{\zeta}_1(x) = V_c(x),$$

and regime (α) again follows by monotonicity. In addition, trivially, case 1 of Lemma A4 applies for $\hat{\zeta} = \hat{\zeta}_n$ and $\hat{\zeta} = \widehat{V}$. □

The following corollary follows immediately from the preceding proof.

Corollary 3. *Regime (β) holds if and only if $\hat{\mathcal{T}}^2\mathbf{0}(x) = \hat{\mathcal{T}}\mathbf{0}(x)$ for all $x \geq x^*$.*

To address the implicit nature of our answers to **M1** and **M2** for the lifetime problem, in the next section, we provide results for the construction and verification of the lifetime value function and corresponding stopping time. For this purpose, we close this section by summarising results obtained above (making use of additional results from Appendix C).

Theorem 3. *In the setting of Theorem 2, assume that regime (α) holds. Then, the lifetime value function $\widehat{V}$ is continuous, is a fixed point of the operator $\hat{\mathcal{T}}$ and $\hat{\mathcal{T}}^n\mathbf{0}$ converges to $\widehat{V}$ exponentially fast in the supremum norm. Moreover, there is $\check{x} < x^*$ such that $\tau_{\check{x}}$ is an optimal stopping time for $\hat{\mathcal{T}}\widehat{V}(x)$ when $x \geq \check{x}$ and, furthermore, $\check{x}$ is the highest price at which the battery operator can buy energy when acting optimally.*

2.4. Construction of the Lifetime Value Function

In this section, we discuss a numerical procedure for solution of the lifetime problem. It is based on the problem's structure as summarised in Theorem 3. Lemma 4 provides a means of constructing the lifetime value function, together with the value $\check{x}$ of Theorem 3, using a one-dimensional search. We assume that regime (α) of Theorem 2 holds.

In the circumstance when the above procedure is not followed, complementary findings in Appendix E enable one to verify if a candidate buy price $\hat{x}$ is optimal for the lifetime problem.

Lemma 4. *The lifetime value function evaluated at x^* satisfies*

$$\widehat{V}(x^*) = \max_{z\in(a,x^*)} y(z), \tag{22}$$

where

$$y(z) := \frac{-z + p_c + \frac{\psi_r(z)}{\psi_r(x^*)}K_c}{\frac{\phi_r(z)}{\phi_r(x^*)} - \frac{\psi_r(z)}{\psi_r(x^*)}A}. \tag{23}$$

Proof. Fix $z \in (a, x^*)$. In the normalised lifetime problem of Section 2.1.3, suppose that the strategy τ_z is used for each energy purchase. Writing y for the total value of this strategy under $\mathbb{P}^{x^*}$, by construction we have the recursion

$$y = \frac{\phi_r(x^*)}{\phi_r(z)}\Big(-z + p_c + \frac{\psi_r(z)}{\psi_r(x^*)}(K_c + Ay)\Big).$$

Rearranging, we obtain (23). By Theorem 3, there exists an optimal strategy $\tau_{\check{x}}$ of the above form under $\mathbb{P}^{x^*}$ and (22) follows. □

Hence, under $\mathbb{P}^{x^*}$, an optimal stopping level $\hat{x}$ can be found by maximising $y(z)$ over $z \in (a, x^*)$. The value $\check{x}$ of Theorem 3 is given by $\check{x} = \max\{x :\ y(x) = \max_{z\in(a,x^*)} y(z)\}$.

3. Results

The general theory presented above provides optimal stopping times for initial EIM prices $x \geq \check{x}$, where $\check{x}$ is the highest price at which the battery operator can buy energy optimally. In this section, for specific models of the EIM price, we derive optimal stopping times for *all possible* initial EIM prices $x \in I$ when the sustainability conditions **S1*** and **S2*** hold. In the examples of this section, the stopping sets Γ for the single and lifetime problems take the form $(a, \check{x}]$ although, in general, stopping sets may have much more complex structure. Interestingly, the stopping sets for the single and lifetime problem are either both half-lines or both compact intervals.

Note that condition **S2*** is ensured by the explicit choice of parameters. Verification of condition **S1*** is straightforward by checking, for example, if the left boundary a of the interval I satisfies $a < p_c + \lim_{x \to a} \frac{\psi_r(x)}{\psi_r(x^*)} K_c$, i.e., that $\limsup_{x \to a} h(x) > 0$. In particular, **S1*** always holds if $a = -\infty$.

Our approach is to combine the above general results with the geometric method drawn from Section 5 of Dayanik and Karatzas (2003). Although Proposition 5.12 of the latter paper gives results for natural boundaries, we note that the same arguments apply to entrance-not-exit boundaries. In particular, we construct the least concave majorant W of the obstacle $H : [0, \infty) \to \mathbb{R}$, where

$$H(y) := \begin{cases} \frac{\hat{h}(F^{-1}(y), \hat{\zeta})}{\phi_r(F^{-1}(y))}, & y > 0, \\ \limsup_{x \to a} \frac{\hat{h}(x, \hat{\zeta})}{\phi_r(x)} = L_c, & y = 0 \end{cases} \tag{24}$$

(the latter equality was given in (A5) in the appendices). Here, the function $F(x) = \psi_r(x)/\phi_r(x)$ is strictly increasing with $F(a+) = 0$. Writing $\hat{\Gamma}$ for the set on which W and H coincide, under appropriate conditions, the smallest optimal stopping time is given by the first hitting time of the set $\Gamma := F^{-1}(\hat{\Gamma})$ (Dayanik and Karatzas 2003, Propositions 5.13 and 5.14).

The Ornstein-Uhlenbeck (OU) process is a continuous-time stochastic process with dynamics

$$dX_t = \theta(\mu - X_t)dt + \sigma dW_t, \tag{25}$$

where $\theta, \sigma > 0$ and $\mu \in \mathbb{R}$. It has two natural boundaries, $a = -\infty$ and $b = \infty$. This process extends the scaled Brownian motion model by introducing a mean reverting drift term $\theta(\mu - X_t)dt$. The mean reversion is commonly observed in commodity price time series and may have several causes (Lutz 2009). In the present context, the mean reversion can also be interpreted as the impact on prices of the system operator's corrective balancing actions. Appendix F collects some useful facts about the Ornstein-Uhlenbeck process. In particular, when constructing W, it is convenient to note that $H'' \circ F$ has the same sign as $(\mathcal{L} - r)h$, where $\mathcal{L}$ is the infinitesimal generator of X defined as in Appendix F.

3.1. OU Price Process

Assume now that the EIM price follows the OU process (25) so that $L_c = 0$ (see Equation (A19) in Appendix F) and, by Lemma 3, case A of Theorem 1 applies. We are able to deal with the single and lifetime problems simultaneously by setting $\hat{\zeta}$ equal to 0 for the single problem and equal to (the positive function) $\hat{V}$ in the lifetime problem. The results of Sections 2.2 and 2.3 yield that, in both problems, the right endpoint of the set $\hat{\Gamma}$ equals $F(\check{x})$ for some $\infty < \check{x} < x^*$. Furthermore, since ψ_r is a solution to $(\mathcal{L} - r)v = 0$ and since $\check{x} < x^*$, for $x \leq x^*$, we have

$$\begin{aligned} (\mathcal{L} - r)\hat{h}(x, \hat{\zeta}) &= (\mathcal{L} - r)\Big(-x + p_c + \frac{\psi_r(x)}{\psi_r(x^*)}(K_c + A\hat{\zeta}(x^*))\Big) & (26) \\ &= (\mathcal{L} - r)(-x + p_c) & (27) \\ &= (r + \theta)x - rp_c - \theta\mu. & (28) \end{aligned}$$

Therefore, the function $(\mathcal{L} - r)\hat{h}(\cdot, \hat{\zeta})$ is negative on $(-\infty, B_0)$ and positive on (B_0, ∞), where $B_0 = \frac{rp_c+\theta\mu}{r+\theta}$. This implies that H is strictly concave on $(0, F(B_0))$ and strictly convex on $(F(B_0), \infty)$. Since the concave majorant W of H cannot coincide with H in any point of convexity, so necessarily $\check{x} < B_0$ and H is concave on $(0, F(\check{x}))$. Hence, we conclude that W is equal to H on the latter interval and so $\Gamma = (-\infty, \check{x}]$.

3.2. General Mean-Reverting Processes

The above reasoning can be extended to mean-reverting processes with general volatility

$$dX_t = \theta(\mu - X_t)dt + \sigma(X_t)dW_t$$

for a measurable function σ such that the above equation admits a unique solution, cf. Section 2, and $L_c = 0$ (cf. (24)). Recall that we assume that (X_t) has two non-exit boundaries a, b (natural or entrance-not-exit boundaries) satisfying $a < x^* < b$. Since $\mathcal{L} = \theta(\mu - x)\frac{d}{dx} + \frac{1}{2}\sigma^2(x)\frac{d^2}{dx^2}$, Equations (26)–(28) still apply. In particular, we see that the diffusion coefficient $\sigma(\cdot)$ does not affect the sign of (28) and thus does not influence the concavity properties of H on $(0, F(x^*))$. Proceeding as above, we argue that case A of Theorem 1 applies and the single and lifetime problems can be solved simultaneously. Particularly, the largest buy price is given by $a < \check{x} < x^*$ (different for the single and lifetime problems). Note that the form of the stopping set is purely determined by μ, θ, the left boundary a and the initial premium p_c. Obviously, the mean price level μ satisfies $\mu > a$ because a is an unreachable boundary.

Lemma 5. *If $p_c > a$, then the stopping sets for the single and lifetime problems are of the form $\Gamma = (a, \check{x}]$.*

Proof. The same arguments as in the OU case are directly applicable to the present setting and, under the assumptions of the lemma, we have $B_0 = \frac{rp_c+\theta\mu}{r+\theta} > a$. Hence, for each problem, the stopping set has the form $\Gamma = (a, \check{x}]$ for some $\check{x} < B_0$. □

In the particular case of the CIR model (Cox et al. 1985)

$$dX_t = \theta(\mu - X_t)dt + \sigma\sqrt{X_t}dW_t, \tag{29}$$

we have $a = 0, b = \infty$. Then:

Corollary 4. *If X is the CIR process (29) with $2\theta\mu \geq \sigma^2$ and $\mu > 0$, then the boundary $a = 0$ is entrance-not-exit. Furthermore, if $p_c > 0$, then the stopping sets for the single and lifetime problems are of the form $\Gamma = (0, \check{x}]$.*

Proof. It follows from (Cox et al. 1985, p. 391) that the condition $2\theta\mu \geq \sigma^2$ is necessary and sufficient for the boundary 0 to be entrance-not-exit. By Lemma 3, we have $L_c = 0$. An application of Lemma 5 concludes. □

Remark 1. *More generally, suppose that the imbalance price process follows*

$$dX_t = \theta(\mu - X_t)dt + \sigma X_t^{\gamma} dW_t$$

for some $\gamma > 0.5$. Then, the left boundary $a = 0$ is entrance-not-exit for any choice of parameters $\theta, \mu, \sigma > 0$ since the scale function p given in (3) converges to negative infinity at 0. Therefore, the arguments in the above corollary apply and the stopping sets for the single and lifetime problems are also of the form $\Gamma = (0, \check{x}]$.

3.3. Shifted Exponential Price Processes

In order to first recover and then generalise previously obtained results (Moriarty and Palczewski 2017), take the following shifted exponential model for the price process:

$$f(z) := D + de^{bz}, \tag{30}$$
$$X_t = f(Z_t), \tag{31}$$

where Z is a regular one-dimensional diffusion with non-exit (natural or entrance-not-exit) boundaries a^Z and b^Z (we will use the superscripts X and Z where necessary to emphasise the dependence on the stochastic process). The idea is that Z models the physical system imbalance process while f represents a *price stack* of bids and offers which is used to form the EIM price. In this case, the left boundary for X is $a = f(a^Z) \geq D$ and, by Lemma 3, $L_c = 0$ and case A of Theorem 1 applies. Rather than working with the implicitly defined process X, however, we may work directly with the process Z by setting:

$$z^* := f^{-1}(x^*), \tag{32}$$
$$h_f(z) := -f(z) + p_c + \begin{cases} \frac{\psi_r^Z(z)}{\psi_r^Z(z^*)} K_c, & z < z^*, \\ K_c, & z \geq z^*, \end{cases} \tag{33}$$
$$\hat{h}_f(z, \hat{\zeta}) := \begin{cases} -f(z) + p_c + \frac{\psi_r^Z(z)}{\psi_r^Z(z^*)} (K_c + A\hat{\zeta}(z^*)), & z < z^*, \\ -f(z) + p_c + K_c + A\hat{\zeta}(z), & z \geq z^*, \end{cases} \tag{34}$$

and modifying the definitions for $\mathcal{T}, \hat{\mathcal{T}}, V_c$ and $\widehat{V}$ accordingly. We then have

Theorem 4. *Taking definitions (30) and (32)–(34), assume that conditions* **S1*** *and* **S2*** *hold. Then,*

$$L_c := \limsup_{z \to a^Z} \frac{-f(z)}{\phi_r^Z(z)} = 0.$$

In addition:

(i) (Single problem) There exists $\hat{z} < z^*$ that maximises $\frac{h_f(z)}{\phi_r^Z(z)}$, the stopping time $\tau_{\hat{z}}$ is optimal for $z \geq \hat{z}$, and

$$V_c(z) = \phi_r^Z(z) \frac{h_f(\hat{z})}{\phi_r^Z(\hat{z})}, \qquad z \geq \hat{z}.$$

(ii) (Lifetime problem) The lifetime value function $\widehat{V}$ is continuous and a fixed point of $\hat{\mathcal{T}}$. There exists $\tilde{z} \in (\hat{z}, z^*)$ which maximises $\frac{\hat{h}(z,\widehat{V})}{\phi_r^Z(z)}$ and $\tau_{\tilde{z}}$ is an optimal stopping time for $z \geq \tilde{z}$ with

$$\widehat{V}(z) = \hat{\mathcal{T}}\widehat{V}(z) = \phi_r^Z(z) \frac{\hat{h}(\tilde{z}, \widehat{V})}{\phi_r^Z(\tilde{z})}, \qquad z \geq \tilde{z}.$$

Proof. The proof follows from the one-to-one correspondence between the process X and the process Z, and direct transfer from Theorems 1 and 3. □

In some cases, explicit necessary and/or sufficient conditions for **S1*** may be given in terms of the problem parameters. Assume that $a^Z = -\infty$ as in the examples studied below. If $p_c > D$ and $K_c \geq 0$, this is sufficient for the condition **S1*** to be satisfied as then $h_f(z) \geq -f(z) + p_c > 0$ for sufficiently small z. When $p_c = D$ and $K_c > 0$, it is sufficient to verify that $e^{bz} = o(\psi_r^Z(z))$ as $z \to -\infty$ since then $h_f(z) = -de^{bz} + \psi_r^Z(z)\, K_c / \psi_r^Z(z^*)$ for $z < z^*$. On the other hand, our assumption that **S1*** holds necessarily excludes parameter combinations with $p_c - D = K_c = 0$, since the reserve contract writer then cannot make any profit because $h_f(z) \leq 0$ for all z.

In Section 3.3.1, we take Z to be the standard Brownian motion and recover results from the single problem of Moriarty and Palczewski (2017) (the lifetime problem is formulated differently in the latter reference, where degradation of the store is not modelled). In Section 3.3.2, we generalise to the case when Z is an OU process.

3.3.1. Brownian Motion Imbalance Process

When the imbalance process $Z = W$, the Brownian motion, we have

$$(\mathcal{L} - r)\hat{h}_f(z, \hat{\zeta}) = (\mathcal{L} - r)(-f(z) + p_c) = de^{bz}\left\{r - \frac{1}{2}b^2\right\} + r(D - p_c).$$

We have several cases depending on the sign of $(D - p_c)$ and $(r - \frac{1}{2}b^2)$.

1. Assume first that $r > \frac{1}{2}b^2$:

   (i) We may exclude the subcase $p_c \leq D$, since then $H(y) = \frac{\hat{h}(z,\hat{\zeta})}{\phi_r^Z(z)}|_{z=(F^Z)^{-1}(y)}$ is strictly convex on $(0, F^Z(z^*))$ for any $\hat{\zeta}$ and Γ cannot intersect this interval, contradicting Theorem 4 and, consequently, violating **S1*** or **S2***.

   (ii) If $p_c > D$, H is concave on $(0, F^Z(B))$ and convex on $(F^Z(B), \infty)$, where

   $$B = \frac{1}{b}\log\left(\frac{r(p_c - D)}{d(r - \frac{1}{2}b^2)}\right).$$

   By Theorem 4 and the positivity of H on $(0, F^Z(\hat{z}))$, we have $\Gamma = (-\infty, \hat{z}]$ and $\Gamma = (-\infty, \tilde{z}]$ for the single and lifetime problems, respectively, with $\tilde{z} < \hat{z} < B$.

2. Suppose that $r < \frac{1}{2}b^2$.

   (i) When $p_c \geq D$, the function H is concave on $(0, \infty)$. Hence, the stopping sets Γ for single and lifetime problems have the same form as in case 1(ii) above.

   (ii) If $p_c < D$, the function H is convex on $(0, F^Z(B))$ and concave on $(F^Z(B), \infty)$. The set Γ must then be an interval, respectively $[\hat{z}_0, \hat{z}]$ and $[\tilde{z}_0, \tilde{z}]$. For explicit expressions for the left and right endpoints for the single problem, as well as sufficient conditions for **S1***, the reader is refered to Moriarty and Palczewski (2017).

3. In the boundary case $r = \frac{1}{2}b^2$, the convexity of H is determined by the sign of the difference $D - p_c$. As above, the possibility $D > p_c$ is excluded since then H is strictly convex. Otherwise, H is concave and the stopping sets Γ have the same form as in case 1(ii) above.

3.3.2. OU Imbalance Process

When Z is the Ornstein-Uhlenbeck process, by adjusting d and b in the price stack function f (see (30)), we can restrict our analysis to the OU process with zero mean and unit volatility, that is:

$$dZ_t = -\theta Z_t dt + dW_t.$$

Then, for $z < z^*$,

$$\begin{aligned}(\mathcal{L} - r)\hat{h}_f(z, \hat{\zeta}) &= (\mathcal{L} - r)(-f(z) + p_c) &(35)\\ &= de^{bz}\left\{b\left(\theta z - \frac{1}{2}b\right) + r\right\} + r(D - p_c) =: \eta(z). &(36)\end{aligned}$$

Differentiating η, we obtain

$$\eta'(z) = db\theta e^{bz}\left(bz + 1 + \frac{r - \frac{1}{2}b^2}{\theta}\right),$$

which has a unique root at $z^{\diamond} = \frac{1}{b}\left(\frac{\frac{1}{2}b^2 - r}{\theta} - 1\right)$. The function η decreases from $r(D - p_c)$ at $-\infty$ until $\eta(z^{\diamond}) = -de^{bz^{\diamond}}\theta + r(D - p_c)$ at $z^{\diamond}$ and then increases to positive infinity.

1. If $p_c \geq D$, then the function η is negative on $(-\infty, u)$, where u is the unique root of η. Hence, H is concave on $(0, F^Z(u))$ and convex on $(F^Z(u), \infty)$. The stopping sets Γ for the single and lifetime problems must then be of the form $(-\infty, \hat{z}]$ and $(-\infty, \tilde{z}]$, respectively, cf. case 1(ii) in Section 3.3.1.
2. The case $p_c < D$ is more complex:

   (i) Let $z^{\diamond} \geq z^*$. We exclude the possibility $\eta(z^*) \geq 0$, since then the function H is convex on $(0, F^Z(z^*))$ and the set Γ has empty intersection with this interval, contradicting Theorem 4 and, consequently, violating **S1*** or **S2***. When $\eta(z^*) < 0$, H is convex on $(0, F^Z(u))$ and concave on $(F^Z(u), F^Z(z^*))$, where u is the unique root of η on $(0, z^*)$. Therefore, the stopping sets Γ for the single and lifetime problems are of the form $[\hat{z}_0, \hat{z}]$ and $[\tilde{z}_0, \tilde{z}]$, respectively, with $\min(\hat{z}_0, \tilde{z}_0) > u$, cf. case 2(ii) in Section 3.3.1.

   (ii) Consider now $z^{\diamond} < z^*$. As above, we exclude the case $\eta(z^{\diamond}) \geq 0$, since then H is convex on $(0, F^Z(z^*))$. The remaining case $\eta(z^{\diamond}) < 0$ implies that the stopping sets Γ have the same form as in case 2(i) above, as H is convex and then concave if $\eta(z^*) \leq 0$, and convex–concave–convex if $\eta(z^*) > 0$.

4. Benchmark Case Study and Economic Implications

In this section, we use a case study to draw qualitative implications from the above results. An OU model is assumed, which captures both the mean reversion and random variability present in EIM prices, and is fitted to relevant data. The interest rate is taken to be 3% per annum, and the degradation factor for the store to be $A = 0.9999$.

Our data is the 'balancing group price' from the German Amprion system operator, which is available for every 15 min period (AMPRION 2016). Summary statistics for the period from 1 June 2012 to 31 May 2016 are presented in Table 1. To address the issue of its extreme range, which impacts the fitting of both volatility and mean reversion in the OU model, the data was truncated at the values -150 and 150. The parameters obtained by maximum likelihood fitting were then $\theta = 68.69$ (the rate of mean reversion), $\sigma = 483.33$ (the volatility), $\mu = 30.99$ (the mean-reversion level). The effect of the truncation step was to approximately halve the fitted volatility.

Table 1. Summary statistics for the 15 min balancing group price per MWh in the German Amprion area, 1 June 2012 to 31 May 2016.

Min.	1st Qu.	Median	Mean	3rd Qu.	Max.
−6002.00	0.27	33.05	31.14	66.97	6344.00

The left panel of Figures 3 and 4 show the lifetime value $\widehat{V}(x^*)$, while the right panel of Figure 3 plots the stopping boundary $\check{x}$, which is the maximum price at which the battery operator can buy energy optimally. These values of $\check{x}$ are significantly below the long-term mean price D, indeed the former value is negative while the latter is positive. Thus, in this example, the battery operator purchases energy when it is in excess supply, further contributing to balancing. To place the negative values on the stopping boundary in Figure 3 in the statistical context, recall from Table 1 that the first quartile of the price distribution is approximately zero. Indeed, negative energy prices usually occur several times per day in the German EIM. In the present dataset of 1461 days, there are only 11 days without negative prices and the longest observed time between negative prices is 41.5 h.

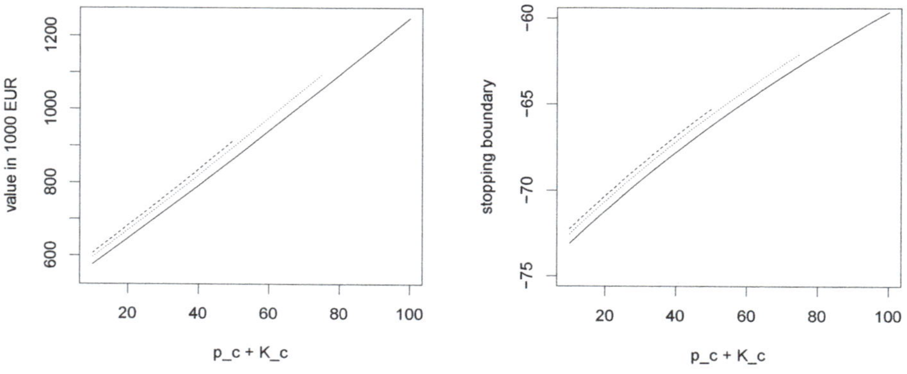

Figure 3. Results obtained with the Ornstein-Uhlenbeck model fitted in Section 4, as functions of the total premium, with interest rate 3% per annum. Solid lines: $x^* = 100$, dotted: $x^* = 75$, dashed: $x^* = 50$. Left: lifetime value $\widehat{V}(x^*)$. Right: the stopping boundary $\check{x}$, the maximum price for which the battery operator can buy energy optimally.

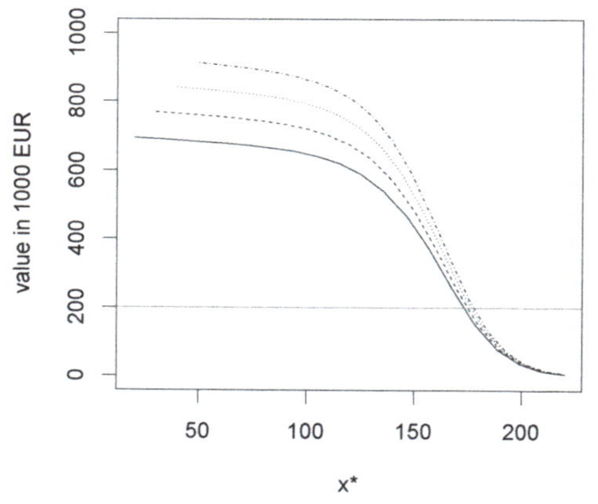

Figure 4. Lifetime value $\widehat{V}(x^*)$ as a function of x^* with the Ornstein-Uhlenbeck model fitted in Section 4, with interest rate 3% per annum. Dashed line: $p_c + K_c = 20$, solid: $p_c + K_c = 30$, dotted: $p_c + K_c = 40$, mixed: $p_c + K_c = 50$. The horizontal grey line indicates the current price of lithium-ion battery storage per MWh (IRENA 2017, Figure 33).

We make the following empirical observations. Firstly, defining the total premium as the sum $p_c + K_c$, altering its distribution between the initial premium p_c (which is received at $x = \check{x}$) and the utilisation payment K_c (which is received at $x = x^*$) results in insignificant changes to the graphs, with relative differences on the vertical axes of the order 10^{-3} (data not shown). It is for this reason that the figures are indexed by the total premium $p_c + K_c$ rather than by individual premia. Secondly, it is seen from the right-hand panel of Figure 3 that the (negative valued) stopping boundary increases with the total premium, making exercise more frequent. Thus, as the total premium increases, both the frequency and size of the cashflows increase, yielding a superlinear relationship in the left-hand panel of Figure 3. This superlinearity is not very pronounced since the stopping boundary is relatively insensitive to the total premium in the range presented in the graphs (see the right hand panel), so that the lifetime value is driven principally by the size of the cashflows. Thirdly, the grey horizontal line of

Figure 4 is placed at a level indicative of recent costs for lithium-ion batteries per MWh (megawatt hour). Thus, the investment case for battery storage providing reserve is significantly positive for a wide range of the contract parameters. Finally, the contours in Figure 4 have an S-shape, the marginal influence of x^* being smaller in the range $x^* < 110$ and larger for greater values of x^* (with the marginal influence eventually decreasing again in the limit of large x^*).

These phenomena are explained by the presence of mean reversion in the OU price model. The timings of the cashflows to the battery operator are entirely determined by the successive *passage times* of the price process between the levels x^* and $\check{x}$. These passage times are relatively short on average for the fitted OU model. This means that the premia are received at almost the same time under each reserve contract, and it is the total premium which drives the real option value. Furthermore, the passage times between x^* and $\check{x}$ may be decomposed into passage times between x^* and D, and between D and $\check{x}$. Since the OU process is statistically symmetric about D, let us compare the distances $|\check{x} - D|$ and $|x^* - D|$. From Figure 3, we have $\check{x} \approx -70$ so that $|\check{x} - D| \approx 100$. Therefore, for $x^* < 110$, we have $|x^* - D| \ll |\check{x} - D|$ and the passage time between D and $\check{x}$, which varies little, dominates that between x^* and D. Correspondingly, we observe in Figure 4 that the value function changes relatively little as x^* varies below 110. Conversely, as x^* increases beyond 110, it is the distance between x^* and D which dominates, and the value function begins to decrease relatively rapidly.

These results provide insights into the suitability of the considered arrangement for correcting differing levels of imbalance. As the distance between x^* and the mean level D grows, the energy price reaches x^* significantly less frequently and the reserve contract starts to provide insurance against rare events, resulting in infrequent power delivery and low utilisation of the battery. These observations suggest that the contractual arrangement studied in this paper is more suitable for the frequent balancing of less severe imbalance. In contrast, the more rapid reduction in the lifetime value for large values of x^* suggests that such arrangements based on real-time markets are not suitable for balancing relatively rare events such as large system disturbances due to unplanned outages of large generators. The system operator may prefer to use alternative arrangements, based, for example, on fixed availability payments, to provide security against such events.

5. Conclusions

In this paper, we investigate the procurement of operating reserve from energy-limited storage using a sequence of physically covered incremental reserve contracts. This leads to the pricing of a real perpetual American swing put option with a random refraction time. We model the underlying energy imbalance market price as a general linear regular diffusion, which, in particular, is capable of modelling the mean reversion present in imbalance prices. Both the optimal operational policy and the real option value of the store are characterised explicitly. Although the solutions are generally not available in an analytical form, we have provided a straightforward procedure for their numerical evaluation together with empirical examples from the German energy imbalance market.

The results of the lifetime analysis in particular have both managerial implications for the battery operator and policy implications for the system operator. From the operational viewpoint, under the setup described in Section 1.1, we have established that the battery operator should purchase energy as soon as the EIM price falls to the level $\check{x}$, which may be calculated as described in Section 2.4. Furthermore, the battery operator should then sell the reserve contract immediately. Our real options valuation may be taken into account when deciding whether to invest in an energy store, and whether to sell such reserve contracts in preference to trading in other markets (for example, performing price arbitrage in the spot energy market).

Turning to the perspective of the system operator, we have demonstrated that the proposed arrangement can be mutually beneficial to the system operator and battery operator. More precisely, the system operator can be protected against guaranteed financial losses from the incremental capacity contract purchase while the battery operator has a quantifiable profit. The analysis also provides information on feedback due to battery charging by determining the highest price $\check{x}$ at which the battery operator buys energy, hence identifying conditions under which the battery operator's operational strategy is aligned with system stability.

We address incremental reserve contracts, which are particularly valuable to the system operator when the margin of electricity generation capacity over peak demand is low. Decremental reserve may also be studied in the above framework, although the second stopping time (action A2) is non-trivial, which leads to a nested stopping problem beyond the scope of the present paper. Furthermore, we assume that the energy storage unit is dedicated to providing incremental reserve contracts, so that the opportunity costs of not operating in other markets or providing other services are not modelled. The extension to a finite expiry time, the lifetime analysis with decremental reserve contracts, and also the opportunity cost of not operating in other markets would be interesting areas for further work.

The methodological advances of this paper reach beyond energy markets. In particular, they are relevant to real options' analyses of storable commodities where the timing problem over the lifetime of the store is of primary interest. The lifetime analysis via optimal stopping techniques, developed in Section 2.3, provides an example of how timing problems can be addressed for rather general dynamics of the underlying stochastic process. In this context, we provide an alternative method to quasi-variational inequalities, which are often dynamics-specific and technically more involved.

Author Contributions: J.M. and J.P. contributed equally to the research and writing of the paper.

Funding: This research was funded by the UK Engineering and Physical Sciences Research Council Grant No. EP/K00557X/2 and MNiSzW grant UMO-2012/07/B/ST1/03298.

Conflicts of Interest: The authors declare no conflict of interest.

Appendix A. Lemmas and Proofs from Section 2

The following three lemmas classify solutions to the stopping problem (7). Note that, if $\sup_x \vartheta(x) \le 0$, then no choice of the stopping time τ gives a value function greater than 0. The optimal stopping time in this case is given by $\tau = \infty$. In what follows, we therefore assume

$$\sup_{x\in(a,b)} \vartheta(x) > 0. \tag{A1}$$

These results can be derived from Beibel and Lerche (2000); however, for the convenience of the reader, we provide simple proofs.

Lemma A1. *Assume that there exists $\hat{x} \in I$ which maximises $\vartheta(x)/\phi_r(x)$ over I. Then, the value function $v(x)$ is finite for all x, and for $x \ge \hat{x}$:*

1. *the stopping time $\tau_{\hat{x}}$ is optimal,*
2. $v(x) = \dfrac{\vartheta(\hat{x})}{\phi_r(\hat{x})}\phi_r(x)$,
3. *any stopping time τ with $\mathbb{P}^x\{\vartheta(X_\tau)/\phi_r(X_\tau) < \vartheta(\hat{x})/\phi_r(\hat{x})\} > 0$ is strictly suboptimal for the problem $v(x)$.*

Proof. Since ϕ_r is r-excessive (Borodin and Salminen 2012, Sec. II.5), for any finite stopping time τ

$$\mathbb{E}^x\{e^{-r\tau}\phi_r(X_\tau)\} \le \phi_r(x).$$

Let now τ be a stopping time taking possibly infinite values. Let b_n be an increasing sequence converging to b with $b_1 > x$, the initial point of the process X. Then, τ_{b_n} is an increasing sequence of stopping times converging to infinity and

$$\phi_r(x) \geq \liminf_{n\to\infty} \mathbb{E}^x\{e^{-r(\tau\wedge\tau_{b_n})}\phi_r(X_{\tau\wedge\tau_{b_n}})\}$$
$$\geq \mathbb{E}^x\{\liminf_{n\to\infty} e^{-r(\tau\wedge\tau_{b_n})}\phi_r(X_{\tau\wedge\tau_{b_n}})\} = \mathbb{E}^x\{e^{-r\tau}\phi_r(X_\tau)\mathbf{1}_{\tau<\infty}\},$$

where $\phi_r(b-) = 0$ was used in the last equality.

For any stopping time τ,

$$\begin{aligned}\mathbb{E}^x\{e^{-r\tau}\vartheta(X_\tau)\mathbf{1}_{\tau<\infty}\} &= \mathbb{E}^x\left\{e^{-r\tau}\phi_r(X_\tau)\frac{\vartheta(X_\tau)}{\phi_r(X_\tau)}\mathbf{1}_{\tau<\infty}\right\} \\ &\leq \frac{\vartheta(\hat{x})}{\phi_r(\hat{x})}\mathbb{E}^x\{e^{-r\tau}\phi_r(X_\tau)\mathbf{1}_{\tau<\infty}\} \leq \frac{\vartheta(\hat{x})}{\phi_r(\hat{x})}\phi_r(x),\end{aligned} \tag{A2}$$

where the final inequality follows from the first part of the proof and (A1) (so $\frac{\vartheta(\hat{x})}{\phi_r(\hat{x})} > 0$). Hence, $v(x)$ is finite for all $x \in I$. To prove claim 1, note from (6) that for $x \geq \hat{x}$ the upper bound is attained by $\tau_{\hat{x}}$, which is therefore an optimal stopping time in the problem $v(x)$. The assumption on τ in claim 3 leads to strict inequality in (A2), making τ strictly suboptimal in the problem $v(x)$. □

It is convenient to introduce the notation

$$L := \limsup_{x\to a} \frac{\vartheta(x)^+}{\phi_r(x)}. \tag{A3}$$

Lemma A2 corresponds to cases when there is no optimal stopping time, but the optimal value can be reached in the limit by a sequence of stopping times.

Lemma A2.

1. *If $L = \infty$, then the value function is infinite and there is no optimal stopping time.*
2. *If $L < \infty$ and $L > \vartheta(x)/\phi_r(x)$ for all $x \in I$, then there is no optimal stopping time and the value function equals $v(x) = L\phi_r(x)$.*

Proof. Assertion 1. Fix any $x \in I$. Then, for any $\hat{x} < x$, we have

$$\mathbb{E}^x\{e^{-r\tau_{\hat{x}}}\vartheta(X_{\tau_{\hat{x}}})\} = \vartheta(\hat{x})\frac{\phi_r(x)}{\phi_r(\hat{x})},$$

which converges to infinity for $\hat{x}$ tending to a over an appropriate subsequence. Since the process is recurrent, the point x can be reached from any other point in the state space with positive probability in a finite time. This proves that the value function is infinite for all $x \in I$.

Assertion 2. Recall that, due to the supremum of $\frac{\vartheta}{\phi_r}$ being strictly positive, we have $L > 0$. From the proof of Lemma A1, for an arbitrary stopping time τ, we have

$$\mathbb{E}^x\{e^{-r\tau}\vartheta(X_\tau)\mathbf{1}_{\tau<\infty}\} = \mathbb{E}^x\{e^{-r\tau}\phi_r(X_\tau)\frac{\vartheta(X_\tau)}{\phi_r(X_\tau)}\mathbf{1}_{\tau<\infty}\} < L\,\mathbb{E}^x\{e^{-r\tau}\phi_r(X_\tau)\mathbf{1}_{\tau<\infty}\} \leq L\phi_r(x).$$

However, one can construct a sequence of stopping times that achieves this value in the limit. Take x_n such that $\lim_{n\to\infty}\vartheta(x_n)/\phi_r(x_n) = L$ and define $\tau_n = \tau_{x_n}$. Then,

$$\lim_{n\to\infty} \mathbb{E}^x\{e^{-r\tau_n}\vartheta(X_{\tau_n})\} = \lim_{n\to\infty} \vartheta(x_n)\frac{\phi_r(x)}{\phi_r(x_n)} = \phi_r(x)L,$$

so $v(x) = \phi_r(x)L$. This together with the strict inequality above proves that an optimal stopping time does not exist. □

The results developed in this section also have a 'mirror' counterpart involving

$$R := \limsup_{x \to b} \frac{\vartheta(x)^+}{\psi_r(x)} \tag{A4}$$

rather than L. In particular, the value function is infinite if $R = \infty$, and

Corollary A1. *If $\hat{x} \in I$ maximises $\vartheta(x)/\psi_r(x)$, then, for any $x \leq \hat{x}$, an optimal stopping time in the problem $v(x)$ is given by $\tau_{\hat{x}}$.*

This also motivates the assumptions of the following lemma which collects results from Dayanik and Karatzas (2003, Sec. 5.2). Again, although those results are obtained under the assumption that both boundaries are natural, their proofs require only that they are non-exit.

Lemma A3. *Assume that $L, R < \infty$ and ϑ is locally bounded. Then, the value function v is finite and continuous on (a, b).*

All the stopping problems considered in this paper have a finite right-hand limit $R < \infty$. Therefore, whenever $L < \infty$, their value functions will be continuous.

Proof of Lemma 2. If **S1*** does not hold, then the payoff from cycle A1–A3 is not profitable (on average) for any value of the EIM price x, so **S1** does not hold. Conversely, if **S1*** holds, then there exists x such that $\hat{\mathcal{T}}\mathbf{0}(x) \geq h(x) > 0$. For any other x', consider the following strategy: wait until the process X hits x and proceed optimally thereafter. This results in a strictly positive expected value: $\hat{\mathcal{T}}\mathbf{0}(x') > 0$ and, by the arbitrariness of x', we have $\hat{\mathcal{T}}\mathbf{0} > 0$.

Suppose that **S2*** holds. Then, the system operator makes a profit on the reserve contract (relative to simply purchasing a unit of energy at the power delivery time $\hat{\tau}_e$, at the price $X(\hat{\tau}_e) \geq x^*$) in undiscounted cash terms. Considering discounting, the system operator similarly makes a profit provided the EIM price reaches the level x^* (or above) sufficiently quickly. Since this happens with positive probability for a regular diffusion, a certain financial loss for the system operator is excluded. When **S2*** does not hold, suppose first that $p_c + K_c > x^*$: then, the system operator makes a loss in undiscounted cash terms, and if the reserve contract is sold when $x \geq x^*$, then this loss is certain. In the boundary case $p_c + K_c = x^*$, the battery operator can only make a profit by purchasing energy and selling the reserve contract when $X_t < x^*$, in which case the system operator makes a certain loss. This follows since instead of buying the reserve contract, the system operator could invest $p_c > 0$ temporarily in a riskless bond, withdrawing it with interest when the EIM price rises to $x^* = p_c + K_c$. The loss in this case is equal in value to the interest payment. □

Appendix B. Lemmas for the Lifetime Problem

It follows from the optimal stopping theory reviewed in Section 2.1.1 and Appendix A that the following definition of an *admissible* continuation function is natural in our setup. In particular, the final condition corresponds to the assumption that the energy purchase occurs at a price below x^*.

Definition A1. *(Admissible continuation value) A continuation value function $\hat{\zeta}$ is* admissible *if it is continuous on $(a, x^*]$ and non-negative on I, with $\frac{\hat{\zeta}(x)}{\phi_r(x)}$ non-increasing on $[x^*, b)$.*

The following result now characterises the possible solution types in the lifetime problem.

Lemma A4. *Assume that conditions **S1*** and **S2*** hold. If $\hat{\zeta}$ is an admissible continuation value function, then*

$$\limsup_{x \to a} \frac{\hat{h}(x, \hat{\zeta})}{\phi_r(x)} = \limsup_{x \to a} \frac{-x}{\phi_r(x)} = L_c, \tag{A5}$$

and with cases A, B, C defined just as in Theorem 1:

1. *In case A, there exists $\hat{x} \leq x^*$ which maximises $\frac{\hat{h}(x,\hat{\zeta})}{\phi_r(x)}$ and $\tau_{\hat{x}}$ is an optimal stopping time for $x \geq \hat{x}$ with value function*
$$v(x) = \hat{\mathcal{T}}\hat{\zeta}(x) = \phi_r(x)\frac{\hat{h}(\hat{x},\hat{\zeta})}{\phi_r(\hat{x})}, \qquad x \geq \hat{x}.$$
Denoting by $\hat{x}_0$ the corresponding $\hat{x}$ in case A of Theorem 1, we have $\hat{x}_0 \leq \hat{x}$.
2. *In case B, either*
   (a) *there exists $x_L \in (a,b)$ with $\frac{\hat{h}(x_L,\hat{\zeta})}{\phi_r(x_L)} \geq L_c$: then, there exists $\hat{x} \in (a, x^*]$ which maximises $\frac{\hat{h}(x,\hat{\zeta})}{\phi_r(x)}$, and $\tau_{\hat{x}}$ is an optimal stopping time for $x \geq \hat{x}$ with value function $v(x) = \phi_r(x)\frac{\hat{h}(\hat{x},\hat{\zeta})}{\phi_r(\hat{x})}$ for $x \geq \hat{x}$; or*
   (b) *there does not exist $x_L \in (a,b)$ with $\frac{\hat{h}(x_L,\hat{\zeta})}{\phi_r(x_L)} \geq L_c$: then, the value function is $v(x) = L_c\,\phi_r(x)$ and there is no optimal stopping time.*
3. *In case C, the value function is infinite and there is no optimal stopping time.*

Moreover, the value function v is continuous in cases A and B.

Proof. Note that
$$h(x) = \hat{h}(x,\mathbf{0}) \leq \hat{h}(x,\hat{\zeta}) = \begin{cases} h(x) + \frac{\psi_r(x)}{\psi_r(x^*)}A\hat{\zeta}(x^*), & x < x^*, \\ h(x) + A\hat{\zeta}(x), & x \geq x^*. \end{cases} \tag{A6}$$

This proves (A5), since $\lim_{x\to a}\psi_r(x)/\phi_r(x) = 0$. We verify from (A6) and the assumptions of the lemma that $R < \infty$ in (A4). Hence, whenever $L_c < \infty$, the value function v is finite and continuous by Lemma A3. As noted previously (in the proof of Theorem 1), h is negative and decreasing on $[x^*, b)$, hence the ratio $h(x)/\phi_r(x)$ is strictly decreasing on that interval. It then follows from (A6) and the admissibility of $\hat{\zeta}$ that the function $x \mapsto \frac{\hat{h}(x,\hat{\zeta})}{\phi_r(x)}$ is strictly decreasing on $[x^*, b)$. Therefore the supremum of $x \mapsto \frac{\hat{h}(x,\hat{\zeta})}{\phi_r(x)}$, which is positive by (A6) and **S1***, is attained on $(a, x^*]$ or asymptotically when $x \to a$. In cases 1 and 2a, the optimality of $\tau_{\hat{x}}$ for $x \geq \hat{x}$ then follows from Lemma A1. To see that $\hat{x}_0 \leq \hat{x}$ in case 1, take $x < \hat{x}_0$. Then, from (A6), we have
$$\frac{\hat{h}(x,\hat{\zeta})}{\phi_r(x)} = \frac{h(x)}{\phi_r(x)} + \frac{\psi_r(x)}{\phi_r(x)}\frac{A\hat{\zeta}(x^*)}{\psi_r(x^*)} < \frac{h(\hat{x}_0)}{\phi_r(\hat{x}_0)} + \frac{\psi_r(\hat{x}_0)}{\phi_r(\hat{x}_0)}\frac{A\hat{\zeta}(x^*)}{\psi_r(x^*)} = \frac{\hat{h}(\hat{x}_0,\hat{\zeta})}{\phi_r(\hat{x}_0)},$$
since $x \mapsto \frac{\psi_r(x)}{\phi_r(x)}$ is strictly increasing. Case 2b follows from Lemma A2 and the fact that $L_c > 0$, while Lemma A2 proves case 3. □

Before proceeding, we note the following technicalities.

Remark A1. *The value function v in cases 1 and 2a of Lemma A4 satisfies the condition that $v(x)/\phi_r(x)$ is non-increasing on $[x^*, b)$. Indeed,*
$$\frac{v(x)}{\phi_r(x)} = \frac{\hat{h}(\hat{x},\hat{\zeta})}{\phi_r(\hat{x})} = const.$$
for $x \geq \hat{x}$.

Remark A2. *For case 3 of Lemma A4, the assumption that $\frac{\hat{\zeta}(x)}{\phi_r(x)}$ is non-increasing on $[x^*, b)$ can be dropped.*

Lemma A5. *The timing of action A2 remains trivial when the cycle A1–A3 is iterated a finite number of times.*

Proof. Let us suppose that action A1 has just been carried out in preparation for selling the first in a chain of n reserve contracts, and that the EIM price currently has the value x. Define τ_{A2} to be the time at which the battery operator carries out action A2. The remaining cashflows are (i) the first contract premium p_c (from action A2), (ii) the first utilisation payment K_c (from A3), and (iii) all cashflows arising from the remaining cycles A1–A3 (there are $n-1$ cycles which remain available to the battery operator). The cashflows (i) and (ii) are both positive and fixed, making it best to obtain them as soon as possible. The cashflows (iii) include positive and negative amounts, so their timing is not as simple. However, it is sufficient to notice that

- their expected net present value is given by an optimal stopping problem, namely, the timing of the *next* action A1:
$$\sup_{\tau \geq \sigma^*} \mathbb{E}^x\{e^{-r\tau} h_{(iii)}(X_\tau)\mathbf{1}_{\tau<\infty}\}, \tag{A7}$$
where $\sigma^* := \inf\{t \geq \tau_{A2} : X_t \geq x^*\}$, for some suitable payoff function $h_{(iii)}$,
- the choice $\tau_{A2} = 0$ minimises the exercise time σ^* and thus maximises the value of component (iii), since the supremum in (A7) is then taken over the largest possible set of stopping times.

It is therefore best to set $\tau_{A2} = 0$, since this choice maximises the value of components (i), (ii) and (iii). □

The next result establishes the existence of, and characterises, the lifetime value function $\widehat{V}$.

Lemma A6. *In cases A and B of Theorem 1,*

1. *For each $n \geq 1$, the function $\hat{\zeta}_n := \hat{\mathcal{T}}^n\mathbf{0}$ is an admissible continuation value function and is decreasing on $[x^*, b)$.*
2. *The functions $\hat{\mathcal{T}}^n\mathbf{0}$ are strictly positive and uniformly bounded in n.*
3. *The limit $\hat{\zeta} = \lim_{n\to\infty} \hat{\mathcal{T}}^n\mathbf{0}$ exists and is a strictly positive bounded function. Moreover, the lifetime value function $\widehat{V}$ coincides with $\hat{\zeta}$.*
4. *The lifetime value function $\widehat{V}$ is a fixed point of $\hat{\mathcal{T}}$.*

Proof. Part 1 is proved by induction. The claim is clearly true for $n = 1$. Assume it holds for n. Then, Lemma A4 applies and $\hat{\zeta}_{n+1}(x)/\phi_r(x) = \hat{h}(\hat{x}, \hat{\zeta}_n)/\phi_r(\hat{x})$ for $x \geq \hat{x}$ when the optimal stopping time exists and $\hat{\zeta}_{n+1}(x)/\phi_r(x) = L_c$ otherwise. Therefore, $\hat{\zeta}_{n+1}(x) = c\phi_r(x)$ for $x \geq x^*$ and some constant $c \geq 0$. Since ϕ_r is decreasing, we conclude that $\hat{\zeta}_{n+1}$ decreases on $[x^*, b)$.

The monotonicity of $\hat{\mathcal{T}}$ guarantees that, if $\hat{\mathcal{T}}\mathbf{0} > 0$, then $\hat{\mathcal{T}}^n\mathbf{0} > 0$ for every n. For the upper bound, notice that

$$\begin{aligned}
\hat{\mathcal{T}}\hat{\zeta}_n(x) &= \sup_\tau \mathbb{E}^x\Big\{e^{-r\tau}\Big(p_c - X_\tau + \mathbb{E}^{X_\tau}\{e^{-r\hat{\tau}_e}(K_c + A\hat{\zeta}_n(X_{\hat{\tau}_e}))\}\Big)\mathbf{1}_{\tau<\infty}\Big\} \\
&\leq \sup_\tau \mathbb{E}^x\Big\{e^{-r\tau}\Big(p_c - X_\tau + K_c\mathbb{E}^{X_\tau}\{e^{-r\hat{\tau}_e}\}\Big)\mathbf{1}_{\tau<\infty}\Big\} + A\hat{\zeta}_n(x^*) = V_c(x) + A\hat{\zeta}_n(x^*),
\end{aligned}$$

where $V_c = \hat{\mathcal{T}}\mathbf{0}$ is the value function for the single problem and the inequality follows from the fact that $\hat{\zeta}_n$ is decreasing on $[x^*, b)$. From the above, we have $\hat{\zeta}_n(x) = \hat{\mathcal{T}}^n\mathbf{0}(x) \leq V_c(x) + \frac{1-A^n}{1-A}V_c(x^*)$. Recalling that $A \in (0,1)$ yields that the $\hat{\zeta}_n(x)$ are bounded by $V_c(x) + \frac{1}{1-A}V_c(x^*)$, so there exists a finite monotone limit $\hat{\zeta} := \lim_{n\to\infty}\hat{\zeta}_n$, and

$$\begin{aligned}\hat{\zeta}(x) = \lim_{n\to\infty} \hat{\mathcal{T}}\hat{\zeta}_n(x) &= \sup_n \sup_\tau \mathbb{E}^x\Big\{e^{-r\tau}\Big(p_c - X_\tau + \mathbb{E}^{X_\tau}\{e^{-r\hat{\tau}_e}(K_c + A\hat{\zeta}_n(X_{\hat{\tau}_e}))\}\Big)\mathbf{1}_{\tau<\infty}\Big\} \\ &= \sup_\tau \lim_{n\to\infty} \mathbb{E}^x\Big\{e^{-r\tau}\Big(p_c - X_\tau + \mathbb{E}^{X_\tau}\{e^{-r\hat{\tau}_e}(K_c + A\hat{\zeta}_n(X_{\hat{\tau}_e}))\}\Big)\mathbf{1}_{\tau<\infty}\Big\} \\ &= \sup_\tau \mathbb{E}^x\Big\{e^{-r\tau}\Big(p_c - X_\tau + \mathbb{E}^{X_\tau}\{e^{-r\hat{\tau}_e}(K_c + A\hat{\zeta}(X_{\hat{\tau}_e}))\}\Big)\mathbf{1}_{\tau<\infty}\Big\} \\ &= \hat{\mathcal{T}}\hat{\zeta}(x),\end{aligned}$$

by monotone convergence. The equality of $\widehat{V}$ and $\hat{\zeta}$ is clear from (14). □

Appendix C. Uniqueness of Fixed Points

Corollary A2 below establishes the uniqueness of the fixed point of $\hat{\mathcal{T}}$. Lemma A8 shows that $\hat{\mathcal{T}}^n\mathbf{0}$ converges exponentially fast to this unique fixed point as $n \to \infty$.

Lemma A7. *Let ξ, ξ' be two continuous non-negative functions with ξ satisfying the assumptions of Lemma A4 together with the bound $\xi \geq \xi'$. In the problem $\hat{\mathcal{T}}\xi$, assume the existence of an optimal stopping time τ^* under which stopping occurs only at values bounded above by $x' < x^*$. Then,*

$$\|\hat{\mathcal{T}}\xi - \hat{\mathcal{T}}\xi'\|_\# \leq \rho\|\xi - \xi'\|_\#,$$

where $\rho = A\frac{\psi_r(x')}{\psi_r(x^*)} < 1$ and $\|f\|_\# = |f(x^*)|$ is a seminorm on the space of continuous functions. Moreover,

$$0 \leq \hat{\mathcal{T}}\xi(x) - \hat{\mathcal{T}}\xi'(x) < \|\xi - \xi'\|_\#. \tag{A8}$$

Note that, in general, an optimal stopping time for $\hat{\mathcal{T}}\xi(x)$ depends on the initial state x. However, under general conditions (cf. Section 2.1.1), $\tau^* = \inf\{t \geq 0 : X_t \in \Gamma\}$, where Γ is the stopping set. Then, the condition in the above lemma writes as $\Gamma \subset (a, x']$ for some $x' < x^*$.

Proof of Lemma A7. By the monotonicity of $\hat{\mathcal{T}}$, for any x, we have

$$\begin{aligned}0 \leq \hat{\mathcal{T}}\xi(x) - \hat{\mathcal{T}}\xi'(x) &\leq \mathbb{E}^x\Big\{e^{-r\tau^*}\Big(-X_{\tau^*} + p_c + (K_c + A\xi(x^*))\frac{\psi_r(X_{\tau^*})}{\psi_r(x^*)}\Big)\Big\} \\ &\quad - \mathbb{E}^x\Big\{e^{-r\tau^*}\Big(-X_{\tau^*} + p_c + (K_c + A\xi'(x^*))\frac{\psi_r(X_{\tau^*})}{\psi_r(x^*)}\Big)\Big\} \\ &= \mathbb{E}^x\Big\{e^{-r\tau^*}A\Big((\xi(x^*) - \xi'(x^*))\frac{\psi_r(X_{\tau^*})}{\psi_r(x^*)}\Big)\Big\} \\ &= \|\xi - \xi'\|_\# A\,\mathbb{E}^x\Big\{e^{-r\tau^*}\frac{\psi_r(X_{\tau^*})}{\psi_r(x^*)}\Big\}.\end{aligned}$$

This proves (A8). In addition, we have

$$A\,\mathbb{E}^{x^*}\Big\{e^{-r\tau^*}\frac{\psi_r(X_{\tau^*})}{\psi_r(x^*)}\Big\} \leq A\frac{\phi_r(x^*)}{\phi_r(x')}\frac{\psi_r(x')}{\psi_r(x^*)} \leq \rho.$$

□

Lemma A8. *Assume that there exists a fixed point $\hat{\zeta}^*$ of $\hat{\mathcal{T}}$ in the space of continuous non-negative functions. In the problem $\hat{\mathcal{T}}\hat{\zeta}^*$, assume the existence of an optimal stopping time under which stopping occurs only at values bounded above by $x' < x^*$ (cf. the comment after the previous lemma). Then, there is a constant $\rho < 1$ such that $\|\hat{\zeta}^* - \hat{\mathcal{T}}^n\mathbf{0}\|_\# \leq \rho^n\|\hat{\zeta}^*\|_\#$ and $\|\hat{\zeta}^* - \hat{\mathcal{T}}^n\mathbf{0}\|_\infty \leq \rho^{n-1}\|\hat{\zeta}^*\|_\#$, where $\|\cdot\|_\infty$ is the supremum norm.*

Proof. Clearly, $\|\hat{\zeta}^* - \mathbf{0}\|_\# < \infty$. By virtue of Lemma A7, we have $\|\hat{\mathcal{T}}^n\mathbf{0} - \hat{\zeta}^*\|_\# \leq \rho^n \|\mathbf{0} - \hat{\zeta}^*\|_\#$ for $\rho = \frac{\psi_r(x')}{\psi_r(x^*)} < 1$. Hence, $\hat{\mathcal{T}}^n\mathbf{0}$ converges exponentially fast to $\hat{\zeta}^*$ in the seminorm $\|\cdot\|_\#$. Using (A8), we have

$$\|\hat{\zeta}^* - \hat{\mathcal{T}}^n\mathbf{0}\|_\infty = \|\hat{\mathcal{T}}\hat{\zeta}^* - \hat{\mathcal{T}} \circ \hat{\mathcal{T}}^{n-1}\mathbf{0}\|_\infty \leq \rho^{n-1}\|\hat{\zeta}^*\|_\#.$$

□

Corollary A2. *Let $\hat{\zeta}^*$ be a fixed point of $\hat{\mathcal{T}}$ and suppose that the problem $\hat{\mathcal{T}}\hat{\zeta}^*$ admits an optimal stopping time $\hat{\tau}^*$ satisfying $X_{\hat{\tau}^*} \leq x' < x^*$, for some constant x'. Such a fixed point $\hat{\zeta}^*$ is unique.*

Proof. By Lemma A8, if $\hat{\zeta}^*$ is a fixed point satisfying the assumptions of the corollary, it is approximated by $\hat{\mathcal{T}}^n\mathbf{0}$ in the supremum norm; hence, it must be unique. □

Appendix D. Note on Lemma 3

The inequality $\lim_{x\to-\infty} \frac{-x}{\phi_r(x)} > 0$ when $a = -\infty$ asserts that the process X escapes to $-\infty$ quickly. Indeed, choosing $z \in I$, we have $\mathbb{E}^z\{e^{-r\tau_x}\} = \frac{\phi_r(z)}{\phi_r(x)}$ for $x \leq z$, hence $\mathbb{E}^z\{e^{-r\tau_x}\} \geq \frac{c}{-x}$ for some constant $c > 0$ and x sufficiently close to $-\infty$. To illustrate the speed of escape, assume for simplicity that X is a deterministic process. Then, the last inequality would imply $\tau_x \leq \frac{1}{r}\big(\log(-x) - \log(c)\big)$, i.e., X escapes to $-\infty$ exponentially quickly.

An example of a model that violates the assumptions of Lemma 3 is the negative geometric Brownian motion: $X_t = -\exp\big((\mu - \sigma^2/2)t + \sigma W_t\big)$ for $\mu, \sigma > 0$. With the generator $\mathcal{A} = \frac{1}{2}\sigma^2 x^2 \frac{d^2}{dx^2} + \mu x \frac{d}{dx}$, we have $\phi_r(x) = (-x)^{\gamma_2}$ and $\psi_r(x) = (-x)^{\gamma_1}$, where $\gamma_1 < 0 < \gamma_2$ are solutions to the quadratic equation $\frac{\sigma^2}{2}\gamma^2 + (\mu - \frac{\sigma^2}{2})\gamma - r = 0$, i.e., $\gamma = B \pm \sqrt{B^2 + 2\frac{r}{\sigma^2}}$ with $B = \frac{1}{2} - \frac{\mu}{\sigma^2}$. Hence, $\lim_{x\to-\infty} \frac{-x}{\phi_r(x)} = \lim_{x\to-\infty}(-x)^{1-\gamma_2} > 0$ if and only if $\gamma_2 \leq 1$. It is easy to check that $\gamma_2 = 1$ for $\mu = r$ and γ_2 is decreasing as a function of μ. Therefore, the condition $\gamma_2 \leq 1$ is equivalent to $\mu \geq r$.

In summary, the negative geometric Brownian motion violates the assumptions of Lemma 3 if $\mu \geq r$. If $\mu = r$, then case B of Theorem 1 applies with $L_c = 1$, while, if $\mu > r$, then $L_c = \infty$ and so case C applies. Both cases may be interpreted heuristically as the negative geometric Brownian motion X escaping 'relatively quickly' to $-\infty$, that is, relative to the value r of the continuously compounded interest rate. In the latter case, this happens sufficiently quickly that the single problem's value function V_c is infinite.

Appendix E. Verification Theorem for the Lifetime Value Function

We now provide a verification lemma which may be used to verify if a given value $\hat{x}$ is an optimal buy price in the lifetime problem. The result is motivated by the following argument using Theorem 3.

We claim that, for all $x \in I$, $\hat{\mathcal{T}}\widehat{V}(x)$ depends on the value function $\widehat{V}$ only through its value at $x = x^*$. The argument is as follows: when the battery operator acts optimally, the energy purchase occurs when the price is not greater than x^*: under $\mathbb{P}^x$ for $x \geq x^*$, this follows directly from Theorem 3; under $\mathbb{P}^x$ for $x < x^*$, the energy is either purchased before the price reaches x^* or one applies a standard dynamic programming argument for optimal stopping problems (see, for example, Peskir and Shiryaev 2006) at x^* to reduce this to the previous case. In our setup, the continuation value is not received until the EIM price rises again to x^* (it is received immediately if the energy purchase occurs at x^*).

Suppose therefore that we can construct functions $V_i : I \to \mathbb{R}$, $i = 1, 2$, with the following properties:

(I) $\hat{\mathcal{T}}V_1 = V_2$,
(II) $V_1(x^*) = V_2(x^*)$,
(III) for $i = 1, 2$, the highest price at which the battery operator buys energy in the problem $\hat{\mathcal{T}}V_i$ is not greater than x^*.

Then, we have $V_2 = \hat{\mathcal{T}}V_1 = \hat{\mathcal{T}}V_2$, so that V_2 is a fixed point of $\hat{\mathcal{T}}$.

We postulate the following form for V_i: given $y > 0$ take

$$V_1(x) = \hat{\xi}_0^y(x) := \mathbf{1}_{x \le x^*} y, \tag{A9}$$

$$V_2(x) = \hat{\xi}^y(x) := \hat{\mathcal{T}}\hat{\xi}_0^y(x). \tag{A10}$$

For convenience, define $\mathfrak{h}(x,y)$ to be the payoff in the lifetime problem when the the continuation value is $\hat{\xi}_0^y$. Thus, we have

$$\mathfrak{h}(x,y) = \hat{h}(x, \hat{\xi}_0^y), \tag{A11}$$

$$\hat{\xi}^y(x) = \hat{\mathcal{T}}\hat{\xi}_0^y(x) = \sup_{\tau} \mathbb{E}^x\{e^{-r\tau}\mathfrak{h}(X_\tau, y)\mathbf{1}_{\tau<\infty}\}. \tag{A12}$$

Lemma A9. *Suppose that $\hat{x} \in (a, x^*)$ satisfies the system*

$$\frac{\mathfrak{h}(\hat{x},y)}{\phi_r(\hat{x})} = \sup_{x\in(a,x^*)} \frac{\mathfrak{h}(x,y)}{\phi_r(x)}, \tag{A13}$$

$$y = \frac{\phi_r(x^*)}{\phi_r(\hat{x})}\mathfrak{h}(\hat{x},y), \tag{A14}$$

$$y > 0. \tag{A15}$$

Then, the function $\hat{\xi}^y$ of (A12) is a fixed point of $\hat{\mathcal{T}}$, is continuous and strictly positive, and

$$\hat{\xi}^y(x) = \frac{\phi_r(x)}{\phi_r(x^*)}y, \quad \text{for } x \ge \hat{x}. \tag{A16}$$

Proof. Consider first the problem (A12) with $x \ge \hat{x}$. By construction, $\hat{\xi}_0^y$ is an admissible continuation value in Lemma A4, and cases 1 or 2a must then hold due to the standing assumption for this section that regime (α) of Theorem 2 is in force. By (A13), the stopping time $\tau_{\hat{x}}$ is optimal, and the problem's value function $\hat{\xi}^y$ has the following three properties. Firstly, $\hat{\xi}^y$ is continuous on I by Lemma A3. Secondly, using (A14), we see that $\hat{\xi}^y$ satisfies (A16). This implies thirdly that $\hat{\xi}^y/\phi_r$ is constant on $[x^*, b)$ and establishes that $\hat{\xi}^y(x^*) = y$, giving property (ii) above. Since $y > 0$ by (A15), the strict positivity of $\hat{\xi}^y$ everywhere follows as in part 1 of the proof of Lemma 2. Our standing assumption **S2*** implies that the payoff $\mathfrak{h}(x,y)$ of (A11) is negative for $x > x^*$, which establishes property (iii) for problem (A12).

The three properties of ξ^y established above make it an admissible continuation value in Lemma A4, so we now consider the problem $\hat{\mathcal{T}}\xi^y$ for $x \ge \hat{x}$. Under $\mathbb{P}^x$ for $x \ge x^*$, claim 2 of Lemma A1 prevents the battery operator from buying energy at prices greater than x^* when acting optimally; under $\mathbb{P}^x$ for $x < x^*$, the dynamic programming principle mentioned above completes the argument. □

The following corollary completes the verification argument, and also establishes the uniqueness of the value y in Lemma A9.

Corollary A3. *Under the conditions of Lemma A9:*

(i) the function $\hat{\xi}^y$ coincides with the lifetime value function: $\widehat{V} = \hat{\xi}^y$,
(ii) there is at most one value y for which the system of equations (A13)-(A14) has a solution $\hat{x} \in (a, x^*)$.

Proof. (i) We will appeal to Lemma A8 by refining property (III) above for the problem $\hat{\mathcal{T}}V_2 = \hat{\mathcal{T}}\hat{\xi}^y$ (as was done in the proof of Corollary 2). Suppose that the battery operator buys energy at the price x^*. Then, since the function $\hat{\xi}^y$ is a fixed point of $\hat{\mathcal{T}}$ under our assumptions, we may consider $\hat{\mathcal{T}}\hat{\xi}^y(x^*) = -x^* + p_c + K_c + \hat{\xi}^y(x^*)$ and then **S2*** leads to $\hat{\mathcal{T}}\hat{\xi}^y(x^*) < \hat{\xi}^y(x^*)$, which is a contradiction.

Thus, from Lemma A8, $\hat{\mathcal{T}}^n\mathbf{0}$ converges to $\hat{\xi}^y$ as $n \to \infty$. As the limit of $\hat{\mathcal{T}}^n\mathbf{0}$ is the lifetime value function, we obtain $\widehat{V} = \hat{\xi}^y$.

(ii) Assume the existence of two such values $y_1 \neq y_2$. Then, (A16) gives $\widehat{V}(x^*) = \hat{\xi}^{y_1}(x^*) = y_1 \neq y_2 = \hat{\xi}^{y_2}(x^*) = \widehat{V}(x^*)$, a contradiction. □

We recall here that, on the other hand, the value $\hat{x}$ in Lemma A9 may not be uniquely determined (cf. part (a) of Corollary 2). In this case, the largest $\hat{x}$ satisfying the assumptions of Lemma A9 is the highest price $\check{x}$ at which the battery operator can buy energy optimally.

Appendix F. Facts about the OU Process

Let us temporarily fix $\mu = 0$ and $\theta = \sigma = 1$. Consider the ordinary differential equation (ODE)

$$w''(z) + \left(\nu + \frac{1}{2} - \frac{1}{4}z^2\right) w(z) = 0.$$

There are two fundamental solutions $D_\nu(z)$ and $D_\nu(-z)$, where D_ν is a parabolic cylinder function. Assume that $\nu < 0$. This function has a multitude of representations, but the following will be sufficient for our purposes (Érdelyi et al. 1953, p. 119):

$$D_\nu(z) = \frac{e^{-z^2/4}}{\Gamma(-\nu)} \int_0^\infty e^{-zt-\frac{1}{2}t^2} t^{-\nu-1} dt.$$

Then, D_ν is strictly positive. Fix $r > 0$. Define

$$\psi_r(x) = e^{\frac{(x-\mu)^2\theta}{2\sigma^2}} D_{-r/\theta}\Big(-\frac{(x-\mu)\sqrt{2\theta}}{\sigma}\Big), \qquad \phi_r(x) = e^{\frac{(x-\mu)^2\theta}{2\sigma^2}} D_{-r/\theta}\Big(\frac{(x-\mu)\sqrt{2\theta}}{\sigma}\Big).$$

By direct calculation, one verifies that these functions solve

$$\mathcal{L}v = rv, \tag{A17}$$

where

$$\mathcal{L}v(x) = \frac{1}{2}\sigma^2 v''(x) + \theta(\mu - x)v'(x) \tag{A18}$$

is the infinitesimal generator of the OU process (25). Setting $\nu = -r/\theta$, we can write

$$\psi_r(x) = \frac{1}{\Gamma(-\nu)} \int_0^\infty e^{(x-\mu)t\frac{\sqrt{2\theta}}{\sigma} - \frac{1}{2}t^2} t^{-\nu-1} dt, \qquad \phi_r(x) = \frac{1}{\Gamma(-\nu)} \int_0^\infty e^{-(x-\mu)t\frac{\sqrt{2\theta}}{\sigma} - \frac{1}{2}t^2} t^{-\nu-1} dt.$$

Hence, ψ_r is increasing and ϕ_r is decreasing in x. In addition, by monotone convergence, $\psi_r(-\infty) = \phi_r(\infty) = 0$ and $\psi_r(\infty) = \phi_r(-\infty) = \infty$. The functions ψ_r and ϕ_r are then fundamental solutions of the Equation (A17). Furthermore, they are strictly convex, which can be checked by passing differentiation under the integral sign (justified by the dominated convergence theorem). Defining $F(x) = \psi_r(x)/\phi_r(x)$, then F is continuous and strictly increasing with $F(-\infty) = 0$ and $F(\infty) = \infty$.

Using the integral representation of ϕ_r and l'Hôpital's rule, we have

$$\begin{aligned}
\lim_{x\to-\infty}\frac{-x}{\phi_r(x)} &= \lim_{x\to-\infty}\frac{-1}{\frac{1}{\Gamma(-\nu)}\int_0^\infty e^{-(x-\mu)t\frac{\sqrt{2\theta}}{\sigma}-\frac{1}{2}t^2}\left(-t\frac{\sqrt{2\theta}}{\sigma}\right)t^{-\nu-1}dt} \\
&= \frac{\sigma}{\sqrt{2\theta}}\lim_{x\to-\infty}\frac{1}{\frac{1}{\Gamma(-\nu)}\int_0^\infty e^{-(x-\mu)t\frac{\sqrt{2\theta}}{\sigma}-\frac{1}{2}t^2}t^{-\nu}dt} \\
&= \frac{\sigma}{\sqrt{2\theta}}\lim_{x\to-\infty}\frac{1}{\frac{\Gamma(-\nu+1)}{\Gamma(-\nu)}\frac{1}{\Gamma(-\nu+1)}\int_0^\infty e^{-(x-\mu)t\frac{\sqrt{2\theta}}{\sigma}-\frac{1}{2}t^2}t^{-\nu}dt} = 0,
\end{aligned} \tag{A19}$$

as the denominator is a scaled version of $\phi_{\tilde{r}}$ corresponding to a new $\tilde{r}$ such that $-\tilde{r}/\theta = \nu - 1 < \nu < 0$, and so it converges to infinity when $x \to -\infty$.

References

(AMPRION 2016) AMPRION. 2016. AMPRION Imbalance Market Data. Available online: http://www.amprion.net/en/control-area-balance (accessed on 9 April 2019).

(Beibel and Lerche 2000) Beibel, Martin, and Hans Rudolf Lerche. 2000. Optimal stopping of regular diffusions under random discounting. *Theory of Probability and Its Applications* 45: 547–57. [CrossRef]

(Benth et al. 2008) Benth, Fred Espen, Jurate Saltyte Benth, and Steen Koekebakker. 2008. *Stochastic Modelling of Electricity and Related Markets*. Singapore: World Scientific, vol. 11.

(Borison 2005) Borison, Adam. 2005. Real options analysis: Where are the emperor's clothes? *Journal of Applied Corporate Finance* 17: 17–31. [CrossRef]

(Borodin and Salminen 2012) Borodin, Andrei N., and Paavo Salminen. 2012. *Handbook of Brownian Motion—Facts and Formulae*. Basel: Birkhäuser.

(Carmona and Dayanik 2008) Carmona, René, and Savas Dayanik. 2008. Optimal multiple stopping of linear diffusions. *Mathematics of Operations Research* 33: 446–60. [CrossRef]

(Carmona and Ludkovski 2010) Carmona, René, and Michael Ludkovski. 2010. Valuation of energy storage: An optimal switching approach. *Quantitative Finance* 10: 359–74. [CrossRef]

(Carmona and Touzi 2008) Carmona, Renè, and Nizar Touzi. 2008. Optimal multiple stopping and valuation of swing options. *Mathematical Finance* 18: 239–68. [CrossRef]

(Cox et al. 1985) Cox, John C., Jonathan E. Ingersoll, and Stephen A. Ross. 1985. A theory of the term structure of interest rates. *Econometrica* 53: 385–407. [CrossRef]

(Dayanik and Karatzas 2003) Dayanik, Savas, and Ioannis Karatzas. 2003. On the optimal stopping problem for one-dimensional diffusions. *Stochastic Processes and their Applications* 107: 173–212. [CrossRef]

(Dixit and Pindyck 1994) Dixit, Avinash K., and Robert S. Pindyck. 1994. *Investment under Uncertainty*. Princeton: Princeton University Press.

(Érdelyi et al. 1953) Érdelyi, Arthur, Wilhelm Magnus, Fritz Oberhettinger, and Francesco G. Tricomi. 1953. *Higher Transcendental Functions*. New York: McGraw Hill, vol. 2.

(Fudenberg et al. 1991) Fudenberg, Drew, and Jean Tirole. 1991. *Game Theory*. Cambridge: MIT Press.

(Ghaffari and Venkatesh 2013) Ghaffari, Reza, and Bala Venkatesh. 2013. Options based reserve procurement strategy for wind generators— Using binomial trees. *IEEE Transactions on Power Systems* 28: 1063–72. [CrossRef]

(IRENA 2017) IRENA. 2017. *Electricity Storageand Renewables: Costs and Markets to 2030*. Technical Report. Abu Dhabi: International Renewable Energy Agency.

(Just and Weber 2008) Just, Sebastian, and Christoph Weber. 2008. Pricing of reserves: Valuing system reserve capacity against spot prices in electricity markets. *Energy Economics* 30: 3198–221. [CrossRef]

(Karatzas and Shreve 1991) Karatzas, Ioannis, and Steven Shreve. 1991. *Brownian Motion and Stochastic Calculus*. New York: Springer.

(King et al. 2011) King, Jack, Brendan Kirby, Michael Milligan, and Steve Beuning. 2011. *Flexibility Reserve Reductions from an Energy Imbalance Market with High Levels of Wind Energy in the Western Interconnection*. Technical Report. Golden: National Renewable Energy Laboratory (NREL).

(Lenhart et al. 2016) Lenhart, Stephanie, Natalie Nelson-Marsh, Elizabeth J. Wilson, and David Solan. 2016. Electricity governance and the Western energy imbalance market in the United States: The necessity of interorganizational collaboration. *Energy Research & Social Science* 19: 94–107.

(Lutz 2009) Lutz, Björn. 2009. *Pricing of Derivatives on Mean-Reverting Assets*. Lecture Notes in Economics and Mathematical Systems. Berlin/Heidelberg: Springer.

(Mastropietro et al. 2018) Mastropietro, Paolo, Fulvio Fontini, Pablo Rodilla, and Carlos Batlle. 2018. The Italian capacity remuneration mechanism: Critical review and open questions. *Energy Policy* 123: 659–69. [CrossRef]

(Moriarty and Palczewski 2017) Moriarty, John, and Jan Palczewski. 2017. Real option valuation for reserve capacity. *European Journal of Operational Research* 257: 251–60. [CrossRef]

(National Grid ESO 2019a) National Grid ESO. 2019. Enhanced Frequency Response. Available online: https://www.nationalgrideso.com/balancing-services/frequency-response-services/enhanced-frequency-response-efr (accessed on 9 April 2019).

(National Grid ESO 2019b) National Grid ESO. 2019. Future of Balancing Services. Available online: https://www.nationalgrideso.com/insights/future-balancing-services (accessed on 9 April 2019).

(New Zealand Electricity Authority 2016) New Zealand Electricity Authority. 2016. What the System Operator Does. Available online: https://www.ea.govt.nz/operations/market-operation-service-providers/system-operator/what-the-system-operator-does/ (accessed on 9 April 2019).

(Ocker and Ehrhart 2017) Ocker, Fabian, and Karl-Martin Ehrhart. 2017. The "German paradox" in the balancing power markets. *Renewable and Sustainable Energy Reviews* 67: 892–8. [CrossRef]

(Peskir and Shiryaev 2006) Peskir, Goran, and Albert Shiryaev. 2006. *Optimal Stopping and Free-Boundary Problems*. Berlin/Heidelberg: Springer.

(Pflug and Broussev 2009) Pflug, Georg C., and Nikola Broussev. 2009. Electricity swing options: Behavioral models and pricing. *European Journal of Operational Research* 197: 1041–50. [CrossRef]

(Szabó and Martyr 2017) Szabó, Dávid Zoltán, and Randall Martyr. 2017. Real option valuation of a decremental regulation service provided by electricity storage. *Philosophical Transactions of the Royal Society of A* 375: 20160300.

(UK Office of Gas and Electricity Markets 2017) UK Office of Gas and Electricity Markets. 2017. Upgrading Our Energy System. Available online: https://www.gov.uk/government/publications/upgrading-our-energy-system-smart-systems-and-flexibility-plan (accessed on 9 April 2019).

(Western EIM 2019) Western EIM. 2019. Western Energy Imbalance Market. Available online: https://www.westerneim.com (accessed on 9 April 2019).

(Xu et al. 2016) Xu, Bolun, Yury Dvorkin, Daniel S. Kirschen, C. A. Silva-Monroy, and Jean-Paul Watson. 2016. A comparison of policies on the participation of storage in U.S. frequency regulation markets. Paper presented at 2016 IEEE Power and Energy Society General Meeting (PESGM), Boston, MA, USA, July 17–21.

(Zervos et al. 2013) Zervos, Mihail, Timothy C. Johnson, and Fares Alazemi. 2013. Buy-low and sell-high investment strategies. *Mathematical Finance* 23: 560–78. [CrossRef]

© 2019 by the authors. Licensee MDPI, Basel, Switzerland. This article is an open access article distributed under the terms and conditions of the Creative Commons Attribution (CC BY) license (http://creativecommons.org/licenses/by/4.0/).

risks

MDPI

Article

Optimal Portfolio Selection in an Itô–Markov Additive Market

Zbigniew Palmowski [1,*], **Łukasz Stettner** [2,3] **and Anna Sulima** [4]

[1] Department of Applied Mathematics, Faculty of Pure and Applied Mathematics, Wrocław University of Science and Technology, 50-370 Wrocław, Poland
[2] Institute of Mathematics, Polish Academy of Sciences, 00-656 Warsaw, Poland; stettner@impan.pl
[3] Vistula University, 02-787 Warsaw, Poland
[4] Faculty of Management, Computer Science and Finance, Wrocław University of Economics, 53-345 Wrocław, Poland; anna.sulima@wp.pl
* Correspondence: zbigniew.palmowski@pwr.edu.pl or zbigniew.palmowski@gmail.com; Tel.: +48-71-320-2012

Received: 8 December 2018; Accepted: 18 March 2019; Published: 25 March 2019

Abstract: We study a portfolio selection problem in a continuous-time Itô–Markov additive market with prices of financial assets described by Markov additive processes that combine Lévy processes and regime switching models. Thus, the model takes into account two sources of risk: the jump diffusion risk and the regime switching risk. For this reason, the market is incomplete. We complete the market by enlarging it with the use of a set of Markovian jump securities, Markovian power-jump securities and impulse regime switching securities. Moreover, we give conditions under which the market is asymptotic-arbitrage-free. We solve the portfolio selection problem in the Itô–Markov additive market for the power utility and the logarithmic utility.

Keywords: Markov additive processes; Markov regime switching market; Markovian jump securities; asymptotic arbitrage; complete market; optimal portfolio

1. Introduction

The portfolio selection problem is an important issue in financial mathematics. The problem is to invest an initial wealth in financial assets so as to maximize the expected utility of the terminal wealth. Markowitz (1952) for the first time used the quantitative methods for the optimal portfolio selection problem and proposed the mean-variance approach for portfolio optimization. Explicit solutions for the portfolio selection problem in continuous time were first given by Merton (1971, 1980).

Although Merton's approach produces significant theoretical results, it has some shortcomings coming from daily practice. The first is related to the assumption that the dynamics of a risky asset follows a geometric Brownian motion. Many investigations (e.g., Black et al. (1972) and Merton (1976)) have suggested that this market model cannot describe perfectly some empirical behaviors of financial markets, such as the asymmetry and heavy-tailedness of the distribution of returns of a time-varying volatility. To model this, the stock price driven by a Lévy process is a better choice. The portfolio selection problem on a Lévy market was considered by Niu (2008) and Corcuera et al. (2006).

The second important assumption in the original Black–Scholes–Merton model is that the coefficients are fixed. However, this assumption may not be satisfied over long time period, where structural changes in macroeconomic conditions may occur several times. Therefore, Markov modulated models (otherwise called regime switching) were proposed instead. In such models, the set of model parameters change in time according to a Markov chain, the transitions of which correspond to changes in the state of the economy. Hence, regime switching models describe perfectly structural macroeconomic changes and various business cycles (Zhang 2001). Hamilton (1989) pioneered econometric applications of regime switching models. These models have many applications in finance (Buffington and Elliott 2002; Di Masi et al. 1994; Elliott et al. 2001, 2003, 2005; Goldfeld and Quandt 1973; Guo 2001; Naik 1993; Tong 1978).

There is a growing literature dealing with portfolio optimization problems in markets with non-constant coefficients. Most of these papers assume that the external process is a diffusion process itself, like in the established volatility model of Heston (1993) or in the Ho–Lee and the Vasicek model of Korn and Kraft (2001). Bäuerle and Rieder (2004) and Rieder and Bäuerle (2005) studied the portfolio optimization problem with an observable and an unobservable Markov-modulated drift, respectively. This problem under stochastic volatility was considered by Pham and Quenez (2001) and Fleming and Hernández-Hernández (2003). In contrast to diffusion volatility, Markov chain volatility has the advantage that many portfolio problems have explicit solution. Moreover, a diffusion process can be approximated arbitrarily closely by a continuous-time Markov chain (Kushner and Dupuis 1992).

Portfolio optimization problems have also been studied in financial markets with regime switching. One of the first papers was by Zariphopoulou (1992), who maximized the utility of consumption under proportional transaction costs in a market where stock returns are determined by a continuous-time Markov chain, and established a viscosity property of the value function. The results of Zariphopoulou were extended by many authors, among them Bäuerle and Rieder (2004, 2007), Fontana et al. (2015), Framstad et al. (2004), Zhang and Yin (2004) and Stockbridge (2002). To solve the problem of maximizing the investor's expected utility of terminal wealth, some authors used numerical methods (Sass and Haussmann 2004; Nagai and Runggaldier 2008; Shen et al. 2012; Fu et al. 2014). Zhang et al. (2010) solved the portfolio selection problem without transition cost in a continuous-time Markovian regime switching Black–Scholes–Merton market. They obtained closed-form solutions for the optimal portfolio strategies when utility function is logarithmic or power-type. Similar results for a Black–Scholes market with regime switching were obtained by Liu (2014), Guo et al. (2005) and Sotomayor and Cadenillas (2013). A discrete time set up was also considered by Yin and Zhou (2004). For the mean-variance portfolio selection problem of this type, we refer to Zhou and Yin (2003). Regime switching was also analyzed by Tu (2010) in a Bayesian setting with model uncertainty and parameter uncertainty. He showed that the economic cost of ignoring regime switching can exceed two percent per year. Bae et al. (2014) constructed a program to optimize portfolios in the above mentioned framework and proved that adding Markov modulation improves risk management. Finally, further applications include large investor models Busch et al. (2013) and optimal productmanagement Korn et al. (2017).

In this paper, we consider a market with the prices of financial assets described by Itô–Markov additive processes, which combine Lévy processes and regime switching models. Such a process evolves as an Itô–Lévy process between changes of states of a Markov chain, that is, its parameters depend on the current state of the Markov chain. In addition, a transition of the Markov chain from state i to state j triggers an additional jump. Itô–Markov additive processes are classical in modeling queues, insurance risks, inventories, data communication, finance, environmental problems and in many other applications (Asmussen 2003; Prabhu 1998, chp. 7, and references therein).

The goal of this paper is to construct a general approach of building the optimal portfolio taking into account the asset jumps and possibility of changing environment by considering asset prices modeled by Itô–Markov additive processes. In particular, we assume that the interest rate and the volatility of the financial assets depend on a continuous-time finite-state Markov chain. Thus, our model takes into account two sources of risk: the jump diffusion risk and the regime switching risk. The jump diffusion risk refers to the source of risk due to fluctuations of market prices modeled by a Poisson random measure, while the regime switching risk refers to the source of risk due to transitions of economic conditions.

Due to the presence of these sources of risk, our market model is incomplete. In this paper, we show how to complete the Itô–Markov additive market model by adding Markovian jump securities, Markovian power-jump securities and impulse regime switching securities. Using these securities, all contingent claims can be replicated by a self-financing portfolio. The main idea of completing a Markovian regime switching market is inspired by Corcuera et al. (2005, 2006), Guo (2001), Karatzas et al. (1991), Niu (2008) and Zhang et al. (2012). However, adding the possibility of jumps of underlying markets when Markov chain changes its state produces more complex analysis that one presented in Corcuera et al. (2005, 2006).Moreover, we give conditions for the market to be asymptotic-arbitrage-free, namely, we find a martingale measure under which all the discounted price processes are martingales.

In this paper, we also consider the problem of identifying the optimal strategy that maximizes the expected value of the utility function of the wealth process at the end of some fixed period. The analysis is conducted for the logarithmic and power utility functions. To solve the main problem of determining the optimal portfolio we do not use dynamic programming but the direct differentiation approach.

This paper is organized as follows. In Section 2, we present the dynamics of the price process in an Itô–Markov additive market. In Section 3, we enlarge this market by Markovian jump securities, Markovian power-jump securities and impulse regime switching securities. In Sections 4 and 5, we show that the enlarged market is asymptotic-arbitrage-free and complete. In Section 6, we state the portfolio optimization problem and solve it for the power utility with risk aversion and the logarithmic utility function. Moreover, Section 7 gives a relationship between finite and infinite markets.

2. Market Model

Let $(\Omega, \mathcal{F}, \mathbb{P})$ be a complete probability space and let $\mathbb{T} := [0, T]$, for fixed $0 < T < \infty$, represent the maturity time for all economic activities. On this probability space, we consider the observable and continuous-time Markov chain $J := \{J(t) : t \in \mathbb{T}\}$ with a finite state space. The role of the Markov chain is to ensure that the parameters change according to the market environment and the different states of the Markov chain represent the different states of the economy. For simplicity, we follow the notation of Elliott et al. (1994) and we identify the state space with the standard basis $E := \{\mathbf{e}_1, \dots, \mathbf{e}_N\}$. Here, $\mathbf{e}_i \in \mathbb{R}^N$ and the jth component of $\mathbf{e}_i$ is the Kronecker delta δ_{ij} for each $i, j = 1, \dots, N$. Moreover, the Markov chain J is characterized by an intensity matrix $[\lambda_{ij}]_{i,j=1}^N$. The element λ_{ij} is the transition intensity of the Markov chain J jumping from state $\mathbf{e}_i$ to state $\mathbf{e}_j$. We assume $\lambda_{ij} > 0$ for $i \neq j$. Note that $\sum_{j=1}^{N} \lambda_{ij} = 0$, thus $\lambda_{ii} < 0$.

2.1. Risk-Free Asset

Now, we describe the dynamic of the price process of risk-free asset B as follows:

$$\mathrm{d}B(t) = r(t)B(t)\mathrm{d}t, \qquad B(0) = 1. \tag{1}$$

Here, r is the interest rate of B and it is modulated by Markov chain J

$$r(t) := \langle \mathbf{r}, J(t) \rangle = \sum_{i=1}^{N} r_i \langle \mathbf{e}_i, J(t) \rangle,$$

where $\mathbf{r} = (r_1, \dots, r_N)' \in \mathbb{R}_+^N$ and $\langle \cdot, \cdot \rangle$ is a scalar product in $\mathbb{R}^N$. The value r_i represents the value of the interest rate when the Markov chain is in the state space $\mathbf{e}_i$.

2.2. Risky Asset

We consider the market with risky asset modeled by (non-anticipative) Itô–Markov additive processes.

A process $(J, X) = \{(J(t), X(t)) : t \in \mathbb{T}\}$ on the state space $\{\mathbf{e}_1, \dots, \mathbf{e}_N\} \times \mathbb{R}$ is a Markov additive process (MAP) if (J, X) is a Markov process and the conditional distribution of $(J(s+t), X(s+t) - X(s))$ for $s, t \in \mathbb{T}$, given $(J(s), X(s))$, depends only on $J(s)$ (Çinlar 1972a, 1972b). Every MAP has a very special structure. It is usually said that X is the additive component and J is the background process representing the environment. Moreover, the process X evolves as a Itô–Lévy process while $J(t) = \mathbf{e}_j$, that is, $X(t) = X^j(t)$ for some Itô–Lévy process $X^j(t)$ with parameters depending on $\mathbf{e}_j$ if $J(t) = \mathbf{e}_j$. In addition, transition of J from $\mathbf{e}_i$ to $\mathbf{e}_j$ triggers a jump of X distributed as $U_n^{(i)}$.

Following Asmussen and Kella (2000), we can decompose the process X as follows:

$$X(t) = \overline{X}(t) + \overline{\overline{X}}(t), \tag{2}$$

where

$$\overline{\overline{X}}(t) := \sum_{i=1}^{N} \Psi_i(t)$$

for

$$\Psi_i(t) := \sum_{n\geq 1} U_n^{(i)} \mathbf{1}_{\{J(T_n-)=\mathbf{e}_i,\, T_n\leq t\}} \tag{3}$$

and for the jump epochs $\{T_n\}$ of J. Here, $U_n^{(i)}$ $(n \geq 1, 1 \leq i \leq N)$ are independent random variables, which are also independent of $\overline{X}$ such that, for every fixed i, the random variables $U_n^{(i)}$ are identically distributed. Note that we can express the process Ψ_i as follows:

$$\Psi_i(t) = \int_0^t \int_{\mathbb{R}} x\, \Pi_U^i(\mathrm{d}s, \mathrm{d}x)$$

for the point measure

$$\Pi_U^i([0,t], \mathrm{d}x) := \sum_{n\geq 1} \mathbf{1}_{\{U_n^{(i)}\in \mathrm{d}x\}} \mathbf{1}_{\{J(T_n)=\mathbf{e}_i,\, T_n\leq t\}}, \quad i = 1, \ldots, N. \tag{4}$$

Moreover, we define the compensated point measure $\bar{\Pi}_U^i(\mathrm{d}t, \mathrm{d}x) := \Pi_U^i(\mathrm{d}t, \mathrm{d}x) - \lambda_i(t)\eta_i(\mathrm{d}x)\mathrm{d}t$ for $\lambda_j(t) := \sum_{i\neq j} \mathbf{1}_{\{J(t-)=\mathbf{e}_i\}}\lambda_{ij}$ and $\eta_i(\mathrm{d}x) = \mathbb{P}(U_n^{(i)} \in \mathrm{d}x)$.

Remark 1. *One can consider jumps $U^{(ij)}$ with distribution depending also on the state $\mathbf{e}_j$ the Markov chain is jumping to by extending the state space to the pairs $(\mathbf{e}_i, \mathbf{e}_j)$ (see Gautam et al. (1999, Thm. 5) for details).*

The first component in the definition in Equation (2) is an Itô–Lévy process and it has the following decomposition (Øksendal and Sulem 2004, p. 5):

$$\overline{X}(t) := \overline{X}(0) + \int_0^t \mu_0(s)\mathrm{d}s + \int_0^t \sigma_0(s)\mathrm{d}W(s) + \int_0^t \int_{\mathbb{R}} \gamma(s-, x)\bar{\Pi}(\mathrm{d}s, \mathrm{d}x), \tag{5}$$

where W denotes the standard Brownian motion independent of J and $\bar{\Pi}(\mathrm{d}t, \mathrm{d}x) := \Pi(\mathrm{d}t, \mathrm{d}x) - \nu(\mathrm{d}x)\mathrm{d}t$ is the compensated Poisson random measure, which is independent of J and W. Furthermore, we define

$$\mu_0(t) := \langle \boldsymbol{\mu}_0, J(t)\rangle = \sum_{i=1}^{N} \mu_0^i \langle \mathbf{e}_i, J(t)\rangle, \tag{6}$$

$$\sigma_0(t) := \langle \boldsymbol{\sigma}_0, J(t)\rangle = \sum_{i=1}^{N} \sigma_0^i \langle \mathbf{e}_i, J(t)\rangle, \tag{7}$$

$$\gamma(t, x) := \langle \boldsymbol{\gamma}(x), J(t)\rangle = \sum_{i=1}^{N} \gamma_i(x) \langle \mathbf{e}_i, J(t)\rangle \tag{8}$$

for some vectors $\boldsymbol{\mu}_0 := (\mu_0^1, \ldots, \mu_0^N)' \in \mathbb{R}^N$, $\boldsymbol{\sigma}_0 := (\sigma_0^1, \ldots, \sigma_0^N)' \in \mathbb{R}_+^N$ with $\sigma_0^j > 0$ and the vector-valued measurable function $\boldsymbol{\gamma}(x) := (\gamma_1(x), \ldots, \gamma_N(x))$. The measure ν is the so-called jump-measure identifying the distribution of the sizes of the jumps of the Poisson measure Π.

The components $\overline{X}$ and $\overline{\overline{X}}$ in Equation (2) are conditionally, on the state of the Markov chain J, independent.

Additionally, we suppose that the Lévy measure satisfies, for some $\varepsilon > 0$ and $\varrho > 0$,

$$\int_{(-\varepsilon,\varepsilon)^c} \exp\left(\varrho|\gamma(s-,x)|\right)\nu(\mathrm{d}x) < \infty, \quad \int_{(-\varepsilon,\varepsilon)^c} \exp(\varrho x)\mathbb{P}(U^{(i)} \in \mathrm{d}x) < \infty, \tag{9}$$

for $i = 1, \ldots, N$. This implies that

$$\int_{\mathbb{R}} |\gamma(s-,x)|^k \nu(\mathrm{d}x) < \infty, \quad \mathbb{E}(U^{(i)})^k < \infty, \quad i = 1, \ldots, N, \ k \geq 2,$$

and that the characteristic function $\mathbb{E}[\exp(kiX)]$ is analytic in a neighborhood of 0. Moreover, X has moments of all orders and the polynomials are dense in $L^2(\mathbb{R}, \mathrm{d}\varphi(t,x))$, where $\varphi(t,x) := \mathbb{P}(X(t) \leq x)$. Itô–Markov additive processes are a natural generalization of Itô–Lévy processes and thus of Lévy processes. Moreover, the structure in Equation (2) explains the used name and can be seen as *Markov-modulated Itô–Lévy process*. Indeed, if $\gamma(s,x) = x$, then X is a Markov additive process. If additionally $N = 1$, then X is a Lévy process. If $U^{(i)} \equiv 0$ and $N > 1$ then X is a Markov modulated Lévy process (Pacheco et al. 2009). If there are no jumps, that is, $\bar{\Pi}(\mathrm{d}s, \mathrm{d}x) = 0$, we have a Markov modulated Brownian motion.

We assume the evolution of the price process of the risky asset S_0 is governed by the Itô–Markov additive process as follows:

$$\begin{cases} \mathrm{d}S_0(t) = S_0(t-)\left[\mu_0(t)\mathrm{d}t + \sigma_0(t)\mathrm{d}W(t) + \int_{\mathbb{R}} \gamma(t-,x)\bar{\Pi}(\mathrm{d}t,\mathrm{d}x) + \sum_{i=1}^{N} \int_{\mathbb{R}} x\bar{\Pi}^i_U(\mathrm{d}t,\mathrm{d}x)\right], \\ S_0(0) = s_0 > 0. \end{cases} \tag{10}$$

To ensure that $S_0(t)$ is non-negative, we additionally assume that

$$\Delta \int_{\mathbb{R}} \gamma(t-,x)\bar{\Pi}(\mathrm{d}t,\mathrm{d}x) > -1, \qquad \Delta \int_{\mathbb{R}} x\bar{\Pi}^i_U(\mathrm{d}t,\mathrm{d}x) > -1, \quad i = 1, \ldots N, \tag{11}$$

where $\Delta Z_t = Z_t - Z_{t-}$ is a jump process related with a processes Z. The last assumption is equivalent to

$$\Delta\Psi_i(t) > -1$$

and it is satisfied when all U^i $(i = 1, \ldots, N)$ have support included in $(-1, +\infty)$. We interpret the coefficient μ_0 defined in Equation (6) as the appreciation rate and σ_0 defined in Equation (7) as the volatility of the risky asset for each $i = 1, \ldots, N$. Similarly, μ_0^i and σ_0^i represent the appreciation rate and the volatility of the risky asset, respectively, when the Markov chain is in state $\mathbf{e}_i$. We assume that

$$\mu_0^i > r_i, \quad i = 1, \ldots, N.$$

Otherwise, stocks would be just a bad investment.

3. Enlarging the Itô–Markov Additive Market

Now, we enlarge the primary market by some financial assets: Markovian jump securities, Markovian power-jump securities and impulse regime switching securities in order to complete the market.

From now, we work with the following filtration on $(\Omega, \mathcal{F}, \mathbb{P})$:

$$\mathcal{F}_t := \mathcal{G}_t \vee \mathcal{N},$$

where $\mathcal{N}$ are the $\mathbb{P}$-null sets of $\mathcal{F}$ and

$$\mathcal{G}_t := \sigma\{J(s), W(s), \Gamma(s), \Pi_U^1([0,s], \mathrm{d}x), \ldots, \Pi_U^N([0,s], \mathrm{d}x); s \leq t\}$$

for

$$\Gamma(t) := \int_0^t \int_{\mathbb{R}} \gamma(s-, x)\Pi(\mathrm{d}s, \mathrm{d}x).$$

Note that the filtration $\{\mathcal{F}_t\}_{t\geq 0}$ is right-continuous (Karatzas and Shreve 1998, Prop. 7.7 and also Protter 2005, Thm. 31). By the same arguments as in the proof of Thm. 3.3. of Liao (2004), the filtration $\{\mathcal{G}_t\}_{t\geq 0}$ can be represented as

$$\sigma\{J(s), \overline{X}(s), \Pi_U^1([0,s], \mathrm{d}x), \ldots, \Pi_U^N([0,s], \mathrm{d}x); s \leq t\}.$$

3.1. Markovian Jump Securities

Let T_n $(n = 1, 2, \ldots)$ denote the jump epochs of the chain J, where $0 < T_1 < T_2 < \ldots$ We observe that the Markov chain J can be represented in terms of a marked point process Φ_j defined by

$$\Phi_j(t) := \Phi([0,t] \times \mathbf{e}_j) = \sum_{n\geq 1} \mathbf{1}_{\{J(T_n)=\mathbf{e}_j,\, T_n \leq t\}}, \ j = 1, \ldots, N.$$

Note that the process Φ_j describes the number of jumps into state $\mathbf{e}_j$ up to time t. Let ϕ_j be the dual predictable projection of Φ_j (sometimes called the compensator). That is, the process

$$\overline{\Phi}_j(t) := \Phi_j(t) - \phi_j(t), \ j = 1, \ldots, N, \tag{12}$$

is an $\{\mathcal{F}_t\}$-martingale and it is called the jth Markovian jump martingale. Note that ϕ_j is unique and

$$\phi_j(t) := \int_0^t \lambda_j(s)\mathrm{d}s,$$

for

$$\lambda_j(t) := \sum_{i\neq j} \mathbf{1}_{\{J(t-)=\mathbf{e}_i\}}\lambda_{ij}; \tag{13}$$

see Zhang et al. (2012, p. 290).

Now, we consider geometric Markovian jump securities S_j (for $j = 1, \ldots, N$) with evolution of prices described by marked point local martingales as follows:

$$\begin{cases} \mathrm{d}S_j(t) = S_j(t-)\left[\mu_j(t)\mathrm{d}t + \sigma_j(t-)\mathrm{d}\overline{\Phi}_j(t)\right], \\ S_j(0) > 0, \end{cases} \tag{14}$$

where the appreciation rate μ_j and the volatility σ_j are given by

$$\mu_j(t) := \langle \boldsymbol{\mu}_j, J(t)\rangle = \sum_{i=1}^N \mu_j^i \langle \mathbf{e}_i, J(t)\rangle,$$

$$\sigma_j(t) := \langle \boldsymbol{\sigma}_j, J(t)\rangle = \sum_{i=1}^N \sigma_j^i \langle \mathbf{e}_i, J(t)\rangle$$

with $\boldsymbol{\mu}_j := (\mu_j^1, \ldots, \mu_j^N)' \in \mathbb{R}^N$ and $\boldsymbol{\sigma}_j := (\sigma_j^1, \ldots, \sigma_j^N)' \in \mathbb{R}_+^N$.

3.2. Markovian Power-Jump Securities

Following Corcuera et al. (2005), we introduce the power-jump processes

$$X^{(k)}(t) := \sum_{0<s\leq t} (\Delta\overline{X}(s))^k, \qquad k \geq 2,$$

where $\Delta\overline{X}(s) = \overline{X}(s) - \overline{X}(s-)$. We set $X^{(1)}(t) = \overline{X}(t)$. The process $X^{(k)}$ is also an Itô–Lévy process with the same jump times as the original process $\overline{X}$ but with their sizes being the kth powers of the jump sizes of $\overline{X}$. From Protter (2005, p. 29), we have

$$\mathbb{E}\left[X^{(k)}(t)|\mathcal{J}_t\right] = \mathbb{E}\Big(\sum_{0<s\leq t} (\Delta\overline{X}(s))^k|\mathcal{J}_t\Big) = \int_0^t \int_{\mathbb{R}} \gamma^k(s-,x)\nu(\mathrm{d}x)\mathrm{d}s < \infty, \mathbb{P} - a.e. \qquad k \geq 2,$$

for $\mathcal{J}_t := \sigma\{J(s) : s \leq t\}$. Hence, the processes

$$\overline{X}^{(k)}(t) := X^{(k)}(t) - \int_0^t \int_{\mathbb{R}} \gamma^k(s-,x)\nu(\mathrm{d}x)\mathrm{d}s, \qquad k \geq 2,$$

are $\{\mathcal{F}_t\}$-martingales (called Teugels martingales of order k; see Schoutens (1999) for details).

We additionally enlarge the market with a series of Markovian kth-power-jump assets $S^{(k)}$ (for $k \geq 2$). The price process of $S^{(k)}$ is described by the stochastic differential equation

$$\begin{cases} \mathrm{d}S^{(k)}(t) = S^{(k)}(t-)\left[\mu^{(k)}(t)\mathrm{d}t + \sigma^{(k)}(t-)\mathrm{d}\overline{X}^{(k)}(t)\right], \\ S^{(k)}(0) > 0, \end{cases} \tag{15}$$

where the coefficients are determined by the Markov chain J, namely:

$$\mu^{(k)}(t) := \langle \boldsymbol{\mu}^{(k)}, J(t)\rangle = \sum_{j=1}^N \mu_j^{(k)}\langle \mathbf{e}_j, J(t)\rangle \quad \text{and} \quad \sigma^{(k)}(t) := \langle \boldsymbol{\sigma}^{(k)}, J(t)\rangle = \sum_{j=1}^N \sigma_j^{(k)}\langle \mathbf{e}_j, J(t)\rangle$$

for $\boldsymbol{\mu}^{(k)} := (\mu_1^{(k)}, \ldots, \mu_N^{(k)})' \in \mathbb{R}^N$ and $\boldsymbol{\sigma}^{(k)} := (\sigma_1^{(k)}, \ldots, \sigma_N^{(k)})' \in \mathbb{R}_+^N$. The positivity of these asset prices follow from assumption in Equation (11).

3.3. Impulse Regime Switching Securities

We will also need power martingales related to the second component of X given in Equation (2), namely to $\overline{\overline{X}}$ or to Ψ_i, defined in Equation (3). For $l \geq 1$ and $i = 1, \ldots, N$ we define

$$\Psi_i^{(l)}(t) := \sum_{n\geq 1} \left(U_n^{(i)}\right)^l \mathbf{1}_{\{J(T_n)=\mathbf{e}_i,\, T_n\leq t\}} = \int_0^t \int_{\mathbb{R}} x^l\, \Pi_U^i(\mathrm{d}s, \mathrm{d}x)$$

for Π_U^i given by Equation (4). The compensated version of $\Psi_i^{(l)}$ is called an impulse regime switching martingale if

$$\overline{\Psi}_i^{(l)}(t) := \Psi_i^{(l)}(t) - \mathbb{E}(U_n^{(i)})^l \phi_i(t) = \int_0^t \int_{\mathbb{R}} x^l\, \bar{\Pi}_U^i(\mathrm{d}s, \mathrm{d}x),$$

where $\bar{\Pi}_U^i(\mathrm{d}t, \mathrm{d}x) = \Pi_U^i(\mathrm{d}t, \mathrm{d}x) - \lambda_i(t)\eta_i(\mathrm{d}x)\mathrm{d}t$ for λ_i defined in Equation (13) and $\eta_i(\mathrm{d}x) = \mathbb{P}(U_n^{(i)} \in \mathrm{d}x)$.

We characterize the evolution of impulse regime switching securities $S_i^{(l)}$ as follows:

$$\begin{cases} \mathrm{d}S_i^{(l)}(t) = S_i^{(l)}(t-)\left[\mu_i^{(l)}(t)\mathrm{d}t + \sigma_i^{(l)}(t-)\mathrm{d}\overline{\Psi}_i^{(l)}(t)\right], \\ S_i^{(l)}(0) > 0, \end{cases} \tag{16}$$

where the coefficients are determined by the Markov chain J, namely:

$$\mu_i^{(l)}(t) := \langle \boldsymbol{\mu}_i^{(l)}, J(t)\rangle = \sum_{j=1}^{N} \mu_{i,j}^{(l)} \langle \mathbf{e}_j, J(t)\rangle; \quad \sigma_i^{(l)}(t) := \langle \boldsymbol{\sigma}_i^{(l)}, J(t)\rangle = \sum_{j=1}^{N} \sigma_{i,j}^{(l)} \langle \mathbf{e}_j, J(t)\rangle$$

for $\boldsymbol{\mu}_i^{(l)} := (\mu_{i,1}^{(l)}, \ldots, \mu_{i,N}^{(l)})' \in \mathbb{R}^N$ and $\boldsymbol{\sigma}_i^{(l)} := (\sigma_{i,1}^{(l)}, \ldots, \sigma_{i,N}^{(l)})' \in \mathbb{R}_+^N$ ($i = 1, \ldots, N$ and $l \geq 1$). The positivity of these asset prices follow from assumption in Equation (11).

Combining Equations (1), (10), (14)–(16), we get an enlarged Itô–Markov additive market:

$$\begin{cases} dB(t) = r(t)B(t)dt, \\ dS_0(t) = S_0(t-)\Big[\mu_0(t)dt + \sigma_0(t)dW(t) + \int_{\mathbb{R}} \gamma(t-, x)\bar{\Pi}(dt, dx) + \sum_{i=1}^{N} \int_{\mathbb{R}} x\bar{\Pi}_U^i(dt, dx)\Big], \\ dS_j(t) = S_j(t-)\Big[\mu_j(t)dt + \sigma_j(t-)d\overline{\Phi}_j(t)\Big], \\ dS^{(k)}(t) = S^{(k)}(t-)\Big[\mu^{(k)}(t)dt + \sigma^{(k)}(t-)d\overline{X}^{(k)}(t)\Big], \\ dS_i^{(l)}(t) = S_i^{(l)}(t-)\Big[\mu_i^{(l)}(t)dt + \sigma_i^{(l)}(t-)d\overline{\Psi}_i^{(l)}(t)\Big], \end{cases} \tag{17}$$

for $i, j = 1, \ldots, N$, $k \geq 2$ and $l \geq 1$. Note that this enlarged market has infinitely many securities. In Section 5, we prove that under a new martingale measure this market is complete. Note that μ_j, $\mu^{(k)}$, $\mu_i^{(l)}$, σ_j, $\sigma^{(k)}$ and $\sigma_i^{(l)}$ are artificial parameters and can be changed later.

Following Corcuera et al. (2005), the use of power-jump assets of order two can be motivated by a quadratic variation process (Barndorff-Nielsen and Shephard 2003, 2004) and so-called realized variance. Contracts on realized variance are traded regularly on OTC markets. Typically, a 3rd-power-jump asset measures a kind of asymmetry ("skewness") and a 4th-power-jump process measures extremal movements ("kurtosis"). This type of contracts could be also traded. Moreover, one can construct an insurance contracts against a crash based on 4th-power-jump (or ith-power-jump, $i > 4$) assets. Power-jumps processes appear in other financial-insurance contracts that hedge Lévy jumps as well, e.g., in COS and CDS contracts.

4. Martingale Measure and Asymptotic Arbitrage

Considering a financial market containing an infinite number of assets, Kabanov and Kramkov (1994) introduced the notion of large financial market. This type of market is described by a sequence of market models with a finite number of securities each, also called small markets. Kabanov and Kramkov (1994) introduced an extension of the classical approach to arbitrage theory, namely arbitrage in a large financial market, called asymptotic arbitrage. A deep study of asymptotic arbitrage was carried out by Kabanov and Kramkov (1998) and Björk and Näslund (1998).

In this section we identify a martingale measure in our Itô–Markov additive market and prove that this market model is asymptotic-arbitrage-free.

Let us start with the definition of *asymptotic arbitrage*. Following (Björk and Näslund 1998, Def. 6.1), we say that there is an asymptotic arbitrage opportunity if we have a sequence of strategies such that, for some real number $c > 0$, the value process V^n on a finite market satisfies:

- $V^n(t) \geq -c$ for each $0 < t \leq T$ and for each $n \in \mathbb{N}$;
- $V^n(0) = 0$ for each $n \in \mathbb{N}$;
- $\liminf_{n\to\infty} V^n(T) \geq 0$, $\mathbb{P}$-a.s; and
- $\mathbb{P}\big(\liminf_{n\to\infty} V^n(T) > 0\big) > 0$.

Proposition 1 (Björk and Näslund 1998, Prop. 6.1). *If there exists a martingale measure $\mathbb{Q}$ equivalent to $\mathbb{P}$, then the market is asymptotic-arbitrage-free.*

In this paper, we formulate the sufficient condition for absence of asymptotic arbitrage in a form of the existence of a martingale measure. Equivalent conditions for the existence of a so-called separated martingale measure can be found in Cuchiero et al. (2016) who introduced *No Asymptotic Free Lunch with Vanishing Risk* (NALFVR) condition (see also Kreps (1981)).

Now, we find a measure $\mathbb{Q}$ under which the discounted price processes are martingales.

Let $\mathcal{L}^2(W)$ be the set of all predictable, $\{\mathcal{F}_t\}$-adapted processes ξ such that $\mathbb{E}\int_0^T \xi^2(s)\mathrm{d}s < \infty$. Similarly, we define $\mathcal{L}^1(\phi_j)$, that is, $\xi \in \mathcal{L}^1(\phi_j)$ iff ξ is predictable, $\{\mathcal{F}_t\}$-adapted and satisfies $\mathbb{E}\int_0^T |\xi(s)|\lambda_j \mathrm{d}s < \infty$.

Proposition 2 (Boel and Kohlmann 1980, p. 515). *Let $\psi_0 \in \mathcal{L}^2(W)$, $\psi_j \in \mathcal{L}^1(\phi_j)$ for all $j = 1, \ldots, N$ and*

$$\psi_j(s) > -1. \tag{18}$$

Then,

$$\ell(t) := \exp\left[\int_0^t \psi_0(s)\mathrm{d}W(s) - \frac{1}{2}\int_0^t \psi_0^2(s)\mathrm{d}s - \sum_{j=1}^{N}\int_0^t \psi_j(s)\phi_j(\mathrm{d}s)\right] \tag{19}$$

$$\times \prod_{j=1}^{N} \prod_{\substack{J(t-)\neq J(t)\\ J(t)=e_j}} (1+\psi_j(t))$$

is a non-negative local martingale. If additionally $\mathbb{E}\ell(t) = 1$, then it is a true martingale.

From now on, we assume that

$$\mathbb{E}\ell(t) = 1. \tag{20}$$

Let $\mathbb{Q}$ be the probability measure defined by the Radon–Nikodym derivative

$$\ell(t) = \left.\frac{\mathrm{d}\mathbb{Q}}{\mathrm{d}\mathbb{P}}\right|_{\mathcal{F}_t}.$$

Then, ℓ, given in Equation (19), is the density process for the new martingale measure $\mathbb{Q}$. By adding a superscript $\mathbb{Q}$, we denote processes observed under this new measure. By a generalized version of Girsanov's theorem for jump-diffusion processes, we have the following theorem:

Theorem 1 (Boel and Kohlmann 1980, p. 517). *The process $\overline{X}$ given in Equation (5) under the new martingale measure $\mathbb{Q}$ has the form*

$$\overline{X}^{\mathbb{Q}}(t) = \int_0^t \sigma_0(s)\mathrm{d}W^{\mathbb{Q}}(s) + \int_0^t \int_{\mathbb{R}} \gamma(s-,x)\bar{\Pi}(\mathrm{d}s,\mathrm{d}x),$$

where

$$W^{\mathbb{Q}}(t) = W(t) - \int_0^t \psi_0(s)\mathrm{d}s$$

is a standard $\mathbb{Q}$-Brownian motion.

Moreover, for $j = 1, \ldots, N$, the process $\overline{\Phi}_j$ given in Equation (12) under the measure $\mathbb{Q}$ is a martingale and takes the form

$$\overline{\Phi}_j^{\mathbb{Q}}(t) = \Phi_j(t) - \int_0^t \Big(1+\psi_j(s)\Big)\phi_j(\mathrm{d}s),$$

that is, the unique predictable projection of Φ_j under $\mathbb{Q}$ is given by

$$\phi_j^{\mathbb{Q}}(t) = \int_0^t \Big(1+\psi_j(s)\Big)\phi_j(\mathrm{d}s).$$

Similarly, for $j = 1, \ldots, N$ and $l \geq 1$, the process $\overline{\Psi}_j^{(l)}$ given in Equation (12) under the measure $\mathbb{Q}$ is a martingale and takes the form

$$\overline{\Psi}_j^{(l),\mathbb{Q}}(t) = \Psi_j^{(l)}(t) - \mathbb{E}(U_n^{(i)})^l \phi_j^{\mathbb{Q}}(t).$$

Remark 2. *If ψ_0 and ψ_j ($j = 1, \ldots, N$) are bounded, then $\mathbb{E}\ell(t) = 1$ (see the Novikov condition in Karatzas and Shreve (1998, Cor. 3.5.13, p. 199) and Resnick (2007, Thm. 5.1, p. 135)).*

Note that $\overline{X}^{(k)}$ for $k \geq 2$ do not change their laws under the new measure $\mathbb{Q}$. Moreover, under $\mathbb{Q}$, the price processes are represented as follows:

$$\begin{cases} dB(t) = r(t)B(t)dt, \\ dS_0(t) = S_0(t-)\Big[\Big(\mu_0(t) + \sigma_0(t)\psi_0(t)\Big)dt + \sigma_0(t)dW^{\mathbb{Q}}(t) + \int\limits_{\mathbb{R}} \gamma(t-,x)\bar{\Pi}(dt,dx) + \sum\limits_{i=1}^{N}\int\limits_{\mathbb{R}} x\bar{\Pi}_U^i(dt,dx)\Big], \\ dS_j(t) = S_j(t-)\Big[\Big(\mu_j(t) + \sigma_j(t)\lambda_j(t)\psi_j(t)\Big)dt + \sigma_j(t-)d\overline{\Phi}_j^{\mathbb{Q}}(t)\Big], \\ dS^{(k)}(t) = S^{(k)}(t-)\Big[\mu^{(k)}(t)dt + \sigma^{(k)}(t-)d\overline{X}^{(k)}(t)\Big], \\ dS_i^{(l)}(t) = S_i^{(l)}(t-)\Big[\mu_i^{(l)}(t)dt + \sigma_i^{(l)}(t-)d\overline{\Psi}_i^{(l),\mathbb{Q}}(t)\Big], \end{cases}$$

for $i, j = 1, \ldots, N$, $k \geq 2$ and $l \geq 1$. Note that in the above equation we can take $r(t) = r(t-)$, $\mu_j(t) = \mu_j(t-)$ and $\sigma_j(t) = \sigma_j(t-)$ (for $j = 0, 1, \ldots, N$). In fact, by stochastic integration by parts, the discounted price processes are governed by

$$\begin{cases} d\tilde{S}_0(t) = \tilde{S}_0(t-)\Big[\Big(\mu_0(t-) + \sigma_0(t-)\psi_0(t) - r(t-)\Big)dt + \sigma_0(t)dW^{\mathbb{Q}}(t) + \int\limits_{\mathbb{R}} \gamma(t-,x)\bar{\Pi}(dt,dx) \\ \quad + \sum\limits_{i=1}^{N}\int\limits_{\mathbb{R}} x\bar{\Pi}_U^i(dt,dx)\Big], \\ d\tilde{S}_j(t) = \tilde{S}_j(t-)\Big[\Big(\mu_j(t-) + \sigma_j(t-)\lambda_j(t)\psi_j(t) - r(t-)\Big)dt + \sigma_j(t-)d\overline{\Phi}_j^{\mathbb{Q}}(t)\Big], \\ d\tilde{S}^{(k)}(t) = \tilde{S}^{(k)}(t-)\Big[\Big(\mu^{(k)}(t) - r(t)\Big)dt + \sigma^{(k)}(t-)d\overline{X}^{(k)}(t)\Big], \\ d\tilde{S}_i^{(l)}(t) = \tilde{S}_i^{(l)}(t-)\Big[\Big(\mu_i^{(l)}(t) - r(t)\Big)dt + \sigma_i^{(l)}(t-)d\overline{\Psi}_i^{(l),\mathbb{Q}}(t)\Big], \end{cases} \tag{21}$$

where $\tilde{S}_0(t) := B^{-1}(t)S_0(t)$, $\tilde{S}_j(t) := B^{-1}(t)S_j(t)$, $\tilde{S}^{(k)}(t) := B^{-1}(t)S^{(k)}(t)$ and $\tilde{S}_i^{(l)}(t) := B^{-1}(t)S_i^{(l)}(t)$. Hence, we require $\tilde{S}_0$, $\tilde{S}_j$, $\tilde{S}^{(k)}$ and $\tilde{S}_i^{(l)}$ to be local martingales (for $i, j = 1, \ldots, N$, $k \geq 2$ and $l \geq 1$). A necessary and sufficient condition for this to hold is given by the following equations:

$$\begin{cases} \mu_0(t-) + \sigma_0(t-)\psi_0(t) - r(t-) = 0, \\ \mu_j(t-) + \sigma_j(t-)\lambda_j(t)\psi_j(t) - r(t-) = 0, \\ \mu^{(k)}(t) - r(t) = 0, \\ \mu_i^{(l)}(t) - r(t) = 0, \\ \psi_j(t) > -1, \end{cases} \tag{22}$$

for $i, j = 1, \ldots, N$, $k \geq 2$ and $l \geq 1$.

Note that $\lambda_j(t) = 0$ if $J(t-) = \mathbf{e}_j$. Thus, in this case, if $\mu_j^j \neq r_j$, the martingale condition would never be satisfied. Therefore, the discounted price processes of all securities in the enlarged market would not be local martingales under $\mathbb{Q}$. Thus, we have to assume that $\mu_j^j = r_j$ for all $j = 1, \ldots, N$

to make the market asymptotic-arbitrage-free. From Equation (22), when $\lambda_j(t) \neq 0$ (i.e., $J(t-) \neq \mathbf{e}_j$), the processes ψ_0 and ψ_j are determined by

$$\begin{cases} \psi_0(t) = \dfrac{r(t-) - \mu_0(t-)}{\sigma_0(t-)}, \\ \psi_j(t) = \dfrac{r(t-) - \mu_j(t-)}{\sigma_j(t-)\lambda_j(t)}, \quad j = 1, \ldots, N, \end{cases} \tag{23}$$

where we assume that

$$r(t-) > \mu_j(t-) - \sigma_j(t-)\lambda_j(t) \tag{24}$$

to satisfy the condition in Equation (18).

Note that ψ_0 and ψ_j $(j = 1, \ldots, N)$ are bounded. Hence, by Remark 2, the density process ℓ is a true martingale. Note that ψ_j $(j = 1, \ldots, N)$ satisfies the assumptions of Proposition 2. We can only determine ψ_j when $J(t-) \neq \mathbf{e}_j$ for $j = 1, \ldots, N$ but this is sufficient to determine the equivalent martingale measure $\mathbb{Q}$. Indeed, if $J(t-) = \mathbf{e}_j$ for $j = 1, \ldots, N$, then $\phi_j(t) = 0$ and ψ_j has no influence on the value of the right side of Equation (19). The above analysis yields the following theorem.

Theorem 2. *Assume that $\mu_j^j = r_j$ for all $j = 1, \ldots, N$ and ψ_0 and ψ_j are given by Equation (23). Then, the discounted price processes of the securities in the enlarged market (Equation (21)) are local martingales under $\mathbb{Q}$ and this market is asymptotic-arbitrage-free.*

From now on, we assume that $\mu_j^j = r_j$ for all $j = 1, \ldots, N$.

5. Asymptotic Completeness of the Enlarged Market

Now, we analyze asymptotic completeness of the enlarged Itô–Markov additive market. A market is said to be complete if each claim can be replicated by a strategy, that is, the claim can be represented as a stochastic integral with respect to the asset prices. We take as class of contingent claims the set $L^2(\Omega, \mathcal{F}, \mathbb{Q})$ of square integrable random variables under the equivalent martingale measure; then, a self-financing strategy is represented as an integrable process and the value of a self-financing portfolio is represented as the stochastic integral of the strategy with respect to the assets. In the case of market models with an infinite number of assets, we define completeness in terms of approximate replication of claims.

For finite market asset, completeness is equivalent to uniqueness of the equivalent martingale measure. In the case of large markets, this property does not occur. Artzner and Heath (1995) constructed a financial market with countably many securities for which there are two equivalent martingale measures under which the market is approximately complete. In the context of a large financial market, Bättig (1999) and Bättig and Jarrow (1999) suggested a definition of completeness that uses neither the notion of arbitrage-free nor equivalent martingale measures. Bättig (1999) constructed an example showing that the existence of an equivalent martingale measure excludes the possibility of replicating a claim, hence proving that the notions of arbitrage-free and completeness could be unrelated to each other in daily practice.

Under $\mathbb{Q}$, the price processes of the securities in the arbitrage-free market have the following representations:

$$\begin{cases} \mathrm{d}B(t) = r(t)B(t)\mathrm{d}t, \\ \mathrm{d}S_0(t) = S_0(t-)\left[r(t)\mathrm{d}t + \sigma_0(t)\mathrm{d}W^{\mathbb{Q}}(t) + \int_{\mathbb{R}} \gamma(t-,x)\bar{\Pi}(\mathrm{d}t,\mathrm{d}x) + \sum_{i=1}^{N} \int_{\mathbb{R}} x\bar{\Pi}_U^i(\mathrm{d}t,\mathrm{d}x)\right], \\ \mathrm{d}S_j(t) = S_j(t-)\left[r(t)\mathrm{d}t + \sigma_j(t-)\mathrm{d}\overline{\Phi}_j^{\mathbb{Q}}(t)\right], \\ \mathrm{d}S^{(k)}(t) = S^{(k)}(t-)\left[r(t)\mathrm{d}t + \sigma^{(k)}(t-)\mathrm{d}\overline{X}^{(k)}(t)\right], \\ \mathrm{d}S_i^{(l)}(t) = S_i^{(l)}(t-)\left[r(t)\mathrm{d}t + \sigma_i^{(l)}(t-)\mathrm{d}\overline{\Psi}_i^{(l),\mathbb{Q}}(t)\right], \end{cases} \tag{25}$$

for $i, j = 1, \ldots, N$, $k \geq 2$ and $l \geq 1$.

We show that the enlarged market (Equation (25)) is asymptotically complete in the sense that for every square-integrable contingent claim A (i.e., a non-negative square-integrable random variable in $L^2(\Omega, \mathcal{F}, \mathbb{Q})$) we can set up a sequence of self-financing portfolios whose final values converge in $L^2(\Omega, \mathcal{F}, \mathbb{Q})$ to A.

These portfolios consist of a finite number of risk-free asset, risky asset, kth-power-jump assets, jth geometric Markovian jump security and impulse regime switching securities. We use the following martingale representation property.

Theorem 3 (Palmowski et al. 2018). *Any square-integrable, $\{\mathcal{F}_t\}$-adapted $\mathbb{Q}$-martingale M can be represented as follows:*

$$\begin{aligned} M(t) \quad &= \quad M(0) + \int_0^t h_0(s)\mathrm{d}X^{\mathbb{Q}}(s) + \sum_{j=1}^{N} \int_0^t h_j(s)\mathrm{d}\overline{\Phi}_j^{\mathbb{Q}}(s) + \sum_{k=2}^{\infty} \int_0^t h^{(k)}(s)\mathrm{d}\overline{X}^{(k)}(s) \\ &\quad + \sum_{i=1}^{N}\sum_{l=1}^{\infty} \int_0^t h_i^{(l)}(s)\mathrm{d}\overline{\Psi}_i^{(l),\mathbb{Q}}(s), \end{aligned} \tag{26}$$

where h_0, h_j, $h^{(k)}$ and $h_i^{(l)}$ are predictable processes (for $i, j = 1, \ldots, N$, $k \geq 2$ and $l \geq 1$).

Remark 3. *The right-hand side of Equation (26) is understood as follows. We take finite sums*

$$\sum_{k=2}^{K} \int_0^t h^{(k)}(s)\mathrm{d}\overline{X}^{(k)}(s) \quad \text{and} \quad \sum_{l=1}^{K} \int_0^t h_i^{(l)}(s)\mathrm{d}\overline{\Psi}_i^{(l),\mathbb{Q}}(s)$$

in $L^2(\Omega, \mathcal{F}, \mathbb{Q})$. Since $L^2(\Omega, \mathcal{F}, \mathbb{Q})$ is a Hilbert space, the right-hand side of Equation (26) is understood as the limit of the above expressions in $L^2(\Omega, \mathcal{F}, \mathbb{Q})$ as $K \to \infty$.

We are ready to prove the main result of this section.

Theorem 4. *The market (Equation (25)) under $\mathbb{Q}$ is asymptotically complete.*

Proof. We consider a square-integrable contingent claim A with maturity T. Let

$$M(t) := E_{\mathbb{Q}}\left[\exp\left(-\int_0^T r(s)\mathrm{d}s\right) A \,\middle|\, \mathcal{F}_t\right]$$

and

$$M^K(t) := M^K(0) + \int_0^t h_0(s)\mathrm{d}X^{\mathbb{Q}}(s) + \sum_{j=1}^{N}\int_0^t h_j(s)\mathrm{d}\overline{\Phi}_j^{\mathbb{Q}}(s) + \sum_{k=2}^{K}\int_0^t h^{(k)}(s)\mathrm{d}\overline{X}^{(k)}(s) \tag{27}$$
$$+\sum_{i=1}^{N}\sum_{l=1}^{K}\int_0^t h_i^{(l)}(s)\mathrm{d}\overline{\Psi}_i^{(l),\mathbb{Q}}(s).$$

By the martingale representation property given in Theorem 3, we see that

$$\lim_{K\to\infty} M^K(t) = M(t) \tag{28}$$

in $L^2(\Omega, \mathcal{F}, \mathbb{Q})$. For $K \geq 2$, we introduce the sequence of portfolios

$$\theta^K(t) := \left(\alpha^K(t), \beta_0(t), \beta_1(t), \ldots, \beta_N(t), \beta^{(2)}(t), \ldots, \beta^{(K)}(t), \beta_1^{(1)}(t), \ldots, \beta_N^{(K)}(t)\right).$$

We assume that all processes in θ^K are predictable and

$$E_{\mathbb{Q}}\int_0^t (\alpha^K(s))^2\mathrm{d}s < \infty,\ E_{\mathbb{Q}}\int_0^t (\beta_0(s))^2\mathrm{d}\langle S_0\rangle(s) < \infty,\ E_{\mathbb{Q}}\int_0^t (\beta_j(s))^2\mathrm{d}\langle S_j\rangle(s) < \infty, \tag{29}$$

$$E_{\mathbb{Q}}\int_0^t (\beta^{(k)}(s))^2\mathrm{d}\langle S^{(k)}\rangle(s) < \infty,\ E_{\mathbb{Q}}\int_0^t (\beta_i^{(l)}(s))^2\mathrm{d}\langle S_i^{(l)}\rangle(s) < \infty. \tag{30}$$

Here, α^K corresponds to the number of risk-free assets, β_0 is the number of stocks, β_j $(j = 1, \ldots, N)$ is the number of units of the jth geometric Markovian jump security, $\beta^{(k)}$ $(k = 2, \ldots, K)$ is the number of assets $S^{(k)}$, and $\beta_i^{(l)}$ $(i = 1, \ldots, N, l = 1, \ldots, K)$ is the number of assets $S_i^{(l)}$.

We construct the portfolio θ^K as follows:

$$\begin{aligned}
\alpha^K(t) &:= M^K(t-) - \beta_0(t)B^{-1}(t)S_0(t-) - \sum_{j=1}^{N}\beta_j(t)B^{-1}(t)S_j(t-) \\
&- \sum_{k=2}^{K}\beta^{(k)}(t)B^{-1}(t)S^{(k)}(t-) - \sum_{i=1}^{N}\sum_{l=1}^{K}\beta_i^{(l)}(t)B^{-1}(t)S_i^{(l)}(t-), \\
\beta_0(t) &:= h_0(t)B(t)S_0^{-1}(t-), \\
\beta_j(t) &:= \frac{h_j(t)}{\sigma_j(t-)}B(t)S_j^{-1}(t-), \\
\beta^{(k)}(t) &:= \frac{h^{(k)}(t)}{\sigma^{(k)}(t-)}B(t)(S^{(k)})^{-1}(t-), \\
\beta_i^{(l)}(t) &:= \frac{h_i^{(l)}(t)}{\sigma_i^{(l)}(t-)}B(t)(S_i^{(l)})^{-1}(t-).
\end{aligned} \tag{31}$$

Observe that for this choice of portfolio, the moment conditions in Equations (29) and (30) are satisfied, hence all stochastic integrals for this portfolio are well-defined. For example, we prove that

$$E_{\mathbb{Q}}\int_0^t (\beta_0(s))^2\mathrm{d}\langle S_0\rangle(s) < \infty. \tag{32}$$

The proofs of other conditions are similar. To show (32) note that

$$d\langle S_0\rangle(s) = S_0^2(t-)\left[\sigma_0^2(t)\mathrm{d}t + \int_{\mathbb{R}}\gamma^2(t-,x)\bar{\Pi}(\mathrm{d}t,\mathrm{d}x) + \sum_{i=1}^{N}\int_{\mathbb{R}}x^2\bar{\Pi}_U^i(\mathrm{d}t,\mathrm{d}x)\right]$$

and this condition is equivalent to requirement that

$$\int_0^\infty h_0^2(t)e^{2r(t)}\sigma_0^2(t)\mathrm{d}t < \infty, \qquad \int_0^\infty h_0^2(t)e^{2r(t)}\lambda_i(t)\int_{\mathbb{R}}\gamma^2(t-,x)\nu(\mathrm{d}x)\mathrm{d}t < \infty,$$

$$\int_{\mathbb{R}} x^2\eta_i(\mathrm{d}x)\int_0^\infty h_0^2(t)e^{2r(t)}\lambda_i(t)\mathrm{d}t < \infty.$$

The above conditions follow from Theorem 3 because $\int_0^\infty h_0^2(t)\mathrm{d}t < \infty$. Note that,

$$\begin{aligned}
\Delta M^K(t) &= h_0(t)\Delta X^{\mathbb{Q}}(t) + \sum_{j=1}^N h_j(t)\Delta\overline{\Phi}_j^{\mathbb{Q}}(t) + \sum_{k=2}^K h^{(k)}(t)\Delta\overline{X}^{(k)}(t) + \sum_{i=1}^N\sum_{l=1}^K h_i^{(l)}(t)\Delta\overline{\Psi}_i^{(l),\mathbb{Q}}(t), \\
\Delta S_0(t) &= S_0(t-)\Delta X^{\mathbb{Q}}(t), \\
\Delta S_j(t) &= S_j(t-)\sigma_j(t-)\Delta\overline{\Phi}_j^{\mathbb{Q}}(t), \\
\Delta S^{(k)}(t) &= S^{(k)}(t-)\sigma^{(k)}(t-)\Delta\overline{X}^{(k)}(t), \qquad \Delta S_i^{(l)}(t) = S_i^{(l)}(t-)\sigma_i^{(l)}(t-)\Delta\overline{\Psi}_i^{(l),\mathbb{Q}}(t).
\end{aligned} \tag{33}$$

We claim that $\{\theta^K, K \geq 2\}$ is the sequence of self-financing portfolios which replicates A. Indeed, by Equations (31) and (33), the value V^K of the portfolio θ^K is expressed by

$$\begin{aligned}
V^K(t) &= \alpha^K(t)B(t) + \beta_0(t)S_0(t) + \sum_{j=1}^N \beta_j(t)S_j(t) + \sum_{k=2}^K \beta^{(k)}(t)S^{(k)}(t) + \sum_{i=1}^N\sum_{l=1}^K \beta_i^{(l)}(t)S_i^{(l)}(t) \\
&= M^K(t)B(t) - \Delta M^K(t)B(t) + \beta_0(t)\Delta S_0(t) + \sum_{j=1}^N \beta_j(t)\Delta S_j(t) + \sum_{k=2}^K \beta^{(k)}(t)\Delta S^{(k)}(t) \\
&\quad + \sum_{i=1}^N\sum_{l=1}^K \beta_i^{(l)}(t)\Delta S_i^{(l)}(t) = M^K(t)B(t).
\end{aligned}$$

Thus, the sequence of portfolios $\{\theta^K, K \geq 2\}$ replicates the claim A. We denote

$$\begin{aligned}
G^K(u) &:= \int_0^u \alpha^K(t)\mathrm{d}B(t) + \int_0^u \beta_0(t)\mathrm{d}S_0(t) + \sum_{j=1}^N\int_0^u \beta_j(t)\mathrm{d}S_j(t) \\
&\quad + \sum_{k=2}^K\int_0^u \beta^{(k)}(t)\mathrm{d}S^{(k)}(t) + \sum_{i=1}^N\sum_{l=1}^K\int_0^u \beta_i^{(l)}(t)\mathrm{d}S_i^{(l)}(t)
\end{aligned} \tag{34}$$

the gain process, i.e., the gains or losses obtained up to time u by following θ^K. We show

$$G^K(u) + M^K(0) = M^K(u)B(u), \tag{35}$$

which implies that the portfolio is self-financing. Note that, from Equation (28), we have

$$\lim_{K\to\infty} G^K(u) = \lim_{K\to\infty} M^K(u)B(u) - \lim_{K\to\infty} M^K(0) = M(u)B(u) - M(0).$$

Thus, the portfolios with infinitely many assets are self-financing as well. Inserting Equation (31) into Equation (34), we derive

$$\begin{aligned} G^K(u) &= \int_0^u M^K(t-)\mathrm{d}B(t) - \int_0^u h_0(t)\mathrm{d}B(t) - \sum_{k=2}^{K}\int_0^u \frac{h^{(k)}(t)}{\sigma^{(k)}(t-)}\mathrm{d}B(t) \\ &- \sum_{j=1}^{N}\int_0^u \frac{h_j(t)}{\sigma_j(t-)}\mathrm{d}B(t) - \sum_{i=1}^{N}\sum_{l=1}^{K}\int_0^u \frac{h_i^{(l)}(t)}{\sigma_i^{(l)}(t-)}\mathrm{d}B(t) + \int_0^u h_0(t)B(t)S_0^{-1}(t-)\mathrm{d}S_0(t) \\ &+ \sum_{j=1}^{N}\int_0^u \frac{h_j(t)}{\sigma_j(t-)}B(t)S_j^{-1}(t-)\mathrm{d}S_j(t) + \sum_{k=2}^{K}\int_0^u \frac{h^{(k)}(t)}{\sigma^{(k)}(t-)}B(t)(S^{(k)})^{-1}(t-)\mathrm{d}S^{(k)}(t) \\ &+ \sum_{i=1}^{N}\sum_{l=1}^{K}\int_0^u \frac{h_i^{(l)}(t)}{\sigma_i^{(l)}(t-)}B(t)(S_i^{(l)})^{-1}(t-)\mathrm{d}S_i^{(l)}(t). \end{aligned} \tag{36}$$

From the martingale representation property given in Theorem 3, the first component of the above sum has the form

$$\begin{aligned} \int_0^u M^K(t-)\mathrm{d}B(t) &= \int_0^u \Big(M^K(0) + \int_0^{t-} h_0(s)\mathrm{d}X^{\mathbb{Q}}(s) + \sum_{j=1}^{N}\int_0^{t-} h_j(s)\mathrm{d}\overline{\Phi}_j^{\mathbb{Q}}(s) \\ &+ \sum_{k=2}^{K}\int_0^{t-} h^{(k)}(s)\mathrm{d}\overline{X}^{(k)}(s) + \sum_{i=1}^{N}\sum_{l=1}^{K}\int_0^{t-} h_i^{(l)}(s)\mathrm{d}\overline{\Psi}_i^{(l)\mathbb{Q}}(s)\Big)\mathrm{d}B(t) \\ &= M^K(0)(B(u)-B(0)) + \int_0^u h_0(s)(B(u)-B(s))\mathrm{d}X^{\mathbb{Q}}(s) + \sum_{j=1}^{N}\int_0^u h_j(s)(B(u)-B(s))\mathrm{d}\overline{\Phi}_j^{\mathbb{Q}}(s) \\ &+ \sum_{k=2}^{K}\int_0^u h^{(k)}(s)(B(u)-B(s))\mathrm{d}\overline{X}^{(k)}(s) + \sum_{i=1}^{N}\sum_{l=1}^{K}\int_0^u h_i^{(l)}(s)(B(u)-B(s))\mathrm{d}\overline{\Psi}_i^{(l),\mathbb{Q}}(s). \end{aligned}$$

Now, using Equation (27) and fact that $B(0) = 1$, we can rewrite the above as follows:

$$\begin{aligned} \int_0^u M^K(t-)\mathrm{d}B(t) &= M^K(0)(B(u)-B(0)) + B(u)(M^K(u)-M^K(0)) - \int_0^u h_0(s)B(s)\mathrm{d}\overline{X}^{\mathbb{Q}}(s) \\ &- \sum_{j=1}^{N}\int_0^u h_j(s)B(s)\mathrm{d}\overline{\Phi}_j^{\mathbb{Q}}(s) - \sum_{k=2}^{K}\int_0^u h^{(k)}(s)B(s)\mathrm{d}\overline{X}^{(k)}(s) - \sum_{i=1}^{N}\sum_{l=1}^{K}\int_0^u h_i^{(l)}(s)B(s)\mathrm{d}\overline{\Psi}_i^{(l),\mathbb{Q}}(s) \\ &= M^K(u)B(u) - M^K(0) - \int_0^u h_0(s)B(s)\mathrm{d}X^{\mathbb{Q}}(s) - \sum_{j=1}^{N}\int_0^u h_j(s)B(s)\mathrm{d}\overline{\Phi}_j^{\mathbb{Q}}(s) \\ &- \sum_{k=2}^{K}\int_0^u h^{(k)}(s)B(s)\mathrm{d}\overline{X}^{(k)}(s) - \sum_{i=1}^{N}\sum_{l=1}^{K}\int_0^u h_i^{(l)}(s)B(s)\mathrm{d}\overline{\Psi}_i^{(l),\mathbb{Q}}(s). \end{aligned}$$

Inserting the above equality into Equation (36), the gain process can be written as:

$$
\begin{aligned}
G^K(u) &= M^K(u)B(u) - M^K(0) - \int_0^u h_0(t)B(t)\mathrm{d}X^{\mathbb{Q}}(t) - \sum_{j=1}^{N}\int_0^u h_j(t)B(t)\mathrm{d}\overline{\Phi}_j^{\mathbb{Q}}(t) \\
&\quad - \sum_{k=2}^{K}\int_0^u h^{(k)}(t)B(t)\mathrm{d}\overline{X}^{(k)}(t) - \sum_{i=1}^{N}\sum_{l=1}^{K}\int_0^u h_i^{(l)}(t)B(t)\mathrm{d}\overline{\Psi}_i^{(l),\mathbb{Q}}(t) - \int_0^u h_0(t)\mathrm{d}B(t) \\
&\quad - \sum_{k=2}^{K}\int_0^u \frac{h^{(k)}(t)}{\sigma^{(k)}(t-)}\mathrm{d}B(t) - \sum_{j=1}^{N}\int_0^u \frac{h_j(t)}{\sigma_j(t-)}\mathrm{d}B(t) - \sum_{i=1}^{N}\sum_{l=1}^{K}\int_0^u \frac{h_i^{(l)}(t)}{\sigma_i^{(l)}(t-)}\mathrm{d}B(t) \\
&\quad + \int_0^u h_0(t)B(t)S_0^{-1}(t-)\mathrm{d}S_0(t) + \sum_{j=1}^{N}\int_0^u \frac{h_j(t)}{\sigma_j(t-)}B(t)S_j^{-1}(t-)\mathrm{d}S_j(t) \\
&\quad + \sum_{k=2}^{K}\int_0^u \frac{h^{(k)}(t)}{\sigma^{(k)}(t-)}B(t)(S^{(k)})^{-1}(t-)\mathrm{d}S^{(k)}(t) + \sum_{i=1}^{N}\sum_{l=1}^{K}\int_0^u \frac{h_i^{(l)}(t)}{\sigma_i^{(l)}(t-)}B(t)(S_i^{(l)})^{-1}(t-)\mathrm{d}S_i^{(l)}(t) \\
&= M^K(u)B(u) - M(0).
\end{aligned}
$$

Thus, Equation (35) holds true and the portfolio θ^K is self-financing. □

6. Optimal Portfolio Selection in an Itô–Markov Additive Market

In this section we solve the optimization problem related to identifying the optimal strategy that maximizes the expected value of the utility function of the wealth process at the end of some fixed period. The analysis is conducted for the logarithmic and power utility functions.

Recall that our Itô–Markov additive market is given by Equation (17). Equations (15) and (16) can be rewritten as follows:

$$
\begin{aligned}
\mathrm{d}S^{(k)}(t) &= S^{(k)}(t-)\left[\mu^{(k)}(t)\mathrm{d}t + \int_{\mathbb{R}} \sigma^{(k)}(t-)\gamma^k(t-,x)\bar{\Pi}(\mathrm{d}t,\mathrm{d}x)\right], \\
\mathrm{d}S_i^{(l)}(t) &= S_i^{(l)}(t-)\left[\mu_i^{(l)}(t)\mathrm{d}t + \int_{\mathbb{R}} x^l\sigma_i^{(l)}(t-)\bar{\Pi}_U^i(\mathrm{d}t,\mathrm{d}x)\right]
\end{aligned}
$$

for $i = 1,\dots,N$, $k \geq 2$ and $l \geq 1$. Note that we consider the price processes with respect the original probability measure $\mathbb{P}$.

We restrict ourselves to self-financing portfolio strategies. Denote by π_0 the proportion of wealth invested in stock. Let π_j $(j = 1,\dots,N)$, $\pi^{(k)}$ $(k \geq 2)$ and $\pi_i^{(l)}$ $(i = 1,\dots,N, l \geq 1)$ be the proportions of wealth invested in the jth geometric Markovian jump security S_j, in the Markovian power-jump securities $S^{(k)}$ and in the impulse regime switching securities $S_i^{(l)}$, respectively. The balance of the investor's wealth is invested in the risk-free asset. We denote by $\pi(t) = (\pi_0(t),\pi_1(t),\dots,\pi_N(t),\pi^{(2)}(t),\dots,\pi_1^{(1)}(t),\pi_2^{(1)}(t),\dots)$ a portfolio strategy. We do allow short selling, but we assume that the wealth process is nonnegative at any instant (Teplá 2000).

Let $K < \infty$ be the number of different assets held by the investor in his portfolio. The wealth process R_π^K for the first K assets is governed by the following stochastic differential equation (for $t \in [0, T]$):

$$\begin{aligned}\frac{dR_\pi^K(t)}{R_\pi^K(t-)} &:= \Big(r(t) + \sum_{j=0}^{N} \pi_j(t)(\mu_j(t) - r(t)) + \sum_{k=2}^{K} \pi^{(k)}(t)(\mu^{(k)}(t) - r(t)) \\ &+ \sum_{i=1}^{N}\sum_{l=1}^{K} \pi_i^{(l)}(t)(\mu_i^{(l)}(t) - r(t))\Big)dt + \pi_0(t)\sigma_0(t-)dW(t) + \sum_{j=1}^{N} \pi_j(t)\sigma_j(t-)d\overline{\Phi}_j(t) \\ &+ \int_{\mathbb{R}} \Big(\pi_0(t)\gamma(t-,x) + \sum_{k=2}^{K} \pi^{(k)}(t)\sigma^{(k)}(t-)\gamma^k(t-,x)\Big)\bar{\Pi}(dt, dx) \\ &+ \sum_{i=1}^{N} \int_{\mathbb{R}} \Big(x\pi_0(t) + \sum_{l=1}^{K} x^l \pi_i^{(l)}(t)\sigma_i^{(l)}(t-)\Big)\bar{\Pi}_U^i(dt, dx).\end{aligned} \tag{37}$$

Note that in Equation (37) we can take $r(t) = r(t-)$, $\mu_j(t) = \mu_j(t-)$ $(j = 0, 1, \ldots, N)$, $\mu^{(k)}(t) = \mu^{(k)}(t-)$ $(k \geq 2)$ and $\mu_i^{(l)}(t) = \mu_i^{(l)}(t-)$ $(i = 1, \ldots, N, l \geq 1)$.

Let $\mathcal{A}$ be the class of admissible portfolio strategies π such that π is predictable, $R_\pi^K > 0$, $\int_0^T |\pi(t)|^2 dt < \infty$ $\mathbb{P}-$a.s., $\int_{\mathbb{R}} (\pi_0(t)\gamma(t-,x) + \sum_{k=2}^{K} \pi^{(k)}(t)\sigma^{(k)}(t-)\gamma^k(t-,x))\bar{\Pi}(dt, dx) < \infty$, $\int_{\mathbb{R}} \sum_{i=1}^{N} (x\pi_0(t) + \sum_{l=1}^{K} x^l \pi_i^{(l)}(t)\sigma_i^{(l)}(t-))\bar{\Pi}_U^i(dt, dx) < \infty$ and π satisfies the following convergence: the wealth process R_π^K converges to a process R_π in $L^2(\Omega, \mathcal{F}, \mathbb{P})$, where R_π^K is the solution of the SDE in Equation (37) (see Itô's formula in Protter (2005, Thm. 32)), that is,

$$\begin{aligned}R_\pi^K(t) &= R_\pi^K(0)\exp\Big[\int_0^t \Big(r(s-) + \sum_{j=0}^{N} \pi_j(s)(\mu_j(s-) - r(s-)) + \sum_{k=2}^{K} \pi^{(k)}(s)(\mu^{(k)}(s) - r(s-)) \\ &+ \sum_{i=1}^{N}\sum_{l=1}^{K} \pi_i^{(l)}(s)(\mu_i^{(l)}(s) - r(s-)) - \frac{1}{2}\pi_0^2(s)\sigma_0^2(s-)\Big)ds \\ &+ \int_0^t \pi_0(s)\sigma_0(s-)dW(s) + \sum_{j=1}^{N} \int_0^t \Big(\log(1 + \pi_j(s)\sigma_j(s-)) - \pi_j(s)\sigma_j(s-)\Big)\lambda_j(s)ds \\ &+ \int_0^t \int_{\mathbb{R}} \log\Big(1 + \pi_0(s)\gamma(s-,x) + \sum_{k=2}^{K} \pi^{(k)}(s)\sigma^{(k)}(s-)\gamma^k(s-,x)\Big)\bar{\Pi}(ds, dx) \\ &+ \int_0^t \int_{\mathbb{R}} \Big(\log\Big(1 + \pi_0(s)\gamma(s-,x) + \sum_{k=2}^{K} \pi^{(k)}(s)\sigma^{(k)}(s-)\gamma^k(s-,x)\Big) - \pi_0(s)\gamma(s-,x) \\ &- \sum_{k=2}^{K} \pi^{(k)}(s)\sigma^{(k)}(s-)\gamma^k(s-,x)\Big)\nu(dx)ds + \sum_{j=1}^{N} \int_0^t \log(1 + \pi_j(s)\sigma_j(s-))d\overline{\Phi}_j(s) \\ &+ \sum_{i=1}^{N} \int_0^t \int_{\mathbb{R}} \log\Big(1 + x\pi_0(s) + \sum_{l=1}^{K} \pi_i^{(l)}(s)\sigma_i^{(l)}(s-)x^l\Big)\bar{\Pi}_U^i(ds, dx) \\ &+ \sum_{i=1}^{N} \int_0^t \int_{\mathbb{R}} \Big(\log\Big(1 + x\pi_0(s) + \sum_{l=1}^{K} \pi_i^{(l)}(s)\sigma_i^{(l)}(s-)x^l\Big) - x\pi_0(s) \\ &- \sum_{l=1}^{K} \pi_i^{(l)}(s)\sigma_i^{(l)}(s-)x^l\Big)\lambda_i(s)\eta(dx)ds\Big].\end{aligned}$$

In other words, for $\pi \in \mathcal{A}$, we require that

$$\lim_{K\to\infty} R_\pi^K(t) = R_\pi(t) \tag{38}$$

in $L^2(\Omega, \mathcal{F}, \mathbb{P})$.

Remark 4. *Note that Equation (38) holds true if*

$$\mathbb{E}_{t,z,i}\big(R_\pi^K(t)\big)^2 < \infty, \ \ \mathbb{E}_{t,z,i}\big(R_\pi(t)\big)^2 < \infty,$$

and

$$\mathbb{E}_{t,z,i}\left| \int_0^t \sum_{k=K+1}^{\infty} \pi^{(k)}(s)\big(\mu^{(k)}(s) - r(s-)\big)\mathrm{d}s \right|^2,$$

$$\mathbb{E}_{t,z,i}\left| \int_0^t \sum_{i=1}^{N} \sum_{l=K+1}^{\infty} \pi_i^{(l)}(s)\big(\mu_i^{(l)}(s) - r(s-)\big)\mathrm{d}s \right|^2,$$

$$\mathbb{E}_{t,z,i}\left| \int_0^t \int_{\mathbb{R}} \log\left(\frac{1+\pi_0(s)\gamma(s-,x) + \sum_{k=2}^{\infty}\pi^{(k)}(s)\sigma^{(k)}(s-)\gamma^k(s-,x)}{1+\pi_0(s)\gamma(s-,x) + \sum_{k=2}^{K}\pi^{(k)}(s)\sigma^{(k)}(s-)\gamma^k(s-,x)}\right)\bar{\Pi}(\mathrm{d}s,\mathrm{d}x) \right|^2,$$

$$\mathbb{E}_{t,z,i}\left| \int_0^t \int_{\mathbb{R}} \left(\log\left(\frac{1+\pi_0(s)\gamma(s-,x) + \sum_{k=2}^{\infty}\pi^{(k)}(s)\sigma^{(k)}(s-)\gamma^k(s-,x)}{1+\pi_0(s)\gamma(s-,x) + \sum_{k=2}^{K}\pi^{(k)}(s)\sigma^{(k)}(s-)\gamma^k(s-,x)}\right) - \sum_{k=K+1}^{\infty}\pi^{(k)}(s)\sigma^{(k)}(s-)\gamma^k(s-,x)\right)\nu(\mathrm{d}x)\mathrm{d}s \right|^2,$$

$$\mathbb{E}_{t,z,i}\left| \int_0^t \int_{\mathbb{R}} \log\left(\frac{1+x\pi_0(s) + \sum_{l=2}^{\infty}\pi_i^{(l)}(s)\sigma_i^{(l)}(s-)x^l}{1+x\pi_0(s) + \sum_{l=2}^{K}\pi_i^{(l)}(s)\sigma_i^{(l)}(s-)x^l}\right)\bar{\Pi}_U^i(\mathrm{d}s,\mathrm{d}x) \right|^2,$$

$$\mathbb{E}_{t,z,i}\left| \sum_{i=1}^{N}\int_0^t \int_{\mathbb{R}} \left(\log\left(\frac{1+x\pi_0(s) + \sum_{l=2}^{\infty}\pi_i^{(l)}(s)\sigma_i^{(l)}(s-)x^l}{1+x\pi_0(s) + \sum_{l=2}^{K}\pi_i^{(l)}(s)\sigma_i^{(l)}(s-)x^l}\right) - \sum_{l=K+1}^{\infty}\pi_i^{(l)}(s)\sigma_i^{(l)}(s-)x^l\right)\lambda_i(s)\eta(\mathrm{d}x)\mathrm{d}s \right|^2$$

tend to 0 *as* $K \to \infty$. *Indeed, the convergence of Equation (38) follows directly from our assumptions: from the triangle inequality and the inequality (Fechner 2008)*

$$2|\exp(a_1) - \exp(a_2)| \leq |a_1 - a_2||\exp(a_1) + \exp(a_2)|, \ \ a_1, a_2 \in \mathbb{R}.$$

Then, we get

$$\mathbb{E}\,|\,R_\pi(t) - R_\pi^K(t)\,|^2 \leq \mathbb{E}\left|\log\frac{R_\pi(t)}{R_\pi^K(t)}\right|^2\Big(\mathbb{E}|R_\pi(t)|^2 + \mathbb{E}|R_\pi^K(t)|^2\Big) < \infty$$

and we can use the following equation

$$\begin{aligned}\log\frac{R_\pi(t)}{R_\pi^K(t)} &= \log\frac{R_\pi(0)}{R_\pi^K(0)} + \Bigg[\int_0^t \Bigg(\sum_{k=K+1}^{\infty}\pi^{(k)}(s)\big(\mu^{(k)}(s) - r(s-)\big) \\ &\quad + \sum_{i=1}^{N}\sum_{l=K+1}^{\infty}\pi_i^{(l)}(s)\big(\mu_i^{(l)}(s) - r(s-)\big) - \frac{1}{2}\pi_0^2(s)\sigma_0^2(s-)\Bigg)\mathrm{d}s\end{aligned}$$

$$
\begin{aligned}
&+\int_0^t \int_{\mathbb{R}} \log\Big(1+\pi_0(s)\gamma(s-,x)+\sum_{k=2}^{\infty}\pi^{(k)}(s)\sigma^{(k)}(s-)\gamma^k(s-,x)\Big)\bar{\Pi}(\mathrm{d}s,\mathrm{d}x)\\
&-\int_0^t \int_{\mathbb{R}} \log\Big(1+\pi_0(s)\gamma(s-,x)+\sum_{k=2}^{K}\pi^{(k)}(s)\sigma^{(k)}(s-)\gamma^k(s-,x)\Big)\bar{\Pi}(\mathrm{d}s,\mathrm{d}x)\\
&+\int_0^t \int_{\mathbb{R}} \Big(\log\Big(1+\pi_0(s)\gamma(s-,x)+\sum_{k=2}^{\infty}\pi^{(k)}(s)\sigma^{(k)}(s-)\gamma^k(s-,x)\Big)\\
&-\sum_{k=K+1}^{\infty}\pi^{(k)}(s)\sigma^{(k)}(s-)\gamma^k(s-,x)\Big)\nu(\mathrm{d}x)\mathrm{d}s\\
&-\int_0^t \int_{\mathbb{R}} \log\Big(1+\pi_0(s)\gamma(s-,x)+\sum_{k=2}^{K}\pi^{(k)}(s)\sigma^{(k)}(s-)\gamma^k(s-,x)\Big)\nu(\mathrm{d}x)\mathrm{d}s\\
&+\sum_{i=1}^{N}\int_0^t \int_{\mathbb{R}} \log\Big(1+x\pi_0(s)+\sum_{l=1}^{\infty}\pi_i^{(l)}(s)\sigma_i^{(l)}(s-)x^l\Big)\bar{\Pi}_U^i(\mathrm{d}s,\mathrm{d}x)\\
&-\sum_{i=1}^{N}\int_0^t \int_{\mathbb{R}} \log\Big(1+x\pi_0(s)+\sum_{l=1}^{K}\pi_i^{(l)}(s)\sigma_i^{(l)}(s-)x^l\Big)\bar{\Pi}_U^i(\mathrm{d}s,\mathrm{d}x)\\
&+\sum_{i=1}^{N}\int_0^t \int_{\mathbb{R}} \Big(\log\Big(1+x\pi_0(s)+\sum_{l=1}^{\infty}\pi_i^{(l)}(s)\sigma_i^{(l)}(s-)x^l\Big)\\
&-\sum_{l=K+1}^{\infty}\pi_i^{(l)}(s)\sigma_i^{(l)}(s-)x^l\Big)\lambda_i(s)\eta(\mathrm{d}x)\mathrm{d}s\\
&-\sum_{i=1}^{N}\int_0^t \int_{\mathbb{R}} \log\Big(1+x\pi_0(s)+\sum_{l=1}^{K}\pi_i^{(l)}(s)\sigma_i^{(l)}(s-)x^l\Big)\lambda_i(s)\eta(\mathrm{d}x)\mathrm{d}s\Bigg].
\end{aligned}
$$

Let U denote a utility function of the investor, which is strictly increasing, strictly concave and twice differentiable, that is, $U' > 0$ and $U'' < 0$.

For each $(t, z) \in \mathbb{T} \times \mathbb{R}^+$ and each $i = 1, \ldots, N$ we define

$$
V^{\pi}(t, z, \mathbf{e}_i) := \mathbb{E}_{t,z,i}\big[U(R_\pi(T))\big],
$$

where $\mathbb{E}_{t,z,i}$ is the conditional expectation given $R_\pi(0) = z$ and $J(t) = \mathbf{e}_i$ under $\mathbb{P}$.

The expectation above is understood in the limiting sense, that is, we limit the set of admissible strategies $\mathcal{A}$ to the strategies π such that $\lim_{K\to\infty} \mathbb{E}_{t,z,i}\big[U(R_\pi^K(T))\big]$ exists and is finite. In other words,

$$
\lim_{K\to\infty} \mathbb{E}_{t,z,i}\big[U(R_\pi^K(T))\big] = \mathbb{E}_{t,z,i}\big[U(R_\pi(T))\big] < \infty. \tag{39}
$$

Then, the value function of the investor's portfolio selection problem is defined by

$$
V(t, z, \mathbf{e}_i) := \sup_{\pi\in\mathcal{A}} V^{\pi}(t, z, \mathbf{e}_i) = \sup_{\pi\in\mathcal{A}} \mathbb{E}_{t,z,i}\big[U(R_\pi(T))\big]. \tag{40}
$$

Lemma 1. *Under the assumption in Equation (38), Equation (39) holds true.*

The proof of this Lemma is given in Appendix A.

Our main goal is to identify the value function given in Equation (40). In what follows, we consider two risk-averse utility functions, namely, the logarithmic utility and the power utility.

6.1. Logarithmic Utility

In this subsection, we derive the optimal portfolio strategy in the case of a logarithmic utility function of wealth, namely

$$U(z) = \log(z).$$

Recall that in $\mathcal{A}$ we consider only the strategies for which

$$\lim_{K\to\infty} \mathbb{E}_{t,z,i}\left[\log R_\pi^K(T)\right] = \mathbb{E}_{t,z,i}\left[\log R_\pi(T)\right] < \infty. \tag{41}$$

Theorem 5. *Assume that there exists a solution*

$$\pi^\star(t) := (\pi_0^\star(t), \pi_1^\star(t), \ldots, \pi_N^\star(t), \pi^{(2)\star}(t), \pi^{(3)\star}(t), \ldots, \pi_1^{(1)\star}(t), \pi_2^{(1)\star}(t), \ldots)$$

of the following system of equations (for $i, j = 1, \ldots, N$, $k \geq 2$ and $l \geq 1$):

$$\begin{aligned}
r(t-) - \mu_0(t-) &= \pi_0^\star(t)\sigma_0^2(t-) + \sum_{i=1}^{N} \frac{r(t-) - \mu_i^{(1)}(t-)}{\sigma_i^{(1)}(t-)} + \int_{\mathbb{R}} \gamma(t-,x)\Big(\Big(1 + \pi_0^\star(t)\gamma(t-,x) \\
&\quad + \sum_{k=2}^{\infty} \pi^{(k)\star}(t)\sigma^{(k)}(t-)\gamma^k(t-,x)\Big)^{-1} - 1\Big)\nu(\mathrm{d}x), \\
\pi_j^\star(t) &= \frac{\mu_j(t-) - r(t-)}{(r(t-) - \mu_j(t-))\sigma_j(t-) + \lambda_j(t)\sigma_j^2(t-)},
\end{aligned} \tag{42}$$

$$\begin{aligned}
\frac{r(t-) - \mu^{(k)}(t-)}{\sigma^{(k)}(t-)} &= \int_{\mathbb{R}} \gamma^k(t-,x)\Big(\Big(1 + \pi_0^\star(t)\gamma(t-,x) \\
&\quad + \sum_{k=2}^{\infty} \pi^{(k)\star}(t)\sigma^{(k)}(t-)\gamma^k(t-,x)\Big)^{-1} - 1\Big)\nu(\mathrm{d}x), \\
\frac{r(t-) - \mu_i^{(l)}(t-)}{\sigma_i^{(l)}(t-)} &= \int_{\mathbb{R}} x^l\Big(\Big(1 + x\pi_0^\star(t) + \sum_{l=1}^{\infty} \pi_i^{(l)\star}(t)\sigma_i^{(l)}(t-)x^l\Big)^{-1} - 1\Big)\lambda_i(t)\eta(\mathrm{d}x),
\end{aligned}$$

which belongs to $\mathcal{A}$, that is, in particular, satisfies Equations (38) and (41). Then, the optimal portfolio strategy for the portfolio selection problem in Equation (40) with logarithmic utility function of wealth is one of those solutions.

Proof. The conditional expectation of the logarithm of the wealth process has the following form (for $t \in [0, T)$):

$$\begin{aligned}
\mathbb{E}_{t,z,i}\left[\log R_\pi(T)\right] &= \log R_\pi(t) + \mathbb{E}_{t,z,i} \int_t^T \Big[r(s-) + \sum_{j=0}^{N} \pi_j(s)(\mu_j(s-) - r(s-)) \\
&+ \sum_{k=2}^{\infty} \pi^{(k)}(s)(\mu^{(k)}(s) - r(s-)) + \sum_{i=0}^{N}\sum_{l=1}^{\infty} \pi_i^{(l)}(s)(\mu_i^{(l)}(s) - r(s-)) - \frac{1}{2}\pi_0^2(s)\sigma_0^2(s-) \\
&+ \sum_{j=1}^{N} \Big(\log(1 + \pi_j(s)\sigma_j(s-)) - \pi_j(s)\sigma_j(s-)\Big)\lambda_j(s) \\
&+ \int_{\mathbb{R}} \Big(\log\Big(1 + \pi_0(s)\gamma(s-,x) + \sum_{k=2}^{\infty} \pi^{(k)}(s)\sigma^{(k)}(s-)\gamma^k(s-,x)\Big) \\
&- \pi_0(s)\gamma(s-,x) - \sum_{k=2}^{\infty} \pi^{(k)}(s)\sigma^{(k)}(s-)\gamma^k(s-,x)\Big)\nu(\mathrm{d}x)
\end{aligned}$$

$$+\sum_{i=1}^{N}\int_{\mathbb{R}}\left(\log\left(1+x\pi_0(s)+\sum_{l=1}^{\infty}\pi_i^{(l)}(s)\sigma_i^{(l)}(s-)x^l\right)-x\pi_0(s)-\sum_{l=1}^{\infty}\pi_i^{(l)}(s)\sigma_i^{(l)}(s-)x^l\right)\lambda_i(s)\eta(\mathrm{d}x)\Bigg]\mathrm{d}s.$$

Therefore, the optimal value function V can be written as

$$V(t,z,\mathbf{e}_i)=\log(z)+\sup_{\pi\in\mathcal{A}}h_\pi(t,\mathbf{e}_i),$$

where

$$h_\pi(t,\mathbf{e}_i):=\mathbb{E}_{t,z,i}\int_t^T F(\pi_0(s),\pi_1(s),\dots,\pi_N(s),\pi^{(2)}(s),\dots,\pi_1^{(1)}(s),\dots)\mathrm{d}s$$

for

$$\begin{aligned}
F(\pi_0(s),\pi_1(s),\dots,\pi_N(s),\pi^{(2)}(s),\dots,\pi_1^{(1)}(s),\dots) &:= r(s-)+\sum_{j=0}^{N}\pi_j(s)(\mu_j(s-)-r(s-))\\
&+\sum_{k=2}^{\infty}\pi^{(k)}(s)(\mu^{(k)}(s)-r(s-))+\sum_{i=0}^{N}\sum_{l=1}^{\infty}\pi_i^{(l)}(s)(\mu_i^{(l)}(s)-r(s-))-\frac{1}{2}\pi_0^2(s)\sigma_0^2(s-)\\
&+\sum_{j=1}^{N}\Big(\log(1+\pi_j(s)\sigma_j(s-))-\pi_j(s)\sigma_j(s-)\Big)\lambda_j(s)\\
&+\int_{\mathbb{R}}\Big(\log\Big(1+\pi_0(s)\gamma(s-,x)+\sum_{k=2}^{\infty}\pi^{(k)}(s)\sigma^{(k)}(s-)\gamma^k(s-,x)\Big)\\
&-\pi_0(s)\gamma(s-,x)-\sum_{k=2}^{\infty}\pi^{(k)}(s)\sigma^{(k)}(s-)\gamma^k(s-,x)\Big)\nu(\mathrm{d}x)\\
&+\sum_{i=1}^{N}\int_{\mathbb{R}}\Big(\log\Big(1+x\pi_0(s)+\sum_{l=1}^{\infty}\pi_i^{(l)}(s)\sigma_i^{(l)}(s-)x^l\Big)-x\pi_0(s)-\sum_{l=1}^{\infty}\pi_i^{(l)}(s)\sigma_i^{(l)}(s-)x^l\Big)\lambda_i(s)\eta(\mathrm{d}x).
\end{aligned}$$

Thus, to determine the optimal portfolio strategy, it is sufficient to maximize F. Indeed, the maximization of the function $F(\pi_0(s),\pi_1(s),\dots,\pi_N(s),\pi^{(2)}(s),\dots,\pi_1^{(1)}(s),\dots)$ at each time point $s\in[0,T]$ maximizes the integral of F on $[0,T]$. By direct differentiation with respect to $\pi_0,\pi_j,\pi^{(k)},\pi_i^{(l)}$ we obtain conditions (Equation (42)) that the optimal strategies have to satisfy. Observe that, from Equation (9), the integrals

$$\begin{aligned}
&\int_{\mathbb{R}}\Big(\log\Big(1+\pi_0(s)\gamma(s-,x)+\sum_{k=2}^{\infty}\pi^{(k)}(s)\sigma^{(k)}(s-)\gamma^k(s-,x)\Big)-\pi_0(s)\gamma(s-,x)\\
&-\sum_{k=2}^{\infty}\pi^{(k)}(s)\sigma^{(k)}(s-)\gamma^k(s-,x)\Big)\nu(\mathrm{d}x)
\end{aligned}$$

and (for $i=1,\dots,N$)

$$\int_{\mathbb{R}}\Big(\log\Big(1+x\pi_0(s)+\sum_{l=1}^{\infty}\pi_i^{(l)}(s)\sigma_i^{(l)}(s-)x^l\Big)-x\pi_0(s)-\sum_{l=1}^{\infty}\pi_i^{(l)}(s)\sigma_i^{(l)}(s-)x^l\Big)\lambda_i(s)\eta(\mathrm{d}x)$$

are well-defined. Hence, by the Leibniz integral rule, we can interchange the above mentioned derivatives and the integrals. □

Remark 5. *We have not been able to prove that a solution of the system in Equation (42) exists and is unique. On a complete Itô–Markov additive market, we have an infinite number of assets, so the optimal portfolio strategy $\pi^\star$ is an infinite dimensional vector. The value function in Equation (40) is understood in the limiting sense and therefore numerically it can be approximated by the finite strategy counterpart. In the case of finite dimensional approximations by Kramkov and Schachermayer (1999, Thm. 2.2), the optimal wealth process exists and is* *unique. Under additional conditions, such as absence of redundant assets, the optimal strategy exists and is unique.*

6.2. Power Utility

In this subsection, we derive the optimal portfolio strategy in the case of the power utility function, namely

$$U(z) = z^\alpha \qquad \text{for } \alpha \in (0,1).$$

We assume that, for each $\pi \in \mathcal{A}$,

$$\lim_{K\to\infty} \mathbb{E}_{t,z,i}\big(R_\pi^K(T)\big)^\alpha = \mathbb{E}_{t,z,i}\big(R_\pi(T)\big)^\alpha < \infty. \tag{43}$$

Theorem 6. *Assume that there exists a solution*

$$\pi^\star(t) := (\pi_0^\star(t), \pi_1^\star(t), \ldots, \pi_N^\star(t), \pi^{(2)\star}(t), \pi^{(3)\star}(t), \ldots, \pi_1^{(1)\star}(t), \pi_2^{(1)\star}(t), \ldots)$$

of the following system of equations (for $i, j = 1, \ldots, N$, $k \geq 2$ and $l \geq 1$):

$$\begin{aligned}
r(t-) - \mu_0(t) &= (\alpha-1)\pi_0^\star(t)\sigma_0^2(t-) + \sum_{i=1}^N \frac{\mu_i^{(1)}(t-) - r(t-)}{\sigma_i^{(1)}(t-)} + \int_{\mathbb{R}} \gamma(t-,x)\bigg(\Big(1 + \pi_0^\star(t)\gamma(t-,x) \\
&\quad + \sum_{k=2}^\infty \pi^{(k)\star}(t)\sigma^{(k)}(t-)\gamma^k(t-,x)\Big)^{\alpha-1} - 1\bigg)\nu(\mathrm{d}x), \\
\pi_j^\star(t) &= \frac{\left(1 - \frac{\mu_j(t-)-r(t-)}{\lambda_i(t)\sigma_j(t-)}\right)^{\frac{1}{\alpha-1}} - 1}{\sigma_j(t-)}, \\
r(t-) - \mu^{(k)}(t) &= \int_{\mathbb{R}} \sigma^{(k)}(t-)\gamma^k(t-,x)\bigg(\Big(1 + \pi_0^\star(t)\gamma(t-,x) \\
&\quad + \sum_{k=2}^\infty \pi^{(k)\star}(t)\sigma^{(k)}(t-)\gamma^k(t-,x)\Big)^{\alpha-1} - 1\bigg)\nu(\mathrm{d}x), \\
r(t-) - \mu_i^{(l)}(t) &= \int_{\mathbb{R}} \sigma_i^{(l)}(t-)x^l\bigg(\Big(1 + x\pi_0^\star(t) + \sum_{l=1}^\infty \pi_i^{\star(l)}(t)x^l\sigma_i^{(l)}(t-)\Big)^{\alpha-1} - 1\bigg)\lambda_i(t)\eta(\mathrm{d}x)\mathrm{d}t,
\end{aligned} \tag{44}$$

which belongs to $\mathcal{A}$, that is, in particular, it satisfies Equations (38) and (43). Then, the optimal portfolio strategy for the portfolio selection problem in Equation (40) with power utility function of wealth is one of those solutions.

Proof. From Itô's formula (see Protter (2005, Thm. 32)) for the power utility function of wealth, we obtain (for $s \in [t, T]$ and $t \in [0, T]$)

$$\begin{aligned}
(R_\pi(T))^\alpha - (R_\pi(t))^\alpha &= \int_t^T \alpha(R_\pi(s))^\alpha\Big(r(s-) + \sum_{j=0}^N \pi_j(s)(\mu_j(s-) - r(s-)) + \sum_{k=2}^\infty \pi^{(k)}(s)(\mu^{(k)}(s) - r(s-)) \\
&+ \sum_{i=0}^N \sum_{l=1}^\infty \pi_i^{(l)}(s)(\mu_i^{(l)}(s) - r(s-))\Big)\mathrm{d}s + \int_t^T \alpha(R_\pi(s))^\alpha \pi_0(s)\sigma_0(s-)\mathrm{d}W(s) \\
&+ \int_t^T \frac{1}{2}\alpha(\alpha-1)(R_\pi(s))^\alpha \pi_0^2(s)\sigma_0^2(s-)\mathrm{d}s + \sum_{j=1}^N \int_t^T \Big((R_\pi(s) + R_\pi(s)\pi_j(s)\sigma_j(s-))^\alpha - (R_\pi(s))^\alpha\Big)\mathrm{d}\overline{\Phi}_j(s) \\
&+ \sum_{j=1}^N \int_t^T \Big((R_\pi(s) + R_\pi(s)\pi_j(s)\sigma_j(s-))^\alpha - (R_\pi(s))^\alpha - \alpha(R_\pi(s))^\alpha \pi_j(s)\sigma_j(s-)\Big)\lambda_j(s)\mathrm{d}s
\end{aligned}$$

$$
\begin{aligned}
&+\int_t^T \int_{\mathbb{R}} \Bigg(\Big(R_\pi(s-) + R_\pi(s) \Big(\pi_0(s)\gamma(s-,x) + \sum_{k=2}^{\infty} \pi^{(k)}(s)\sigma^{(k)}(s-)\gamma^k(s-,x) \Big) \Big)^{\alpha} \\
&- (R_\pi(s-))^{\alpha} - \alpha (R_\pi(s-))^{\alpha} \Big(\pi_0(s)\gamma(s-,x) + \sum_{k=2}^{\infty} \pi^{(k)}(s)\sigma^{(k)}(s-)\gamma^k(s-,x) \Big) \Bigg) \nu(\mathrm{d}x)\mathrm{d}s \\
&+\int_t^T \int_{\mathbb{R}} \Bigg(\Big(R_\pi(s-) + R_\pi(s) \Big(\pi_0(s)\gamma(s-,x) + \sum_{k=2}^{\infty} \pi^{(k)}(s)\sigma^{(k)}(s-)\gamma^k(s-,x) \Big) \Big)^{\alpha} - (R_\pi(s-))^{\alpha} \Bigg) \bar{\Pi}(\mathrm{d}s,\mathrm{d}x) \\
&+\sum_{i=1}^{N} \int_t^T \int_{\mathbb{R}} \Bigg(\Big(R_\pi(s-) + R_\pi(s) \Big(x\pi_0(s) + \sum_{l=1}^{\infty} x^l \pi_i^{(l)}(s)\sigma_i^{(l)}(s-) \Big) \Big)^{\alpha} - (R_\pi(s-))^{\alpha} \\
&- \alpha (R_\pi(s-))^{\alpha} \Big(x\pi_0(s) + \sum_{l=1}^{\infty} x^l \pi_i^{(l)}(s)\sigma_i^{(l)}(s-) \Big) \Bigg) \lambda_i(s)\eta(\mathrm{d}x)\mathrm{d}s \\
&+\sum_{i=1}^{N} \int_t^T \int_{\mathbb{R}} \Bigg(\Big(R_\pi(s-) + R_\pi(s) \Big(x\pi_0(s) + \sum_{l=1}^{\infty} x^l \pi_i^{(l)}(s)\sigma_i^{(l)}(s-) \Big) \Big)^{\alpha} - (R_\pi(s-))^{\alpha} \Bigg) \bar{\Pi}_U^i(\mathrm{d}s,\mathrm{d}x).
\end{aligned}
$$

From this and Equation (40), the value function is given by

$$
\begin{aligned}
V(t,z,\mathbf{e}_i) \quad = \quad & z^{\alpha} + \sup_{\pi\in\mathcal{A}} \mathbb{E}_{t,z,i} \int_t^T z^{\alpha} \Bigg[\alpha \Big(r(s-) + \sum_{j=0}^{N} \pi_j(s)(\mu_j(s-) - r(s-)) + \sum_{k=2}^{\infty} \pi^{(k)}(s)(\mu^{(k)}(s) - r(s-)) \\
&+ \sum_{i=0}^{N}\sum_{l=1}^{\infty} \pi_i^{(l)}(s)(\mu_i^{(l)}(s) - r(s-)) + \frac{1}{2}(\alpha-1)\pi_0^2(s)\sigma_0^2(s-) \Big) \\
&+ \sum_{j=1}^{N} \Big((1+\pi_j(s)\sigma_j(s-))^{\alpha} - 1 - \alpha\pi_j(s)\sigma_j(s-) \Big) \lambda_j(s) \\
&+ \int_{\mathbb{R}} \Bigg(\Big(1 + \pi_0(s)\gamma(s-,x) + \sum_{k=2}^{\infty} \pi^{(k)}(s)\sigma^{(k)}(s-)\gamma^k(s-,x) \Big)^{\alpha} \\
&- 1 - \alpha \Big(\pi_0(s)\gamma(s-,x) + \sum_{k=2}^{\infty} \pi^{(k)}(s)\sigma^{(k)}(s-)\gamma^k(s-,x) \Big) \Bigg) \nu(\mathrm{d}x) \\
&+ \sum_{i=1}^{N} \int_{\mathbb{R}} \Bigg(\Big(1 + x\pi_0(s) + \sum_{l=1}^{\infty} x^l \pi_i^{(l)}(s)\sigma_i^{(l)}(s-) \Big)^{\alpha} - 1 \\
&- \alpha \Big(x\pi_0(s) + \sum_{l=1}^{\infty} x^l \pi_i^{(l)}(s)\sigma_i^{(l)}(s-) \Big) \Bigg) \lambda_i(s)\eta(\mathrm{d}x) \Bigg] \mathrm{d}s.
\end{aligned}
$$

By direct differentiation with respect to each strategy, this supremum is attained if the strategies satisfy the system in Equation (44). Observe that, from Equation (9), the integrals

$$
\begin{aligned}
&\int_{\mathbb{R}} \Bigg(\Big(1 + \pi_0(s)\gamma(s-,x) + \sum_{k=2}^{\infty} \pi^{(k)}(s)\sigma^{(k)}(s-)\gamma^k(s-,x) \Big)^{\alpha} \\
&- 1 - \alpha \Big(\pi_0(s)\gamma(s-,x) + \sum_{k=2}^{\infty} \pi^{(k)}(s)\sigma^{(k)}(s-)\gamma^k(s-,x) \Big) \Bigg) \nu(\mathrm{d}x)
\end{aligned}
$$

and (for $i = 1, \ldots, N$)

$$
\int_{\mathbb{R}} \Bigg(\Big(1 + x\pi_0(s) + \sum_{l=1}^{\infty} x^l \pi_i^{(l)}(s)\sigma_i^{(l)}(s-) \Big)^{\alpha} - 1 - \alpha \Big(x\pi_0(s) + \sum_{l=1}^{\infty} x^l \pi_i^{(l)}(s)\sigma_i^{(l)}(s-) \Big) \Bigg) \lambda_i(s)\eta(\mathrm{d}x)
$$

are well-defined. Hence, by the Leibniz integral rule, we can interchange the derivatives and integrals. □

Remark 6. *We have not been able to prove that a solution of Equation (44) exists and is unique. However, if we consider a finite market, then this solution exists and is unique and must be the optimal portfolio by Kramkov and Schachermayer (1999, Thm. 2.2). In $\pi_j^*(t)$, one can observe the dependence of this strategy on Sharpe ratio.*

Remark 7. *If the prices of assets in the Black–Scholes–Merton market are described by processes without jumps (that is, $\bar{\Pi}(\mathrm{d}t, \mathrm{d}x) = 0$ and $\bar{\Pi}_U^i(\mathrm{d}t, \mathrm{d}x) = 0$), then we obtain closed-form solutions to the optimal portfolio selection problem in Equation (40) for the logarithmic and power utilities (Zhang et al. 2010). In addition, the value function in the primary market is the same as in the enlarged market, while in our market this does not occur.*

7. Optimal Portfolio Selection in the Original Market

In this section, we find conditions for optimal portfolio strategies in the original market, i.e., in the market with one risk-free asset and one share.

Let $\tilde{\pi}_0$ be the proportion of wealth invested in share S_0 in the original market. Then, the corresponding wealth process, denoted as $R^{\tilde{\pi}_0}$, is given by the stochastic differential equation

$$\begin{aligned} \frac{\mathrm{d}R_{\tilde{\pi}_0}(t)}{R_{\tilde{\pi}_0}(t-)} &:= \Big(r(t-) + \tilde{\pi}_0(t)\big(\mu_0(t-) - r(t-)\big)\Big)\mathrm{d}t + \tilde{\pi}_0(t)\sigma_0(t-)\mathrm{d}W(t) \\ &\quad + \tilde{\pi}_0(t)\int_{\mathbb{R}} \gamma(t-,x)\bar{\Pi}(\mathrm{d}t,\mathrm{d}x) + \tilde{\pi}_0(t)\sum_{i=1}^{N}\int_{\mathbb{R}} x\bar{\Pi}_U^i(\mathrm{d}t,\mathrm{d}x). \end{aligned}$$

Let $\mathcal{A}_0$ be the class of admissible portfolio strategies $\tilde{\pi}_0$ such that $\tilde{\pi}_0$ is predictable, $\{\mathcal{F}_t\}$-adaptable and satisfies the condition $\int_t^T |\tilde{\pi}_0(s)|^2\mathrm{d}s < \infty, \mathbb{P}-$ a.s. Similar to the definition of the value function in the enlarged market, we define the value function in the original incomplete market as

$$V_0(t,z,\mathbf{e}_i) := \sup_{\tilde{\pi}_0\in\mathcal{A}_0} \mathbb{E}_{t,z,i}\big[U(R^{\tilde{\pi}_0}(T))\big]. \tag{45}$$

We assume $\mathbb{E}_{t,z,i}\big[U(R_{\tilde{\pi}_0}(T))\big] < \infty$ for $i = 1, \ldots, N$.

First, we consider the logarithmic utility function. We have

$$\begin{aligned} \mathbb{E}_{t,z,i}\big[\log R_{\tilde{\pi}_0}(T)\big] &= \log z + \mathbb{E}_{t,z,i}\int_t^T \Big[r(s-) + \tilde{\pi}_0(s)\big(\mu_0(s-) - r(s-)\big) - \frac{1}{2}\tilde{\pi}_0^2(s)\sigma_0^2(s-) \\ &\quad + \int_{\mathbb{R}}\Big(\log\big(1 + \tilde{\pi}_0(s)\gamma(s-,x)\big) - \tilde{\pi}_0(s)\gamma(s-,x)\Big)\nu(\mathrm{d}x) \\ &\quad + \sum_{i=1}^{N}\int_{\mathbb{R}}\Big(\log\big(1 + x\tilde{\pi}_0(s)\big) - x\tilde{\pi}_0(s)\Big)\lambda_i(s)\eta(\mathrm{d}x)\Big]\mathrm{d}s, \end{aligned}$$

that is, for the logarithmic utility, the value function V_0 can be written as follows:

$$\begin{aligned} V_0(t,z,\mathbf{e}_i) &= \log z + \sup_{\tilde{\pi}_0\in\mathcal{A}_0} \mathbb{E}_{t,z,i}\int_t^T \Big[r(s-) + \tilde{\pi}_0(s)\big(\mu_0(s-) - r(s-)\big) - \frac{1}{2}\tilde{\pi}_0^2(s)\sigma_0^2(s-) \\ &\quad + \int_{\mathbb{R}}\Big(\log\big(1 + \tilde{\pi}_0(s)\gamma(s-,x)\big) - \tilde{\pi}_0(s)\gamma(s-,x)\Big)\nu(\mathrm{d}x) \\ &\quad + \sum_{i=1}^{N}\int_{\mathbb{R}}\Big(\log\big(1 + x\tilde{\pi}_0(s)\big) - x\tilde{\pi}_0(s)\Big)\lambda_i(s)\eta(\mathrm{d}x)\Big]\mathrm{d}s. \end{aligned}$$

From Equation (9), the integrals

$$\int_{\mathbb{R}}\Big(\log\big(1 + \tilde{\pi}_0(s)\gamma(s-,x)\big) - \tilde{\pi}_0(s)\gamma(s-,x)\Big)\nu(\mathrm{d}x)$$

and (for $i = 1, \ldots, N$)

$$\int_{\mathbb{R}} \Big(\log\left(1 + x\tilde{\pi}_0(s)\right) - x\tilde{\pi}_0(s) \Big) \lambda_i(s)\eta(\mathrm{d}x)$$

are well-defined. Hence, by the Leibniz integral rule, we can differentiate the above integrals with respect to $\tilde{\pi}_0$. The above supremum is attained if $\tilde{\pi}_0$ solves the equation

$$\begin{aligned} &\mu_0(s-) - r(s) - \sigma_0^2(s-)\tilde{\pi}_0(s) + \int_{\mathbb{R}} \left(\frac{\gamma(s-,x)}{1 + \tilde{\pi}_0(s)\gamma(s-,x)} - \gamma(s-,x) \right) \nu(\mathrm{d}x) \\ &+ \sum_{i=1}^{N} \int_{\mathbb{R}} \left(\frac{x}{1 + x\tilde{\pi}_0(s)} - x \right) \lambda_i(s)\eta(\mathrm{d}x) = 0. \end{aligned} \tag{46}$$

In the case of the power utility, the value function V_0 can be written as

$$\begin{aligned} V_0(t,z,\mathbf{e}_i) &= z^\alpha + \sup_{\tilde{\pi}_0 \in \mathcal{A}_0} \mathbb{E}_{t,z,i} \int_t^T \Bigg[\alpha z^\alpha \Big(r(s-) + \tilde{\pi}_0(s)\left(\mu_0(s-) - r(s-)\right) + \frac{1}{2}(\alpha - 1)\tilde{\pi}_0^2(s)\sigma_0^2(s-) \Big) \\ &+ \int_{\mathbb{R}} z^\alpha \bigg(\Big(1 + \tilde{\pi}_0(s)\gamma(s-,x)\Big)^\alpha - 1 - \alpha\tilde{\pi}_0(s)\gamma(s-,x) \bigg) \nu(\mathrm{d}x) \\ &+ \sum_{i=1}^{N} \int_{\mathbb{R}} z^\alpha \bigg(\Big(1 + x\tilde{\pi}_0(s)\Big)^\alpha - 1 - \alpha x\tilde{\pi}_0(s) \bigg) \lambda_i(s)\eta(\mathrm{d}x) \Bigg] \mathrm{d}s. \end{aligned}$$

Note that, from Equation (9), the integrals

$$\int_{\mathbb{R}} z^\alpha \bigg(\Big(1 + \tilde{\pi}_0(s)\gamma(s-,x)\Big)^\alpha - 1 - \alpha\tilde{\pi}_0(s)\gamma(s-,x) \bigg) \nu(\mathrm{d}x)$$

and (for $i = 1, \ldots, N$)

$$\int_{\mathbb{R}} z^\alpha \bigg(\Big(1 + x\tilde{\pi}_0(s)\Big)^\alpha - 1 - \alpha x\tilde{\pi}_0(s) \bigg) \lambda_i(s)\eta(\mathrm{d}x)$$

are well-defined. By direct differentiation in Equation (47) with respect to $\tilde{\pi}_0$, we get

$$\begin{aligned} &\mu_0(s-) - r(s) - (\alpha - 1)\sigma_0^2(s-)\tilde{\pi}_0(s) + \int_{\mathbb{R}} \Big(\gamma(s-,x)\left(1 + \tilde{\pi}_0(s)\gamma(s-,x)\right)^{\alpha-1} - \gamma(s-,x) \Big) \nu(\mathrm{d}x) \\ &+ \sum_{i=1}^{N} \int_{\mathbb{R}} \Big(x\left(1 + x\tilde{\pi}_0(s)\right)^{\alpha-1} - x \Big) \lambda_i(s)\eta(\mathrm{d}x) = 0. \end{aligned} \tag{47}$$

Lemma 2. *The solutions of Equations (46) and (47) are optimal strategies for the portfolio selection problem in Equation (45) for the logarithmic and power utilities, respectively.*

Proof. We prove that solutions of Equations (46) and (47) are optimal portfolio strategies; their existence was proved by Kramkov and Schachermayer (1999). Let $\tilde{\pi}_0^\varepsilon := \tilde{\pi}_0 + \varepsilon$ be a perturbed portfolio strategy for $\varepsilon > 0$.

We define the value function V_0^ε related to the strategy $\tilde{\pi}_0^\varepsilon$ (Fouque et al. 2017a, 2017b; Mokkhavesa and Atkinson 2002) as follows:

$$V_0^\varepsilon(t,z,\mathbf{e}_i) := \sup_{\tilde{\pi}_0^\varepsilon \in \mathcal{A}_0} \mathbb{E}_{t,z,i}\left[U(R_{\tilde{\pi}_0^\varepsilon}(T))\right].$$

In the case of the logarithmic utility,

$$\begin{aligned} V_0^\varepsilon(t,z,\mathbf{e}_i) &= \log z + \sup_{\tilde{\pi}_0 \in \mathcal{A}_0} \mathbb{E}_{t,z,i} \int_t^T \Big[r(s-) + (\tilde{\pi}_0(s)+\varepsilon)\big(\mu_0(s-) - r(s-)\big) - \frac{1}{2}(\tilde{\pi}_0(s)+\varepsilon)^2\sigma_0^2(s-) \\ &+ \int_{\mathbb{R}} \Big(\log\left(1 + (\tilde{\pi}_0(s)+\varepsilon)\gamma(s-,x)\right) - (\tilde{\pi}_0(s)+\varepsilon)\gamma(s-,x)\Big)\nu(\mathrm{d}x) \\ &+ \sum_{i=1}^N \int_{\mathbb{R}} \Big(\log\left(1 + x(\tilde{\pi}_0(s)+\varepsilon)\right) - x(\tilde{\pi}_0(s)+\varepsilon)\Big)\lambda_i(s)\eta(\mathrm{d}x)\Big]\mathrm{d}s, \end{aligned}$$

and for the power utility,

$$\begin{aligned} V_0^\varepsilon(t,z,\mathbf{e}_i) &= z^\alpha + \sup_{\tilde{\pi}_0 \in \mathcal{A}_0} \mathbb{E}_{t,z,i} \int_t^T \Big[\alpha z^\alpha \Big(r(s-) + (\tilde{\pi}_0(s)+\varepsilon)\big(\mu_0(s-) - r(s-)\big) \\ &+ \frac{1}{2}(\alpha-1)(\tilde{\pi}_0(s)+\varepsilon)^2\sigma_0^2(s-)\Big) \\ &+ \int_{\mathbb{R}} z^\alpha \Big(\Big(1 + (\tilde{\pi}_0(s)+\varepsilon)\gamma(s-,x)\Big)^\alpha - 1 - \alpha(\tilde{\pi}_0(s)+\varepsilon)\gamma(s-,x)\Big)\nu(\mathrm{d}x) \\ &+ \sum_{i=1}^N \int_{\mathbb{R}} z^\alpha \Big(\Big(1 + x(\tilde{\pi}_0(s)+\varepsilon)\Big)^\alpha - 1 - \alpha x(\tilde{\pi}_0(s)+\varepsilon)\Big)\lambda_i(s)\eta(\mathrm{d}x)\Big]\mathrm{d}s. \end{aligned}$$

Note that $\tilde{\pi}_0$ is a portfolio strategy that maximizes the value function, so $\frac{\partial}{\partial\varepsilon}V_0^\varepsilon\Big|_{\varepsilon=0} = 0.$ Calculating this derivative for V_0^ε in both cases, we get Equations (46) and (47).

Thus, the optimal portfolio strategies solve these equations. The existence and uniqueness of the optimal strategies follows from Kramkov and Schachermayer (1999). In that paper, the main assumption concerns the utility function, which has to have asymptotic elasticity strictly less than 1, that is,

$$\overline{\lim_{z\to\infty}} \frac{zU'(z)}{U(z)} < 1.$$

Note that the power and logarithmic utilities satisfy this condition. □

Remark 8. *In a general semi-martingale market model, Goll and Kallsen (2000, 2003) obtained the optimal solution explicitly in terms of semi-martingale characteristics of the price process for the logarithmic utility.*

Author Contributions: Methodology, Z.P. and Ł.S.; Formal Analysis, A.S., Z.P. and Ł.S.; Investigation, A.S., Z.P. and Ł.S.; Writing—Original Draft Preparation, A.S.; Writing—Review and Editing, A.S., Z.P. and Ł.S.; Visualization, A.S.; Supervision, Z.P. and Ł.S.; Project Administration, Z.P. and Ł.S.; and Funding Acquisition, Z.P.

Funding: This paper was supported by the National Science Centre under the grant 2016/23/B/HS4/00566 (2017–2020).

Acknowledgments: Anna Sulima would like to thank Monique Pontier (Université Paul Sabatier, Toulouse) for plenty of helpful suggestions that improved this paper.

Conflicts of Interest: The authors declare no conflict of interest. The funders had no role in the design of the study; in the collection, analyses, or interpretation of data; in the writing of the manuscript, or in the decision to publish the results.

Appendix A

Proof of Lemma 1. We define

$$U_M(z) := U(z)\mathbf{1}_{\{z:|U(z)|\le M\}}.$$

The convergence of R_π^K to R_π in $L^2(\Omega,\mathcal{F},\mathbb{P})$ given in Equation (38) implies the convergence in probability of R_π^K to R_π as $K\to\infty$ (see Jacod and Protter (2004, Thm. 17.2)).

Thus, for the bounded and continuous function U_M given above, we have

$$\lim_{K\to\infty}\mathbb{E}_{t,z,i}\big[U_M(R_\pi^K(T))\big]=\mathbb{E}_{t,z,i}\big[U_M(R_\pi(T))\big] \tag{A1}$$

(see Jacod and Protter (2004, Thm. 18.1)). Note that

$$\mathbb{E}_{t,z,i}\big[U(R_\pi^K(T))\big]=\mathbb{E}_{t,z,i}\big[U_M(R_\pi^K(T))\big]+\mathbb{E}_{t,z,i}\big[U(R_\pi^K(T))\mathbf{1}_{\{R_\pi^K(T):|U(R_\pi^K(T))|>M\}}\big]. \tag{A2}$$

From the concavity of U, it follows that $U(z)\le b+cz$ for each $z\ge 0$ and some real $b,c\ge 0$. Thus, the second term on the right-hand side of Equation (A2) satisfies

$$\mathbb{E}_{t,z,i}\big[U(R_\pi^K(T))\mathbf{1}_{\{R_\pi^K(T):|U(R_\pi^K(T))|>M\}}\big] \;\le\; b+c\,\mathbb{E}_{t,z,i}\big[R_\pi^K(T)\mathbf{1}_{\{R_\pi^K(T):|U(R_\pi^K(T))|>M\}}\big].$$

Now, we prove that

$$\lim_{K\to\infty}\mathbb{E}_{t,z,i}\big[R_\pi^K(T)\mathbb{I}^K(T)\big]=\mathbb{E}_{t,z,i}\big[R_\pi(T)\mathbb{I}(T)\big], \tag{A3}$$

where

$$\mathbb{I}^K(T):=\mathbf{1}_{\{R_\pi^K(T):|U(R_\pi^K(T))|>M\}} \text{ and } \mathbb{I}(T):=\mathbf{1}_{\{R_\pi(T):|U(R_\pi(T))|>M\}}.$$

Note that

$$\begin{aligned}
&\mathbb{E}_{t,z,i}\big|R_\pi^K(T)\mathbb{I}^K(T)-R_\pi(T)\mathbb{I}(T)\big|\\
\le\;&\Big[\mathbb{E}_{t,z,i}\big(R_\pi^K(T)-R_\pi(T)\big)^2\Big]^{\frac12}\Big[\mathbb{E}_{t,z,i}\big(\mathbb{I}(T)\big)\Big]^{\frac12}\\
&+\Big[\mathbb{E}_{t,z,i}\big(R_\pi(T)\big)^2\Big]^{\frac12}\Big[\mathbb{E}_{t,z,i}\big(\mathbb{I}(T)-\mathbb{I}^K(T)\big)^2\Big]^{\frac12}\\
&+\Big[\mathbb{E}_{t,z,i}\big(R_\pi^K(T)\big)^2\Big]^{\frac12}\Big[\mathbb{E}_{t,z,i}\big(\mathbb{I}^K(T)-\mathbb{I}(T)\big)^2\Big]^{\frac12}\\
&+\Big[\mathbb{E}_{t,z,i}\big(R_\pi(T)\big)^2\Big]^{\frac12}\Big[\mathbb{E}_{t,z,i}\big(\mathbb{I}^K(T)-\mathbb{I}(T)\big)^2\Big]^{\frac12}.
\end{aligned} \tag{A4}$$

Indeed, from the triangle inequality, we obtain

$$\begin{aligned}
&\mathbb{E}_{t,z,i}\big|R_\pi^K(T)\mathbb{I}^K(T)-R_\pi(T)\mathbb{I}(T)\big|\\
\le\;&\mathbb{E}_{t,z,i}\big|R_\pi^K(T)\mathbb{I}^K(T)-R_\pi^K(T)\mathbb{I}(T)\big|+\mathbb{E}_{t,z,i}\Big|R_\pi^K(T)\mathbb{I}(T)-R_\pi(T)\mathbb{I}^K(T)\Big|\\
&+\mathbb{E}_{t,z,i}\Big|R_\pi(T)\mathbb{I}^K(T)-R_\pi(T)\mathbb{I}(T)\Big|.
\end{aligned} \tag{A5}$$

Moreover, using Hölder's inequality, we get

$$\mathbb{E}_{t,z,i}\Big|R_\pi^K(T)\mathbb{I}^K(T)-R_\pi^K(T)\mathbb{I}(T)\Big|\le\Big[\mathbb{E}_{t,z,i}\big(R_\pi^K(T)\big)^2\Big]^{\frac12}\Big[\mathbb{E}_{t,z,i}\big(\mathbb{I}^K(T)-\mathbb{I}(T)\big)^2\Big]^{\frac12} \tag{A6}$$

and

$$\mathbb{E}_{t,z,i}\left|R_\pi(T)\mathbb{I}^K(T)-R_\pi(T)\mathbb{I}(T)\right| \le \left[\mathbb{E}_{t,z,i}(R_\pi(T))^2\right]^{\frac{1}{2}}\left[\mathbb{E}_{t,z,i}(\mathbb{I}^K(T)-\mathbb{I}(T))^2\right]^{\frac{1}{2}}. \tag{A7}$$

Finally, from the triangle inequality and Hölder's inequality, we derive

$$\begin{aligned}
&\mathbb{E}_{t,z,i}\left|R_\pi^K(T)\mathbb{I}(T)-R_\pi(T)\mathbb{I}^K(T)\right| \\
\le\ & \left[\mathbb{E}_{t,z,i}(R_\pi^K(T)-R_\pi(T))^2\right]^{\frac{1}{2}}\left[\mathbb{E}_{t,z,i}(\mathbb{I}(T))\right]^{\frac{1}{2}} \\
&+\left[\mathbb{E}_{t,z,i}(R_\pi(T))^2\right]^{\frac{1}{2}}\left[\mathbb{E}_{t,z,i}(\mathbb{I}(T)-\mathbb{I}^K(T))^2\right]^{\frac{1}{2}}.
\end{aligned} \tag{A8}$$

Combining Equations (A5)–(A8), we get the inequality in Equation (A4).

Now, we prove that

$$\mathbb{I}^K \to \mathbb{I} \tag{A9}$$

in $L^2(\Omega,\mathcal{F},\mathbb{P})$ as $K\to\infty$.

First, we verify this convergence in probability. Indeed, for any $\varepsilon>0$, there exists $\delta>0$ such that

$$\begin{aligned}
\mathbb{P}(|\mathbb{I}^K(T)-\mathbb{I}(T)|>\varepsilon) &= \mathbb{P}(\{U(R_\pi^K(T))>M, U(R_\pi(T))<M\}\cup\{U(R_\pi^K(T))<M, U(R_\pi(T))>M\}) \\
&\le \mathbb{P}(|U(R_\pi^K(T))-U(R_\pi(T))|>\delta).
\end{aligned}$$

The right-hand side of the above inequality tends to zero as $K\to\infty$, since the convergence in probability of R_π^K to R_π yields the convergence in probability of $U(R_\pi^K)$ to $U(R_\pi)$ (see Jacod and Protter (2004, Thm. 17.5)).

Moreover, we have

$$\mathbb{I}^K(T)\le 1,$$

thus $\{\mathbb{I}^K\}_{K=2}^\infty$ is uniformly integrable and

$$\lim_{K\to\infty}\mathbb{I}^K(T)=\mathbb{I}(T)$$

in $L^2(\Omega,\mathcal{F},\mathbb{P})$ (see Gut (2005, Thm. 4.5, p. 216 and Thm. 5.4, p. 221)). This completes the proof of Equation (A9).

By Equations (38) and (A9), the right-hand side of the inequality in Equation (A4) tends to 0 as $K\to\infty$. This completes the proof of Equation (A3).

From Equation (A3), it follows that

$$\overline{\lim_{K\to\infty}}\,\mathbb{E}_{t,z,i}\left[U\left(R_\pi^K(T)\right)\mathbf{1}_{\{R_\pi^K(T):|U(R_\pi^K(T))|>M\}}\right]$$

is well-defined. Thus, as $M\to\infty$, the second term on the right-hand side of Equation (A2) tends to zero. Moreover, the first term converges to $\mathbb{E}_{t,z,i}\left[U\left(R_\pi(T)\right)\right]$ by (A1). This completes the proof. □

References

Artzner, Philippe, and David Heath. 1995. Approximate completeness with multiple martingale measures. *Mathematical Finance* 5: 1–11.

Asmussen, Søren. 2003. *Applied Probability and Queues*, 2nd ed; Berlin and Heidelberg: Springer.

Asmussen, Søren, and Offer Kella. 2000. Multi-dimensional martingale for Markov additive processes and its applications. *Advances in Applied Probability* 32: 376–80. [CrossRef]

Bae, Geum, Woo Chang Kim, and John M. Mulvey. 2014. Dynamic asset allocation for varied financial markets under regime switching framework. *European Journal of Operational Research* 234: 450–58. [CrossRef]

Barndorff-Nielsen, Ole E., and Neil Shephard. 2003. Realised power variation and stochastic volatility models. *Bernoulli* 9: 243–65. [CrossRef]

Barndorff-Nielsen, Ole E., and Neil Shephard. 2004. *Financial Volatility: Stochastic Volatility and Lévy Based Models*. Cambridge: Cambridge University Press.

Bättig, Robert. 1999. Completeness of securities market models-an operator point of view. *Annals of Applied Probability* 9: 529–66. [CrossRef]

Bättig, Robert, and Robert A. Jarrow. 1999. The second fundamental theorem of asset pricing: A new approach. *The Review of Financial Studies* 12: 1219–35. [CrossRef]

Bäuerle, Nicole, and Ulric Rieder. 2004. Portfolio optimization with Markov-modulated stock prices and interest rates. *IEEE Transactions on Automatic Control* 49: 442–47. [CrossRef]

Bäuerle, Nicole, and Ulric Riede. 2007. Portfolio optimization with jumps and unobservable intensity process. *Mathematical Finance* 17: 205–24. [CrossRef]

Björk, Tomas, and Bertil Näslund. 1998. Diversified portfolios in continuous time. *European Financial Review* 1: 361–87. [CrossRef]

Black, Fischer, Michael C. Jensen, and Myron Scholes. 1972. Some Empirical Tests, Studies in the Theory of Capital Markets. In *Studies in the Theory of Capital Markets*. Edited by M. Jensen. New York: Praeger, pp. 79–121.

Boel, René, and Michael Kohlmann. 1980. Semimartingale models of stochastic optimal control, with applications to double Martingales. *SIAM Journal on Control and Optimization* 18: 511–33. [CrossRef]

Buffington, John, and Robert J. Elliott. 2002. American options with regime switching. *International Journal of Theoretical and Applied Finance* 5: 497–514. [CrossRef]

Busch, Michael, Ralf Korn, and Frank Thomas Seifried. 2013. Optimal consumption and investment for a large investor: An intensity-based control framework. *Mathematical Finance* 23: 687–717. [CrossRef]

Çinlar, Erhan. 1972a. Markov additive processes: I. *Zeitschrift Wahrscheinlichkeitstheorie und verwandte Gebiete* 24: 85–93. [CrossRef]

Çinlar, Erhan. 1972b. Markov additive processes: II. *Zeitschrift Wahrscheinlichkeitstheorie und verwandte Gebiete* 24: 95–121. [CrossRef]

Corcuera, José Manuel, Joao Guerra, David Nualart, and Wim Schoutens. 2006. Optimal investment in a Lévy market. *Applied Mathematics and Optimization* 53: 279–309. [CrossRef]

Corcuera, José Manuel, David Nualart, and Wim Schoutens. 2005. Completion of a Lévy market by power-jump assets. *Finance and Stochastics* 9: 109–27. [CrossRef]

Cuchiero, Christa, Irene Klein, and Josef Teichmann. 2016. A new perspective on the fundamental theorem of asset pricing for large financial markets. *Theory of Probability and its Applications* 60: 561–79. [CrossRef]

Di Masi, Giovanni Battista, Yuri M. Kabanov, and Wolfgang J. Runggaldier. 1994. Mean variance hedging of options on stocks with Markov volatility. *Theory of Probability and Applications* 39: 173–81. [CrossRef]

Elliott, Rogemar J., Lakhdar Aggoun, and John B. Moore. 1994. *Hidden Markov Models: Estimation and Control*. Berlin: Springer.

Elliott, Rogemar J., Leunglung Chan, and Tak Kuen Siu. 2005. Option pricing and esscher transform under regime switching. *Annals of Finance* 1: 423–32. [CrossRef]

Elliott, Rogemar J., William C. Hunter, and Barbara M. Jamieson. 2001. Financial signal processing: A self calibrating model. *International Journal of Theoretical and Applied Finance* 4: 567–84. [CrossRef]

Elliott, Rogemar J., W. P. Malcolm, and Allanus H. Tsoi. 2003. Robust parameter estimation for asset price models with Markov modulated volatilities. *Journal of Economic Dynamics and Control* 27: 1391–409. [CrossRef]

Fechner, Włodzimierz. 2008. Some inequalities connected with the exponential function. *Archivum Mathematicum (Brno)* 44: 217–22.

Fleming, Wendell H., and Daniel Hernández-Hernández. 2003. An optimal consumption model with stochastic volatility. *Finance and Stochastics* 7: 245–62. [CrossRef]

Fontana, Claudio, Bernt Øksendal, and Agnès Sulem. 2015. Market viability and martingale measures under partial information. *Methodology and Computing in Applied Probability* 17: 15–39. [CrossRef]

Fouque, Jean-Pierre, Andrew Papanicolaou, and Ronnie Sircar. 2017a. Perturbation Analysis for Investment Portfolios Under Partial Information with Expert Opinions. *SIAM Journal on Control and Optimization* 55: 1534–66. [CrossRef]

Fouque, Jean-Pierre, Ronnie Sircar, and T. Zariphopoulou. 2017b. Portfolio optimization and stochastic volatility asymptotics. *Mathematical Finance* 27: 704–45. [CrossRef]

Framstad, Nils Chr., Bernt Øksendal, and Agnes Sulem. 2004. Sufficient stochastic maximum principle for the optimal control of jump diffusions and applications to finance. *Journal of Optimization Theory and Applications* 121: 77–98. [CrossRef]

Fu, Jun, Jiaqin Wei, and Hailiang Yang. 2014. Portfolio optimization in a regime-switching market with derivatives. *European Journal of Operational Research* 233: 184–92. [CrossRef]

Gautam, Natarajan, Vidyadhar Kulkarni, Zbigniew Palmowski, and Tomasz Rolski. 1999. Bounds for fluid models driven by semi-Markov inputs. *Probability in Engineering and Information Sciences* 13: 429–75. [CrossRef]

Goldfeld, Stephen M., and Richard E. Quandt. 1973. A Markov model for switching regressions. *Journal of Econometrics* 1: 3–16. [CrossRef]

Goll, Thomas, and Jan Kallsen. 2000. Optimal portfolios for logarithmic utility. *Stochastic Processes and their Applications* 89: 31–48. [CrossRef]

Goll, Thomas, and Jan Kallsen. 2003. A complete explicit solution to the log-optimal portfolio problem. *The Annals of Applied Probability* 13: 774–99.

Guo, Xin. 2001. Information and option pricings. *Quantitative Finance* 1: 38–44. [CrossRef]

Guo, Xin, Jianjun Miao, and Erwan Morellec. 2005. Irreversible investments with regime shifts. *Journal of Economic Theory* 122: 37–59. [CrossRef]

Gut, Allan. 2005. *Probability: A Graduate Course*. New York: Springer.

Hamilton, James D. 1989. A new approach to the economics analysis of non-stationary time series. *Econometrica* 57: 357–84. [CrossRef]

Heston, Steven. 1993. A closed-form solution for options with stochastic volatility with applications to bond and currency options. *Review of Financial Studies* 6: 327–43. [CrossRef]

Jacod, Jean, and Philip Protter. 2004. *Probability Essentials*, 2nd ed. Berlin and Heidelberg: Springer.

Kabanov, Yuri, and Dmitry Kramkov. 1994. Large financial markets: Asymptotic arbitrage and contiguity. *Probability Theory and Its Applications* 39: 222–29. [CrossRef]

Kabanov, Yuri, and Dmitry Kramkov. 1998. Asymptotic arbitrage in large financial markets. *Finance and Stochastics* 2: 143–72. [CrossRef]

Karatzas, Ioannis, John P. Lehoczky, Steven E. Shreve, and Gan-Lin Xu. 1991. Martingale and duality methods for utility maximization in an incomplete market. *SIAM Journal on Control and Optimization* 29: 702–30. [CrossRef]

Karatzas, Ioannis, and Steven E. Shreve. 1998. *Brownian Motion and Stochastic Calculus*. Berlin, Heidelberg and New York: Springer.

Korn, Ralf, Yaroslav Melnyk, and Frank Thomas Seifried. 2017. Stochastic impulse control with regime-switching dynamics. *European Journal of Operational Research* 260: 1024–42. [CrossRef]

Korn, Ralf, and H. Kraft. 2001. A stochastic control approach to portfolio problems with stochastic interest rates. *SIAM Journal on Control and Optimization* 40: 1250–69. [CrossRef]

Kramkov, Dmitry, and Walter Schachermayer. 1999. The asymptotic elasticity of utility functions and optimal investment in incomplete markets. *Annals of Applied Probability* 9: 904–50. [CrossRef]

Kreps, David M. 1981. Arbitrage and equilibrium in economies with infinitely many commodities. *Journal of Mathematical Economics* 8: 15–35. [CrossRef]

Kushner, Harold J., and Paul G. Dupuis. 1992. *Numerical Methods for Stochastic Control Problems in Continuous Time*. New York: Springer.

Liao, Ming. 2004. *Lévy Processes in Lie Groups*. Cambridge Tracts in Mathematics. Cambridge: Cambridge University Press, vol. 162.

Liu, Ruihua. 2014. Optimal investment and consumption with proportional transaction costs in regime-switching model. *Journal of Optimization Theory and Applications* 163: 614–41. [CrossRef]

Markowitz, Harry M. 1952. Portfolio selection. *The Journal of Finance* 7: 77–91.

Merton, Robert C. 1971. Optimal consumption and portfolio rules in a continuous time model. *Journal of Economic Theory* 3: 373–413. [CrossRef]

Merton, Robert C. 1976. Option pricing when underlying stock returns are discontinuous. *Journal of Financial Economics* 3: 125–44. [CrossRef]

Merton, Robert C. 1980. On estimating the expected return on the market. *Journal of Financial Economics* 8: 323–61. [CrossRef]

Mokkhavesa, Sutee, and Colin Atkinson. 2002. Perturbation solution of optimal portfolio theory with transaction costs for any utility function. *IMA Journal of Management Mathematics* 13: 131–51. [CrossRef]

Nagai, Hideo, and Wolfgang J. Runggaldier. 2008. PDE Approach to Utility Maximization for Market Models with Hidden Markov Factors. In *Seminar on Stochastic Analysis, Random Fields and Applications V, Progress in Probability*. Edited by R. C. Dalang, M. Dozzi and F. Russo. Basel: Birkhuser Verlag, vol. 59, pp. 493–506.

Naik, Vasanttilak. 1993. Option valuation and hedging strategies with jumps in the volatility of asset returns. *Journal of Finance* 48: 1969–84. [CrossRef]

Niu, Liqun. 2008. Some stability results of optimal investment in a simple Lévy market. *Insurance Mathematics Economics* 42: 445–52. [CrossRef]

Øksendal, Bernt, and Agnès Sulem. 2004. *Applied Stochastic Control of Jump Diffusions*. Berlin and Heidelberg: Springer.

Pacheco, António, Loon Ching Tang, and Narahari U. Prabhu. 2009. *Markov-Modulated Processes and Semigenerative Phenomena*. Hackensack: World Scientific.

Palmowski, Zbigniew, Łukasz Stettner, and Anna Sulima. 2018. A note on chaotic and predictable representations for Itô-Markov additive processes. *Stochastic Analysis and Applications* 36: 622–38. [CrossRef]

Pham, Huyên Pham, and Marie-Claire Quenez. 2001. Optimal portfolio in partially observed stochastic volatility models. *The Annals of Applied Probability* 11: 210–38. [CrossRef]

Prabhu, Narahari U. 1998. *Stochastic Storage Processes: Queues, Insurance Risk, Dams, and Data Communication*, 2nd ed. Berlin and Heidelberg:Springer.

Protter, Philip E. 2005. *Stochastic Integration and Differential Equations: A New Approach*, 2nd ed. Berlin: Springer.

Resnick, Sidney I. 2007. *Heavy-Tail Phenomena. Probabilistic and Statistical Modeling*. New York: Springer.

Rieder, Ulrich, and Nicole Bäuerle. 2005. Portfolio optimization with unobservable markov-modulated drift process. *Journal of Applied Probability* 42: 362–78. [CrossRef]

Sass, Jörn, and Ulrich G. Haussmann. 2004. Optimizing the terminal wealth under partial information: The drift process as a continuous time markov chain. *Finance and Stochastics* 8: 553–77. [CrossRef]

Schoutens, Wim. 1999. *Stochastic Processes and Orthogonal Polynomials*. Lecture Notes in Statistics. New York: Springer, vol. 146.

Shen, Yang, and Tak Kuen Siu. 2012. Asset allocation under stochastic interest rate with regime switching. *Economic Modelling* 29: 1126–36. [CrossRef]

Sotomayor, Luz R., and Abel Cadenillas. 2013. Stochastic impulse control with regime switching for the optimal dividend policy when there are business cycles, taxes and fixed costs. *Stochastics: An International Journal of Probability and Stochastic Processes* 85: 707–22. [CrossRef]

Stockbridge, Richard. 2002. Portfolio optimization in markets having stochastic rates. In *Lecture Notes in Control and Information Sciences: Stochastic Theory and Control*. Edited by B. Pasik-Duncan. Berlin: Springer, vol. 280, pp. 447–58.

Teplá, Lucie. 2000. Optimal portfolio policies with borrowing and shortsale constraints. *Journal of Economic Dynamics and Control* 24: 1623–39. [CrossRef]

Tong, Howell. 1978. *Threshold Models in Non-linear Time Series Analysis*. Berlin: Springer.

Tu, Jun. 2010. Is regime switching in stock returns important in asset allocations? *Management Science* 56: 1198–215. [CrossRef]

Yin, George, and Xun Yu Zhou. 2004. Markowitz's mean-variance portfolio selection with regime switching: From discrete-time models to their continuous-time limits. *IEEE Transactions on Automatic Control* 49: 349–60. [CrossRef]

Zariphopoulou, Thaleia. 1992. Investment-consumption models with transaction fees and markov-chain parameters. *SIAM Journal on Control and Optimization* 30: 613–36. [CrossRef]

Zhang, Xin, Robert J. Elliott, Tak Kuen Siu, and Junyi Guo. 2012. Markovian regime-switching market completion using additional Markov jump assets. *IMA Journal of Management Mathematics* 23: 283–305. [CrossRef]

Zhang, Qing. 2001. Stock trading: An optimal selling rule. *SIAM Journal on Control and Optimization* 40: 64–87. [CrossRef]

Zhang, Xin, Tak Kuen Siu, and Qingbin Meng. 2010. Porfolio selection in the enlarged Markovian regime-switching market. *SIAM Journal on Control and Optimization* 48: 3368–88. [CrossRef]

Zhou, Xun Yu, and George Yin. 2003. Markowitz's Mean-Variance Portfolio Selection with Regime Switching: A Continuous Time Model. *SIAM Journal on Control and Optimization* 42: 1466–82. [CrossRef]
Zhang, Qing, and George Yin. 2004. Nearly-optimal asset allocation in hybrid stock investment models. *Journal of Optimization Theory and Applications* 121: 197–222. [CrossRef]

© 2019 by the authors. Licensee MDPI, Basel, Switzerland. This article is an open access article distributed under the terms and conditions of the Creative Commons Attribution (CC BY) license (http://creativecommons.org/licenses/by/4.0/).

risks

MDPI

Article

Dealing with Drift Uncertainty: A Bayesian Learning Approach

Carmine De Franco [1], **Johann Nicolle** [1,2] **and Huyên Pham** [2,*]

[1] OSSIAM, 75017 Paris, France; carmine.de-franco@ossiam.com
[2] LPSM, Université Paris Diderot, 75013 Paris, France; johann.nicolle@ossiam.com
* Correspondence: pham@math.univ-paris-diderot.fr; Tel.: +33-157-279-106

Received: 20 November 2018; Accepted: 4 January 2019; Published: 9 January 2019

Abstract: One of the main challenges investors have to face is model uncertainty. Typically, the dynamic of the assets is modeled using two parameters: the drift vector and the covariance matrix, which are both uncertain. Since the variance/covariance parameter is assumed to be estimated with a certain level of confidence, we focus on drift uncertainty in this paper. Building on filtering techniques and learning methods, we use a Bayesian learning approach to solve the Markowitz problem and provide a simple and practical procedure to implement optimal strategy. To illustrate the value added of using the optimal Bayesian learning strategy, we compare it with an optimal nonlearning strategy that keeps the drift constant at all times. In order to emphasize the prevalence of the Bayesian learning strategy above the nonlearning one in different situations, we experiment three different investment universes: indices of various asset classes, currencies and smart beta strategies.

Keywords: Bayesian learning; Markowitz problem; optimal portfolio; portfolio selection

---

1. Introduction

The seminal work by Markowitz (1952) initiated modern portfolio theory and provided a solution to the portfolio selection problem according to a mean-variance criterion. The mean-variance optimal portfolio is the one that maximizes its expected return at a given level of risk, measured by its variance, or conversely the one that minimizes its risk at a given level of expected return. This one period model has known multiple extensions, among them the discrete time multi-period model by Samuelson (1969) and the continuous time model by Merton (1969).

Initially, the parameters of these models have been considered known and constant, especially the parameters that drive the behavior of the assets: drifts and covariances. It not only oversimplifies the reality but also it raises the question of estimating these parameters. The most basic and widely used method consists of estimating drifts and covariances from past data and fix them once and for all. Estimating volatility in this way appears to give relatively good results in practice, while estimating the drift seems to be more difficult or even impossible, see Merton (1980). Moreover, optimal portfolios are very sensitive to the level of expected returns, as shown in Best and Grauer (1991), and a wrong estimation can result in very suboptimal portfolios a posteriori. See also Elliott et al. (1998) and Siegel and Woodgate (2007) for more details about these issues.

This explains the development of the literature on parameters uncertainty in portfolio analysis, see for instance Barry (1974) and Klein and Bawa (1976), and especially on Bayesian statistics, see (Aguilar and West 2000; Avramov and Zhou 2010; Bodnar et al. 2017; Frost and Savarino 1986). Nonetheless, these models remain static and cannot benefit from the flow of information which results in a nonadaptive strategy, unable to process the most recent information conveyed by the assets market prices. It is one of the main reasons why literature on filtering and learning techniques in a partial information framework has developed, see (Cvitanić et al. (2006); Rogers (2001); Lakner 1995, 1998).

The Bayesian learning approach consists of modeling the uncertainty of a set of parameters by a prior distribution, representing the beliefs of the investor on the potential values of the parameters, which is updated with incoming information, for instance assets market prices. In particular, in our companion paper De Franco et al. (2018), we have solved the multidimensional Markowitz problem in the case of an uncertain drift using Bayesian learning with a Gaussian prior and have provided a brief analysis of sensitivities of the optimal solution w.r.t. the different parameters.

In this paper, we adapt the results in De Franco et al. (2018) to implement the strategy in practice. Indeed, the solution provided is in continuous time and the amounts invested in the assets are unconstrained. Of course, in reality, trading is discrete and amounts invested in assets are limited, so we discretize the optimal solution of the continuous Markowitz problem, turn amounts into proportions and cap the optimal proportions to be invested in order to fit the portfolio management constraints. Our purpose is to show the prevalence of the Bayesian learning strategy above the nonlearning one which considers the drift constant. To do so, we illustrate our point by confronting both strategies to different datasets representing different investment universes. First, we use a panel of major indices in four different asset classes: corporate bonds, sovereign bonds, commodities and equities completed with cash. Then, we consider bank accounts in foreign banks that pay the local interest rate but are valued in EUR, in order to study the performance of both strategies with respect to foreign exchange rates. Finally, we implement both strategies in an investment universe composed of smart beta strategies. Moreover, using the first dataset, we provide a sensitivity analysis of both strategies to various parameters: the uncertainty in the model, the impact of the leverage, the review frequency and the rebalancing frequency. We do not show this analysis for the two other datasets since we would find similar results.

The paper is organized as follows. Section 2 details the model and the discretized optimal strategies while Section 3 depicts the market data and the workflow. Section 4 shows the results in the case of the first dataset, and Section 5 is about the sensitivity analysis of the Bayesian learning and the nonlearning strategies applied to this dataset. Finally, Section 6 deals with foreign exchange rates and Section 7 with smart beta strategies.

2. The Framework

We consider a financial market consisting of one risk-free asset, whose return is denoted by r^f, and n risky assets whose returns $\boldsymbol{r}_t$ are modeled by

$$\begin{cases} \boldsymbol{r}_t &= \boldsymbol{B} + \sigma \boldsymbol{\xi}_t \\ \boldsymbol{\xi}_t &\sim N(0, I_n). \end{cases} \tag{1}$$

We shall assume that the random vectors $\boldsymbol{\xi}_t$ are independent for all t. Model (1) includes major linear models available in the financial literature, such as CAPM (Lintner 1965; Sharpe 1964), discrete-time Black-Scholes (Black and Scholes 1973) or Fama-French models (Fama and French 1993, 2015, 2016). $\boldsymbol{B} \in \mathbb{R}^n$ is the vector of the expected returns of the risky assets, while $\boldsymbol{\Sigma} := \sigma\sigma' \in \mathbb{R}^{n \times n}$ is the covariance matrix of the risky assets. We assume that σ^{-1} exists. We denote by $\mathcal{A}$ the set of admissible investment strategies. An admissible strategy $\mathbf{w} = (\mathbf{w_t})_t \in \mathcal{A}$ represents the fraction of wealth invested in the assets at any time t. Recalling from the self-financing condition that,

$$X_{s+1} = X_s \left(1 + \mathbf{w_s'r_{s+1}} + \left(1 - w_s'1\right) r^f\right), \quad s = 0, \ldots, T-1,$$

we write the wealth at maturity $T > 0$ as

$$X_T^{\mathbf{w}} = X_0 \prod_{s=0}^{T-1} \left(1 + \mathbf{w_s'r_{s+1}} + \left(1 - w_s'1\right) r^f\right).$$

We consider an investor who is aiming to solve the Markowitz problem:

$$\begin{cases} \max_{\mathbf{w}\in\mathcal{A}} \mathbb{E}\left[X_T^{\mathbf{w}}\right] \\ \\ \mathrm{Var}\left(X_T^{\mathbf{w}}\right) \leq \vartheta, \end{cases} \tag{2}$$

where $\vartheta > 0$ is the risk tolerance for the investor.

The initial version of the Markowitz problem (Markowitz 1952), which was stated for a single period, has been widely studied and solutions in the multi-period framework (such ours) in both discrete and continuous time have been provided (see e.g., Karatzas et al. (1987); Merton 1969, 1975; Samuelson (1969) among others). The common assumptions in previous works are that both expected return and volatility coefficients ($\boldsymbol{B}$ and $\boldsymbol{\Sigma}$ in our framework) are known. In practice, these parameters are not directly observable and must be estimated from the data or input by the investor at inception. In both cases, biased parameters can significantly affect ex-post performance of the optimal strategy. Although the parameter $\boldsymbol{\Sigma}$ can be estimated from the data with some degree of confidence, the estimation of $\boldsymbol{B}$ turns out to be quite difficult, if not impossible. Because the optimal strategy strongly depends on both $\boldsymbol{B}$ and $\boldsymbol{\Sigma}$, a wrong estimation could significantly affect the optimal strategy.

To get closer to reality and account for model uncertainty, we assume reasonably that the investor has an a priori view on the risky assets and their expected returns, but she is uncertain about how good her forecast is. Introducing uncertainty into the problem brings it closer to the real-life situation, where not only does the investor not know the parameters of the model, but is also forced to admit that her estimates are uncertain. More precisely, the investor does not observe $\boldsymbol{B}$ and only assumes that $\boldsymbol{B} \sim \mu$, where μ is a probability distribution in $\mathbb{R}^n$ centered at $\boldsymbol{b_0}$ ($\mathbb{E}\left[\boldsymbol{B}\right] = \boldsymbol{b_0}$). The parameter $\boldsymbol{b_0}$ is the vector of returns the investor is expecting, while μ translates her uncertainty about it.

Remark 1. *When $\mu = \delta_{\boldsymbol{b_0}}$—the Dirac distribution at $\boldsymbol{b_0}$—the investor has no uncertainty about her forecast.*

Remark 2 (Discretization). *Implementing optimal strategies in practice leads to continuous adjustments to the optimal solutions in time and makes them suboptimal. Here, we discretize the continuous optimal solutions and controls, and cap them. To propose a solution to Problem (2), we suggest confronting the discretized continuous optimal Bayesian learning and nonlearning solutions since the investor can observe assets prices nearly continuously but trades in discrete time.*

The paper De Franco et al. (2018) solved the continuous-time version of problem (1) for a large class of distributions μ with $\mathbb{E}[|B|^2] < \infty$ in a Bayesian framework using dynamic programming techniques. We report here the discretized version of the results in the Gaussian case $\mu = N(\boldsymbol{b_0}, \boldsymbol{\Sigma_0})$: Let $\mu = N(\boldsymbol{b_0}, \boldsymbol{\Sigma_0})$ with $\boldsymbol{\Sigma_0} > 0$. Then, the discretized version of the continuous-time optimal solution of the Bayesian–Markowitz problem is given by (the Bayesian learning case, *BL*)

$$\mathbf{w}_s^{BL} = \alpha\left(s, X_s, \hat{\boldsymbol{B}}_s\right) / X_s \tag{3}$$

where X_s is the wealth process at time s and

- $\hat{\boldsymbol{B}}_s = \left(\boldsymbol{\Sigma_0}^{-1} + s\boldsymbol{\Sigma}^{-1}\right)\left(\boldsymbol{\Sigma_0}^{-1}\boldsymbol{b_0} + (\boldsymbol{\sigma}')^{-1}\boldsymbol{Y}_s\right)$,
- $\boldsymbol{Y}_s$ is defined as $[\boldsymbol{\sigma}\boldsymbol{Y}_s]^i = \prod_{u=0}^{s-1}\left(1 + \boldsymbol{r}_u^i\right) + \frac{s}{2}\boldsymbol{\Sigma}_{ii}$,
- $\alpha\left(s, x, \boldsymbol{b}\right) = \left(x_0 - x + \sqrt{\vartheta}\frac{e^{R(0,\boldsymbol{b_0})}}{\sqrt{e^{R(0,\boldsymbol{b_0})} - 1}}\right)\left(\boldsymbol{\Sigma}^{-1}\boldsymbol{b} - \left(\boldsymbol{\psi}(s)\boldsymbol{\sigma}^{-1}\right)'\nabla_b R(s, \boldsymbol{b})\right)$,
- $\boldsymbol{\psi}(s) = \boldsymbol{\Sigma_0}\left(\boldsymbol{\Sigma} + s\boldsymbol{\Sigma_0}\right)^{-1}\boldsymbol{\sigma}$,
- R is the unique solution to the following semi-linear parabolic PDE

$$\begin{cases} 0 = -\partial_t R - \frac{1}{2}\mathrm{tr}\left(\psi\psi' D_b^2 R\right) + 2\left(\psi\sigma^{-1}b\right)' \nabla_b R - \frac{1}{2}\left|\psi'\nabla_b R\right|^2 - \left|\sigma^{-1}b\right|^2, \\ 0 = R(T,b), \end{cases}$$

which in the case of a Gaussian prior proves to be of the form $R(s,\boldsymbol{b}) = \boldsymbol{b}'\boldsymbol{M}(s)\boldsymbol{b} + r(s)$, where $\boldsymbol{M}$ is the solution to a multidimensional Riccati equation, for which the solution can be found explicitly, and r is the solution to a first-order linear differential equation depending on $\boldsymbol{\psi}$ and $\boldsymbol{M}$, which can also be explicitly calculated. See De Franco et al. (2018) for further details.

The process $\hat{\boldsymbol{B}}$ is the conditional expectation of $\boldsymbol{B}$ given the current observation of the assets returns, which are given by $\boldsymbol{Y}$. The matrix $\boldsymbol{\Sigma}_0$ represents the uncertainty around $\boldsymbol{b}_0$. As time goes by, we observe more returns which in turns improves our knowledge of $\boldsymbol{B}$, as one can see from the fact that when $s \to T$, more weight is put on $\boldsymbol{\Sigma}^{-1}$ in the definition of $\hat{\boldsymbol{B}}$. The matrix valued function $\boldsymbol{\psi}$ is linked to the conditional covariance of $\boldsymbol{B}$ given $\boldsymbol{Y}$.

Remark 3. *When there is no uncertainty ($\mu = \delta_{\boldsymbol{b}_0}$), or when the investor directly inputs her estimate $\boldsymbol{b}_0$, the structure of the discretized version of the optimal continuous solution is simplified as follows (the nonlearning case,* NL*):*

$$\mathbf{w}_s^{NL} = \alpha^{NL}\left(s, X_s\right) / X_s \tag{4}$$

where

- $\alpha^{NL}\left(s,x\right) = \left(x_0 - x + \sqrt{\vartheta}\frac{e^{R(0,\boldsymbol{b}_0)}}{\sqrt{e^{R(0,\boldsymbol{b}_0)}-1}}\right)\boldsymbol{\Sigma}^{-1}\boldsymbol{b}_0,$
- $R(s,b) = \boldsymbol{b}'\boldsymbol{\Sigma}^{-1}\boldsymbol{b}(T-s).$

The main differences between the Bayesian learning and the nonlearning strategies arise from

- the *market risk premium* R in the leverage coefficient,
- the *correction* term $\left(\boldsymbol{\psi}(\boldsymbol{s})\sigma^{-1}\right)' \nabla_b R(s,\boldsymbol{b})$ which is zero for the nonlearning strategy.

As time goes by, we observe realized returns and we learn more about $\boldsymbol{B}$. Indeed, with uncertainty, the Bayesian learning strategy is updated with $\hat{\boldsymbol{B}}$, which is the conditional expectation of $\boldsymbol{B}$ given the current observation (new knowledge). The trade $\boldsymbol{\Sigma}^{-1}\hat{\boldsymbol{B}}$ is modified with the corrective term $\left(\boldsymbol{\psi}(\boldsymbol{s})\sigma^{-1}\right)' \nabla_b R(s,\hat{\boldsymbol{B}})$.

Both $\mathbf{w}^{BL}$ and $\mathbf{w}^{NL}$ are unconstrained. In order to provide a realistic analysis on both strategies, we consider capped versions of them.

Definition 1. *The capping operator for an investment strategy $\mathbf{w}$ with a leverage $l > 0$ is*

$$c(\mathbf{w}, l) := w1_{|\mathbf{w}|_1 \le l} + \frac{l}{|\mathbf{w}|_1} w1_{|\mathbf{w}|_1 > l},$$

where $|\mathbf{w}|_1 = \sum_{i=1}^{n} |\mathbf{w}_i|$.

In Section 3, we will implement both the Bayesian learning and the nonlearning strategies in the context of asset allocation with real market data, to get insights on the effect of learning and its value added (*value of information*).

3. Market Data

We consider four asset classes across different regions, each of which is represented by a well-known market index detailed in Table 1, and the EONIA rate as the risk-free rate for an investor whose base currency is the Euro.

Table 1. Major market indices relative to each currency and asset class.

Bloomberg Ticker	Name	Currency	Asset Class
SPDYCITR Index	S&P GSCI Dynamic Roll TR	USD	Commodity
GOLDLNPM Index	LBMA Gold Price PM	USD	Commodity
LECPTREU Index	Bloomberg Barclays Euro Aggregate Corporate TR Index	EUR	Corporate Bonds
IBOXHY Index	iBoxx USD Liquid High Yield Index	USD	Corporate Bonds
IBOXIG Index	iBoxx USD Liquid Investment Grade Index	USD	Corporate Bonds
IBOXXMJA Index	EUR Corporate Liquid Hight Yield	EUR	Corporate Bonds
SPTR500N Index	S&P 500 Net TR Index	USD	Equity
SX5T Index	Eurostoxx 50 Net TR Index	EUR	Equity
TUKXG Index	FTSE 100 TR Index	GBP	Equity
NDUEEGF Index	MSCI Emerging Net TR Index	USD	Equity
SPTPXN Index	S&P Topix 150 NR	JPY	Equity
LUATTRUU Index	Bloomberg Barclays US Treasury TR Unhedged Index	USD	Sovereign Bonds
LEATTREU Index	Bloomberg Barclays EurAgg Treasury TR Unhedged Index	EUR	Sovereign Bonds
JPEICORE Index	JP Morgan EMBI Global Core Index	USD	Sovereign Bonds
FTFIBGT Index	FTSE Actuaries UK Conv. GILTs All Stocks TR Index	GBP	Sovereign Bonds
EONIA Index	EMMI EURO Overnight Index average	EUR	Cash

Non-Euro-denominated indices are hedged against the Euro simply by implementing a monthly rolled hedging overlay with one-month forward contracts. We collected data from December 1998, except for the EUR Corporate Liquid High Yield for which we only obtained data from January 2006. Prices were sourced from Bloomberg, while currency spot and forward rates came from Datastream and both refer to the 4 p.m. London fixing. Our choice of market indices is motivated by their popularity among investors, their liquidity, and the wide range of financial products available in the market that give exposures to these indices (such as listed futures and ETFs). While limited in number, they provide well-diversified exposures to major global asset classes. Therefore, this suits the underlying premises of the Markowitz problem which is less suited for asset allocation in presence of many underlyings.

The testing period is from January 2000 to June 2018. To implement both *BL* and *NL*, we iteratively followed the workflow outlined below and Table 2 collects the parameters (in bold in the workflow) used for our test.

Work Flow 1.

- *Let* $\mathbf{T} > 0$ *and consider the time-frame* $\{t_0 < t_1 < \cdots t_n = T\}$.
- *We call* t_0 *a* Review *date since at this date we estimate all the parameters and calculate the function* R *that define* $\mathbf{w}^{BL}$ *in* (3) *and* $\mathbf{w}^{NL}$ *in* (4). *To ensure a realistic implementation of both strategies, all data-based estimations are performed with data available before the* Review *date* t_0 *and ending on* $t_0 - \mathbf{Lag}$. *The first* ***Review*** *date is 21 January 2000.*
- *We call* t_k *a* Rebalancing *date if, at this date, we updated the portfolio weights according to* (3) *and* (4). *To limit turnover and transaction costs, the subsets of* Rebalancing *dates in* $[0, T]$ *is relatively small. We assume that both* Review *and* Rebalancing *dates are Fridays, so that the number of* Rebalancing *dates in the* $[0, T]$ *period is given by the frequency* **Freq**.
- $\mathbf{b_0}$ *is estimated as the sample mean over the past* $r^{\mathbf{w}}$ *days ending on* $t_0 - \mathbf{Lag}$ *or over the maximum data available with a minimum of 30 data points.* $\mathbf{\Sigma}$ *is estimated as the sample covariance matrix over* $s^{\mathbf{w}}$ *days ending on* $t_0 - \mathbf{Lag}$ *or over the maximum data available with a minimum of 30 data points.*
- *We consider a parametric function for* ϑ *as follows:*

$$\vartheta = \vartheta(\mathbf{d}) := T\,(\mathbf{d} \times X_{t_0})^2 \,/\, \left(1.96^2\right), \quad \mathbf{d} \in (0,1).$$

The motivation behind our choice comes from Problem (2). *Indeed, we expect that*

$$X_T \succeq \mathbb{E}\,[X_T] - 1.96 \times \sqrt{\frac{Var\,(X_T)}{T}} \geq \mathbb{E}\,[X_T] - 1.96 \times \sqrt{\frac{\vartheta}{T}},$$

and we set ϑ so that within our confidence interval, the gap to the expected value of X_T is a fraction of the initial wealth

$$1.96 \times \sqrt{\frac{\vartheta}{T}} \sim \mathbf{d} \times X_{t_0}.$$

- *The uncertainty around the estimate $\boldsymbol{b_0}$ is measured by $\boldsymbol{\Sigma_0}$. We assume $\boldsymbol{\Sigma_0}$ to be diagonal. Therefore, each diagonal entry measures the degree of confidence we have on the relative entry of $\boldsymbol{b_0}$. Each diagonal entry is modeled as follows:*

$$\Sigma_0^{ii} = \Sigma_0^{ii}(\mathbf{unc}) := \mathbf{unc} \times \left(\frac{pct_{95}^i - pct_5^i}{2} \right)^2,$$

  where pct_{95}^i (pct_5^i) is the 95% (5%) quantile of the empirical distribution of the return r^i. To calculate these quantiles, we consider the time series of the returns r^i spanning for r^q days and ending on $t_0 - \mathbf{Lag}$. Up to the parameter $\mathbf{unc}$, the square root of Σ_0^{ii} is half of the segment, centered at the median, that contains 90% of the empirical distribution over r^q days.
- *Strategies $\mathbf{w}^{BL}$ and $\mathbf{w}^{NL}$ are considered in their capped versions according to Definition 1 with a maximum leverage $\mathbf{L}$.*
- *At time T, we rerun the workflow by setting $t_0 = T$ and update all parameters according to the new data available.*

It should be noted that the choice of diagonal $\boldsymbol{\Sigma_0}$ does not imply that assets are uncorrelated. The matrix $\boldsymbol{\Sigma_0}$ represents the uncertainty the investor has around her initial prior $\boldsymbol{b_0}$. While assets are correlated, we assume that the investor makes her initial expectations on $\boldsymbol{B}$ and she only includes her anticipated error due to uncertainty on her expectations. To simplify, we do not include off-diagonal terms (uncertainty on pairwise cross-expectations), because this allows for a simple, one-parameter modeling of uncertainty in $\boldsymbol{\Sigma_0}$.

Our choice of Σ_0^{ii} reflects the assumption that investors anticipate the assets returns to be equal to $\boldsymbol{b_0} + error$, and the error, which is unknown and represents their uncertainty around the expectation $\boldsymbol{b_0}$, depends on the width of the empirical distribution of returns. In practice, if we decide to proxy expected returns with the average of past returns (which of course is known to be a very poor indicator of future returns), then the width of the empirical distribution, here measured by the difference between the 95% and 5% quantiles, serves as a proxy for uncertainty. The fine-tuning parameter *unc* is a simple way to increase the uncertainty in the initial guess $\boldsymbol{b_0}$.

Table 2. Parameters used in the implementation of *BL* and *NL* as defined in the workflow.

Parameter	Value
X_0	100
T	3 months
Lag	1 day
Freq	Monthly, 3rd Friday of each month.
r^w	750 days
s^w	125 days
d	10%
unc	100
r^q	125
L	200%

The workflow above and Table 2 represent the *Base Case*. In Section 4, we report the results for both the Bayesian learning (*BL*) and the nonlearning (*NL*) strategies over the last 18 years. In Section 5, we will assess the sensitivity of both strategies to changes in the parameters of the *Base Case* to get a better grasp of the value added of learning in the context of portfolio construction.

4. The Base Case Result

We implemented the workflow to build the wealth processes X^{BL} and X^{NL} as in (2) related to the *BL* and *NL* strategies in the Base Case framework (Table 2). For the sake of simplicity, we refer to *BL* as either the strategy weights $\mathbf{w}^{BL}$ or the associated wealth process X^{BL} and we do the same for *NL*. Table 3 collects some long term statistics for both strategies. Although our choice of statistics is limited and many other interesting properties could have been easily derived, such as skew, kurtosis, VaR, CVaR or turnover (as e.g., in Scaillet (2004)), we prefer to show the statistics that are usually considered at any initial due diligence for investment strategies, such as annualized performance, volatility, maximum drawdown, Sharpe ratios and information ratios. The main reason behind our choice is to provide evidence on the effect of learning in the improvement of long-term performance.

Table 3. Statistics for the *BL* and *NL* strategies. The Sharpe Ratio is calculated as the ratio between annualized performance and annualized volatility. In this case, the difference is given in relative terms. Data from January 2000 to June 2018.

Statistics	*BL*	*NL*	Difference
Ann. Performance	5.96%	3.96%	2.00%
Ann. Volatility	5.51%	4.92%	0.59%
Max. Drawdown	−8.51%	−11.2%	2.70%
Sharpe ratio	1.08	0.80	34.26%
Information ratio	0.55	-	-

Over the period from January 2000 to June 2018, *BL* delivered an annualized performance of 5.96% while *NL* reached 3.96%. Incorporating uncertainty and learning from the data yielded an annualized 2% excess return. In terms of risk metrics, annualized volatility is slightly higher for *BL* (0.59% difference) but also shows a better maximum drawdown figure (−8.51% for *BL* versus −11.20% for *NL*). Finally, the Sharpe ratio is 1.08 for *BL* versus 0.80 for *NL*, or a 34.26% improvement in relative terms. The information ratio of *BL* over *NL* is about 0.55, meaning that the performance of *BL* comes from a better ability to process incoming information.

Figure 1a shows the historical levels of the wealth processes *BL* and *NL*, while Figure 1b provides the relative strength of *BL* over *NL* as well as the growth line. An increasing relative strength index signals outperformance of *BL* over *NL*, while a decreasing index shows underperformance.

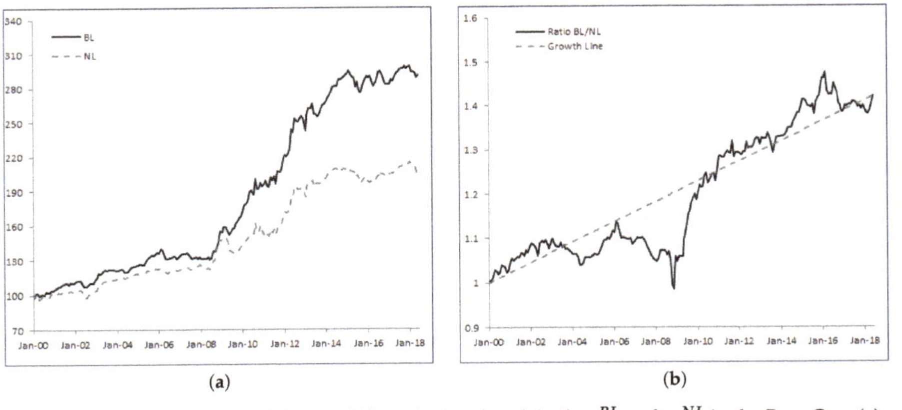

Figure 1. Historical values of the portfolios calculated with both $\mathbf{w}^{BL}$ and $\mathbf{w}^{NL}$ in the Base Case (**a**) and their ratio (**b**).

Looking at Figure 1b, *BL* mostly delivers a more robust and more regular performance than *NL*. Integrating uncertainty in the drift, learning from the data and adjusting the strategy accordingly clearly adds value over time. Specifically, we identify three distinct periods: from inception until February 2006 the ratio BL/NL has an upward trend at moderate pace, reaching 1.13 (or equivalently 13% cumulated outperformance); then *BL* underperforms *NL* until October 2008; and finally, from October 2008 to June 2018, *BL* strongly dominates *NL* with 40% of cumulated outperformance.

5. Sensitivity Analysis

In the following paragraphs, we will stress-test the *BL* strategy by measuring the effects of the main parameters on long term results. Our stress-test methodology consists in fixing all but one of the parameters detailed in Table 2 and varying the remaining parameter across plausible values.

5.1. Impact of Uncertainty

Here, we study the effect of the uncertainty parameter *unc* in the strategy. Higher values of *unc* signal a higher volatility of the estimate $\boldsymbol{b}_0$, hence a higher uncertainty on the estimate of the expected returns. We study the *BL*strategy for $unc \in \{10, 50, 100, 200, 300\}$, where the value $unc = 100$ corresponds to the Base Case detailed in Section 4. Table 4 shows the results.

Table 4. Statistics for *BL* strategies with different values of *unc* and *NL* as defined in the workflow. The Sharpe ratio improvement is relative to *NL*.

			BL			NL
unc	10	50	100	200	300	
Ann. Performance	4.59%	5.76%	5.96%	6.41%	6.51%	3.96%
Ann. Volatility	5.25%	5.49%	5.51%	5.62%	5.76%	4.92%
Max. Drawdown	−10.21%	−8.56%	−8.51%	−8.27%	−8.58%	−11.2%
Sharpe ratio	0.87	1.05	1.08	1.14	1.13	0.8
Sharpe ratio impr.	8.64%	30.45%	34.26%	41.72%	40.54%	-
Information ratio	0.34	0.58	0.55	0.57	0.54	-

Intuitively, among the *BL* strategies detailed in Table 4, the strategy with $unc = 10$ is the closest to *NL* and this is confirmed by the performance and volatility figures. Indeed, with such a low level of uncertainty, we are confident in our initial estimate $\boldsymbol{b}_0$. As we increase *unc*, the confidence we place in $\boldsymbol{b}_0$ decreases.

Very interestingly, as *unc* increases, the excess return of the corresponding *BL* strategy over *NL* increases without significantly increasing the risk. Therefore, Sharpe ratios increase with *unc* from 0.87 for $unc = 10$ to 1.13 for $unc = 300$. More striking is the relative increase in Sharpe ratios with respect to *NL*—for $unc = 10$ we only have an increase of 8.64% and for $unc = 300$ the relative increase is 40.54%. Finally, the Information ratio rapidly stabilizes around 0.5.

Figure 2a,b graphically renders the increase in both annualized performances, excess returns and Sharpe ratios with respect to *NL* as a function of *unc*.

Figure 3 shows the historical levels of the strategy *BL* with $unc = 10$ (minimum uncertainty), $unc = 300$ (high uncertainty) and $unc = 100$ (Base Case) compared to *NL*. The *BL* strategies share the same profile, but the higher the *unc* parameter, the higher the excess return we find in the long run.

Clearly, the standard solution to the Markowitz problem suffers from the poor estimate of $\boldsymbol{b}_0$, while the *BL* strategy is able to adjust and react to new observable data. Moreover, the higher the uncertainty, the better *BL* behaves compared to *NL*.

Unreported tests showed us that with this particular dataset, we can increase the *unc* parameter even further. At some point though, around 10,000, the *BL* strategy underperforms *NL*. Indeed, when uncertainty is extremely high, the matrix $\boldsymbol{\Sigma}_0$ that controls the a priori knowledge we have on $\boldsymbol{B}$ is simply uninformative because we are allowing $\boldsymbol{B}$ to span too vast a region of potential values. Therefore, the learning process, over a relatively short period of time of three months, is slow and does not add value.

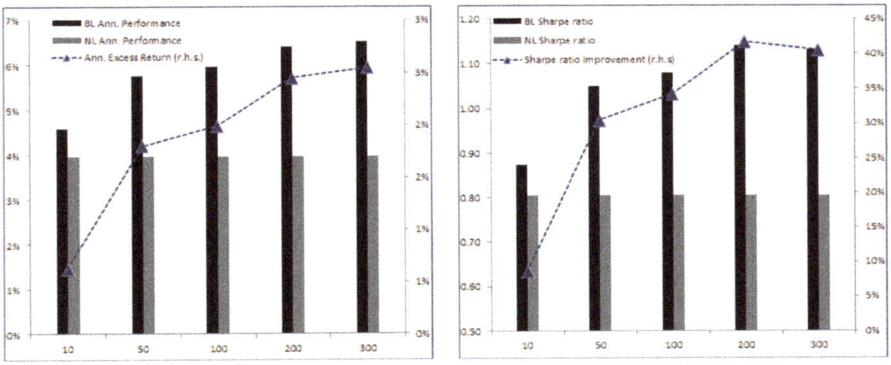

(**a**) (**b**)

Figure 2. Annualized performances and excess returns of *BL* as a function of *unc* (**a**); Sharpe ratios and relative improvement (**b**).

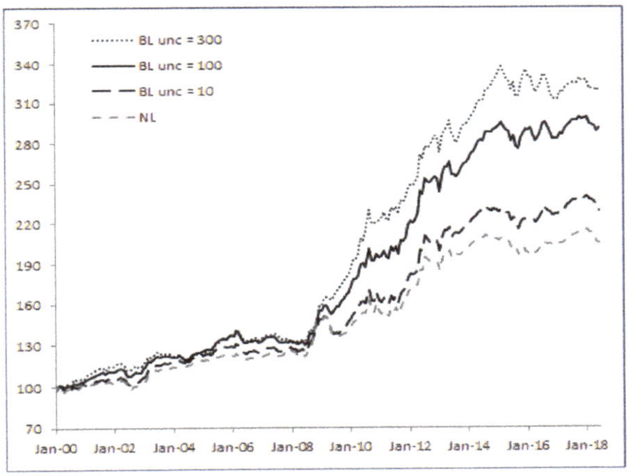

Figure 3. Historical values of the *BL* portfolios calculated with $unc = 10, 100, 300$ and *NL*.

5.2. Impact of Leverage

We now look at the maximum leverage parameter L in both strategies. Higher values of L make both $c(\mathbf{w}^{BL}, L)$ and $c(\mathbf{w}^{NL}, L)$ closer to the unconstrained weights. We test $L \in \{100\%, 150\%, 200\%, 250\%, 300\%\}$, where the value $L = 200\%$ corresponds to the Base Case detailed in Section 4. Table 5 collects the results, while Figure 4a,b gives a graphical overview of the impact on long term statistics.

Table 5. Statistics for *BL* and *NL* strategies with different levels of maximum leverage *L*. The Sharpe ratio improvement is calculated as the relative difference between *BL* and *NL* Sharpe ratios for the same level of maximum leverage.

L	100%		150%		200%		250%		300%	
	BL	*NL*	*BL*	*NL*	*BL*	*NL*	*BL*	*NL*	*BL*	*NL*
Ann. Performance	3.78%	2.48%	4.89%	3.23%	5.96%	3.96%	7.06%	4.39%	7.96%	5.00%
Ann. Volatility	2.78%	2.48%	4.12%	3.64%	5.51%	4.92%	6.85%	6.09%	8.11%	7.23%
Max. Drawdown	−3.96%	−5.59%	−5.92%	−8.43%	−8.51%	−11.2%	−12.49%	−13.01%	−16.33%	−14.07%
Sharpe ratio	1.36	1	1.19	0.89	1.08	0.8	1.03	0.72	0.98	0.69
Sharpe ratio impr.	36.36%	-	33.96%	-	34.26%	-	42.89%	-	41.88%	-
Information Ratio	0.69	-	0.65	-	0.55	-	0.58	-	0.53	-

As the maximum leverage L increases, the corresponding excess return of the *BL* strategy over *NL* increases. For $L = 100\%$, the excess return is 1.30% and goes up to 2.96% for $L = 300\%$.

Clearly, and as expected, the excess return increases with the leverage and on average we observe that adding 100% of leverage brings 0.80% in extra excess return. When we look at the Sharpe ratios, we see that *BL* always outperforms *NL* but the relation is more complex than the previous one. Both *BL* and *NL* Sharpe ratios decrease with L. Indeed, as L increases, we observe higher performances but also higher volatilities, and the volatility grows faster than the performance. This is obvious, because when L increases the strategy becomes more sensitive to any error in the estimated parameters, which is reflected in higher volatility. As $L \to \infty$, the strategies become unconstrained and bring all the instability that is well known to go alongside with price-based strategies. On a relative basis, the improvement in the Sharpe ratios first decreases as L reaches 200% and then increases.

To conclude, it appears that the impact of the maximum leverage L is as expected—it brings extra performance at the cost of higher risk. Because we know real data do not need to follow model (1), unconstrained *BL* and *NL* (as any price-based strategies) tend to amplify any model error, making the leverage constraint a wise feature to consider.

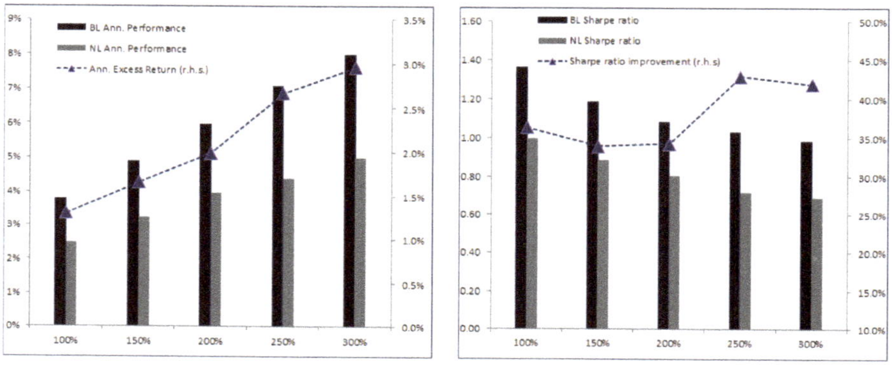

(**a**) (**b**)

Figure 4. Annualized performances and excess returns of *BL* as a function of L (**a**); Sharpe ratios and relative improvement (**b**).

5.3. Impact of the Review Frequency

Probably one of the most important features of the learning effect on the portfolio is the frequency at which we recalibrate the parameters of the model. We have chosen a three-month frequency in the Base Case. In other words, every three months we compute new estimates of $\boldsymbol{b}_0$ and $\boldsymbol{\Sigma}$ and input a new matrix $\boldsymbol{\Sigma}_0$, driving the uncertainty. We expected that the lower the frequency, the better *BL* would compare to *NL*. The main reason behind this thesis is that the strategy *NL* will be stuck with parameters $\boldsymbol{b}_0$ and $\boldsymbol{\Sigma}$ for a long period of time, during which we know that they will most likely become obsolete as the market evolves and new information is processed. As investors know very well, forecasting is difficult and outdated forecasts are badly suited for portfolio construction[1]. On the other side, *BL* can adapt over time because it embeds uncertainty about $\boldsymbol{b}_0$.

1 *It's tough to make predictions, especially about the future.* The quote, which clearly applies in the context of portfolio construction, has been reported by many different people. According to https://quoteinvestigator.com/2013/10/20/no-predict/, it first appeared in Danish documents, but well known personalities such as Neils Bohr, Mark Kac, Stanislaw M. Ulam, and, probably misattributed, Mark Twain and Yogi Berra.

Let us consider the frequency parameter *Freq* in both strategies varying from three to twelve months, $Freq \in \{3\,M, 6\,M, 9\,M, 12\,M\}$, where the value $Freq = 3\,M$ corresponds to the Base Case detailed in Section 4. Table 6 shows the results.

Table 6. Statistics for *BL* and *NL* strategies with different levels of the review frequency *Freq*. The Sharpe ratio improvement is calculated as the relative difference between *BL* and *NL* Sharpe ratios for the same review frequency.

Freq	3 *M*		6 *M*		9 *M*		12 *M*	
	BL	*NL*	*BL*	*NL*	*BL*	*NL*	*BL*	*NL*
Ann. Performance	5.96%	3.96%	4.74%	3.25%	4.28%	2.41%	4.75%	2.21%
Ann. Volatility	5.51%	4.92%	5.5%	5.35%	5.71%	5.45%	5.36%	4.5%
Max. Drawdown	−8.51%	−11.2%	−11.62%	−13.71%	−12.44%	−16.15%	−8.9%	−16.05%
Sharpe ratio	1.08	0.8	0.86	0.61	0.75	0.44	0.89	0.49
Sharpe ratio impr.	34.26%	-	41.74%	-	69.38%	-	80.4%	-
Information Ratio	0.55	-	0.33	-	0.35	-	0.57	-

As we lower the review frequency, we see the performances of both *BL* and *NL* decreasing. Nevertheless, the excess return of *BL* over *NL* actually increases at frequencies lower than 6-month. The fact that it is not monotonic is related to the timing effect. The best metric to assess the value added of the learning feature remains the relative improvement in Sharpe ratios, as shown in Figure 5b. Here we see that as the frequency lowers, more risk-adjusted value added comes from the learning effect: at 3 months, the relative improvement in Sharpe ratio between *BL* and *NL* is 34.26%. At 6 months it goes up to 41.47%, then 69.38% at 9 months and finally 80.4% relative improvement at the 12-month frequency. Clearly, *BL* outperforms *NL* if we do not review the parameters of the model quite often, and this is clearly attributable to the fact that *BL* can adjust over time according to the data observed and the adjustments it can make on the a priori distribution of $\boldsymbol{B}$.

For the sake of simplicity, we do not report the results here, but it is possible to increase the efficiency of *BL* compared to *NL* if we simultaneously modify the frequency *Freq* and the uncertainty parameter *unc* in $\boldsymbol{\Sigma}_0$. Over long investment horizons, the investor would definitely habr more uncertainty on her a priori estimate $\boldsymbol{b}_0$, therefore it makes perfect sense to consider *Freq* = 12 coupled with *unc* = 1600 or higher[2].

[2] We suggest 1600 simply as a rule of thumb: the ratio of frequency between 3 M and 12 M is 4 so that we pass a $4^2 = 16$ factor in *unc*. Of course, we do not expect this parameter to be the best choice since, empirically, uncertainty grows more than linearly with time, but even this, provides slightly higher Sharpe ratio improvements.

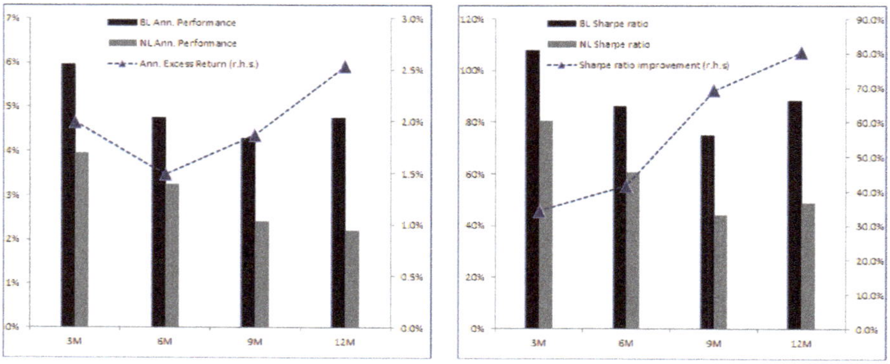

(a) (b)

Figure 5. Annualized performances and excess returns of *BL* as a function of *L* (**a**); Sharpe ratios and relative improvement (**b**).

5.4. Impact of Rebalancing Frequency

We conclude this section with an overview on the impact of the rebalancing frequency on both *BL* and *NL*. This exercise is only theoretical, since within the Base Case we only performed three trades (one each month before the next review). A lower rebalancing frequency of trading would mean that we do not fully exploit the power of learning by adjusting the portfolio. Higher rebalancing frequency carries a turnover (and transaction cost) issue, that would make any benefit only hypothetical. Furthermore, when we rebalance too often, we embark significant amount of noise coming from daily, short term, price movements. Usually, practitioners consider higher rebalancing frequencies only for a small portion of the portfolio, i.e., they only rebalance a fraction x of their portfolio while keeping the remaining $1 - x$ unchanged and they roll over. Because this goes beyond the scope of this paper, we limit ourselves to monthly versus biweekly rebalancing frequency. Table 7 collects summary statistics for *BL* and *NL* when the optimal weights in the Base Case are implemented on both monthly and biweekly frequencies.

Table 7. Statistics for *BL* and *NL* strategies with different rebalancing frequencies *Reb Freq*, monthly versus biweekly. The Sharpe ratio improvement is calculated as the relative difference between *BL* and *NL* Sharpe ratios for the same rebalancing frequency.

Reb Freq	**Monthly**		**Bi-Weekly**	
	BL	***NL***	***BL***	***NL***
Ann. Performance	5.96%	3.96%	5.42%	2.43%
Ann. Volatility	5.51%	4.92%	5.18%	4.93%
Max. Drawdown	−8.51%	−11.2%	−13.62%	−14.08%
Sharpe ratio	1.08	0.8	1.05	0.49
Sharpe ratio impr.	34.26%	-	112.01%	-
Information Ratio	0.55	-	0.77	-

As we go from the monthly to the biweekly rebalancing frequency, we observe a small decrease in annualized performance of *BL*, while the drop is more significant for *NL*. Although these numbers should not be taken as very informative due to the timing effect, there is clearly not a strong incentive for *BL* to rebalance more often, since performance goes down slightly, as does volatility. In the end, the Sharpe ratio seems fairly stable. On the other hand, *NL* experiences a large drop in performance as well as an important increase in its maximum drawdown. Indeed, when we look at the structure of the strategy *NL* in (4), we see that the trade $\boldsymbol{\Sigma}^{-1}\boldsymbol{b}_0$ does not change at higher frequency. So, *NL* will implement the same trade (up to the maximum leverage). If, for example, the *NL* strategy was successful in the first two weeks, at the next rebalancing it will most likely reverse this successful trade because of the $x_{t_0} - x_t$ part of $\mathbf{w}^{NL}$. Conversely, if the *NL* strategy was unsuccessful over a two-week period with a trade, at the next rebalancing it will increase this trade for the same reason. Therefore, *NL* tends to have a reversal feature at short horizon/high frequency.

As far as *BL* is concerned, because of uncertainty, the strategy can accommodate for larger deviation of the process B relatively to the forecast $\boldsymbol{b}_0$, so that it does not necessarily have to reverse a successful trade or leverage an unsuccessful one. Indeed, when we look at (3), a successful trade will lower the leverage, but this can be compensated by the corrective term in the trade, which depends on ψ and $\nabla_b R$, so that in theory *BL* does not systematically have a reversal feature.

Finally, given our dataset and the fact that the momentum premium (see for example Asness et al. (2013); Blitz and Van Vliet (2008); Carhart (1997); Geczy and Samonov (2017)) exists in the multi-asset framework, it is not surprising that *NL* experiences a drop in performance while *BL* is almost unaffected.

This is confirmed by the significant Sharpe ratio improvement: from a +34.26% in the Base Case, we improve the final Sharpe ratio at the biweekly frequency by 112.01% (mainly driven by the drop in *NL* Sharpe ratio). Furthermore, we see how *BL* is able to extract more information (or *alpha*) from the market because the Information ratio increases from 0.55 with the monthly rebalancing to 0.77 (a 40% increase) with the biweekly rebalancing.

6. Investing in Foreign Currencies

In our second example, we consider investing in different currencies: the Australian Dollar (AUD), the Canadian Dollar (CAD), the Euro (EUR), the British Pound (GBP), the Japanese Yen (JPY) and the U.S. Dollar (USD). Usually set by the central banks, the local risk-free interest rate, such as the federal funds rate in the U.S., together with the foreign exchange rate of currencies versus the Euro are the sources of performance for the investor. Therefore, the underlying assets available to the investor are bank accounts in foreign banks that pay the local interest rate but are valued in EUR. Details are collected in Table 8.

Table 8. Currency and their reference rates.

Currency	Rate	Source
AUD	Thomson Reuters Australian Dollar Overnight Deposit	Thomson Reuters
CAD	Canada Money Market Overnight	Bank of Canada
EUR	Eonia (Euro OverNight Index Average)	European Banking Federation
GBP	United Kingdom Sonia	Wholesale Markets Brokers' Association
JPY	Japan Uncollateralized Overnight	Bank of Japan
USD	United States Federal Funds Effective Rate	Federal Reserve, United States

The workflow detailed in Section 3 was implemented with the parameters listed in Table 9.

Table 9. Parameters used in the implementation of *BL* and *NL* as defined in the workflow for the foreign currency strategy.

Parameter	Value
X_0	100
T	12 months
Lag	1 day
Freq	Weekly, Friday
r^w	60 days
s^w	250 days
d	10%
unc	100
r^q	30
L	100%

With respect to Table 2, here we consider a longer investment horizon (one year), we rebalance more often (weekly) because of reduced transaction costs in highly liquid foreign currencies, we consider short windows for estimating the drift parameter and we do not allow leverage.

The result of the *BL* and *NL* strategies from January 2002 to June 2018 are reported in Table 10, while the historical performance is shown in Figure 6.

Table 10. Statistics for the *BL* and *NL* strategies. The Sharpe Ratio is calculated as the ratio between annualized performance and annualized volatility. For this case, the difference is given in relative terms. Data from January 2002 to June 2018.

	BL	*NL*	**Difference**
Ann. Performance	4.00%	2.83%	1.17%
Ann. Volatility	5.97%	4.93%	1.04%
Max. Drawdown	−14.17%	−10.51%	−3.66%
Sharpe ratio	0.67	0.57	17.5%
Information Ratio	0.42	-	-

Over the period used, *BL* outperformed *NL* by 1.17% annualized. This is quite impressive given the low yields of developed countries' currencies (mainly EUR and JPY) that can usually be observed in the market. Therefore, the effect of learning clearly brings value to the investor by adding extra performance, although this comes at slightly higher risk (roughly 1% more volatile and 3.66% larger maximum drawdown). Nevertheless, the improvement in the Sharpe ratio is consistent. Figure 6b shows the relative strength of *BL* over *NL* and the growth line. We can see that, except for a few months in the second half of 2008 where *BL* strongly underperformed, after that time it regularly outperformed *NL*.

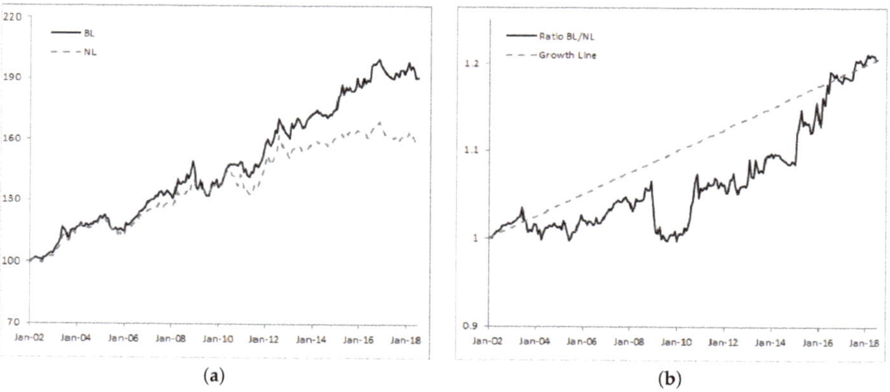

Figure 6. Historical values of the portfolios calculated with both $\mathbf{w}^{BL}$ and $\mathbf{w}^{NL}$ under the Base Case (**a**) and their ratio (**b**).

7. Investing in Factor Strategies

In the last few years, investors have embraced alternative strategies that target specific, well-established equity factors (such as size, value, volatility or momentum). These strategies offer an efficient and direct exposure to the main driving factors of equity markets and allow for an optimal allocation across factors. The main challenge is to invest in the right factor at the right time, as their performance usually shows cyclical patterns. Table 11 contains more details on the strategies we considered. All of them are based on the U.S. large capitalization equity market.

Table 11. Factor-based strategies and cash. For the volatility factor, we chained two strategies on 18 December 2009. Data in USD.

Factor	Name	Source
Dividend	S&P 500 Dividend Aristocrats Net Total Return Index	S&P
Growth	MSCI USA Growth Net Total Return Index	MSCI
Momentum	MSCI USA Momentum USD Net Total Return Index	MSCI
Quality	MSCI USA Quality Net Total Return Index	MSCI
Size	MSCI USA Small Cap Net Total Return Index	MSCI
Value	Shiller Barclays CAPE US Sector Value Net TR Index	Barclays
Volatility	Ossiam US Minimum Variance Index Net Return/ ESG US Minimum Variance Index	S&P, Solactive
Cash	United States Federal Funds Effective Rate	Federal Reserve, United States

We follow the workflow of Section 3 with the parameters listed in Table 12 to derive both *BL* and *NL* strategies.

Table 12. Parameters used in the implementation of the *BL* and *NL* factor rotation strategies as defined in the workflow.

Parameter	Value
X_0	100
T	12 months
Lag	1 day
$Freq$	Monthly, 3rd Friday of each month.
r^w	90 days
s^w	250 days
d	10%
unc	100
r^q	60
L	100%

The results from January 2002 to June 2018 are shown in Table 13. In this example as well, the *BL* strategy has significantly outperformed the *NL* strategy. Again, the learning effect clearly brings value to the investor. On an annualized basis, *BL* improves the performance by a bit more than 2%, with a lower maximum drawdown (−8.24% versus −10.43% for *NL*) but a slightly higher annualized volatility (3.61% for *BL* versus 2.26% for *NL*).

Table 13. Statistics for the *BL* and *NL* strategies. The Sharpe Ratio is calculated as the ratio between annualized performance and annualized volatility. For this case, the difference is given in relative terms. Data from January 2002 to June 2018.

	BL	*NL*	Difference
Ann. Performance	3.1%	1.03%	2.07%
Ann. Volatility	3.61%	2.26%	1.34%
Max. Drawdown	−8.24%	−10.43%	2.2%
Sharpe ratio	0.86	0.45	91.11%
Information Ratio	0.55	-	-

The improvement in the Sharpe ratio is particularly high—0.86 for the *BL* factor rotation strategy versus 0.45 for the *NL* strategy (an improvement of 91.11%). Figure 7 shows the historical performance (Figure 7a) and the strength ratio (Figure 7b) of the *BL* strategy over *NL*. Clearly, learning over time produces regular outperformance, as shown by the regular upwardly increasing ratio between *BL* and *NL*.

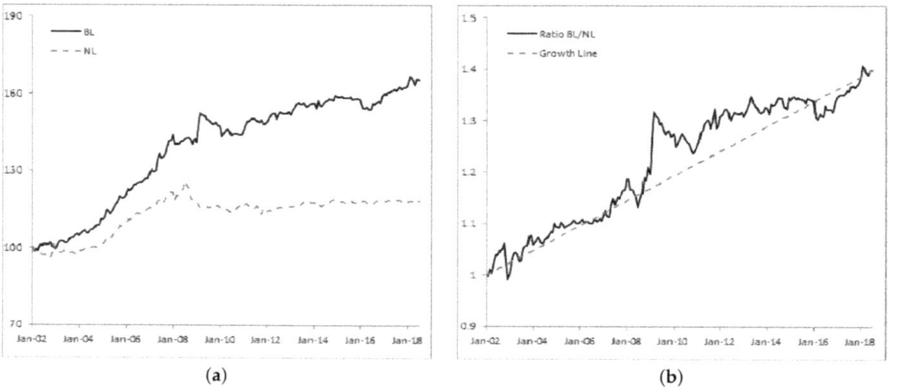

Figure 7. Historical values of the portfolios calculated with both $\mathbf{w}^{BL}$ and $\mathbf{w}^{NL}$ under the Base Case (**a**) and their ratio (**b**).

Author Contributions: C.D.F. designed the experiments; C.D.F. and J.N. performed the experiments; C.D.F. and J.N. analyzed the data; C.D.F., J.N. and H.P. contributed to the mathematical analysis; H.P. designed the theoretical framework of this study.

Funding: This research received no external funding.

Acknowledgments: This work is issued from a CIFRE collaboration between OSSIAM and LPSM.

Conflicts of Interest: The authors declare no conflict of interest.

Abbreviations

The following abbreviations are used in this manuscript:

CAPM	Capital Asset Pricing Model
AUD	Australian Dollar
BL	Bayesian learning (strategy)
CAD	Canadian Dollar
CAPE	Cyclically Adjusted Price-to-Earnings
Conv.	Conventional
EONIA	Euro OverNight Index Average
ETF	Exchange-Traded Fund
FTSE	Financial Times Stock Exchange
EMBI	Emerging Markets Bond Index
EMMI	European Money Markets Institute
EUR	Euro
EurAgg	Euro Aggregate
GBP	Great British Pound
GSCI	Goldman Sachs Commodities Index
JPY	Japanese Yen
LBMA	London Bullion Market Association
MSCI	Morgan Stanley Capital International
NL	nonlearning (strategy)
NR	Net Return
S&P	Standard and Poors
Topix	Tokyo Stock Price Index
TR	Total Return

References

Aguilar, Omar, and Mike West. 2000. Bayesian dynamic factor models and portfolio allocation. *Journal of Business & Economic Statistics* 18: 338–57.

Asness, Clifford S., Tobias J. Moskowitz, and Lasse Heje Pedersen. 2013. Value and momentum everywhere. *Journal of Finance* 68: 929–86. [CrossRef]

Avramov, Doron, and Guofu Zhou. 2010. Bayesian portfolio analysis. *Annual Review of Financial Economics* 2: 25–47. [CrossRef]

Barry, Chistopher B. 1974. Portfolio analysis under uncertain means, variances, and covariances. *The Journal of Finance* 29: 515–22. [CrossRef]

Best, Michael J., and Robert R. Grauer. 1991. On the sensitivity of mean-variance-efficient portfolios to changes in asset means: Some analytical and computational results. *The Review of Financial Studies* 4: 315–42. [CrossRef]

Black, Fisher, and Myron Scholes. 1973. The pricing of options and corporate liabilities. *Journal of Political Economy* 81: 637–54. [CrossRef]

Blitz, David, and Pim Van Vliet. 2008. Global tactical cross-asset allocation: Applying value and momentum across asset classes. *Journal of Portfolio Management* 35: 23–28. [CrossRef]

Bodnar, Taras, Stepan Mazur, and Yarema Okhrin. 2017. Bayesian estimation of the global minimum variance portfolio. *European Journal of Operational Research* 256: 292–307. [CrossRef]

Carhart, Mark M. 1997. On persistence in mutual fund performance. *The Journal of Finance* 52: 57–82. [CrossRef]

Cvitanić, Jakša, Ali Lazrak, Lionel Martellini, and Fernando Zapatero. 2006. Dynamic portfolio choice with parameter uncertainty and the economic value of analysts? recommendations. *The Review of Financial Studies* 19: 1113–56. [CrossRef]

De Franco, Carmine, Johann Nicolle, and Huyên Pham. 2018. Bayesian Learning for Markowitz Portfolio Selection Problem. Working paper, Cornell University, Ithaca, NY, USA, arXiv:1811.06893.

Elliott, Robert J., William C. Hunter, and Barbara M. Jamieson. 1998. Drift and volatility estimation in discrete time. *Journal of Economic Dynamics and Control* 22: 209–18. [CrossRef]

Fama, Eugene F., and Kenneth R. French. 1993. Common risk factors in the returns on stocks and bonds. *Journal of Financial Economics* 33: 3–56. [CrossRef]

Fama, Eugene F., and Kenneth R. French. 2015. A five-factor asset pricing model. *Journal of Financial Economics* 116: 1–22. [CrossRef]

Fama, Eugene F., and Kenneth R. French. 2016. Dissecting anomalies with a five-factor model. *The Review of Financial Studies* 29: 69–103. [CrossRef]

Frost, Peter A., and James E. Savarino. 1986. An empirical bayes approach to efficient portfolio selection. *Journal of Financial and Quantitative Analysis* 21: 293–305. [CrossRef]

Geczy, Christopher, and Mikhail Samonov. 2017. Two Centuries of Multi-Asset Momentum (Equities, Bonds, Currencies, Commodities, Sectors and Stocks). Available online: http://dx.doi.org/10.2139/ssrn.2607730 (accessed on 20 May 2015).

Karatzas, Ioannis, John P. Lehoczky, and Steven E. Shreve. 1987. Optimal portfolio and consumption decisions for a "small investor" on a finite horizon. *SIAM Journal on Control and Optimization* 25: 1557–86. [CrossRef]

Klein, Roger W., and Vijay S. Bawa. 1976. The effect of estimation risk on optimal portfolio choice. *Journal of Financial Economics* 3: 215–31. [CrossRef]

Lakner, Peter. 1995. Utility maximization with partial information. *Stochastic Processes and Their Applications* 56: 247–73. [CrossRef]

Lakner, Peter. 1998. Optimal trading strategy for an investor: The case of partial information. *Stochastic Processes and Their Applications* 76: 77–97. [CrossRef]

Lintner, John. 1965. The valuation of risk assets and the selection of risky investments in stock portfolios and capital budgets. *The Review of Economics and Statistics* 47: 13–37. [CrossRef]

Markowitz, Harry. 1952. Portfolio Selection. *The Journal of Finance* 7: 77–91.

Merton, Robert C. 1969. Lifetime portfolio selection under uncertainty: The continuous-time case. *The Review of Economics and Statistics* 51: 247–57. [CrossRef]

Merton, Robert C. 1975. Optimum consumption and portfolio rules in a continuous-time model. In *Stochastic Optimization Models in Finance*. New York: Elsevier, pp. 621–61.

Merton, Robert C. 1980. On estimating the expected return on the market: An exploratory investigation. *Journal of Financial Economics* 8: 323–61. [CrossRef]

Rogers, Leonard. C. G. 2001. The relaxed investor and parameter uncertainty. *Finance and Stochastics* 5: 131–54. [CrossRef]

Samuelson, Paul. 1969. Lifetime Portfolio Selection by Dynamic Stochastic Programming. *The Review of Economics and Statistics* 51: 239–46. [CrossRef]

Scaillet, Olivier. 2004. Nonparametric estimation and sensitivity analysis of expected shortfall. *Mathematical Finance* 14: 115–29. [CrossRef]

Sharpe, William F. 1964. Capital asset prices: A theory of market equilibrium under conditions of risk. *The Journal of Finance* 19: 425–42.

Siegel, Andrew F., and Artemiza Woodgate. 2007. Performance of portfolios optimized with estimation error. *Management Science* 53: 1005–15. [CrossRef]

© 2019 by the authors. Licensee MDPI, Basel, Switzerland. This article is an open access article distributed under the terms and conditions of the Creative Commons Attribution (CC BY) license (http://creativecommons.org/licenses/by/4.0/).

risks

MDPI

Article

On the Failure to Reach the Optimal Government Debt Ceiling

Abel Cadenillas [1,*] **and Ricardo Huamán-Aguilar** [2]

[1] Department of Mathematical and Statistical Sciences, University of Alberta, Central Academic Building 639, Edmonton, AB T6G 2G1, Canada
[2] Department of Economics, Pontificia Universidad Católica del Perú, Av. Universitaria 1801, San Miguel, Lima 32, Peru; rhuaman@pucp.pe
* Correspondence: abel@ualberta.ca; Tel.: +1-780-492-0572

Received: 19 September 2018; Accepted: 27 November 2018; Published: 4 December 2018

Abstract: We develop a government debt management model to study the optimal debt ceiling when the ability of the government to generate primary surpluses to reduce the debt ratio is limited. We succeed in finding a solution for the optimal debt ceiling. We study the conditions under which a country is not able to reduce its debt ratio to reach its optimal debt ceiling, even in the long run. In addition, this model with bounded intervention is consistent with the fact that, in reality, countries that succeed in reducing their debt ratio do not do so immediately, but over some period of time. To the best of our knowledge, this is the first theoretical model on the debt ceiling that accounts for bounded interventions.

Keywords: debt crisis; government debt management; optimal government debt ceiling; government debt ratio; stochastic control; decision analysis; risk management

---

1. Introduction

1.1. Economic Motivations

The recent debt crisis in the world has proved that controlling the debt ratio of a country is of paramount importance. The literature on public debt management is abundant, from classical theoretical references such as Domar (1944); Barro (1989, 1999); and Dornbusch and Draghi (1990), to more applied ones such as Wheeler (2004); IMF (2002); IMF and World Bank (2001); IMF and World Bank (2003); Ghosh et al. (2013); Huamán-Aguilar and Cadenillas (2015); Woo and Kumar (2015) and Shah (2005). The theoretical literature deals with the optimal tax problem, and the effects of government debt. The applied references provide useful guidelines for practitioners.

There is also literature on debt sustainability. There are two interpretations of this term: the long-term meaning and the short-term meaning. The long-term meaning states that debt is sustainable if the total discounted path of governments expenses equals the total discounted path taxes. The medium term meaning defines that debt is sustainable if the debt-to-GDP ratio converges toward a target ratio over some period of time. Among theoretical references, we have, for example, Bohn (1995) and Blanchard et al. (2003). Among applied literature, we have, for instance, Balassone and Franco (2000) and Neck and Sturm (2008).

As Balassone and Franco (2000) point out, "the absence of a clear-cut theoretical benchmark to assess sustainability has often favoured the use of ad hoc definitions". In 1992, the Maastricht Treaty selected 60% as the upper bound for the debt-to-GDP ratio for countries to be members of the European

Union[1]. In the USA, the nominal debt (measured in USA dollars, not debt-to-GDP ratio) has a ceiling that is determined by its Congress. However, the selection of the debt ceiling by politicians is not necessarily optimal. Indeed, Gersbach (2014) points out the following: "Politicians tend to push the amount of public debt beyond socially desirable levels in order to increase their reelection chances".

Inspired by the preceding discussion, we define *debt ceiling* as the maximum level of debt ratio at which government intervention is not required. That is, if the debt ratio of a country is larger than its debt ceiling, the government should reduce the debt ratio by generating fiscal surpluses. Otherwise, the debt is said to be under control and there is no reason for interventions. This definition is consistent with the intended meaning given to the 60% in the Maastricht Treaty (Article 104c). We remark that the government debt ceiling that we study in this paper is different from the following topics related to government debt management: optimal debt, credit ceiling, and debt limit[2].

Uctum and Wickens (2000) study the debt sustainability for some countries considering the 60% ceiling. In that research the debt ceiling is treated as exogenous. The literature in which the government debt ceiling is endogenous is scarce. As far as we know, the only mathematically rigorous research on the optimal government debt ceiling problem has been done by Cadenillas and Huamán-Aguilar (2016) and Ferrari (2018). In both papers, the government debt ceiling is endogenous. Cadenillas and Huamán-Aguilar (2016) study the optimal debt ceiling assuming that the interventions of a government to reduce its debt ratio are *unbounded*[3]. They succeed in finding an explicit formula for the optimal debt ceiling as a function of important macro-financial variables. Ferrari (2018) incorporates inflation in the model of Cadenillas and Huamán-Aguilar (2016) but does not present an explicit solution.

We consider a country whose government wants to impose an upper bound on its debt ratio. We assume that debt generates a disutility for the government of the country, which is an increasing and convex function of the debt ratio. On the other hand, the government can reduce its debt ratio, but there is a cost generated by this intervention. The government wants to minimize the expected total discounted cost (the cost of debt reduction plus the disutility of debt) taking into account that its ability to generate primary surpluses to reduce its debt ratio is limited. In such theoretical framework, we have found a solution for the optimal debt ceiling, which depends on key macro-financial variables, such as the interest rate on debt, the debt volatility, and the rate of economic growth. Moreover, we have obtained an optimal debt policy based on the optimal debt ceiling. It works in the following way. If the actual debt ratio of a country is below its optimal debt ceiling, then it is optimal for the government not to intervene. Otherwise, the government should intervene at the maximal rate to reduce its debt ratio. Given the constraint on the generation of primary surpluses, the controlled debt ratio may be sometimes or always above the optimal debt ceiling. Having in mind a country with

---

1 That 60% was simply the median of the debt ratios of those European countries. Although it was not binding, it was considered as a reference value. For more details, please see Footnote 3 of this paper.

2 *Optimal debt* is the debt ratio that arises as a result of welfare analysis considering that debt, on the one hand, smooths consumption and, on the other hand, has negative effects in wealth distribution; see, for example, Aiyagari and McGrattan (1998) or Barro (1999). *Credit ceiling* is the level of debt above which the country is not allowed to borrow in the financial markets; see, for example, Eaton and Gersovitz (1981). *Debt limit* is the debt level at which a debt crises takes place; see, for instance, Ostry et al. (2010).

3 Article 104c of the Maastricht Treaty Council of the European Communities (1992) says the following: "2. The Commission shall monitor the development of the budgetary situation and of the stock of government debt in the Member States with a view to identifying gross errors. In particular, it shall examine compliance with budgetary discipline on the basis of the following two criteria: (a) whether the ratio of the planned or actual government deficit to gross domestic product exceeds a reference value, unless either the ratio has declined substantially and continuously and reached a level that comes close to the reference value;—or, alternatively, the excess over the reference value is only exceptional and temporary and the ratio remains close to the reference value; (b) whether the ratio of government debt to gross domestic product exceeds a reference value, unless the ratio is sufficiently diminishing and approaching the reference value at a satisfactory pace. The reference values are specified in the protocol on the excessive deficit procedure annexed to this Treaty". In the Maastricht Treaty, the "ratio of the planned or actual government deficit to gross domestic product" is the debt ratio, and the "reference value" is the debt ceiling (which was selected as 60%). Thus, the Maastricht Treaty does not mention explicitly any bound for the government interventions. Similarly, the debate in the USA Senate about the selection of the debt ceiling does not mention any bound for the government interventions.

debt problems, we also study the time to reach its debt ceiling (not necessarily its optimal debt ceiling) assuming that the current debt ratio is above its debt ceiling.

1.2. Contributions

We improve the results of Cadenillas and Huamán-Aguilar (2016) by studying the optimal debt ceiling when the government interventions to reduce its debt ratio have an upper bound. The motivation is that it is difficult for a country to obtain primary surpluses to reduce its debt ratio. The 60% ceiling set in the Maastricht Treaty was part of the "convergence criteria", in the understanding that countries whose debt ratio were above that threshold should reach the 60% over a number of years. The model presented in this paper accounts for the important fact that countries in reality may or may not succeed in reaching their optimal debt ceilings. If they do, it takes some time to reach that goal. Our quantitative results differ from those of Cadenillas and Huamán-Aguilar (2016). For example, the optimal debt ceiling in our model is always smaller than the optimal debt ceiling in the unbounded case. Our qualitative results differ as well. Indeed, if the bound on government intervention is very large, then the debt ceiling is an increasing function of the volatility. That coincides with the unbounded case studied by Cadenillas and Huamán-Aguilar (2016). However, if the bound on government intervention is small, then the debt ceiling is a decreasing function of the volatility. That differs from the unbounded case studied by Cadenillas and Huamán-Aguilar (2016). We find that if the constraint to generate primary surpluses is severe (very low upper bound), a country may not be able to reach its optimal debt ceiling, even in the long run. For those countries which succeed in reaching their optimal debt ceiling, it may take some time to accomplish that goal. These findings are some of the main results of this research.

This paper is organized as follows: we present the model for bounded government debt management in Section 2. In Section 3, we present a verification theorem which states a sufficient condition for a debt control policy to be optimal. In Section 4, we find a candidate for solution and then verify that this candidate is indeed the solution. We study the time to reach a debt ceiling in Section 5. In Sections 6 and 7, we perform an interesting economic analysis of the debt policy based on the government debt ceiling. We write the conclusions in Section 8.

2. The Bounded Government Intervention Model

We use a Brownian motion to model the uncertainty in the debt ratio. Formally, we consider a complete probability space $(\Omega, \mathcal{F}, P)$ together with a filtration $\{\mathcal{F}_t\} = \{\mathcal{F}_t, t \in [0, \infty)\}$, which is the P-augmentation of the filtration generated by a one-dimensional Brownian motion W.

We study the debt ratio $X = \{X_t, t \in [0, \infty)\}$ of a country, which is defined by

$$X_t := \frac{\text{gross public debt at time t}}{\text{gross domestic product (GDP) at time t}}.$$

This definition of the debt ratio is standard in the economics literature (see, for example, Uctum and Wickens (2000)).

Let r denote the interest rate on debt and g the rate of economic growth. Section 22.2 (p. 460) of Blanchard (2017), a standard reference on macroeconomics, states that

$$\begin{aligned} &\text{change of the debt ratio at time } t \\ &= (r-g)(\text{debt ratio at time } t) + \frac{\text{primary deficit at time } t}{\text{gross domestic product (GDP) at time } t}. \end{aligned}$$

He assumes a discrete-time deterministic model in which r and g are constants.

The continuous-time version of Blanchard (2017) can be written in integral form as

$$X_t = x + \int_0^t (r-g) X_s ds - \int_0^t u_s ds, \tag{1}$$

where $x \in (0, \infty)$ is the initial debt ratio, $r \in [0, \infty)$ is the interest rate on debt, $g \in (-\infty, +\infty)$ is the rate of economic growth, and $u = \{u_t, t \in [0, \infty)\}$ is the rate of the primary balance (equivalently, the negative of the primary deficit).

Motivated by the uncertainty of the economy, we generalize the deterministic model (1) to the stochastic model

$$X_t = x + \int_0^t (r - g) X_s ds + \int_0^t \sigma X_s dW_s - \int_0^t u_s ds. \tag{2}$$

The term $\int_0^t \sigma X_t \, dW_s$ above accounts for the uncertainty in the economy, and models the empirical fact that the bigger the debt, the bigger the risk. Here, $\sigma \in (0, \infty)$ is the debt volatility.

The government intervenes to manage its debt ratio via the control process $u = \{u_t, t \in [0, \infty)\}$. This process represents the rate of intervention of the government, and it is associated with the generation of primary surpluses with the specific goal of reducing the debt ratio. Unlike Cadenillas and Huamán-Aguilar (2016), we assume that this control process is bounded. Indeed, for a fixed $\overline{U} > 0$, we assume that

$$u_t \in [0, \overline{U}], \; \forall t \geq 0,$$

which means that the ability of the government to produce primary surpluses is limited, as it is in reality. We allow each country to have a different bound $\overline{U}$, which depends on its structural economic and political characteristics.

The intervention of the government to reduce its debt ratio has a cost. This cost is generated by fiscal adjustments, which can take the form of reducing expenses or raising taxes. We denote the marginal cost of debt ratio reduction by k. That is, the government has to pay the cost $k > 0$ for each unit of debt ratio reduction. Let λ stand for the government discount rate. Thus, $\int_0^\infty e^{-\lambda t} k \, u_t \, dt$ represents the cumulative discounted cost of reducing the debt ratio.

There are also costs for having debt. High public debt has negative effects on the economy. According to Blanchard (2017), high public debt means less growth of the capital stock and more tax distortions. Furthermore, it can make the fiscal policy extremely difficult. Moreover, Das et al. (2010) claim that it can generate a debt crisis, which, in turn, may lead to an economic crisis. On the other hand, having public debt may be beneficial for the economy, see, for example, Holmstrong and Tirole (1998). Since we are modelling a country that faces a debt problem, we disregard the positive effect of debt.

We assume that the government has a disutility function $h : [0, \infty) \to [0, \infty)$ defined by

$$h(y) = \alpha y^{m+1}, \quad \text{where } m \in \{1, 2, 3, \cdots\}.$$

Here, the parameter m represents the aversion of the government towards the debt ratio y. For example, countries which have never had a default (such as Canada and USA) have a lower parameter m than countries which have suffered debt crises (such as Argentina and Greece). The function h has the property of constant relative risk aversion (CRRA) equal to m (see Remark 1 below). We point out that this disutility function generalizes the quadratic function that is widely used in economics (see, for instance, Kydland and Prescott 1977, Taylor 1979, and Cadenillas and Zapatero 1999). On the other hand, the importance of debt for the government is represented by the parameter α, and it is measured in monetary units. The more important the debt, the larger the parameter α. The debt importance reflects the concern of the government to debt, and is usually determined in its economic plan.

Remark 1. *For a utility function $u(y)$, the risk aversion is defined to be $-yu''(y)/u'(y)$ (see, for instance, MasCollel et al. (1995) or Pratt (1964)). Similarly, for a disutility function $h(y)$, we define the relative risk aversion to be $yh''(y)/h'(y)$.*

Thus, the expected total discounted cost (the cost of debt reduction plus the disutility of debt) is given by

$$J(x;u) := E_x\left[\int_0^\infty e^{-\lambda t}h(X_t)dt + \int_0^\infty e^{-\lambda t}k\, u_t\, dt\right].$$

Here, E_x represents the conditional expected value given that $X_0 = x$.

Definition 1. *An adapted process $u : [0,\infty) \times \Omega \to [0,\overline{U}]$ is called an admissible stochastic control if $J(x;u) < \infty$. The set of all admissible controls is denoted by $\mathcal{A}(x)$.*

Problem 1. *The government wants to select the control $u \in \mathcal{A}(x)$ that minimizes the functional $J(x;\cdot)$.*

Thus, we can think of J as a loss function, a function that the government wants to minimize.

Proposition 1. *For every $x \in (0,\infty)$, $\mathcal{A}(x)$ is a convex set and the function $J(x;\cdot)$ is strictly convex. Furthermore, Problem 1 has at most one solution.*

Proof. See Appendix A. □

We observe that for every $u \in \mathcal{A}(x)$:

$$\lim_{T\to\infty} E_x\left[e^{-\lambda T}X_T^{m+1}\right] = 0, \tag{3}$$

because

$$\int_0^\infty e^{-\lambda t}E_x\left[\alpha X_t^{m+1}\right]dt = \int_0^\infty e^{-\lambda t}E_x\left[h(X_t)\right]dt = E_x\left[\int_0^\infty e^{-\lambda t}h(X_t)dt\right] < \infty.$$

We will use condition (3) in the proof of Theorem 1 below. Condition (3) is a classical transversality condition.

We denote $\mu = r - g$. Since we want the nonintervention policy to be admissible (see details in Section 6.1), we assume the following condition on the discount rate:

$$\lambda > \sigma^2 m(m+1)/2 + \mu(m+1). \tag{4}$$

This condition is consistent with the empirical observation that for governments the present is more important than the future. Condition (4) is similar to the ones imposed in economic models with infinite horizon (see, for instance, Romer 2002).

3. The Value Function and the Verification Theorem

The value function $V : (0,\infty) \to \mathbb{R}$ is defined by

$$V(x) := \inf_{u\in\mathcal{A}(x)} J(x;u).$$

It measures the minimum loss for the government because it is the smallest cost that can be achieved when the initial debt ratio is x and we consider all the admissible controls.

Proposition 2. *The value function is nonnegative, increasing and convex. Furthermore, $V(0+) = 0$, and it satisfies the polynomial growth condition*

$$V(x) \leq Mx^{m+1}, \tag{5}$$

for some constant $M \in (0,\infty)$.

Proof. See Appendix B. □

We state a sufficient condition for a policy to be optimal. First, we introduce the corresponding Hamilton–Jacobi–Bellman equation (HJB).

Let $\varphi : (0,\infty) \to \mathbb{R}$ be a function in $C^2(0,\infty)$. The differential operator $\mathcal{L}$ is defined by

$$\mathcal{L}^u(\varphi(x)) \;:=\; \frac{1}{2}\sigma^2 x^2 \varphi''(x) + \mu x \varphi'(x) - u\,\varphi'(x) - \lambda\varphi(x). \tag{6}$$

We consider the Hamilton-Jacobi-Bellman (HJB) equation

$$\inf_{0 \le u \le \overline{U}} \left\{ \mathcal{L}^u(v(x)) + k\,u + h(x) \right\} = 0, \tag{7}$$

where $v : (0,\infty) \to \mathbb{R}$ is a function in $C^2(0,\infty)$.

We next present a verification theorem that will be used to obtain the solution. Other verification theorems for classical stochastic control problems can be found, for instance, in Fleming and Soner (2006).

Theorem 1. *Let $v \in C^2((0,\infty);[0,\infty))$ be a convex function. If v satisfies the HJB Equation (7) and the polynomial growth condition*

$$v(x) \;\le\; Mx^{m+1}, \tag{8}$$

for some constant $M > 0$, then for every $u \in \mathcal{A}(x)$:

$$v(x) \le J(x;u).$$

Moreover, if the control u^v, defined by

$$u^v := u^v(X_t) = arg \inf_{u \in [0,\overline{U}]} \left\{ \mathcal{L}^u(v(X_t)) + k\,u + h(X_t) \right\}, \tag{9}$$

is admissible, then

$$v(x) = J(x;u^v).$$

That is, $\hat{u} := u^v$ is the optimal control and $V := v$ is the value function for Problem 1.

Proof. Let $u \in \mathcal{A}(x)$, and let $X_0 = x > 0$. Since v is twice continuously differentiable, we may apply Ito's formula to obtain for every $s > 0$:

$$v(x) = e^{-\lambda s} v(X_s) \;-\; \int_0^s e^{-\lambda t} \left\{ \mathcal{L}^{u_t}(v(X_t)) \right\} dt \;+\; \int_0^s e^{-\lambda t} v'(X_t)\sigma dW_t, \tag{10}$$

where $\mathcal{L}$ is defined in Equation (6). From the HJB Equation (7), we have $\mathcal{L}^{u_t}(v(X_t)) + k\,u_t + h(X_t) \ge 0$. Thus,

$$v(x) \;\le\; e^{-\lambda s} v(X_s) + \int_0^s e^{-\lambda t} h(X_t) dt + \int_0^s e^{-\lambda t} k\,u_t dt + \int_0^s e^{-\lambda t} v'(X_t)\sigma dW_t. \tag{11}$$

Let $c \in \mathbb{R}$, such that $x < c < \infty$. We define $\tau_c := \inf\{t \ge 0 : X_t = c\}$. We denote $a \wedge b := \min(a,b)$, where a and b are real numbers. Then, for every $T \ge 0$,

$$v(x) \;\;\le\;\; e^{-\lambda(T\wedge\tau_c)} v(X_{T\wedge\tau_c}) + \int_0^{T\wedge\tau_c} e^{-\lambda t} h(X_t) dt + \int_0^{T\wedge\tau_c} e^{-\lambda t} k\,u_t dt + \int_0^{T\wedge\tau_c} e^{-\lambda t} v'(X_t)\sigma dW_t.$$

Taking conditional expectation given that $X_0 = x$, we obtain

$$\begin{aligned} v(x) \;&\le\; E_x\left[e^{-\lambda(T\wedge\tau_c)}v(X_{T\wedge\tau_c})\right] + E_x\left[\int_0^{T\wedge\tau_c} e^{-\lambda t}h(X_t)dt\right] + E_x\left[\int_0^{T\wedge\tau_c} e^{-\lambda t}k\,u_t dt\right] \\ &\quad + E_x\left[\int_0^{T\wedge\tau_c} e^{-\lambda t}v'(X_t)\sigma dW_t\right]. \end{aligned} \tag{12}$$

Since $v \in C^2((0,\infty);[0,\infty))$ and v is convex, we have $v'(X_t) \le v'(c)$ for every $t \in [0, T\wedge\tau_c]$. Thus,

$$E_x\left[\int_0^{T\wedge\tau_c}\left(e^{-\lambda t}v'(X_t)\sigma\right)^2 dt\right] \le (v'(c))^2\sigma^2\int_0^T e^{-2\lambda t}dt < \infty.$$

Consequently, the stochastic integral

$$\int_0^{T\wedge\tau_c} e^{-\lambda t}v'(X_t)\sigma dW_t = \int_0^T e^{-\lambda t}v'(X_t)\sigma I_{\{t\in[0,\tau_c]\}}dW_t =: N_T$$

is a square integrable martingale, and hence $E_x[N_T] = N_0 = 0$. Here, I_A is the indicator function of A.

Since v is a continuous function,

$$\lim_{c\to\infty} e^{-\lambda(T\wedge\tau_c)}v(X_{T\wedge\tau_c}) = e^{-\lambda T}v(X_T), \quad P-a.s.$$

Moreover, due to the polynomial growth condition (8), the family of random variables $\{e^{-\lambda(T\wedge\tau_c)}v(X_{T\wedge\tau_c}) : c > x\}$ is uniformly integrable (see Appendix D in Fleming and Soner 2006), and hence

$$\lim_{c\to\infty} E_x\left[e^{-\lambda(T\wedge\tau_c)}v(X_{T\wedge\tau_c})\right] = E_x\left[e^{-\lambda T}v(X_T)\right].$$

The Monotone Convergence Theorem implies

$$\lim_{c\to\infty} E_x\left[\int_0^{T\wedge\tau_c} e^{-\lambda t}h(X_t)dt\right] = E_x\left[\int_0^T e^{-\lambda t}h(X_t)dt\right]$$

and

$$\lim_{c\to\infty} E_x\left[\int_0^{T\wedge\tau_c} e^{-\lambda t}k\,u_t dt\right] = E_x\left[\int_0^T e^{-\lambda t}k\,u_t dt\right].$$

Taking the limit as $c \to \infty$ in (12),

$$v(x) \;\le\; E_x\left[e^{-\lambda T}v(X_T)\right] + E_x\left[\int_0^T e^{-\lambda t}h(X_t)dt\right] + E_x\left[\int_0^T e^{-\lambda t}k\,u_t dt\right]. \tag{13}$$

In view of (3), and the polynomial growth condition (8),

$$\lim_{T\to\infty} E_x\left[e^{-\lambda T}v(X_T)\right] = 0.$$

Taking the limit as $T \to \infty$ in (13), by the Monotone Convergence Theorem, we conclude

$$v(x) \le E_x\left[\int_0^\infty e^{-\lambda t}h(X_t)dt + \int_0^\infty e^{-\lambda t}k\,u_t\,dt\right] = J(x;u). \tag{14}$$

This proves the first part of this theorem.

Next, we consider the second part of the theorem. Since $u := u^v$ satisfies $\mathcal{L}^u(\varphi(x)) + ku + h(x) = 0$, inequality (11) becomes an equality. Hence, the inequality in (14) becomes an equality for the admissible control $u = u^v$. This completes the proof. □

4. The Solution

4.1. Construction of the Solution

Our goal in this subsection is to find a function that satisfies the conditions of Theorem 1. We note that the HJB Equation (7) can be expressed equivalently as

$$\left\{\frac{1}{2}\sigma^2 x^2 v''(x) + \mu x v'(x) - \lambda v(x) + \inf_{u\in[0,\overline{U}]} \left[\left(k - v'(x)\right) u\right] + h(x)\right\} = 0. \tag{15}$$

Thus, we want to find a control that has the following form:

$$\hat{u}_t := \arg \inf_{u\in[0,\overline{U}]} \left[\left(k - v'(X_t)\right) u_t\right] = \begin{cases} 0, & \text{if } v'(X_t) < k, \\ \overline{U}, & \text{if } v'(X_t) \geq k. \end{cases} \tag{16}$$

Consequently, to solve the HJB Equation (15) is equivalent to solve

$$\frac{1}{2}\sigma^2 x^2 v''(x) + \mu x v'(x) - \lambda v(x) + h(x) = 0, \tag{17}$$

for $v'(x) < k$; and

$$\frac{1}{2}\sigma^2 x^2 v''(x) + \mu x v'(x) - \lambda v(x) + \left(k - v'(x)\right)\overline{U} + h(x) = 0, \tag{18}$$

for $v'(x) \geq k$.

Thus, a solution v of the HJB equation defines the regions $\mathcal{C} = \mathcal{C}^v$ and $\Sigma = \Sigma^v$ by

$$\mathcal{C} := \left\{x > 0 : \frac{1}{2}\sigma^2 x^2 v''(x) + \mu x v'(x) - \lambda v(x) + h(x) = 0,\ v'(x) < k\right\}, \tag{19}$$

$$\Sigma := \left\{x > 0 : \frac{1}{2}\sigma^2 x^2 v''(x) + \mu x v'(x) - \lambda v(x) + \left(k - v'(x)\right)\overline{U} + h(x) = 0,\ v'(x) \geq k\right\}. \tag{20}$$

We observe that the control $\hat{u}$ takes the value zero on the region $\mathcal{C}$, whereas it takes the value $\overline{U}$ on the region Σ. We conjecture that there exists a threshold $b \in (0, \infty)$ such that the government should intervene with $\hat{u} = \overline{U}$ when the debt ratio $X \geq b$, and should not intervene (equivalently, $\hat{u} = 0$) when the debt ratio $X < b$. Accordingly, if v satisfies the HJB equation, we will call $\mathcal{C} = (0, b)$ the continuation region and $\Sigma = [b, \infty)$ the intervention region. Thus, it is natural to define the debt ratio ceiling as follows.

Definition 2. *Let v be a function that satisfies the HJB Equation (15), and $\mathcal{C}$ the corresponding continuation region. If $\mathcal{C} \neq \emptyset$, the debt ratio ceiling b is*

$$b := \sup\{x \in (0, \infty) \mid x \in \mathcal{C}\}.$$

Furthermore, if v is equal to the value function, then b is said to be the optimal debt ceiling.

Hence, we need to find the value function to obtain the optimal debt ceiling. The general solution of the HJB equation depends on whether we consider the continuation region $\mathcal{C}$ or the intervention region Σ. We have applied the power series method to obtain the solution on the region Σ.

To simplify the notation, we consider the power series

$$Hypergeometric_1F_1(\theta;\eta;z) := \left[1 + \sum_{n=1}^{\infty} \frac{(\theta)_n}{(\eta)_n} \frac{1}{n!} z^n\right], \quad K(\theta;\eta;x) := \left[1 + \sum_{n=1}^{\infty} \frac{(\theta)_n}{(\eta)_n} \frac{1}{n!} \left(-\frac{2\overline{U}}{\sigma^2 x}\right)^n\right]. \tag{21}$$

Here, $\theta \in (-\infty,\infty)$ and $\eta \in (-\infty,\infty)$ are constants, and we denote

$$(a)_n := \Pi_{j=0}^{n-1}(a+j) = a(a+1)(a+2)\cdots(a+n-1), \quad a \in \mathbb{R},\, n \in \mathbb{N}.$$

This function $Hypergeometric_1F_1(\theta;\eta;z)$ belongs to the family of hypergeometric functions. For a reference of these functions, and their relationship to second order differential equations, see, for example, Bell (2004) and Kristensson (2010).

Thus, the solution of the HJB equation is given by

$$v(x) = \begin{cases} A_1\, x^{\gamma_1} + A_2\, x^{\gamma_2} + \alpha\, \xi\, x^{m+1}, & \text{if } x \in \mathcal{C} = (0,b), \\ f(x), & \text{if } x \in \Sigma = [b,\infty), \end{cases}$$

with

$$\begin{aligned} f(x) &= \sum_{j=0}^{m+1} \zeta_j\, x^j + B_1\, x^{\gamma_2} \left(\frac{\sigma^2}{2\overline{U}}\right)^{\gamma_2} \left[1 + \sum_{n=1}^{\infty} \frac{(-\gamma_2)_n}{(c_2)_n} \frac{1}{n!} \left(\frac{-2\overline{U}}{\sigma^2\, x}\right)^n\right] \\ &\quad + B_2 \left(\frac{2\overline{U}}{\sigma^2\, x}\right)^{c_3} \left[1 + \sum_{n=1}^{\infty} \frac{(c_3)_n}{(2-c_2)_n} \frac{1}{n!} \left(\frac{-2\overline{U}}{\sigma^2\, x}\right)^n\right] \\ &= \sum_{j=0}^{m+1} \zeta_j\, x^j + B_1\, x^{\gamma_2} \left(\frac{\sigma^2}{2\overline{U}}\right)^{\gamma_2} K\left(-\gamma_2, c_2, x\right) + B_2 \left(\frac{2\overline{U}}{\sigma^2\, x}\right)^{c_3} K\left(c_3, 2-c_2, x\right), \end{aligned} \tag{22}$$

where A_1, A_2, B_1 and B_2 are some constants to be found. Furthermore, we define

$$\tilde{\mu} := \mu - \frac{1}{2}\sigma^2, \tag{23}$$

$$\gamma_1 := \frac{-\tilde{\mu} - \sqrt{\tilde{\mu}^2 + 2\lambda\sigma^2}}{\sigma^2} < 0, \tag{24}$$

$$\gamma_2 := \frac{-\tilde{\mu} + \sqrt{\tilde{\mu}^2 + 2\lambda\sigma^2}}{\sigma^2} > 0, \tag{25}$$

$$\xi := \frac{1}{\lambda - \sigma^2 m(m+1)/2 - \mu(m+1)} > 0, \tag{26}$$

$$c_2 := 2\left(1 - \gamma_2 - \frac{\mu}{\sigma^2}\right), \tag{27}$$

$$c_3 := \gamma_2 + 2\frac{\tilde{\mu}}{\sigma^2}, \tag{28}$$

$$\zeta_j := -\binom{m+1}{j} \frac{\alpha\,(m+1-j)!\,\overline{U}^{m+1-j}}{\Pi_{i=j}^{m+1}\left(i\mu + i(i-1)\sigma^2/2 - \lambda\right)}, \quad \forall j \in \{2,3,\cdots,m+1\}, \tag{29}$$

$$\zeta_1 := \frac{2\overline{U}}{\mu - \lambda}\zeta_2, \tag{30}$$

$$\zeta_0 := \frac{k\,\overline{U}}{\lambda} - \frac{\overline{U}}{\lambda}\zeta_1. \tag{31}$$

Remark 2. *By definition (21), one can verify that*

$$\lim_{x\to\infty} K(-\gamma_2, c_2, x) = 1,$$

$$\lim_{x\to\infty} K(c_3, 2-c_2, x) = 1.$$

To guarantee the existence of the parameters $\{\zeta_j : j = 2, 3, \cdots, m+1\}$ defined in (29), in addition to condition (4), we need to assume

$$\lambda \neq j(j-1)\frac{\sigma^2}{2} + j\mu, \quad j \in \{2, 3, \cdots, m\}. \tag{32}$$

We observe that, in the special case $\mu \geq 0$, the inequality (4) implies (32).

Lemma 1. *The parameters of the model satisfy the following conditions:*

(i) $\xi > 0$,
(ii) $\lambda > \mu$,
(iii) $\gamma_2 > m+1$,
(iv) $c_3 > 0$.

Proof. Part (i) follows immediately from (4). Part (iv) follows directly from the definition of γ_2. Let us show (ii). If $\mu > 0$, then condition (4) implies that $\lambda > \mu$. If $\mu \leq 0$, then $\lambda > 0 \geq \mu$.

To prove (iii), we define

$$\tilde{f}(y) = \frac{\sqrt{\tilde{\mu}^2 + 2y\sigma^2}}{\sigma^2} - \frac{\tilde{\mu}}{\sigma^2}, \tag{33}$$

where $\tilde{\mu} = \mu - 0.5\sigma^2$. We note that $\tilde{f}$ is strictly increasing. By definition, $\gamma_2 = \tilde{f}(\lambda)$. If $\tilde{\mu} + \sigma^2(m+1) \geq 0$, then $\gamma_2 = \tilde{f}(\lambda) > \tilde{f}\Big((m+1)^2\sigma^2/2 + \tilde{\mu}(m+1)\Big) = m+1$, where the inequality follows from (4). If $\tilde{\mu} + \sigma^2(m+1) < 0$, then $\gamma_2 = \tilde{f}(\lambda) > \tilde{f}(0) > 2(m+1)$, since $\lambda > 0$. □

We recall that Proposition 2 implies $V(0+) = 0$, and that the value function V satisfies the polynomial growth condition (5). Furthermore, we conjecture that v is twice continuously differentiable. Then, the five constants A_1, A_2, B_1, B_2 and b can be found from the following five conditions:

$$v(0+) = 0, \tag{34}$$

$$v(x) \leq Mx^{m+1}, \tag{35}$$

$$v(b+) = v(b-), \tag{36}$$

$$v'(b+) = v'(b-), \tag{37}$$

$$v''(b+) = v''(b-). \tag{38}$$

From Equations (19) and (20), we see that Equation (37) is equivalent to $v'(b-) = k$, which in turn is equivalent to

$$A_2\gamma_2 b^{\gamma_2 - 1} + (m+1)\alpha\xi b^m = k. \tag{39}$$

Since $\gamma_1 < 0$, condition (34) implies $A_1 = 0$ in the equation for v. Moreover, in the lemma below, we show that $B_1 = 0$.

Lemma 2. *Suppose f, defined in (22), is non-negative and satisfies the polynomial growth condition*

$$f(x) \leq Mx^{m+1},$$

for some $M > 0$. Then, $B_1 = 0$.

Proof. See Appendix C. □

Hence, the candidate for value function is defined by

$$v(x) = \begin{cases} A_2\, x^{\gamma_2} + \alpha\, \xi\, x^{m+1}, & \text{if } x \in \mathcal{C} = (0, b), \\ f_1(x), & \text{if } x \in \Sigma = [b, \infty), \end{cases} \tag{40}$$

with

$$f_1(x) \quad := \quad \sum_{j=0}^{m+1} \zeta_j\, x^j \, + \, B_2 \left(\frac{2\overline{U}}{\sigma^2\, x} \right)^{c_3} K\Big(c_3, 2 - c_2, x\Big), \tag{41}$$

where the remaining three constants A_2, B_2 and b are found by solving the system of nonlinear Equations (36)–(38).

In summary, our candidate for value function is given by (40), and our candidate for optimal control is given by $\hat{u}_t := \begin{cases} 0, & \text{if } X_t < b, \\ \overline{U}, & \text{if } X_t \geq b. \end{cases}$ Moreover, our candidate for optimal debt ceiling is b. Naturally, we expect b to depend on the underlying parameters of the model $(\mu, \sigma, \lambda, k, \alpha, m, \overline{U})$, where $\mu = r - g$.

Now, we describe a procedure to solve the system (36)–(38). Noting that

$$\begin{aligned} K'(\theta; \eta; x) &= \sum_{n=1}^{\infty} \frac{(\theta)_n}{(\eta)_n} \frac{1}{(n-1)!} \frac{\sigma^2}{2\overline{U}} \left(-\frac{2\overline{U}}{\sigma^2\, x} \right)^{n+1}, \\ K''(\theta; \eta; x) &= \sum_{n=1}^{\infty} \frac{(\theta)_n}{(\eta)_n} \frac{(n+1)}{(n-1)!} \left(\frac{\sigma^2}{2\overline{U}} \right)^2 \left(-\frac{2\overline{U}}{\sigma^2\, x} \right)^{n+2}, \end{aligned}$$

we have

$$f_1'(x) = \sum_{j=0}^{m} (j+1)\zeta_{j+1} x^j - B_2 c_3 \left(\frac{2\overline{U}}{\sigma^2\, x} \right)^{c_3+1} K(c_3; 2 - c_2; x) + B_2 \left(\frac{2\overline{U}}{\sigma^2\, x} \right)^{c_3} K'(c_3; 2 - c_2; x),$$

$$\begin{aligned} f_1''(x) &= \sum_{j=0}^{m-1} (j+2)(j+1)\zeta_{j+2} x^j + B_2 c_3 (c_3+1) \left(\frac{2\overline{U}}{\sigma^2\, x} \right)^{c_3} \frac{1}{x^2} K(c_3; 2 - c_2; x) \\ &\quad - B_2 c_3 \left(\frac{\sigma^2}{2\overline{U}} + \frac{\sigma^2}{(2\overline{U})^2} \right) \left(\frac{2\overline{U}}{\sigma^2\, x} \right)^{c_3+1} K'(c_3; 2 - c_2; x) + B_2 \left(\frac{2\overline{U}}{\sigma^2\, x} \right)^{c_3} K''(c_3; 2 - c_2; x) \\ &= \sum_{j=0}^{m-1} (j+2)(j+1)\zeta_{j+2} x^j \\ &\quad + B_2 \left\{ c_3(c_3+1) \left(\frac{2\overline{U}}{\sigma^2\, x} \right)^{c_3} \frac{1}{x^2} K(c_3; 2 - c_2; x) - c_3 \left(\frac{\sigma^2}{2\overline{U}} + \frac{\sigma^2}{(2\overline{U})^2} \right) \left(\frac{2\overline{U}}{\sigma^2\, x} \right)^{c_3+1} K'(c_3; 2 - c_2; x) + \left(\frac{2\overline{U}}{\sigma^2\, x} \right)^{c_3} K''(c_3; 2 - c_2; x) \right\}. \end{aligned}$$

To simplify the notation, consider the functions R and S defined by

$$\begin{aligned} R(x) &:= \left(\frac{2\overline{U}}{\sigma^2\, x} \right)^{c_3} K(c_3; 2 - c_2; x), \\ S(x) &:= c_3(c_3+1) \left(\frac{2\overline{U}}{\sigma^2\, x} \right)^{c_3} \frac{1}{x^2} K(c_3; 2 - c_2; x) \\ &\quad - c_3 \left(\frac{\sigma^2}{2\overline{U}} + \frac{\sigma^2}{(2\overline{U})^2} \right) \left(\frac{2\overline{U}}{\sigma^2\, x} \right)^{c_3+1} K'(c_3; 2 - c_2; x) \\ &\quad + \left(\frac{2\overline{U}}{\sigma^2\, x} \right)^{c_3} K''(c_3; 2 - c_2; x). \end{aligned}$$

Then, Equation (36) can be rewritten as

$$A_2\, b^{\gamma_2} + \alpha\, \xi\, b^{m+1} = \sum_{j=0}^{m+1} \zeta_j b^j + B_2 R(b)$$

and Equation (38) can be rewritten as

$$A_2\, \gamma_2(\gamma_2 - 1) b^{\gamma_2 - 2} + \alpha\, \xi (m+1) m b^{m-1} = \sum_{j=0}^{m-1} (j+2)(j+1)\zeta_{j+2} x^j + B_2 S(b).$$

Thus, Equations (36) and (38) are equivalent to

$$\begin{aligned} A_2 &= A_2(b) \\ &= \frac{(\sum_{j=0}^{m+1} \zeta_j b^j - \alpha\, \xi\, b^{m+1}) S(b) + (\alpha\, \xi (m+1) m b^{m-1} - \sum_{j=0}^{m-1} (j+2)(j+1)\zeta_{j+2} b^j) R(b)}{b^{\gamma_2} S(b) - \gamma_2(\gamma_2 - 1) b^{\gamma_2 - 2} R(b)}, \end{aligned} \tag{42}$$

$$\begin{aligned} B_2 &= B_2(b) \\ &= \frac{A_2(b) b^{\gamma_2} + \alpha\, \xi\, b^{m+1} - \sum_{j=0}^{m+1} \zeta_j b^j}{R(b)}. \end{aligned} \tag{43}$$

Then, Equation (37), or equivalently Equation (39), can be rewritten as

$$A_2(b)\gamma_2 b^{\gamma_2 - 1} + (m+1)\alpha\xi b^m = k.$$

Let us consider the function $w : (0, \infty) \longmapsto (-\infty, \infty)$ defined by

$$w(y) := A_2(y)\gamma_2 y^{\gamma_2 - 1} + (m+1)\alpha\xi y^m.$$

The procedure to solve Equations (36)–(38) is first to solve equation

$$w(b) = k, \tag{44}$$

and then obtain A_2 and B_2 from Equations (42) and (43), respectively.

4.2. Verification of the Solution

In this subsection, we will prove rigorously that our candidate for optimal control is indeed the optimal control, and our candidate for value function is indeed the value function.

Theorem 2. *Let b be solution of Equation (44), and A_2 and B_2 be constants determined by (42) and (43). Let us define the function $V : (0, \infty) \to [0, \infty)$ by*

$$V(x) = v(x) = \begin{cases} A_2\, x^{\gamma_2} + \alpha\, \xi\, x^{m+1}, & \text{if } x \in (0, b), \\ f_1(x), & \text{if } x \in [b, \infty), \end{cases} \tag{45}$$

with f_1 defined by Equation (41). Furthermore, let us define the process $\hat{u}$ by

$$\hat{u}_t := \overline{U}\, I_{\{\hat{X}_t \geq b\}}(t) = \begin{cases} 0, & \text{if } \hat{X}(t) < b, \\ \overline{U}, & \text{if } \hat{X}(t) \geq b. \end{cases} \tag{46}$$

If

$$\forall x \in (0, \infty) : \quad V''(x) > 0, \tag{47}$$

then V is the value function, b is the optimal debt ceiling, and $\hat{u}$ is the debt policy generated by the optimal debt ceiling. Here, I_A is the indicator function of A.

Proof. It is sufficient to show that all the conditions of Theorem 1 are satisfied. We observe that $V(0+) = 0$. By construction, we get immediately that $V \in C^2(0,\infty)$. In view of (47), V is strictly convex. Thus, $V'(x)$ is strictly increasing. Next, we will show that $V'(0+) = 0$. We note that for every $x \in (0,b)$:

$$V'(x) = x^m\Big((m+1)\alpha\xi + A_2\gamma_2 x^{\gamma_2-m-1}\Big).$$

We recall that $\gamma_2 > m+1$ by Lemma 1. Thus, $V'(0+) = 0$. Consequently, $V'(x) > 0$ for every $x > 0$. Hence, V is strictly increasing.

Next, we will show that V satisfies the HJB Equation (7). We recall that condition (39) is equivalent to $V'(b) = k$. Since $V'(x) > 0$ for every $x \in (0,\infty)$, we conclude $0 < V'(x) < k$ for every $x \in (0,b)$, and $V'(x) > k$ for every $x \in (b,\infty)$. By construction, V satisfies (17) on $(0,b)$, and (18) on (b,∞). Hence, V satisfies the HJB equation for all $x \in (0,\infty)$. This also shows that indeed $\mathcal{C} = (0,b)$ and $\Sigma = [b,\infty)$. Regarding the value function, it remains to verify that V satisfies the polynomial growth condition (8). Since

$$\lim_{x\to\infty} K\left(c_3, 2-c_2, x\right) = 1$$

by Remark 2, and $c_3 > 0$ by Lemma 1, we obtain

$$\lim_{x\to\infty} B_2\left(\frac{2\overline{U}}{\sigma^2 x}\right)^{c_3} K\Big(c_3, 2-c_2, x\Big) = 0.$$

This implies that V is bounded above by a polynomial of degree $m+1$ on the interval $[b,\infty)$. On the other hand, on the interval $(0,b)$, the function V is bounded above by $|A_2|b^{\gamma_2} + \alpha\xi b^{m+1}$. Hence, V satisfies the polynomial growth condition (8). Consequently, by Theorem 1, V is the value function. Since

$$J(x;\hat{u}) \leq J(x;0) + E_x\left[\int_0^\infty e^{-\lambda t}\,\overline{U}dt\right] = \alpha\xi x^{m+1} + \overline{U}\frac{1}{\lambda} < \infty,$$

by Section 6.1, we conclude that $\hat{u}$ is admissible. Therefore, $\hat{u}$ is the optimal debt policy. By Definition 2, the constant b is the optimal debt ceiling. This completes the proof of this theorem. □

4.3. The Debt Policy Generated by the Optimal Debt Ceiling

We observe that under the debt policy (46) generated by the optimal debt ceiling, the optimal debt ratio is given by

$$\hat{X}_t = x + \int_0^t (r-g)\hat{X}_s ds + \int_0^t \sigma\hat{X}_s\, dW_s - \int_0^t \bar{U}\, I_{\{\hat{X}_s\geq b\}}\, ds. \tag{48}$$

When the actual debt ratio $\hat{X}_t$ is below the optimal debt ceiling b, the definition of debt control given in Equation (46) states that $\hat{u}(t) = 0$. Hence, the government does not generate primary surpluses to reduce its debt ratio. When the debt ratio reaches b and tries to cross it, the optimal control states that $\hat{u}_t = \overline{U}$. In other words, the government intervenes to reduce the debt ratio with the maximal rate $\overline{U}$ allowed. When the actual debt ratio $\hat{X}_t$ is strictly greater than the optimal debt ceiling b, the optimal debt policy in the bounded model states that the government reduces its debt ratio with the maximal rate $\overline{U}$.

Suppose that the actual debt ratio is below the optimal debt ceiling b. Then, the government might or might not succeed in preventing the debt ratio from crossing b, the result depends on the values of the underlying parameters of the model, in particular on $\overline{U}$. Specifically, the higher the parameter $\overline{U}$, the more likely the controlled debt ratio will remain below the optimal debt ceiling b (see Section 5). This result differs from the unbounded case of Cadenillas and Huamán-Aguilar (2016) in which the optimal policy states that once the actual debt ratio is below or equal to its debt ceiling, it will remain there all the time.

On the other hand, if the current debt ratio is strictly greater than the optimal debt ceiling b, the optimal debt policy states that the government should reduce the debt ratio with the maximal rate $\overline{U}$. Certainly, there is no guarantee that the resulting debt ratio will equal the debt ceiling b immediately because it may take some time to accomplish that goal, if that ever happens. Indeed, in Section 5, we present Example 2 in which the expected time to reach the optimal debt ceiling is strictly positive. Furthermore, if the government constraint is too severe (very low $\overline{U}$), there is a high probability that the country will never reach its optimal debt ceiling (see Example 3 in Section 5). In contrast, in the unbounded model of Cadenillas and Huamán-Aguilar (2016), the optimal debt ceiling is reached immediately.

4.4. Numerical Solutions

The solution of the problem involves the numerical solution of the system of three Equations (36)–(38) with three unknowns: A_2, B_2 and b. We have written a program in *Mathematica 11.0* to solve numerically those equations (see Appendix E). We get immediate solutions in a standard personal computer. We now present an example to illustrate the solution.

Example 1. *Let us consider the parameter values*

$$r = 0.10,\ g = 0.05,\ \sigma = 0.05,\ \lambda = 0.7,\ k = 1,\ \overline{U} = 0.05,\ m = 3,\ \alpha = 1. \tag{49}$$

Solving numerically the Equation (44), we obtain $b = 54.2756\%$. *Alternatively, we can solve numerically the system of Equations (36)–(38).*

The graph of the corresponding value function is shown in Figure 1. We observe that condition (47) is satisfied. Thus, the value function is increasing, strictly convex, and twice continuously differentiable.

The optimal debt ratio ceiling is 54.2756%. Thus, the corresponding debt policy is given by

$$\hat{u}_t = \begin{cases} 0, & \text{if } X_t < 54.2756\%, \\ 0.05, & \text{if } X_t \geq 54.2756\%. \end{cases} \tag{50}$$

That is, if the actual debt ratio is below the level 54.2756%, the government should not intervene. Otherwise, the government should intervene with the maximal allowed rate of 0.05. Given such constraint, there is no guarantee that the resulting debt ratio after intervention of the government will remain below 54.2756%; it may be the case that sometimes the debt ratio is above that threshold.

Remark 3. *We conjecture that condition (47) in Theorem 2 is satisfied for every solution of the system of Equations (36)–(38). This is actually the case in all the numerical examples that we have studied to calculate the optimal debt ceiling (see Sections 4.4, 5.4, 6.2 and 6.3).*

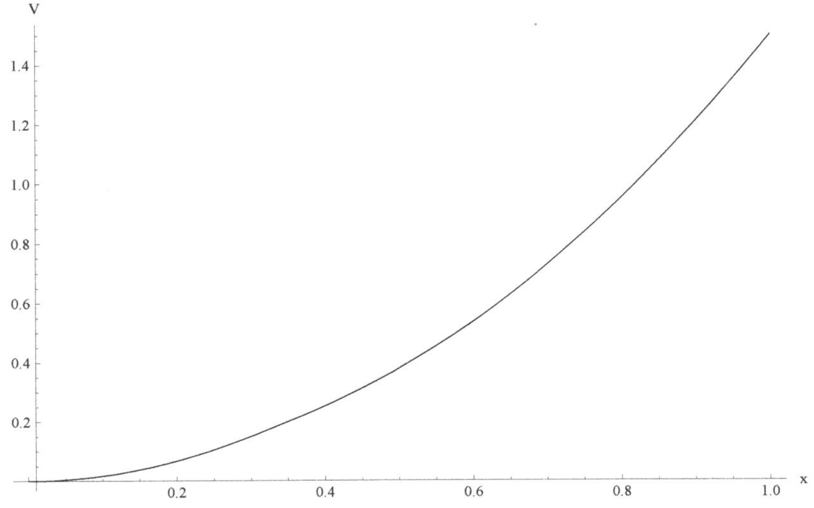

Figure 1. The value function V.

5. Time to Reach the Debt Ceiling

We study the time to reach a debt ceiling c considering that the government follows the debt policy $u^{(c)}$ defined by

$$u_t^{(c)} := \begin{cases} 0, & \text{if } X_t < c, \\ \overline{U}, & \text{if } X_t \geq c. \end{cases} \tag{51}$$

We define the stopping time

$$\tau \ := \ \inf\{t > 0 \ : \ X(t) \ = \ c\} \ .$$

In this section, $c > 0$ is a constant real number that represents a ceiling for the debt ratio. We emphasize that c is any debt ceiling, not necessarily the optimal debt ceiling found in the previous section. In particular, c could be equal to the ceiling 60% imposed by the Maastricht Treaty for the European Union.

5.1. The Theoretical Result

In general, the current or initial debt ratio of a country $X_0 = x$ could be below or above the debt ceiling c. If a country selects c as its debt ceiling, and follows the debt policy $u^{(c)}$, the dynamics of the debt ratio (2) becomes

$$X_t^{(c)} \ = \ \begin{cases} x\exp\left\{(r-g-0.5\sigma^2)t + \sigma W_t\right\}, & \text{if } x \ < \ c, \ t \leq \tau, \\ x\exp\left\{(r-g-0.5\sigma^2)t + \sigma W_t\right\} - \overline{U}\int_0^t \frac{V_t}{V_u}du, & \text{if } x \ > \ c, \ t \leq \tau, \end{cases}$$

where

$$V_t \ := \ \exp\left\{(r-g-0.5\sigma^2)t + \sigma W_t\right\}.$$

We can study the time τ to reach the debt ceiling for both cases, i.e., $x < c$ or $x > c$. However, given the debt problems that motivate this research, it is compelling to study the time to reach the debt ceiling assuming $x > c$.

We recall that $\tilde{\mu} := r - g - \frac{1}{2}\sigma^2$. We need to distinguish two cases: $\tilde{\mu} \leq 0$ and $\tilde{\mu} > 0$.

Proposition 3. *Suppose $x > c$. The following assertions are valid:*
(i) If $\tilde{\mu} \leq 0$ or, equivalently, $r - g \leq \sigma^2/2$, then

$$P_x\{\tau < \infty\} = 1. \tag{52}$$

(ii) If $\tilde{\mu} > 0$ or, equivalently, $r - g > \sigma^2/2$, then

$$P_x\{\tau < \infty\} = \frac{\Gamma(\nu-1) - \Gamma(\nu-1, \beta/x)}{\Gamma(\nu-1) - \Gamma(\nu-1, \beta/c)}, \tag{53}$$

where $\nu = 2\mu/\sigma^2$ and $\beta = 2\overline{U}/\sigma^2$, $\Gamma(\cdot)$ is the Gamma function, and $\Gamma(\cdot,\cdot)$ is the incomplete Gamma function defined by

$$\Gamma(a,z) := \int_z^\infty t^{(a-1)} e^{-t} dt, \quad z \geq 0,\ a > 0.$$

Furthermore,

$$\lim_{\overline{U}\to\infty} P_x\{\tau < \infty\} = 1. \tag{54}$$

Proof. See Appendix D. □

Proposition 3 provides different conclusions depending on the parameters of the economy. Part (i) is associated with countries that have a big economic growth, and Part (ii) with countries with moderate economic growth.

5.2. Application 1: Countries with Big Economic Growth

If

$$g + \sigma^2/2 \geq r, \tag{55}$$

Part (i) of Proposition 3 states that the debt ceiling is reached with probability one, regardless of the level $\bar{U}$ of maximal rate. In other words, if the interest rate is lower that the rate of economic growth, plus an adjustment by volatility, then the debt ratio tends to decrease until it reaches the debt ceiling with probability one. The intuition behind the result is that the economic growth is big enough to control the debt ratio. This is a consequence of the definition of debt ratio, namely, debt ratio = debt in nominal currency/gross domestic product. Consequently, economies in which the rate of economic growth satisfy the above condition will be successful in reaching the debt ceiling.

For economies that satisfy the above condition (55), we can compute the expected time to reach the debt ceiling c. We illustrate this point in the following example.

Example 2. *We consider a country with parameter values*

$$r = 0.05, \quad g = 0.10, \quad \sigma = 0.05, \quad \overline{U} = 0.01,$$

and initial debt ratio $x = 100\%$. Suppose that this country selects $c = 80\%$ as its debt ceiling.

For the above parameters, the expected time to reach the debt ceiling is $E[\tau] = 3.58$, with a 95% confidence interval given by $[3.5540, 3.6136]$. We have performed Monte Carlo simulations with 10,000 sample paths and time steps equal to 0.001. That is, it takes 3.58 years on average to reach the debt ceiling 80%, starting at the initial debt ratio of 100%, and assuming that the government can decrease the debt ratio at the maximal rate. For a reference on Monte Carlo simulations see, for instance, Brandimarte (2002).

5.3. Application 2: Countries with Moderate Economic Growth

Now consider Part (ii) of Proposition 3. It refers to countries that have moderate economic growth in the sense that they satisfy the condition $\tilde{\mu} > 0$, which is equivalent to

$$g + \sigma^2/2 < r. \tag{56}$$

The probability to reach the optimal debt ceiling is given by the formula (53) that depends on $(r, g, \sigma, \overline{U}, c)$. To illustrate the role played by the parameter $\overline{U}$, we present a numerical example.

Example 3. *To study the role played by $\bar{U}$ on the probability of reaching c, we set $c = 60\%$, which is the ceiling proposed by the Maastricht Treaty for the European Union. We consider the set of parameter values*

$$r = 0.10, \quad g = 0.05, \quad \sigma = 0.05.$$

We consider two countries: Country A with initial debt ratio of 70% (approximately the current debt ratio of Germany) and Country B with initial debt ratio of 170% (approximately the current debt ratio of Greece). For simplicity, we assume that the other parameters values are the same for both countries.

In Table 1, we observe that, regardless of the type of country, there exist levels of the maximal rate of intervention $\overline{U}$ for which a country has very low probability of reaching the debt ceiling. For instance, if $\bar{U} = 2.5\%$, then Country *B* has zero probability of reaching the debt ceiling, while Country *A* has only around 20% of probability of reaching it. That is, severe constraints to generate primary surpluses lead to a high probability of never reaching the debt ceiling. Even worse, countries with severe constraints and high initial debt ratios, such as Country *B*, have probabilities close to zero of ever reaching their debt ceilings.

In addition, in Table 1, we observe that, as expected, the higher the maximal rate of intervention $\overline{U}$, the greater the probability of reaching the debt ceiling, regardless of the type of country. In addition, there is a finite level of $\bar{U}$ such that the probability of reaching the optimal debt ceiling is one. For Country *B*, such level is $\bar{U} = 0.15$ and for Country *A* it is around $\bar{U} = 0.05$.

Table 1. Effects of $\overline{U}$ on the probability of reaching the debt ceiling c (*).

	c	Country A	Country B
$\overline{U} = 0.010$	0.60	0.01538	0.00000
$\overline{U} = 0.025$	0.60	0.19876	0.00000
$\overline{U} = 0.050$	0.60	0.99542	0.00215
$\overline{U} = 0.100$	0.60	1.00000	0.89679
$\overline{U} = 0.150$	0.60	1.00000	0.99998

(*) The other parameters used in these computations are those of Example 3.

5.4. Application 3: Time to Reach the Optimal Debt Ceiling

Now, we study the time to reach the optimal debt ceiling *b* for countries with moderate economic growth. That is, we consider the setting of Part (ii) of Proposition 3, taking $c = b$. To compute the optimal debt ceiling, we consider the parameters (r, g, σ) given in Example 3, and in addition the following parameter values:

$$\lambda = 0.7, \quad k = 1, \quad m = 1, \quad \alpha = 0.5. \tag{57}$$

As in the previous subsection, we consider Country A with initial debt ratio 70%, and Country B with initial debt ratio 170%.

In Table 2, we present the optimal debt ceiling that corresponds to the parameters given above, and the value of $\bar{U}$ given in the first column of that table. Then, for each set of parameters $(r, g, \sigma, \bar{U}, b)$, we perform the calculations of the probability of reaching the optimal debt ceiling using Formula (53), with $c = b$. The probabilities of reaching the optimal debt ceiling b for Country A and Country B are presented in columns 3 and 4, respectively.

We note that the conclusions from Table 2 are the same as those from Table 1, namely, severe constraints on $\bar{U}$ imply that a country may not be able to reach its optimal debt ceiling, and the probability of eventually reaching its optimal debt ceiling increases with the value of $\bar{U}$.

Table 2. Effects of $\overline{U}$ on the probability of reaching the optimal debt ceiling b (*).

	b	Country A	Country B
$\overline{U} = 0.010$	0.60982	0.02356	0.00000
$\overline{U} = 0.025$	0.62576	0.29127	0.00000
$\overline{U} = 0.050$	0.64324	0.99598	0.00215
$\overline{U} = 0.100$	0.65495	1.00000	0.89679
$\overline{U} = 0.150$	0.65808	1.00000	0.99998

(*) The other parameters used in these computations are those of Example 3, and Equation (57).

For a country with no severe constraint, that is able to reach its optimal debt ceiling, we have computed the expected time to reach its optimal debt ceiling by Monte Carlo simulations. For instance, for Country A with $\bar{U} = 0.1$, the expected time of reaching its debt ceiling is 0.6877, while for Country B, with $\bar{U} = 0.15$, such value is 11.98.

To sum up, we conclude that countries with severe constraints to generate primary surpluses (very low $\overline{U}$) have zero or very low probability of ever reaching their debt ceilings. This is one of the main results of this research, and represents a dramatic difference with the work of Cadenillas and Huamán-Aguilar (2016), in which the corresponding optimal debt ceiling is reached immediately with probability one.

6. Comparative Statics Analysis

In this section, we consider different parameter values in order to analyze the debt policy associated with the optimal debt ceiling. Specifically, we are going to make the following three analyses:

1. Compare the results of the debt policy associated with the optimal debt ceiling with the policy of non-government intervention.
2. Compare the results of the debt policy associated with the optimal debt ceiling presented in this paper with the policy derived in the unbounded model of Cadenillas and Huamán-Aguilar (2016).
3. Analyze the effects of some parameters on the optimal debt ceiling.

Unless otherwise stated, the basic parameter values that we will use in this section are given in the following example.

Example 4. *Let us consider the basic parameter values:*

$$\mu = 0.05, \quad \sigma = 0.05, \quad \lambda = 0.7, \quad k = 1, \quad \overline{U} = 0.01, \quad m = 1, \quad \alpha = 1.$$

Solving numerically Equations (36)–(38), we obtain $b = 31.04266\%$.

We remark that, as Examples 1 and 4 show, the 60% proposed by the Maastricht Treaty is not necessarily an optimal debt ceiling. In contrast to the 60% proposed by the Maastricht Treaty, the optimal debt ceiling proposed in our paper depends on the specific characteristics of the country, which are reflected in the parameters' values. We recall that that 60% was simply the median of the debt ratio of some European countries.

6.1. The Debt Policy Associated with the Optimal Debt Ceiling versus the Non-Intervention Policy

We want to compare the policy obtained in Section 4 with the non-intervention policy. The latter can be modeled as $u \equiv 0$, that is, $u(t) = 0$ for all $t \geq 0$. If the government never intervenes, then

$$X_t = x \exp\left\{ \left(\mu - \frac{1}{2}\sigma^2 \right) t + \sigma W_t \right\}. \tag{58}$$

The total cost function is

$$\begin{aligned} J(x;0) &= E_x \left[\int_0^\infty e^{-\lambda t} h(X_t) dt \; + \; 0 \right] = E_x \left[\int_0^\infty e^{-\lambda t} (\alpha X_t^{m+1}) dt \right] \\ &= \int_0^\infty e^{-\lambda t} \alpha E_x \left[X_t^{m+1} \right] dt = \alpha \int_0^\infty e^{-\lambda t} x^{m+1} \exp\left\{ (\sigma^2 m/2 + \mu) t (m+1) \right\} dt \\ &= \alpha \, \xi \, x^{m+1}, \end{aligned}$$

due to condition (4).

We recall that the value function V represents the minimum expected total discounted cost, and is a function of the initial debt ratio. Thus, the cost $J(x;0)$ is greater than or equal to $V(x)$. Indeed, using the parameter values of Example 4 with $\overline{U} = 0.05$, we plot these functions in Figure 2. We observe that the expected relation is satisfied. Hence, we confirm that it is better to intervene optimally than to not intervene at all. We point out that the larger the initial debt ratio, the greater the benefits of the optimal intervention.

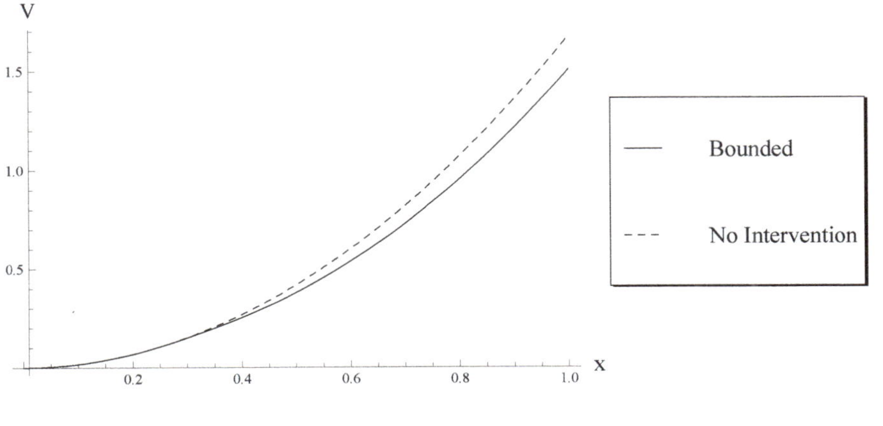

Figure 2. The value function (for the bounded-intervention model) versus the total cost of the non-intervention policy.

6.2. The Bounded Model versus the Unbounded Model

In this subsection, we compare our results to the ones obtained by Cadenillas and Huamán-Aguilar (2016) for their model with unbounded government intervention. They proved that the optimal debt ceiling $\tilde{b}$ for the unbounded intervention model is given by

$$\tilde{b} = \left(\frac{1}{\alpha \xi} \frac{k(\gamma_2 - 1)}{(\gamma_2 - m - 1)(m+1)} \right)^{\frac{1}{m}} > 0, \tag{59}$$

where

$$\begin{aligned}
\tilde{\mu} &= \mu - \frac{1}{2}\sigma^2, \\
\gamma_2 &= \frac{-\tilde{\mu} + \sqrt{\tilde{\mu}^2 + 2\lambda\sigma^2}}{\sigma^2} > 0, \\
\xi &= \frac{1}{\lambda - \sigma^2 m(m+1)/2 - \mu(m+1)} > 0.
\end{aligned}$$

In Table 3, we study the effect of the maximal rate of intervention $\overline{U}$ on the optimal debt ceiling. We notice that the optimal debt ceiling b in the bounded model is always smaller than the optimal debt ceiling $\tilde{b}$ in the unbounded case $\overline{U} = \infty$, given by Equation (59). Moreover, we observe that, as the maximal rate $\overline{U}$ increases, the optimal debt ceiling b for the bounded model increases towards the optimal debt ceiling $\tilde{b}$ for the unbounded model. It is worth remarking that $\tilde{b}$ is an upper bound for b. Furthermore, we conclude that, other things being equal, countries with severe constraints to control their debt ratios should have low optimal debt ceilings.

Table 3. Effect of $\overline{U}$ on the optimal debt ceiling b (*).

	$\overline{U} = 0.001$	$\overline{U} = 0.01$	$\overline{U} = 1$	$\overline{U} = 5$	$\overline{U} = \infty$
b	0.300024	0.310426	0.331213	0.331325	0.331352

(*) The other parameters used in these computations are those of Example 4. The unbounded case $\overline{U} = \infty$ is calculated using the explicit Formula (59).

6.3. The Effects of α, g, and σ on the Optimal Debt Ceiling

We recall that α represents the importance of government debt. In Table 4 we observe that the more important the government debt, the lower the optimal debt ceiling. In other words, the more concerned the government is about its debt, the more control should be exerted. We note that this result holds for every value of the maximal rate of intervention $\overline{U}$.

Table 4. Effect of α, μ and σ on the optimal debt ceiling b (*).

	$\alpha = 0.5$	$\alpha = 1$	$\alpha = 1.3$
$\overline{U} = 0.01$	0.609820	0.310426	0.241035
$\overline{U} = 2.00$	0.662425	0.331283	0.254845
$\overline{U} = \infty$	0.662704	0.331352	0.254886
	$\mu = 0.05$	$\mu = 0.10$	$\mu = 0.14$
$\overline{U} = 0.01$	0.310426	0.263990	0.253090
$\overline{U} = 2.00$	0.331283	0.303408	0.282346
$\overline{U} = \infty$	0.331352	0.303466	0.282397
	$\sigma = 0.05$	$\sigma = 0.13$	$\sigma = 0.17$
$\overline{U} = 0.01$	0.310426	0.301363	0.295110
$\overline{U} = 2.00$	0.331283	0.349697	0.359007
$\overline{U} = \infty$	0.331352	0.350220	0.359954

(*) The other parameters used in these computations are those of Example 4. The unbounded case $\overline{U} = \infty$ is calculated using the explicit Formula (59).

We recall the definition $\mu := r - g$ in order to analyze the effect of the rate of economic growth. In Table 4, we observe that the larger the rate of economic growth, the larger the optimal debt ceiling.

In other words, since the economic growth reduces the debt ratio (see Domar 1944), countries with high economic growth are allowed to have a high debt ceiling. We point out that this behavior holds regardless of the value of the maximal rate of intervention $\overline{U}$.

In Table 4, we also show the effects of volatility. We observe mixed results. If the maximal rate of intervention $\overline{U}$ is large, then the higher the debt volatility the larger the optimal debt ceiling. This is consistent with the unbounded model ($\overline{U} = \infty$) of Cadenillas and Huamán-Aguilar (2016). However, if the maximal rate of intervention $\overline{U}$ is small, then the higher the debt volatility, the lower the optimal debt ceiling. This establishes a dramatic difference with the unbounded model ($\overline{U} = \infty$) of Cadenillas and Huamán-Aguilar (2016).

We have also studied the effects of the parameters on the value function. We have found out that an increase in the importance of the debt α for the government, or in the debt volatility σ, implies an increase in the value function, thereby generating a bad result for the government. By contrast, an increase in the rate of economic growth reduces the value function and, hence, improves the government welfare.

7. Summary of Analysis

We have confirmed that the debt policy associated with the optimal debt ceiling is better than the non-intervention policy. Furthermore, as expected, the debt policy associated with the optimal debt ceiling under the bounded intervention model determines a higher cost than the debt policy associated with the optimal debt ceiling for the unbounded intervention model.

In addition, we have studied the time to reach any debt ceiling (including the optimal debt ceiling), when the initial debt ratio is higher than the debt ceiling. We have found out that a country may or may not succeed in reaching its debt ceiling. Indeed, we have found out that countries with strong constraints to generate primary superavits (low maximal rate $\overline{U}$ of intervention) may not be able to reduce their debt ratios, and hence may not succeed in reaching their corresponding debt ceilings. On the contrary, for countries with less constraints, we have estimated their finite expected times to reach their debt ceilings. That is, governments that succeed in reducing their debt ratios to their debt ceiling levels do not do so immediately, but over some period of time. These are the main results of this research.

We have observed that our quantitative results are different from those of Cadenillas and Huamán-Aguilar (2016) for the unbounded intervention model ($\overline{U} = \infty$). For example, the optimal debt ceiling in our model is smaller than the optimal debt ceiling in the unbounded case. Another important difference is that the optimal debt policies differ and, hence, produce different results. Suppose the initial debt ratio of a country is below the optimal debt ceiling. Then, as pointed out in Section 4.3, sometimes the controlled debt ratio may be above its corresponding optimal debt ceiling, whereas, in the unbounded model, it will always be equal to or less than the optimal debt ceiling.

We have also analyzed the effects of some parameters on the optimal debt ceiling. We have shown that, when the importance of debt for the government increases (large α), the optimal debt ceiling decreases. An increase in the rate of economic growth (large g) has the same qualitative effect. However, the effect of the volatility (σ) on the optimal debt ceiling depends on the maximal rate ($\overline{U}$) of intervention. We have shown that, if the maximal rate of intervention $\overline{U}$ is large, then the higher the debt volatility, the larger the optimal debt ceiling. Nevertheless, if the maximal rate of intervention $\overline{U}$ is small, then the higher the debt volatility, the lower the optimal debt ceiling. This result is different from the one obtained by Cadenillas and Huamán-Aguilar (2016).

8. Conclusions

In this paper, we study the optimal government debt ceiling considering that the generation of primary superavits to reduce the debt ratio is bounded. The goal of the government is to find a debt reduction policy that minimizes the expected total cost, given by the cost of reducing the debt ratio plus the cost (disutility) of having debt. The debt problem is set as a stochastic control problem in continuous time with infinite horizon. We succeed in obtaining the optimal control debt policy. The main contribution of this paper is to present for the first time a model that not only allows us to compute analytically the optimal debt ceiling (as a function of macro-financial variables), but also accounts for the constraints that governments face in reducing their debt ratios. We have shown that this constraint plays a key role in explaining, for instance, why many countries fail to reduce their debt ratios to their debt ceilings.

For future research, it would be interesting to generalize our model to the case in which the interest rate and the GDP growth rate are stochastic processes. This could be complemented by empirical tests.

Author Contributions: A.C. and R.H.-A. have both contributed to this paper.

Funding: The research of Abel Cadenillas was funded by The Social Sciences and Humanities Research Council of Canada, grant number SSHRC IG 435-2017-0511.

Acknowledgments: We dedicate this paper to the memory of Professor Ramón García-Cobián. Preliminary versions of this paper have been presented at ETH (Zurich) Risk Center, Université de Lausanne (Faculté des hautes études commerciales (HEC)), Humboldt Universität zu Berlin, and 2018 INFORMS Annual Meeting. We are grateful to the seminars and conference participants for their comments. We are also grateful for the comments of the associate editor and the five referees.

Conflicts of Interest: The authors declare no conflict of interest. The founding sponsor had no role in the design of the study; in the collection, analyses, or interpretation of data; in the writing of the manuscript, and in the decision to publish the results.

Appendix A. Proof of Proposition 1

Proof. Let us consider the controls u^1 and u^2 with $u^1 \neq u^2$. Let us denote by X^{u^i} the debt ratio controlled by $u^i, i \in \{1,2\}$. Let $\beta \in (0,1)$. From Equation (2), we observe that the debt ratio controlled by $\beta u^1 + (1-\beta)u^2$ is given by

$$X^{\beta u^1+(1-\beta)u^2} = \beta X^{u^1} + (1-\beta)X^{u^2}.$$

Since h is a strictly convex function,

$$h(X_t^{\beta u^1+(1-\beta)u^2}) = h(\beta X_t^{u^1} + (1-\beta)X_t^{u^2}) < \beta h(X_t^{u^1}) + (1-\beta)h(X_t^{u^2}).$$

Then, for every $x \in (0,\infty)$:

$$\begin{aligned} J(x, \beta u^1 + (1-\beta)u^2) &= E_x\left[\int_0^\infty e^{-\lambda t} h(X_t^{\beta u^1+(1-\beta)u^2}) + \int_0^\infty e^{-\lambda t} k(\beta u_t^1 + (1-\beta)u_t^2)dt\right] \\ &< \beta J(x;u^1) + (1-\beta)J(x;u^2). \end{aligned}$$

This proves that, if $u^1 \in \mathcal{A}(x)$ and $u^2 \in \mathcal{A}(x)$, then $\beta u^1 + (1-\beta)u^2 \in \mathcal{A}(x)$. Hence, $\mathcal{A}(x)$ is a convex set. Furthermore, the function $J(x,\cdot)$ is strictly convex.

Suppose that $u^1 \in \mathcal{A}(x)$ and $u^2 \in \mathcal{A}(x)$, with $u^1 \neq u^2$, are two optimal controls. Then, $J(x;u^1) = J(x;u^2) \in (0,\infty)$. Since $\frac{1}{2}u^1 + \frac{1}{2}u^2 \in \mathcal{A}(x)$ and $J(x,\cdot)$ is strictly convex,

$$J\left(x, \frac{1}{2}u^1 + \frac{1}{2}u^2\right) < \frac{1}{2}J(x;u^1) + \frac{1}{2}J(x;u^2) = J(x;u^1).$$

This contradicts that $u^1 \in \mathcal{A}(x)$ and $u^2 \in \mathcal{A}(x)$ are optimal controls. Therefore, Problem 1 has at most one solution. □

Appendix B. Proof of Proposition 2

Proof. Since J is nonnegative, the value function V is nonnegative as well.

Consider $x_1 < x_2$ and $u^{(2)} \in \mathcal{A}(x_2)$. Since h is a strictly increasing function, we have

$$V(x_1) \leq J(x_1, u^{(2)}) < J(x_2, u^{(2)}).$$

This implies $u^{(2)} \in \mathcal{A}(x_1)$ and then $V(x_1) \leq V(x_2)$. Hence, V is increasing.

Consider $x_1 \leq x_2$ with associated controls $u^{(1)} \in \mathcal{A}(x_1)$ and $u^{(2)} \in \mathcal{A}(x_2)$, and $\gamma \in [0,1]$. We define $u^{(3)} := \gamma u^{(1)} + (1-\gamma)u^{(2)}$ and $x_3 := \gamma x_1 + (1-\gamma)x_2$. For every $i = 1,2,3$, we denote by $X^{(i)}$ the trajectory that starts at x_i and is determined by the control $u^{(i)}$. Thus, for every $t \geq 0$:

$$X_t^{(3)} = \gamma X_t^{(1)} + (1-\gamma)X_t^{(2)}.$$

The convexity of the function h implies

$$\begin{aligned} \int_0^\infty e^{-\lambda t} h(X_t^{(3)})dt &\leq \int_0^\infty e^{-\lambda t}\Big(\gamma h(X_t^{(1)}) + (1-\gamma)h(X_t^{(2)})\Big)dt \\ &= \gamma\Big(\int_0^\infty e^{-\lambda t} h(X_t^{(1)})dt\Big) + (1-\gamma)\Big(\int_0^\infty e^{-\lambda t} h(X_t^{(2)})dt\Big). \end{aligned}$$

This implies

$$J(x_3; u^{(3)}) \leq \gamma J(x_1; u^{(1)}) + (1-\gamma)J(x_2; u^{(2)}),$$

and hence $u^{(3)} \in \mathcal{A}(x_3)$. Thus,

$$\begin{aligned} V\Big(\gamma x_1 + (1-\gamma)x_2\Big) &\leq J\Big(\gamma x_1 + (1-\gamma)x_2, \gamma u^{(1)} + (1-\gamma)u^{(2)}\Big) \\ &= J(x_3; u^{(3)}) \\ &\leq \gamma J(x_1, u^{(1)}) + (1-\gamma)J(x_2, u^{(2)}). \end{aligned}$$

Therefore,

$$V\Big(\gamma x_1 + (1-\gamma)x_2\Big) \leq \gamma V(x_1) + (1-\gamma)V(x_2),$$

which proves that V is a convex function.

It remains to prove that $V(0+) = 0$. Since $V(x)$ is nonnegative, $V(0+) \geq 0$. On the other hand, by the result found in Section 6.1, we have

$$V(x) \leq J(x; 0) = \xi\, \alpha\, x^{m+1},$$

which implies $V(0+) \leq 0$. Furthermore, there exists $M = \xi\alpha \in (0, \infty)$ such that $\forall x \in (0, \infty)$:

$$V(x) \leq M x^{m+1}.$$

This completes the proof of this proposition. □

Appendix C. Proof of Lemma 2

Proof. Let us consider the functions G and H defined by

$$G(x) := x^{\gamma_2}\left(\frac{\sigma^2}{2\overline{U}}\right)^{\gamma_2} K\left(-\gamma_2, c_2, x\right)$$

and

$$H(x) := \left(\frac{2\overline{U}}{\sigma^2\, x}\right)^{c_3} K\left(c_3, 2 - c_2, x\right).$$

The function f, defined in (22), can be written as

$$f(x) = \sum_{j=0}^{m+1} \zeta_j x^j + B_1 G(x) + B_2 H(x), \quad \forall x \in [b, \infty).$$

By Lemma 1, we note that $\gamma_2 > m+1$ and $c_3 > 0$. Then, Remark 2 implies

$$\lim_{x \to \infty} B_2 H(x) = 0.$$

Consequently, there exists $\bar{x} > b$, such that for all $x > \bar{x}$, we have $-1 < B_2 H(x) < 1$. Thus,

$$\underline{f}(x) := \sum_{j=0}^{m+1} \zeta_j x^j + B_1 G(x) - 1 < f(x) < \overline{f}(x) := \sum_{j=0}^{m+1} \zeta_j x^j + B_1 G(x) + 1.$$

Since $\gamma_2 > m+1$, using Remark 2, it follows that G does not satisfy any polynomial growth condition of degree $m+1$. That is, for every $M_2 > 0$, there exists x_{M_2} such that $G(x) > M_2(1 + x^{m+1})$ for every $x > x_{M_2}$.

Now, for a contradiction, suppose $B_1 > 0$. Then, $\underline{f}$ does not satisfy the polynomial growth condition of Lemma 2. However, this, in turn, implies that f does not satisfy that polynomial growth condition either. This contradiction implies that $B_1 \leq 0$. Next, we show $B_1 \geq 0$. For a contradiction, suppose $B_1 < 0$. Then, there exists x big enough such that $\overline{f}(x) < 0$. However, this contradicts the fact that f is non-negative. Then, there must be the case that $B_1 \geq 0$. Combining these two results, we conclude that $B_1 = 0$. □

Appendix D. Proof of Proposition 3

Proof. Proof of Part (i). Since $x > c$, we can rewrite τ as

$$\tau = \inf\{t > 0 \,:\, X_t \leq c\}.$$

By definition of the debt policy $u^{(c)}$, the debt ratio ceiling follows

$$X_t^{(c)} = x + \int_0^t \mu X_s^{(c)} ds + \int_0^t \sigma X_s^{(c)} dW_s - \overline{U}\, t.$$

We define the auxiliary process $\{Y_t\}$ by

$$Y_t = x + \int_0^t \mu Y_s ds + \int_0^t \sigma Y_s dW_s,$$

and the auxiliary stopping time:

$$\theta := \inf\{t > 0 \,:\, Y(t) \leq c\}.$$

Since $\overline{U} > 0$, we have $X_t^{(c)} \leq Y_t$. Then, $\tau \leq \theta$. Hence, $P_x\{\theta < \infty\} \leq P_x\{\tau < \infty\}$. Thus, it suffices to show that $P_x\{\theta < \infty\} = 1$.

The stopping time θ can be written as

$$\begin{aligned}\theta &= \inf\{t > 0 \,:\, x \exp\{\tilde{\mu}\, t + \sigma W_t\} \leq c\} \\ &= \inf\{t > 0 \,:\, -\tilde{\mu}\, t + \sigma(-W_t) \geq \log x - \log c\}.\end{aligned}$$

Since $-W$ is also a Brownian motion, the process $-\tilde{\mu}\, t + \sigma\,(-W_t)$ is a Brownian motion with drift. We may apply the methods in Section 8.4 of Ross (1996), and Section 7.5 of Karlin and Taylor (1975), to show that if $\tilde{\mu} \leq 0$, then $P_x\{\theta < \infty\} = 1$. This completes the proof of Part (i).

Proof of Part (ii). For $-\infty < c < x < n < \infty$, let us define the auxiliary stopping time

$$\theta(c,n) := \inf\left\{ t > 0 \;:\; x + \int_0^t \mu X_s^{(c)} ds + \int_0^t \sigma X_s^{(c)}\, dW_s - \overline{U}\, t \;\notin\; (c,n) \right\}.$$

We claim that

$$P_x\{\tau < \infty\} = 1 - \lim_{n\to\infty} P_x\{X^{(c)}_{\theta(c,n)} = n\}.$$

Let us prove the claim. We note that, for $n \in \mathbb{N}$,

$$\bigcup_{n>c} \{X^{(c)}_{\theta(c,n)} = c\} = \{X^{(c)}_\tau = c\} = \{\tau < \infty\}.$$

Since the events in the above union are monotone increasing in n, we have

$$P_x\{\tau < \infty\} \;=\; \lim_{n\to\infty} P_x\{X^{(c)}_{\theta(c,n)} = c\} \;=\; 1 \;-\; \lim_{n\to\infty} P_x\{X^{(c)}_{\theta(c,n)} = n\}. \tag{A1}$$

Our goal now is to find an analytic expression for $P_x\{X^{(c)}_{\theta(c,n)} = n\}$ as a function of n, and the other parameters. Let us define the functional f by

$$f(x) \;:=\; P_x\{X^{(c)}_{\theta(c,n)} = n\},$$

and the differential operator $\mathcal{A}$ by

$$\mathcal{A}\psi(y) \;:=\; \frac{1}{2}\sigma^2 y^2 \frac{d^2\psi(y)}{dy^2} + (\mu y - \bar{U})\,\frac{d\psi(y)}{dy}.$$

According to Section 3, Chapter 15 of Karlin and Taylor (1981), f satisfies the ordinary differential equation,

$$\mathcal{A}f(y) \;=\; 0,$$

with the boundary conditions $f(c) = 0$ and $f(n) = 1$. The solution of this differential equation is

$$f(x) \;=\; \frac{\Gamma(\alpha-1,\beta/c) - \Gamma(\alpha-1,\beta/x)}{\Gamma(\alpha-1,\beta/c) - \Gamma(\alpha-1,\beta/n)},$$

where $\Gamma(a,z)$ is the incomplete Gamma function, defined by

$$\Gamma(a,z) \;=\; \int_z^\infty t^{(a-1)} e^{-t} dt, \quad z \geq 0,\; a > 0.$$

Taking the limit, we obtain

$$\lim_{n\to\infty} f(x) \;=\; \frac{\Gamma(\alpha-1,\beta/c) - \Gamma(\alpha-1,\beta/x)}{\Gamma(\alpha-1,\beta/c) - \Gamma(\alpha-1)}.$$

Here, $\Gamma(a) := \Gamma(a,0)$, the Gamma function. From Equation (A1), the proof of (53) is complete.

Finally, let us show that

$$\lim_{\overline{U}\to\infty} P_x\{\tau < \infty\} = 1.$$

By definition of the incomplete Gamma function, we have that $\Gamma(a,z) \downarrow 0$ as $z \uparrow \infty$. Then, the result follows. □

Appendix E. Mathematica Code

Here is the Mathematica 11.0 code for solving numerically Equations (36)–(38). We create the function ceiling whose output is the optimal debt ceiling b. As an illustration, on the bottom part of the code, we apply that function to the parameter values of Example 1.

```
ceiling[U0_, μ0_, σ0_, λ0_, k0_, m0_, α0_] :=
 Module[{U = U0, μ = μ0, σ = σ0, λ = λ0, k = k0, m = m0,
   α = α0, γ2, c2, c3, ξ, ξ0, ξ1, ξ2, μ1, v1, v2, A2, B2, n},
  μ1 = μ - (1/2) σ^2; (* corresponds to μ tilde in the paper *)
  γ2 = (-μ1 + Sqrt[(μ1)^2 + 2 λ σ^2]) / σ^2; c2 = 2 (1 - γ2 - μ/σ^2);
  c3 = γ2 + 2 μ1/σ^2; ξ2 = -Binomial[m + 1, 2] (2^m α U^(m-1) Factorial[m - 1]) /
     Product[(-2 λ + 2 i μ - i σ^2 + i^2 σ^2), {i, 2, m + 1}];
  ξ1 = (2 U)/(μ - λ) ξ2; ξ0 = (k U)/λ - U/λ ξ1;
  ξ = 1 / (λ - m (m + 1) σ^2 / 2 - μ (m + 1));
  If[ξ > 0, v1[x_, A2_] := A2 x^γ2 + α ξ x^(m + 1);
   v2[x_, B2_] := B2 ((2 U)/(x σ^2))^c3 Hypergeometric1F1[c3, 2 - c2, -(2 U)/(x σ^2)] +
     ξ0 + ξ1 x + Sum[((x^n (-α) U^(m + 1 - n) Binomial[m + 1, n] Factorial[m + 1 - n]) /
         (Product[(j μ + j (j - 1) σ^2 / 2 - λ), {j, n, m + 1}])), {n, 2, m + 1}];
   FindRoot[
     {v1[b, A2] - v2[b, B2] == 0, D[v1[b, A2], b] - D[v2[b, B2], b] == 0,
      D[v2[b, B2], {b, 2}] - D[v1[b, A2], {b, 2}] == 0},
     {{b, 0.3}, {A2, 1.0}, {B2, 1.0}}, (* initial values*)
     AccuracyGoal → 6
    ][[1]],
   Print["Condition is not satisfied"]]]

In[63]:= (* executing the code for Example 1 *)
 U = 0.05; r = 0.1; g = 0.05; μ = r - g; σ = 0.05; λ = 0.7; k = 1; m = 3; α = 1;
 output = ceiling[U, μ, σ, λ, k, m, α]

Out[64]= b → 0.542756
```

References

Aiyagari, S. Rao, and Ellen R. McGrattan. 1998. The optimum quantity of debt. *Journal of Monetary Economics* 42: 447–69. [CrossRef]

Balassone, Fabrizio, and Daniele Franco. 2000. Assessing fiscal sustainability: A review of methods with a view to EMU. In *Fiscal Sustainability*. Edited by Banca d'Italia. Rome: Bank of Italy, pp. 21–60.

Barro, Robert J. 1989. The Ricardian approach to budget deficits. *Journal of Economic Perspectives* 3: 37–54. [CrossRef]

Barro, Robert J. 1999. Notes on optimal debt management. *Journal of Applied Economics* 2: 281–89.

Bell, William Wallace. 2004. *Special Functions for Scientists and Engineers*. Mineola: Dover Publications Inc.

Blanchard, Olivier J., Jean-Claude Chouraqui, Robert Hagemann, and Nicola Sartor. 1990. The sustainability of fiscal policy: New answers to an old question. *OECD Economic Studies* 15: 7–36. [CrossRef]

Blanchard, Olivier. 2017. *Macroeconomics*, 7th ed. Boston, USA: Pearson Ed. Inc.

Bohn, Henning. 1995. The sustainability of budget deficits in a stochastic economy. *Journal of Money, Credit, and Banking* 27: 257–71.

Brandimarte, Paolo. 2002. *Numerical Methods in Finance: A MATLAB-Based Introduction*. Hoboken: John Wiley & Sons.

Cadenillas, Abel, and Ricardo Huamán-Aguilar. 2016. Explicit formula for the optimal government debt ceiling. *Annals of Operations Research* 247: 415–49. [CrossRef]

Cadenillas, Abel, and Fernando Zapatero. 1999. Optimal Central Bank intervention in the foreign exchange market. *Journal of Economic Theory* 87: 218–42. [CrossRef]

Council of the European Communities. 1992. *Treaty on European Union*. Brussels and Luxembourg: ECSC-EEC-EAEC.

Das, Udaibir S., Michael Papapioannou, Guilherme Pedras, Faisal Ahmed, and Jay Surti. 2010. Managing Public Debt and Its Financial Stability Implications. Working Paper 10/280, Washington, DC, USA: IMF.

Domar, Evsey D. 1944. The "Burden of the Debt" and the National Income. *The American Economic Review* 34: 798–827.

Dornbusch, Rudiger, and Mario Draghi, eds. 1990. *Public Debt Management: Theory and History*. Cambridge: Cambridge University Press.

Eaton, Jonathan, and Mark Gersovitz. 1981. Debt with potential repudiation: Theoretical and empirical analysis. *Review of Economic Studies* 48: 289–309.

Ferrari, Giorgio. 2018. On the Optimal Management of Public Debt: A Singular Stochastic Control Problem. *SIAM Journal on Control and Optimization* 56: 2036–73. [CrossRef]

Fleming, Wendell H., and Halil Mete Soner. 2006. *Control Markov Processes and Viscosity Solutions*, 2nd ed. New York: Springer. [CrossRef]

Gersbach, Hans. 2014. Government Debt-Threshold Contracts. *Economic Enquiry* 52: 444–58.

Ghosh, Atish, Jun I. Kim, Enrique Mendoza, Jonathan Ostry, and Mahvash Qureshi. 2013. Fiscal Fatigue, Fiscal Space and Debt Sustainability in Advanced Economies. *The Economic Journal* 123: 4–30.

Holmstrong, Bengt, and Jean Tirole. 1998. Private and public supply of liquidity. *The Journal of Political Economy* 106: 1–40. [CrossRef]

Huamán-Aguilar, Ricardo, and Abel Cadenillas. 2015. Government Debt Control: Optimal Currency Portfolio and Payments. *Operations Research* 63: 1044–57. [CrossRef]

IMF and World Bank. 2001. *Guidelines for Public Debt Management*. Discussion Paper. Washington: IMF and World Bank. [CrossRef]

IMF and World Bank. 2003. *Guidelines for Public Debt Management*, Amended Version. Discussion Paper. Washington: IMF and World Bank.

IMF. 2002. *Assessing Sustainability*. Washington: IMF. [CrossRef]

Karlin, Samuel, and Howard Taylor. 1975. *A First Course in Stochastic Processes*, 2nd ed. New York: Academic Press.

Karlin, Samuel, and Howard Taylor. 1981. *A Second Course in Stochastic Processes*. New York: Academic Press.

Kristensson, Gerhard. 2010. *Second Order Differential Equations, Special Functions and Their Classification*. New York: Springer.

Kydland, Finn E., and Edward C. Prescott. 1977. Rules rather than discretion: The inconsistency of optimal plans. *Journal of Political Economy* 85: 473–91.

Mas-Colell, Andreu, Michael Dennis Whinston, and Jerry R. Green. 1995. *Microeconomic Theory*. New York: Oxford University Press. [CrossRef]

Neck, Reinhard, and Jan-Egbert Sturm, eds. 2008. *Sustainability of Public Debt*. Cambridge: MIT Press. [CrossRef]

Ostry, Jonathan David, Atish R. Ghosh, Jun I. Kim, and Mahvash S. Qureshi. 2010. *Fiscal Space*. Staff Position Paper no SPN/10/11. Washington DC, USA: IMF.

Pratt, John W. 1964. Risk aversion in the small and in the large. *Econometrica* 32: 122–36.

Romer, David. 2002. *Advanced Macroeconomics*, 2nd ed. New York: McGraw-Hill/Irwin.

Ross, Sheldon M. 1996. *Stochastic Processes*, 2nd ed. New York: John Wiley & Sons, Inc. [CrossRef]

Shah, Anwar, ed. 2005. *Fiscal Management*. Washington: The World Bank. [CrossRef]

Taylor, John B. 1979. Estimation and control of a macroeconomic model with rational expectations. *Econometrica* 47: 1267–86.

Uctum, Merih, and Michael R. Wickens. 2000. Debt and Deficit Ceilings, and Sustainability of Fiscal Policies: An Intertemporal Analysis. *Oxford Bulletin of Economics and Statistics* 62: 197–222.

Wheeler, Graeme. 2004. *Sound Practice in Government Debt Management*. Washington, DC: The World Bank.

Woo, Jaejoon, and Manmohan S. Kumar. 2015. Public Debt and Growth. *Economica* 82: 705–739.

© 2018 by the authors. Licensee MDPI, Basel, Switzerland. This article is an open access article distributed under the terms and conditions of the Creative Commons Attribution (CC BY) license (http://creativecommons.org/licenses/by/4.0/).

MDPI
St. Alban-Anlage 66
4052 Basel
Switzerland
Tel. +41 61 683 77 34
Fax +41 61 302 89 18
www.mdpi.com

Risks Editorial Office
E-mail: risks@mdpi.com
www.mdpi.com/journal/risks

www.ingramcontent.com/pod-product-compliance
Lightning Source LLC
Chambersburg PA
CBHW061503210926
51850CB00008B/1801
9783039360581